BROTHERHOOD
OF THE
CAULDRON

BROTHERHOOD OF THE CAULDRON

Irishmen in the 1st Airborne Division from North Africa to Arnhem

David Truesdale

REDCOAT
Publishing

First published in 2002

British Library Cataloguing in Publication Data

A catalogue record for this book is available from the British Library.

ISBN 0 9538367 1 1

Published by

Redcoat Publishing
16 Shiralee Drive
Newtownard
Co Down
BT23 4BA

in association with

Silver Link Publishing Ltd
The Trundle
Ringstead Road
Great Addington
Kettering
Northants
NN14 4BW

Printed and bound in Great Britain

Unless otherwise credited, all illustrations are from the archive of the Airborne Battle Study Group.

CONTENTS

Foreword   7
Preface   9
Introduction   11

1 'By tradition we are united'   13

2 The formation of the
    1st Airborne Division   19
    Support units of the Airborne Division   23
    1st Parachute Brigade   31
    4th Parachute Brigade   42
    1st Air-Landing Brigade   46
    The Glider Pilot Regiment   49

3 North Africa   57

4 Sicily   66
    Operation 'Ladbroke'   69
    Operation 'Fustian'   71

5 Italy   75

6 Into the cauldron – Arnhem   80
    The plan   81
    The enemy   85
    Sunday 17 September – the first day   86
    Monday 18 September – the second day   106
    Tuesday 19 September – the third day   120
    Wednesday 20 September – the fourth day   126
    Thursday 21 September – the fifth day   132

Friday 22 September – the sixth day   137
Saturday 23 September – the seventh day   142
Sunday 24 September – the eighth day   146
Monday 25 September – the ninth day   149
Operation 'Berlin'   151

7 Aftermath   157
    Operation 'Pegasus'   160
    Norwegian interlude   161
    Going home   167
    Palestine   174
    A traitor?   175
    The films   176

8 The last word   181

Appendix 1   Roll of Irishmen who served
    in or with the 1st Airborne Division
    1942-45   185

Appendix 2   The danger of the three-lift
    attack, and 'the phrase'   227

Appendix 3   1st Airborne Division Order
    of Battle 1944   228

Acknowledgements   230
Bibliography and sources   233
Glossary   236
Index   238

I sit beside my lonely fire,
And pray for wisdom yet –
For calmness to remember
Or courage to forget.

Charles Hamilton 1830-1906

Coronach

O quiet lie the goodly men of Antrim,
O soundly sleep the gallant lads of Down.
No more they make grey Derry echo to them,
Or ring their gladness through the murk of Belfast Town.
Cloud shadows sweep across the breast of Sperrin,
And up the Mourne, the homing salmon runs.
No spring shall call them up the Gap of Gortin,
Nor summer bring again to dark Tyrone her sons.

Favourite poem of L/Sgt Jack Fryer, 1st Parachute Battalion

FOREWORD

by Paul Clark
Producer and presenter, *Let Erin Remember*

That great commander of the British Army in the 19th century, the Duke of Wellington, said he was glad the Irish were on his side at Waterloo, because he would hate to have been fighting against them. After the battle, a French general is reported to have said, 'I have seen Russian, Prussian and French bravery, but anything to equal the stubborn bravery of the regiment with castles, I have never before witnessed.' He was referring to the 27th (Inniskilling) Regiment, later the Royal Inniskilling Fusiliers, who, according to Wellington, '...saved the centre of my line at Waterloo.' Irish regiments have always found a home in the 'British Army', and the Irish soldier has served in every regiment in the Army.

Throughout history, Irish soldiers have discharged their duty with distinction, in every generation. Army Order 77 issued in April 1900 reads, 'Her Majesty The Queen, having deemed it desirable to commemorate the bravery shown by the Irish regiments in the recent operations in South Africa, has been graciously pleased to command that an Irish regiment of Foot Guards be formed. This regiment will be designated the Irish Guards.'

During the First World War, politicians in Ireland could have learned much from Irish soldiers at the front. Major Willie Redmond – a Nationalist MP, and an officer in the Royal Irish Regiment – told the Commons in December 1916 that the Nationalist and Unionist soldiers were a brotherhood of Irishmen. 'They came together in the trenches and they were friends. Get them together on the floor of an assembly in Ireland, and a similar result will follow.'

The creation of the Irish Free State in 1922 resulted in the disbandment of the southern Irish regiments. Names like the Royal Irish Regiment, Connaught Rangers, the Munster Fusiliers, the Leinsters, the Royal Dublin Fusiliers and the South Irish Horse passed into history. But Irishmen continued to flock to the colours of the British Army – not for them a state of neutrality!

In his excellent book *Irish Men and Women in the Second World War*, Richard Doherty uncovered a double embarrassment, which was deliberately hidden by the governments in Dublin and Belfast. At Stormont Unionist ministers in the government of John Andrews found to their dismay that not as many 'Loyal Ulsterman' as they would have hoped had flocked to the colours. And at Dail Eireann, Eamon De Valera and his ministers were equally embarrassed when they discovered that large numbers of Irishmen and women had gone to England to 'join up'. Nor did they do it for 'the King's shilling' alone!

It is against this background that Irishmen of differing religions and political persuasions fought a common enemy. They were on the beaches at Dunkirk, at sea during the Battle of the Atlantic, and in the sky during the Battle of Britain. They were in the skies again in September 1944, among thousands of airborne soldiers descending behind enemy lines – their goal, to secure bridges across the rivers in Holland so that the Allied Army could advance rapidly northwards and turn into the lowlands of Germany, skirting around the defensive Siegfried Line.

This daring plan, named Operation 'Market Garden', did not achieve the expected result. After nine days of bitter fighting, the operation ended with the evacuation of the remainder of the 1st British Airborne Division. 'Market Garden' failed for a number of reasons – not least the bad weather and the presence of the II SS Panzer Corps in the Arnhem area. But it had been one of the boldest and most imaginative of the war.

This was yet another chapter in the story of the Irish soldier. It was not an isolated incident of war, but a further bonding of two nations – Irish and British – whose past and future are inextricably linked. It is a history to which countless Irish soldiers have contributed, in life and death. It is a proud history and a shared history of which I am privileged to be a part.

'The Irish soldier has served in every regiment in the British Army': Sergeants of the 55th (Westmorland) Regiment of Foot at the Barracks, Newry, Ireland, in November 1871. *Border & King's Own Royal Border Regiment Museum*

PREFACE

*When historians write today of wars gone by, they
beat the drum with the bones of dead men!
If the writer has done his job well you will long
remember the tune.*

I first became aware of the Battle of Arnhem in
1965. As new recruits in one of the then Junior
Leader Battalions, my platoon was taken one
afternoon into a dusty wooden classroom for a
viewing of the 1945 film *Theirs Is The Glory*. This
film had been made with the assistance of survivors
of the 1st Airborne Division and today, nearly 60
years later, is still in my opinion the best portrayal of
the battle. I was struck by the fact that, of the ten
leading characters portrayed in the film, four were
Irishmen. This led to an increasing interest in the
Irish connection with the battle that has lasted to
this day. One of my instructors at that time had
fought at Arnhem, and as he stood at the back of
the room it was possible to see a teardrop at the
corner of his eye as the final credits appeared. While
this was not in itself surprising, the total silence and
rapt attention from some 30 15-year-olds
throughout the entire film, was.

While this is the story of those and other
Irishmen in that and other battles, it is not another
Arnhem book, but rather a book about Arnhem.
Irishmen served in almost all units present in the 1st
Airborne Division and in all ranks from Private to
Brigadier, with bravery awards ranging from a
Mention-in-Despatches to the Victoria Cross.

For the majority of these men their story began in
the hills of North Africa where they drew first
blood against their enemies, who were defeated
there and in Sicily and Italy. The following year they
fought the Germans again, in the streets and woods
around Arnhem, still the better soldiers, defeated
only by superior firepower and numbers. For some
of the men I interviewed the first shots had been
fired in France in 1940. For one, Spain was his
baptism of fire, while others had fought the Pathans
on the North West Frontier. However, for many
others their first time in action would be that warm
Sunday in September 1944, in Holland. From the
red mud of Tamara to the suburbs of Oosterbeek
and beyond, these are the individual stories told in
their own words by the men who were there.

This book does not seek to demean in any way
the actions of any other men who served in the 1st
Airborne Division; these are simply the stories I
know best. Ten years ago I made a promise and this
is my attempt for better or worse to fulfil it. While
many others assisted in the research for this book, as
the list of acknowledgements will show, any
mistakes are mine alone.

Today the number of 'Arnhem Men' is much
fewer, but I have been privileged to meet some of
them and they have become my friends. Their
stories have intrigued and captivated me over the
last ten years and in the retelling I hope the reader
will be equally intrigued and captivated.

David Truesdale
July 2002

'The family business': Major George Cecil Brooke, 1st Battalion The Border Regiment, killed in action at Gallipoli on 28 April 1915, aged 44. He was the only son of Brigadier-General Henry Francis Brooke of Ashbrooke, Brookborough, Co Fermanagh, killed in action at Kandahar in 1880 during the Second Afghan War. *Border & King's Own Royal Border Regiment Museum*

INTRODUCTION

I was very flattered when David asked me to write the introduction to his book. I first met him in 1993, shortly after taking up my job as Curator of the Border and King's Own Royal Border Regiment Museum in Carlisle Castle. He visited the Museum with friends to research archive material relating to the 1st Battalion The Border Regiment's involvement in the Battle of Arnhem. Since then I have been aware of his broad and varied research on military subjects and was happy to provide background information for his book of *The Irish Winners of the Victoria Cross*, co-authored with Richard Doherty. I have been closely associated with the creation of this book and am acutely aware of the time, patience and research that he has committed to it and the support that he has received from so many veterans of the Second World War, their families, historians, researchers and many other individuals from the UK and abroad.

Over the last 30 years, the recollections of ordinary soldiers have become recognised as vital sources of history and have made important contributions to many military books, both regimental and unit histories and broader works on military campaigns. Moreover, official records and the vast number of books on military campaigns by their nature do not always dwell on ordinary things such as training, general experiences of military life, what the soldier carried, or personal views of comradeship. As I know from my own research the view from one man's foxhole can be very different from that of his neighbour, who was perhaps only a few yards away. Such memories sometimes conflict with the official records or established views of what

happened, but it is important to realise that however well the official records have been compiled, there is much left unrecorded. This is particularly true of battles such as Arnhem, where more than two-thirds of the 1st Airborne Division did not return across the Rhine.

This book recounts the experiences of individuals from the broad range of units that served in the 1st Airborne Division 1942-45 and particularly during the fighting at Arnhem and Oosterbeek. It is still a common failing of documentaries about the battle of Arnhem not to mention the range of units that made up the 1st Airborne Division and what its objectives were. The Division comprised six battalions of paratroopers, three glider-borne infantry battalions, and a host of support units including a Recce Squadron, Medics, Engineers, Signallers and Gunners, together with almost 1,000 glider pilots, who, having flown in the troops with their vehicles, trailers, guns and other equipment, fought as ground troops. In addition, the Division had the support of the Polish Independent Parachute Brigade group. While the road bridge at Arnhem was the principal objective, the Division's task was to hold a wide perimeter on the north bank of the Rhine from Arnhem road bridge, stretching over 3 miles to the western outskirts of Oosterbeek. This provided a broad front for XXX Corps to cross the river, whether or not the road and rail bridges, or a ferry, were intact. Given all that went wrong with the operation it makes the efforts to hold the bridge and defend the Oosterbeek perimeter all the more remarkable.

David Truesdale has collated what these men remembered of their experiences during a momentous period in their own lives and that of the world as a whole. In the changing and uncertain world in which we now live, and with a growing interest in history, it is vital to record such experiences while some of the participants in these events are still alive. The reader should also realise that many former servicemen do not regard their own experiences as particularly significant and most are very humble about the role they played during the Second World War. For them, at a time when so many were involved in the war effort, they were just doing their bit. May succeeding generations be ever mindful of that.

Stuart Eastwood
July 2002

Major Algernon Montgomerie Caulfield DSO DCM, Northumberland Fusiliers, circa 1888. As a Private in the 66th Foot (Berkshire Regiment) he won a DCM for saving the lives of two wounded officers in the Second Afghan War. Promoted Sergeant, he was commissioned into the 5th Northumberland Fusiliers in 1881, served in Burma, and was awarded the DSO in 1887. In 1889 he transferred to the Border Regiment and retired in 1902. He rejoined his Regiment as second-in-command of the 6th (Service) Battalion and was killed in action at Suvla, Gallipoli, on 9 August 1915, aged 57. He was the fourth son of Lt-Col Montgomerie Stewart Caulfield of Monkstown, Co Dublin. *Border & King's Own Royal Border Regiment Museum*

1 'BY TRADITION
WE ARE UNITED'

With the successful evacuation of British and French troops from Dunkirk in June 1940, Britain stood alone against the might of the German Blitzkrieg. It is somehow ironic therefore to remember that what was left of the British Army at this time was committed by Winston Churchill into the care of the great Irish Generals: Harold Alexander, Claude Auchinleck, Alan Brooke, Sir John Dill and Bernard Montgomery. All were destined to hold Field Marshal rank and, together with men like Richard O'Connor, Brian Horrocks and Eric Dorman-Smith, would win initial victories in the Western Desert and move on to greater triumphs.[1]

Harold Alexander had been born in London, the son of a noted County Tyrone family that had come to Ulster from Scotland during the Plantation years. From schooldays at Harrow he went to Sandhurst and was placed 85th out of 172. He was commissioned into the Irish Guards and joined them at Chelsea Barracks on 23 September 1911. He served throughout the First World War on the Western Front, and when peace was declared he held the rank of Lieutenant-Colonel. Between the wars he served in a variety of posts, each of which brought him closer to the rank of Field Marshal.

The 'Auk', Field Marshal Sir Claude Auchinleck, also had his roots buried in Irish earth. For 200 years the Auchinleck clan had played a not unimportant part in Scottish history. With the fall of the clans the family took the advice of James I of England and with other clan chieftains sought

Field Marshals Harold Alexander, Alan Brooke and Bernard Mont-gomery, somewhere in France in 1944. It would have been a severe blow to the Allied cause had a wandering German pilot spotted this target of opportunity! The driver of the staff car is reported to be Private 'Paddy' Boyle from Dublin. *Mick Hamilton*

---

[1] Churchill did not particularly want Brooke, but was forced to accept him by the Army, which recognised his exceptional abilities. *War Diaries 1939-1945*, Field Marshal Lord Alanbrooke (Weidenfeld & Nicolson, London)

other lands in Ireland. They settled in County Fermanagh, with some sons taking Holy Orders, whole others elected for a career under arms. In the early 1800s the two sons of the Reverend John Auchinleck chose the army, both sons being commissioned into the Royal Horse Artillery. The first born, William, had an uneventful career and retired as a Colonel, while his brother John served with distinction in the Indian Mutiny and later in the Second Afghan War of 1878. John was Claude Auchinleck's father. Claude was schooled at Wellington College and later Sandhurst, but, due to reduced financial circumstances, opted for the Indian Army, where a subaltern could just about exist on his army pay. He sailed for the subcontinent in March 1903, and began the journey towards a Field Marshal's baton.

Sir John Dill, a native of Lurgan, County Armagh, had served in both the South African and the First World Wars before serving in France in 1940 as a corps commander. He was appointed Chief of Staff in 1940, but the near constant conflict with the views of Winston Churchill, who found him overcautious, ended with him being sent to Washington as the head of the British military mission. Dill's charm, integrity and professional ability gained him prestige in US military circles, and the trust and friendship he engendered with both President Roosevelt and General Marshall did nothing but good for Britain. Sir John Dill passed away on 4 November 1944, while in Washington; he was considered to have died on active service and consequently was buried in Arlington National Cemetery with full military honours. The tradition of Irishmen serving in the Regular Army goes back to the reign of James II, who in 1662 raised a regiment of 'Irish Guards', part of which would go on to form the cadre of the Royal Irish Regiment, although there are those who would claim that Elizabeth I had her share of Irishmen under arms. As this book will show, many of the men who served in or with the 1st Airborne Division were simply

carrying on what Brigadier 'Shan' Hackett called 'the family business', and succeeded in doing it well.

As a way of attempting to show the depth of tradition associated with Irishmen in the service of the Crown, the following is a potted history of some of the names associated with the battle and the part played by them in the annals of the British Army.

Five hundred years prior to Operation 'Market Garden' another 'British' army had set out from England under its King and won undying fame on the field of Agincourt. King Henry's army consisted not only of English knights, yeomen and archers, but a fair number of Welsh, Scots and Irish. One such unit was a component of Irish hoblairs. This force of light cavalry, some 1,500 strong, had left the port of Cork under the command of Thomas Butler, Prior of Kilmainham, and served with the King throughout his campaign in France[2], although by the time of Agincourt the numbers remaining would have been much fewer. In the ranks of the archers was one named Matthew Gough.

During the Napoleonic Wars the Gough name would again find fame. Major Hugh Gough led the 2nd Battalion of the 87th Regiment of Foot (later the Royal Irish Fusiliers) at the Battle of Barrosa on 5 March 1811. It was here that a French 'Eagle' was captured for the first time in battle. Prior to this the only 'Eagles' in British hands were those taken when French garrisons had surrendered or been captured after a siege. The Barrosa 'Eagle' was captured from the French 8th Regiment by the combined efforts of Ensign Keogh and Sergeant Patrick Masterson. In the bloody struggle Keogh was killed, but Masterson succeeded in taking the prized standard. As a reward for his behaviour that day Masterson was offered a commission, which he accepted.[3] The 87th were not the only Irishmen on the field at Barrosa that day. In the 28th Foot the Regimental Colours were borne by two brothers from Ireland, Robert and Henry Mitchell. They carried the colours until Henry was killed at the Battle of Vittoria on 21 June 1813. The 67th Foot could almost be described as another

---

[2] *The Irish Soldier*, Bredin (Century Books, Belfast, 1987)

[3] A descendent of the 'Eagle Taker' was James Edward Ignatius Masterson, who had enlisted in the Royal Irish Fusiliers as a Private in 1881. He received a commission in the Devonshire Regiment and was awarded the Victoria Cross for his actions at Wagon Hill, Ladysmith, during the Boer War.

'Irish' regiment. Led by Lieutenant Colonel William Prevost, the battalion had been raised in Ireland in January 1804, its nominal roll of 460 rank and file showing only 23 English and six Scots. At Barrosa the battalion fielded 500 men and was still mainly Irish.

Hugh Gough had fought in more campaigns than almost any soldier of his generation. He was much loved by his troops and always wore a white coat in action so he could be instantly recognised by the men. Gough ended his career as a Field Marshal. Charles John Stanley Gough and his brother Hugh were both awarded the Victoria Cross for their actions during the Indian Mutiny of 1857/58. Charles was awarded the medal for no fewer than four occasions of outstanding bravery, one of which was the rescue of his brother Hugh. John Edmund Gough, son of Charles, won the third family VC in Somaliland in 1903 in one of the small wars of the Empire fought against one Mohammed-bin-Abdullah Hassan, otherwise known as the 'Mad Mullah'.[4] By 1913 he had been promoted to Brigadier-General and the following year he accompanied the British Expeditionary Force to France. It quickly became apparent that Gough was one of the finest brains in the Army at that time and his popularity with the men was second to none. It was therefore a tragedy not only for his family, but also for the British Army in general, when this fine officer was hit by a sniper's bullet on 20 February 1915 near Faquissant, France; he died of his wounds two days later. Unusually, he was posthumously knighted on 22 April 1915, 12 years to the day after he won his Victoria Cross. He is buried in the communal cemetery at Estaires.

Johnny Gough was not the only member of the family to serve during the First World War. General Sir Hubert Gough was in command of the Fifth Army in July 1916. In 1918 the main German attack fell on his army and, unable to hold the line, he withdrew to take up a shorter and more easily defended position. This action was held responsible for the initial German success and Gough was relieved of his command. Subsequent research into the battle showed that this was the only sensible course of action that could have been taken at the time. Now after all those years of service to the Crown another Gough was to take the field in the service of his King – Major 'Freddie' Gough MC would lead the 1st Airborne Reconnaissance Squadron at Arnhem.

The name Bermingham goes back a long way in Irish military history. It can be found on the Waterloo Roll Call as Private Patrick Bermingham of the 73rd Foot.[5] Patrick Bermingham was born at Templemore, County Tipperary, and left his trade as a labourer to enlist in the regiment on 3 April 1813. Described as 5ft 7in tall, with a fair complexion, sandy hair and grey eyes, he served in Number 7 Company and was wounded on Sunday 18 June 1815 at Waterloo. He was discharged on 27 February 1816, aged 33, with a pension of ninepence per day; the reason given for his discharge was a gunshot wound to the left wrist received at that battle. The nominal roll of the Battalion at Waterloo shows 558 other ranks present for duty on 18 June 1815, of which 114 were Irish. Many other battalions on the field that day contained similar percentages of Irishmen.

At Gallipoli there was Lieutenant William Arthur Bermingham of the Royal Irish Fusiliers; he was killed in action on 9 August 1915, has no known grave and is commemorated on the Helles memorial. The Gallipoli campaign involved many Irishmen, the vast majority of whom served in the 10th (Irish) Division, although many other battalions boasted an Irish contingent. The Lancashire Fusiliers, famous for their 'six VCs before breakfast', owed one of them to the actions of Private William Keneally from Wexford. For 'Market Garden' the Army would have Sergeant John Bermingham from Dublin, an ex-Royal Ulster Rifleman with previous service on the North West Frontier, who would serve in the 1st Parachute Battalion.

The Hackett name is familiar to students of military history. During the Indian Mutiny

---

[4] *Irish Winners of the Victoria Cross*, p101

[5] The 73rd Foot was listed on the 1815 Army List as a Highland Regiment, but had in fact abandoned Highland dress in 1808. At Waterloo only the Battalion's piper, Hugh McKay, was permitted to wear the kilt.

Lieutenant Thomas Bernard Hackett from County Tipperary served with the 23rd Royal Welch Fusiliers. On 8 November 1857 he led a rescue party that recovered a fellow wounded officer of the 23rd from certain death. The officer had been lying in the open, exposed to enemy fire, and Hackett and his men arrived just in time to save his life. Later that day the Lieutenant climbed on to the roof of a bungalow his men were defending and cut away the thatch to prevent it being set alight by the mutineers. Eventually rising to the rank of Lieutenant-Colonel, he returned to Ireland after his military career. His younger brother, Robert Henry, had served in the Zulu War of 1879 and had been wounded in action serving with the 90th Foot at the Battle of Khambula in 1879. A gunshot from a Zulu rifle had left him blind in both eyes and Thomas devoted a lot of his time to looking after his brother. It was therefore a double tragedy when Thomas died as the result of an accident, when the breech of his gun exploded while out shooting near his home at Arrabeg, King's County, in 1890. The 4th Parachute Brigade was lucky to have a professional such as 'Shan' Hackett as its commander during 'Market Garden'.

Vittoria was the final major battle fought by Wellington in Spain. After spending the winter of 1812 reorganising and strengthening his forces, Wellington set out from Portugal and marched his army across the mountains of northern Spain to engage the 58,000-strong army of Marshal Jourdan deployed between the rivers Douro and Tagus. The French were compelled to retreat, hotly pursued by Wellington's men, who marched hard to cut off the French from the road back to France. On 21 June 1813 Wellington launched a three-column attack against the French at Vittoria. After some ferocious fighting General Picton's 3rd Division broke Jourdan's centre. The remainder of the French Army crumbled in the face of determined attacks and its retreat abruptly became a rout. Jourdan's losses amounted to 8,000 killed and wounded, 2,000 prisoners and 154 artillery pieces. Wellington's losses were put at 4,500 killed or wounded. The following December British troops were encamped on French soil. An officer highly praised for his actions at Vittoria was one Captain Frederick Vandeleur of the 87th Regiment. He was severely wounded during the battle and died of wounds on 6 July 1813.[6]

In September 1944 the advance by XXX Corps up the single road from the Belgian border towards Arnhem would be led by the tanks of the Guards Armoured Division. They in turn would be led by the Irish Guards Group, commanded by Lieutenant-Colonel J. O. E. Vandeleur, with his brother Giles in command of the 2nd Battalion.

An Irishman would lead XXX Corps in its attempt to reach Arnhem. Brian Horrocks was the son of a Lancastrian doctor who had joined the Royal Army Medical Corps and been posted to India. Here he met his future wife, an Ulster Presbyterian and also from a family of doctors. The couple married in 1894 and Horrocks was born a year later at Ranniket, a hill station in India. In October 1912 this 'rash, impetuous' student entered the Royal Military College, Sandhurst, bottom but one! While Horrocks excelled at games, his military studies were less than successful. He was foreordained to remain a 'gentleman cadet' (equivalent to a private soldier) throughout his time at Sandhurst.

Four days after the declaration of war, Horrocks found himself reporting for duty with a militia battalion of the Middlesex Regiment. Two weeks later he led a draft of reinforcements for the 1st Battalion, then in France, to the shores of the continent. When this august body eventually joined up with the Battalion it was taking part in the retreat from Mons. During this confused time Horrocks remained in command until after the Battle of the Aisne, a month later. When the reinforcements were allotted to their companies Horrocks was made a platoon commander. On 21 October 1914, during the 1st Battle of Ypres, the enemy surrounded Horrocks and his platoon. In the ensuing mêlée Horrocks was wounded in the lower stomach and became a prisoner-of-war, bringing an end to his military career for the next four years. Horrocks always maintained that his time spent in prison camp was the best apprenticeship for the difficult lessons of command in war. The most

---

[6] PRO WO 25/2965. Obituary in *The Gentleman's Magazine*, November 1813, p504.

important of these was self-reliance: without superior officers to take responsibility, or junior ranks on which to depend, prisoners were forced to account for their own actions, and mistakes had to be lived with. At the end of the First World War, Horrocks returned to his Regiment, then stationed in Germany. It was here that he saw at first hand the horrors of inflation on an economy and became convinced that any sacrifice was worthwhile in order to stop what he called 'this economic cancer'.[7]

Shortly thereafter he found himself seconded for duty in Russia, a period he found both fearful and fascinating, especially his time as a prisoner of the Red Army. During the inter-war years he served in England, doing duty in connection with the coal strike, in Ireland in connection with the never-ending 'troubles', and in Silesia during the plebiscite to decided the frontiers between Poland and Germany. In 1924 the Olympic Games were held in Paris and Horrocks represented Great Britain in the modern pentathlon. Despite being superbly fit, the competition was such that he finished well down in the order of merit.

During the Dunkirk campaign Horrocks commanded the 2nd Battalion Middlesex Regiment, a machine-gun battalion. During the retreat from their position in Belgium to the French coast at Dunkirk, Horrocks had nothing but the highest regard for the behaviour of the men under his command. He maintained that while other armies have men just as brave and professional in arms, none has the sense of humour of the British fighting soldier, and it is this humour that sees him through all adversity.

After the withdrawal from France, Horrocks spent the next two years in England, then in August 1942 he was given command of XIII Corps and posted to North Africa. Throughout the desert campaign he performed well and it was sheer bad luck that his military career was once again put on hold in June 1943. He was at the port of Bizerta to watch the 46th Division carry out a full-scale rehearsal for the assault on the Salerno beaches. As the air raid siren sounded Horrocks and other staff officers went outside to see if the famous American

Brian Horrocks, the man who led XXX Corps in its failed attempt to relieve the 1st Airborne Division at Arnhem. This photograph of him in the full-dress uniform of the Middlesex Regiment was taken shortly after his promotion to Major.

smokescreen worked as well as they claimed. Everything seemed to be going well, and the thick smoke rolled over the town, but not before a lone German fighter made a strafing run and deposited a bullet through Horrocks's chest, severely wounding him. He was still suffering from the effects of this injury when he led XXX Corps northwards from the Dutch-Belgian border in September 1944.

Before finishing this very brief history it would be remiss not to mention Field Marshal Bernard Law Montgomery, instigator of 'Market Garden'. Once again it is necessary to go back in history to find the origins of an 'Irish' soldier.

The Battle of Hastings, fought on 14 October 1066, saw the Norman Army under the command

[7] *A Full Life*, Lt General Sir Brian Horrocks (Collins, 1960)

of William, Duke of Normandy, inflict a terrible defeat on the English under King Harold, a victory that led to Norman rule in Britain. Sir Roger de Montgomeri, a distinguished and successful soldier who led the vanguard of the Norman Army, was a member of a family that owned large estates in the area of Caen, Falaise and Argentan. As a result of his success at Hastings and elsewhere, Sir Roger was rewarded with various titles and estates, one of which was situated on the Welsh border near Shrewsbury. His youngest son, Arnold, crossed the Irish Sea and married Lafracotte, daughter of the King of Munster in Ireland. In turn Arnold's son crossed into Scotland early in the 12th century and became ancestor to all the Montgomeri families in Scotland. When the Protestant plantation of the north began, many of the Montgomeri families moved across the Irish Sea to the nine counties. Just when the Field Marshal's family arrived in Ulster is unknown, but it is assumed to have been around 1628. They settled on an estate in south-west Donegal between the villages of Killybegs and Killaghtee. The use of the word 'settled' in this case is defined as riding about on a big horse with a sharp sword to forcibly evict the previous Catholic landowners. This was a widespread custom at the time and believed by many to be the basic cause of all 'troubles' in Ireland today.[8]

By now the spelling of the family name had changed to Montgomery, and they showed a marked leaning towards the Church. Thankfully when Bernard was born fate decided that his future would lie with the Army. He went to Sandhurst in 1907, just after his 19th birthday, and initially did quite well. Despite several setbacks, some quite serious, he left the Academy in July 1908. At first he hoped to join the Indian Army, but fate decided otherwise and he was commissioned into the Royal Warwickshire Regiment, joining its 1st Battalion.

On 13 October 1914 the now Lieutenant Montgomery led his platoon against the enemy at Meteren near the Somme. Leading his men forward, sword in hand, he was shot in the chest by an enemy sniper and fell, badly wounded. A member of his platoon ran forward with a shell dressing, and kneeling by the wounded officer he attempted to apply the bandage and was in turn shot by the sniper. The dead soldier fell across Montgomery's body, protecting him from further bullets fired by the rifleman, who had recognised Montgomery as an officer. Despite this protection he was hit later in the day by another bullet, this time in the knee. When recovered by stretcher-bearers later still, he was assumed to be dead and a field grave was dug for him. When signs of life were discovered he was quickly taken to hospital where immediate surgery saved his life. For his actions at Meteren, Montgomery was promoted to Captain and awarded the DSO. By July 1918 he was GSO1 of the 47th Infantry Division, with the rank of Lieutenant-Colonel. The path towards Field Marshal was well and truly set, and the 'family business' was going strong.

The contribution towards the British Army from Ireland, both 'loyal' north and 'neutral' south, has been investigated in great detail by Richard Doherty in his book *Irish Men and Women in the Second World War*.[9] Through exhaustive research he has arrived at a total of 52,174 from Northern Ireland, while 78,826 volunteered from Eire. Although Ireland (Eire) remained neutral during the Second World War, it was a biased neutrality, prompting one of de Valera's ministers to ask, 'Just who are we neutral against?'[10] A few weeks before this book went to press the author received a list of some 5,000 men who deserted from the Irish Defence Force during the Second World War, or as it was known in Ireland, 'the emergency'. Among these names can be found men who served in the ranks of the 1st Airborne Division and other units. Desertion is usually defined as leaving a place of danger to seek safety elsewhere. It is therefore somewhat ironic that these men left the comparative 'safety' of garrison duty in Ireland to serve in all three services within the British Army in all theatres and for so many to have died on active service.

---

[8] Quoted in a letter written by Brian Montgomery, the Field Marshal's brother.
[9] Four Courts Press, Dublin, 1999
[10] *Neutral Ireland and the Third Reich*, John P. Duggan (Gill & Macmillan, 1989)

2 THE FORMATION OF THE 1ST AIRBORNE DIVISION

The story of how British Airborne Forces came into being began in late 1940, with the penning of a memorandum from the Prime Minister, Winston Churchill, to the War Office suggesting the formation of a corps of airborne troops of at least 5,000 men. This was in reply to the success enjoyed by the German paratroopers in the invasion of Denmark, Belgium and Holland in the summer of 1940.

On 9 April 1940 some 500 German aircraft delivered troops on to selected targets in Denmark. Although the actual parachute contingent was relatively small, it was a foretaste of things to come. The following month, on 10 May, a glider-borne assault on the border fortress of Eben Emael ensured a successful German crossing of the Albert Canal into Belgium. This fortress, believed to be the strongest in the world, fell to a handful of lightly armed men, but men who came from an unexpected direction and had an élan not yet seen in this war. On the same day, 580 JU52 transport aircraft carried elements of the German airborne forces into Holland, and despite initial setbacks, they were again victorious.

In turn the Germans had taken a lesson from the Russians, who had pioneered the dropping of large numbers of paratroopers in the 1930s. In the coming war the Russians would fail to use their paratroopers in any strategic role; rather they would drop groups of men to carry out sabotage or in support of partisan units.

The first British unit was known as the 11th Special Air Service Battalion, which was formed from No 2 Commando on 21 November 1940.[11] One of those responsible for the training of No 2 Commando in its airborne role was Charles Ivor Jackson. 'Jacko' Jackson was born on 7 February 1902 in County Cavan, and attended Campbell College, Belfast, before going to the Royal Military Academy, Sandhurst. His was a varied military career. Commissioned into the Royal Tank Corps in February 1923, he joined its 3rd Battalion, then stationed with the Rhine Army in Germany. He later transferred to No 5 Armoured Car Company in India. In 1927 he joined the Royal Air Force and as a Flight Lieutenant performed various duties throughout his service until posted to 54 Training Regiment in April 1940. 'Jacko' then returned to the Army, and on 3 July 1940 reported to Ringway to take command of No 2 Commando.

He led the unit throughout its training and provided superb leadership in those early days, culminating in the unit's inaugural action in Italy. This was Operation 'Colossus', an airborne attack on the Tragino aqueduct in the south of the country, carried out on the night of 10 February 1941. While the operation was a success in that the aqueduct was destroyed, those personnel involved were all captured; nevertheless valuable lessons were learned for future operations.[12] Shortly after this 'Jacko' handed over command to Lieutenant-Colonel Eric 'Dracula' Down, while he went to act as second-in-

---

[11] Not to be confused with the Special Air Service formed in North Africa by Colonel David Stirling.

[12] Fortunato Picchi, the Italian guide on the raid, was also captured and handed over to the Fascist militia. Despite torture he refused to reveal any details of the operation and was executed by a firing squad.

command of the Westminster Dragoons. By the end of his military service he was again serving in Germany, retiring from the Army with the rank of Lieutenant-Colonel in 1948.

In July 1941 it was decided to form the 1st Parachute Brigade, and the 11th SAS Battalion was re-designated as the 1st Battalion of the new Brigade. The following September the 2nd, 3rd and 4th Battalions were added. By the end of the year it was decided that a further brigade would be added, these troops being transported to battle by glider, and on 31 October 1941 1st Air-Landing

With Britain's Sky Troops

Belfast Man on His Experiences

SOLDIERS who receive extra pay; who aren't ordered about in the usual military manner, because they have only to be told, nicely, what's wanted of them; soldiers who vary sharpshooting practice with athletics and swimming lessons, etc.; who are supremely fit, and who are given endurance tests that would qualify them as Arctic explorers.

Such are the men of Britain's new corps d'élite—the parachutists.

I have just had a chat with one of these boys (writes the "Telegraph" military correspondent). He is a former Belfast boxer, who almost attained championship class in Ireland before departing for Canada, where he lived for a few years prior to the outbreak of war.

TO say that he is a husky-looking specimen is putting it mildly. His cheeks glowed with health, his teeth positively gleamed, and in his special parachutist's boots his step had the spring of a ballet dancer's.

"Bob"—that's as much of his name as I will give—told me something, when he called at the "Telegraph" office, of his life in the "sky-jumpers" corps since he got tired of his desk job in the Royal Army Service Corps after the campaign in France, and decided to aspire to higher things.

I asked him how long he had been a parachutist.

"You sort of measure your length of service by the number of jumps you have made," he explained in his pleasing Ulster-Canadian drawl.

"I have made nine up to the present," he added matter-of-factly.

"It's the weirdest feeling imaginable, baling out of a plane," Bob went on. "Every time you jump you're scared stiff—but once you have made one jump it fascinates you. You actually develop a craving for it. No matter how many times you've jumped, you always want to make another."

Every precaution, he said, was taken against accidents.

"Yes, it's a funny feeling to be up in a plane and sitting looking at the hole you've got to jump through," he con-

" The Parachutist Corps is the finest in the Service," this Belfast member says.

fessed. "The section sit round the hole, and when the time comes we go at the rate of one every second. You feel a touch on the shoulder, and you know it's your turn to hop, and off you go!

"THE curious thing is that you don't mind so much when you jump in company. You bale out quite happily, but, doing it yourself, you don't feel so good.

"Yes, it's a case of gritting your teeth then. A pilot baling out because his plane is out of control or on fire knows he has no alternative. But to have to jump when everything's hunky-dory and you're making it alone. No, sir. It's not so hot, believe me."

Bob was naturally inclined to "keep mum" about a lot of details connected with the life of a military parachutist, but just to show how keen he is he informed me that, although boxing was

encouraged as an excellent "toughening" sport, he now took merely an onlooker's interest in the gentle art.

"The way I look at it," he explained, "is that I've boxed for a good few years, and taken all the hard knocks coming to me via a glove, but now I don't want to get knocked up even for a week or so by a chance punch, as can happen in the friendliest bout, and perhaps not be fit and ready for anything when a real job of work comes along. So I just watch the other fellows."

Parachutists are, of course, picked men. They must have an above the average education. They must be young and adaptable. Their character and record, both in the Army and in civilian life, must bear strictest investigation. They must be absolutely physically fit. And they must have a zest for adventure—high adventure!

THEY receive special training, physical jerks, map-reading, etc. Parachutists have to be adepts at skating, swimming, and other accomplishments. And in everything they do they are trained to use the utmost initiative in whatever situation they may find themselves.

"And sometimes we do find ourselves in funny situations," said Bob, grinning. "For instance, when you bale out and get caught in the air-stream of the plane and find yourself upside-down in the air. The ground looks a bit odd when you're that way."

Volunteers come from all branches of the Army, he told me. "A newcomer may be a corporal, sergeant, or warrant officer, but once he's enrolled he finds that we are all free and equal among ourselves. Nobody would dream of ordering others about. It's just not done. We don't require ordering. We're told what's wanted of us—and we jump to it."

Bob rose from his seat and shook hands, preparatory to taking his departure.

"There's just one other thing I want to tell you," he said. "The Parachutist Corps is the finest corps in the Service."

'With Britain's Sky Troops', an undated cutting from a local newspaper.

Soldiers of the 2nd Battalion Ox and Bucks board their Horsa glider for a training flight in 1942. This early Mark of Horsa had the small door on the port side; later models had a large door wide enough to load a jeep through, and a removable tail section. *Border & King's Own Royal Border Regiment Museum*

Brigade was formed from 31st Independent Infantry Brigade. Command was given to Brigadier G. F. Hopkinson OBE MC. Initially the Brigade consisted of the 1st Battalion Border Regiment, 2nd Battalion South Staffordshire Regiment, 2nd Battalion Oxfordshire and Buckinghamshire Light Infantry and the 1st Battalion Royal Ulster Rifles.[13] The Brigade support units were comprised of 31st Independent Reconnaissance Company, 9th Field Company RE, 181 Field Ambulance RAMC, 31 Brigade Ordnance Workshop and Field Park, an RASC Company, Brigade HQ, Brigade Signals, and an Anti-Tank Battery. Both Brigades were formed into a divisional unit, and by the end of October 1941 Headquarters 1st Airborne Division came into being at Hardwick Hall in Derbyshire.

Various changes in the formation were made in 1942 and 1943. Apart from 181 Field Ambulance, all the other support units of the 1st Air-Landing Brigade became Divisional units. In 1943 the Royal Ulster Rifles and the Ox and Bucks were transferred to the 6th Airborne Division to form

the 6th Air-Landing Brigade and were joined later by the 12th Battalion Devonshire Regiment.

In July 1942 it was decided to form a second parachute brigade for the Airborne Division, and the 4th Battalion of the 1st Brigade was detached to form the cadre of the new organisation. Due to a shortfall in the number of volunteers coming forward it was decided that converting two existing infantry battalions into the airborne role would provide the required number of men. Therefore the 7th Battalion The Queen's Own Cameron Highlanders and the 10th Battalion The Royal Welch Fusiliers became the 5th (Scottish) and 6th (Royal Welch) Parachute Battalions of the 2nd Parachute Brigade. In 1943 the Brigade left the 1st Airborne Division and was replaced by the 4th Parachute Brigade, which had been formed in North Africa in 1942.

The 2nd Brigade was designated the 2nd Independent Parachute Brigade Group and fought as infantry throughout the long bitter winter of 1943-44 in Italy. From March to May of 1944, the Brigade fought at Cassino, in Italy. In June 1944

---

[13] Usually referred to as 1 Border, 1RUR, 1 Ox and Bucks, and 2 South Staffords.

A training cadre at Bulford Camp in the winter of 1942. The men are mostly from the Royal Ulster Rifles. On the extreme left of the third row from the rear is Victor Hughes, a veteran of the North West Frontier who would serve at Arnhem with the 3rd Parachute Battalion. *V. Hughes*

some 60 men of the 6th Battalion took part in Operation 'Hasty', a diversionary attack on German demolition targets near the town of Rimini. To combat the efforts of the raiders an entire German brigade was sent to hunt them down. At the same time a division was held in reserve to reinforce the rear areas against attack. The operation was deemed a total success, with a very small number of men being lost.

The Brigade formed part of the 1st Airborne Task Force during Operation 'Anvil', the invasion of the south of France, on 15 August 1944. This brigade was made up of parachute troops from Britain, Canada and the United States, and despite a widely dispersed drop, all objectives were attained. By 17 August a link had been established with Allied ground forces and on 26 August the Brigade was returned to Italy.

By October 1944 the Brigade was stationed in Greece, and with the withdrawal of the Germans it found itself in the middle of a civil war as communist and royalist forces fought for control of the country. The Task Force was again called into action and the result was Operation 'Manna'. The objective of this operation was to occupy Athens in the wake of the German withdrawal and attempt to

prevent the outbreak of civil war between the communist and royalist forces. The operation began on 12 October, with a drop on Megara airfield by the 4th Battalion. Many casualties were incurred, not by enemy action but due to the high winds.

Despite the intervention of British forces, civil war could not be avoided and British troops found themselves a new enemy when there were clashes between paratroopers and ELAS (the communist guerrilla army). After service in Greece the Brigade was sent to Palestine to join with the 6th Airborne Division for more 'peacekeeping' duties.

The weapon that would become the British 1st Airborne Division was forged in the hills of Tunisia in 1942 and was destroyed in the suburbs of a Dutch town in 1944. The units that made up the Division and some of the Irishmen who served in these units are described below.

For Operation 'Market Garden' the 1st Airborne Division consisted of two parachute brigades, each of three battalions, an air-landing brigade, also of three battalions, and accompanying divisional troops. Some of the men involved would be going into action for the first time, while others had served from the creation of airborne forces and had fought in North Africa, Sicily and Italy. The 1st Polish Independent Parachute Brigade Group, under the command of General Stanislaw Sosabowski, consisting of three battalions with their own support troops, would be attached. Arnhem was the first and last airborne operation in which the Polish Brigade would take part.

Command of the Division went to Major-General Robert Elliot Urquhart DSO, who was appointed in January 1944. Urquhart, known to his colleagues as Roy, was a Highland Light Infantryman, with recent experience in the Middle East. At 43 years of age he was considered by some to be too old for airborne command and there was a certain resentment that he was brought in from outside the 'airborne brotherhood'. There were also those who felt that if an 'airborne' Brigadier been promoted to command the Division, stronger opposition would have been raised against the choice of landing and drop zones at Arnhem. Nevertheless Urquhart was an experienced officer and by September 1944 the men of the Division had accepted him.

SUPPORT UNITS OF THE AIRBORNE DIVISION

The Oxford English Dictionary defines the word pathfinder as 'one who discovers a way or path, an explorer'. The pathfinders of 1st Airborne Division were embodied in the 21st Independent Parachute Company, and they would mark out the landing and drop zones to the west of Arnhem for the troops scheduled to arrive on both Sunday and Monday. This Company had been the brainchild of Major John Lander TD[14], and had been formed in June 1942 to act as 'Pathfinders' for any large-scale airborne landings. Despite previous action in North Africa, Sicily and Italy, where they had fought mainly as infantry, Operation 'Market Garden' was the first time the Company would act in its planned role. The 22nd Independent Parachute Company had successfully performed a similar role for the 6th

Airborne Division during the D-Day operation in Normandy the previous June. For Arnhem, command of the Company went to Major Bernard Alexander 'Boy' Wilson, at 45 years of age the oldest paratrooper in the 1st Airborne Division.

The 21st was independent in more than name; it contained a large number of German Jews and a strong Irish influence. The core of the Company arrived in 1943 in the shape of a contingent from the 70th (Young Soldiers) Battalion of the Inniskilling Fusiliers under the command of Sergeant Gordon 'Slim' Summerville from Belfast. These battalions had been raised from the beginning of 1940, when the War Office decided to accept volunteers from 18 years of age. Recruits were not considered for duty overseas, but after initial training were deployed in the home defence role, for example in airfield light anti-aircraft duties. Some of these units became known as 'Borstal Battalions' as they contained a good many of what could be described as the hooligan element of society. Nevertheless there were a number who had a genuine interest in becoming professional soldiers and it was just such a group that Sergeant Summerville took into the 21st Independent Parachute Company. In the campaigns of North Africa, Sicily and Italy, these men proved their worth at all times.

They included James Cameron from Carrickfergus, County Antrim, whose father Thomas had served in the Royal Irish Rifles in the First World War. William 'Barney' Moore came from McMaster Street, Belfast, and had attended Templemore Primary School before taking an apprenticeship in the Harland & Wolff shipyard. When other local men began to enlist it was only natural that 'Barney' would follow suit, and being too young for active service, he joined the Young Soldiers Battalion of the Inniskillings. He would be remembered in the ranks of the 21st as a fine singer, his rendering of 'Galway Bay', being a particular favourite.

Dennis Ivan 'Danny' Gillespie had lied about his age in several attempts at joining the British Army;

---

[14] Major Lander was killed during operations on Sicily. The letters after his name refer to the Territorial Decoration, not that he was an Irish MP!

Private 'Jimmy' Cameron from Carrickfergus, County Antrim. A former 'Young Soldier' with the Royal Inniskilling Fusiliers, he was one of the original members of the 21st Independent Parachute Company. Wounded in action during the fighting in Oosterbeek, he died on 26 September 1944. *Cameron family*

Private Dennis Ivan 'Danny' Gillespie of the 21st Independent Parachute Company. He is wearing the maroon beret with the cap badge of his original regiment, the Royal Inniskilling Fusiliers, and has the Inniskilling shoulder title on his battledress blouse. The shoulder titles were going to war for the second time – they had been worn by Danny's father in the Great War. *D. Gillespie*

he was 16 at the time. He was working as an apprentice in a local engineering firm and in the evenings acting as a bicycle messenger for the ARP. During his time with the ARP he met another messenger, a 15-year-old girl named Joan. It was the beginning of a relationship that was to last a very long time indeed! He had tried, unsuccessfully, to enlist in the Royal Inniskilling Fusiliers, the Royal Navy and the Royal Air Force, being told on each occasion that he was too young.

He was more fortunate with the Ulster Home Guard, and soon he had exchanged his ARP armband for one bearing the letters LDV. The Local Defence Volunteers was the original name given to the Home Guard, but was changed at the insistence of Winston Churchill, as he felt the words 'home' and 'guard' would generate a more patriotic emotion. Danny remembers the letters standing for 'Look Duck and Vanish'. His Home Guard platoon, 30 men strong, met in the premises of a local undertaker on the Upper Newtownards Road in East Belfast. They carried out their field training exercises across the rather neatly mowed grass of Knock Golf Links situated

near the village of Dundonald in County Down, much to the displeasure of the club secretary. The platoon was armed with a variety of weapons, including old Lee-Metford rifles and single-shot carbines as well as the standard issue Lee Enfield .303 rifle.

Danny, as he was known, particularly enjoyed the unarmed combat training, and there was a constant striving between him and his mate, 'Big Hugh' Petrie, to see who would be the best. Their service careers from this time followed a similar path, but always with Petrie one step behind. When Danny joined the Inniskillings, Petrie followed only to find Danny had transferred to Airborne. When Petrie was accepted for airborne training, Danny had moved on to the 21st. On his first leave after gaining his prized red beret, Petrie turned up at Danny's mother's house only to be told that Danny

Above No 1 Platoon of the 21st Independent Parachute Company, Italy, 1943. Second from the left in the back row is William 'Barney' Moore from McMaster Street, Belfast; fourth from the left is Jimmy Gamble from Coleraine, County Londonderry; second row third from the left is Don McArthur, who left the unit to serve on Operation 'Anvil'; eighth from the left is Dennis 'Danny' Gillespie; seated row, second from the left, is Corporal 'Paddy' Cockings from Eire, who served at Arnhem as a Sergeant; front row fifth from the left is James Cameron from Carrickfergus, County Antrim. *21st Independent Parachute Company Club*

Right Third from the left in this photograph is 'Red' Magee of the 21st Independent Parachute Company. James Patrick Magee came from a County Wicklow family and rose through the ranks from private soldier to Lieutenant-Colonel. He was always quite thankful that during his time in Airborne Forces he never had to do a combat parachute jump. *James Magee*

was 'away fighting' in North Africa. Rifleman Hugh Petrie settled for the remainder of the war with the 6th Airborne Division.

Others in the 21st were Richard 'Dick' Rodgers from County Londonderry, who had enlisted in 1940 when he was 17 years old, and Tommy Scullion from Ballymena, County Antrim, whose sister was married to another paratrooper, Boyde Black of the 2nd Parachute Battalion. Tommy had been born in Ballymena in 1923 and had volunteered for the Royal Inniskilling Fusiliers on the outbreak of war. He would survive the battles of North Africa, Italy and Arnhem and, like three

other Irishmen, go on to be a 'film star'. Jimmy Gamble, from Coleraine, County Londonderry, would be one of the lucky ones to escape across the Rhine at the end of the 'Market Garden'.

From outside the Inniskillings came 'Paddy' Cockings, an ex-member of the Royal Horse Artillery, who was to serve at Arnhem as a Sergeant; Jim Fiely from Dublin, ex-Berkshire Regiment; and Redmond from somewhere in Eire, who had an identity crisis![15] There was also 'Curley' Cowan, a

---

[15] Many men from Ireland, for various reasons, served under assumed names.

volunteer from one of the British battalions serving with the Indian Army, covered in tattoos and with spiky jet-black hair that made it look as though he had a hedgehog on his head.

Lance-Corporal Edward Delaney O'Sullivan, another Irishman, was ill and confined to hospital when the 21st Independent left for North Africa. When he recovered he was retained in England, and, because he was a fully trained Pathfinder, he was posted to the newly formed 22nd Independent Parachute Company of the 6th Airborne Division. He jumped with the 22nd in the early hours of D-Day on 6 June 1944, and was killed in action shortly after landing. He was subsequently buried in Touffreville Churchyard, where the village square was later named in his honour.

For Operation 'Market Garden' the 21st would deploy 186 men organised into three platoons and a headquarters. They would fly from Fairford airfield in 12 specially adapted Stirling bombers, the first time they had jumped from this type of aircraft. If the responsibility of getting the Division down on the correct landing zones lay with the 21st Independent, once on the ground the 'eyes' of the Division would be the responsibility of the 1st Airborne Reconnaissance Squadron, commanded by Major Charles Frederick Howard Gough MC.

This unit had been formed in January 1941 as the 31st Independent Reconnaissance Company, the reconnaissance unit of 31st Independent Infantry Brigade, and had joined the 1st Air-Landing Brigade with other support units. In April 1942 it left the Brigade, was re-designated the 1st Airborne Reconnaissance Squadron and became a divisional unit. The men now landed by parachute, and their vehicles travelled by glider. The Squadron's first commanding officer was Major T. B. H. Otway. Terence Brandram Hastings Otway was an Ulster Rifleman, who led the outstanding attack against the Merville Battery on D-Day, winning a well-deserved DSO for his actions.

The Reconnaissance Squadron was equipped with Jeeps and motor-cycles and played its part in the invasion of Italy by a landing from the sea. During the Squadron's advance immediately after the disembarkation in Italy, it was found prudent to carry an Italian officer sitting on the bonnet of the leading jeep to deter any interference from those Italian troops that did not realise they were now on the side of the Allies. 'Freddy' Gough was considered an old man by airborne standards; he celebrated his 43rd birthday the evening before Arnhem. At Arnhem Bridge he would have the chance of earning not only further glory for his family, but also their fourth Victoria Cross. Freddy had served in the Royal Navy as a midshipman in the First World War, had commanded a provost section with the British Expeditionary Force in

From the field of Agincourt to the present day, the Gough family has served in the ranks of the British Army. In August 1945 Freddy Gough returned to Arnhem to play a part in the film *Theirs Is The Glory*. *The Rank Organisation*

France in 1940, and was one of the lucky ones to be evacuated from the beaches of Dunkirk.

For 'Market Garden' his squadron jeeps and their drivers would travel by glider while the remainder of the men would parachute in. The un-armoured jeeps were fitted with a single machine-gun, the Vickers K.[16] Apart from two 3-inch mortars, the only other heavy weapons available to the Reconnaissance Squadron were two 20mm Polsten cannon, a version of the Swiss-manufactured Oerlikon anti-aircraft guns. They had a rate of fire of 450 rounds per minute, and had been adapted for ground use on what was probably one of the most complicated platforms ever devised for a gun! Mounted on a light two-wheeled carriage, the weapons were towed by jeeps of Support Troop.

Gough's attempt to procure twin machine-gun mountings for his jeeps, like his attempt to 'borrow' some Tetrarch light tanks from the 6th Airborne Division, had not been successful; he later blamed a dearth of interest in the higher command of the 1st Airborne Division. Gough's original plan had been to send his three troops, each of eight vehicles, to scout ahead of the three parachute battalions of the 1st Parachute Brigade. Gough stressed that 'information not assault' was the regiment's normal role, but both General Urquhart and Brigadier Lathbury had other ideas; they wanted Gough to launch a coup de main against the bridge, a role to which the Reconnaissance Squadron was totally unsuited.

On the other hand, had Gough been allowed the Tetrarchs he would have had an armoured vehicle with a three-man crew capable of 40mph on roads and armed with a 40mm gun. With eight of these vehicles, as there had been in Normandy, backed up by the Reconnaissance jeeps, a coup de main operation against Arnhem Bridge would in all probability have been successful, with both ends being taken at once and the proposed Polish landing zone secured. Later events would prove that infantry faced with tanks, even lightly armed near-obsolete tanks, would suffer severe psychological pressure, albeit for a short time.

Sergeant Leslie McCreedie from Newtownards, County Down. An ex-Royal Ulster Rifleman, he had served in the Airborne Reconnaissance Squadron since its inception. Wounded during Operation 'Market Garden', he was successfully evacuated across the Rhine at the end of the battle.

Within the Reconnaissance Squadron was Sergeant Leslie McCreedie, an ex-GPO worker from Newtownards, County Down, serving in the Mortar Platoon of Support Company. A veteran of North Africa, Sicily and Italy, he had completed four years service by September 1944. There was also Trooper H. A. Kerr from Newry, County Down, and Sergeant Peter Quinn, an ex-Royal Ulster Rifleman from Athlone.

Artillery support to the Division would come in the form of the 1st Air-Landing Light Regiment, Royal Artillery. This had been formed on 13 February 1943, and by May of the same year it was in action in North Africa. Originally equipped with the 3.7-inch Pack Howitzer, this had been replaced by the American 75mm gun in time for the North African campaign. The howitzer, despite its small size, had a range of 9,600 yards and fired high explosive, smoke and anti-tank shells. It was deemed by the Americans to be very accurate, but they found the shells' explosive power to be too light

---

[16] The Vickers K was an ex-aircraft machine-gun with a distinctive circular top-fitted magazine. It was a dependable weapon with a high rate of fire and a favourite of the Special Air Service, which favoured the guns mounted in pairs.

The Airborne 75mm Gun/Howitzer as used by the 1st Air-Landing Light Regiment RA in Italy and at Arnhem. Two gliders carried each gun detachment into action; the first carried the gun itself, a jeep and an ammunition trailer, while the second carried another jeep and two more ammunition trailers. The crew would be split between the two gliders. Each detachment carried 137 rounds of ammunition, consisting of 125 high-explosive, six armour-piercing and six smoke. It was a good gun, easy to operate and handle with a good rate of fire, but its shell was too light to deal with strong emplacements or heavy vehicles. *Lori Woollacott*

when dealing with armoured vehicles or prepared emplacements. Nevertheless the sight and sound of friendly artillery falling on enemy positions was a great morale-booster, if nothing else.

For Arnhem the plan was that Nos 1 and 3 Batteries would fly in on the first day to be in a position to lend immediate support, while No 2 Battery would land the following day. Forward Observation units would drop with both the parachute battalions and land with the glider elements to ensure that all battalions could call on artillery support when needed. Each Horsa glider allocated to the Regiment carried a jeep, gun and trailer, or a jeep and two trailers, with one jeep-mounted radio per battery. In the history of the Royal Artillery this was the first time that a regiment had flown into battle. For this they were allocated 87 gliders, the first lift flying from Harwell, Keevil, Manston and Fairford, and the second from Down Ampney and Manston. Those glider pilots who would fly the regiment into

Arnhem would stay with them to fight as infantry, and, under the command of Major Bob Croute, the officer commanding 'G' Squadron GPR, they would prove to be an invaluable asset in the days to come.[17]

Among those Irishmen who served with the gunners was John Daly, a native of Waterford; he had enlisted in the Royal Inniskilling Fusiliers before transferring to the 1st Air-Landing Light Regiment. As the Regiment embarked for North Africa, sailing from the River Clyde in Scotland, Sergeant Daly caused some consternation to the other men in the battery when he told them of the last time he had sailed that stretch of water. Dressed in civilian clothes, because he was going home on leave to Wexford in neutral Eire, he had taken the ferry from Stranraer to Larne in Northern Ireland. As they had crossed the Irish Sea a German U-boat had sunk the ferry. He said it totally spoiled his suit, and his leave.

Donald Siggins was born at Northlands,

---

[17] Unlike their British counterparts, American glider pilots were not trained as infantrymen, and when the landings were completed, they had to be returned to the rear as quickly as possible, with regular infantry detailed to act as escorts. When they did elect to stay and fight they performed very well indeed.

Colcraine, in County Londonderry. He was the grandson of the Reverend Foy of Fort Gray, Lisnadill, County Armagh, and had attended the Royal School, Armagh, where the Duke of Wellington had been a pupil, and Methodist College, Belfast. For 'Market Garden' Lieutenant Siggins was to serve as an Assistant Command Post Officer with 'A' Troop 1st Air-Landing Light Battery. Other men who served in the Regiment were Gunner Samuel Gough, from County Londonderry, and Gunner Thomas L Hamilton, also from County Armagh.

To kill enemy tanks the Regiment depended on the guns of the 1st and 2nd Air-Landing Anti-Tank Batteries RA and the anti-tank platoons of the three Air-Landing Brigade Battalions. The normal anti-tank gun for the Division was the 6-pounder, which had a calibre of 57mm and could penetrate up to 73mm of armour at just under 1,000 yards. The ordinary 6-pounder anti-tank gun was difficult to fit into a Horsa glider and the 'airborne' version had folding trail legs, a narrower axle and smaller gun-shield. Each of the Air-Landing Anti-Tank Batteries had one troop of 17-pounder guns, which

Men of the 1st Air-Landing Light Regiment RA at an advanced airstrip (B82) at Kent, a village near Grave. According to Dutch sources, this photograph was probably taken on 26 September 1944. The Sergeant lying at the front left is John Daly from Waterford, who was awarded the Distinguished Conduct Medal for his gallantry at Arnhem. *Lori Woollacott*

HM King George VI views a demonstration by the 2nd Air-Landing Anti-Tank Battery on a visit to the 1st Airborne Division on 16 March 1944. Brigadier Hackett is standing to the left of the King, Major-General Urquhart is to the right, and behind him on the extreme right is General Browning. *IWM H36709*

A 17-pounder anti-tank gun sitting on the west side of the Airborne Museum, Hartenstein, one of 16 such guns taken to Arnhem, of which 11 were used in the actual battle, the others being lost for various reasons. A Hamilcar glider landed this particular gun on 17 September 1944 near Wolfheze, and it saw most of its action near the Oosterbeek Church. On 21 September the gun was hit and the recoil mechanism damaged as the gun recoiled. The result was a shell case jammed in the breech. The gun was moved to its present position after the war. *David Orr*

were the heaviest anti-tank guns in British service and the only weapon in the arsenal of the 1st Airborne Division that could penetrate the armour of the German Tiger tank. They would prove quite a surprise to the Germans at Arnhem.

The 17-pounders had their own towing vehicle[18], which not only towed the gun but also carried the crew and a limited supply of ammunition. Sixteen of these guns were taken to Arnhem, carried in the giant Hamilcar glider. Some guns were lost, even as they were being landed, but the remainder would play a vital part in the defence of the Division's perimeter around Oosterbeek. The guns were continuously in action to repel German armoured attacks, particularly around the Divisional Headquarters and in the lower part of Oosterbeek village.

Medical care was provided by the 16 Parachute Field Ambulance RAMC, attached to the 1st Parachute Brigade, and the 133 Parachute Field Ambulance RAMC, attached to 'Shan' Hackett's 4th Parachute Brigade, while the 181 Air-Landing Field Ambulance RAMC would arrive by glider together with the Air-Landing Brigade on 18 September. A total of approximately 400 men would treat many times their own number, quite often in the most appalling conditions. Corporal J. R. Atkinson from Belfast was one of those men; he

was captured together with nearly all the medics and spent time in Fallingbostel prison camp, not returning home until April 1945.

The Division would take its own police force to Arnhem. The 1st (Airborne) Divisional Provost Company under the command of Captain W. B. Gray led a total of 61 men into 'Market Garden', ostensibly for the guarding of prisoners and traffic control, but these men, like nearly all others, would find themselves in the firing line. They included Tom 'Paddy' Breen, another 'neutral' from Eire; 26 years old, prior to joining the Corps of Military Police he had seen service in Iceland, North Africa and Italy with the Royal Engineers. 'Mick' Cox was another Eire man who volunteered for Airborne Forces. For Arnhem this Dublin man was a Lance-Corporal in No 1 Section of the Provost Corps attached to the 1st Parachute Brigade. Lieutenant W. D. Morley and Sergeant H. L. 'Cab' Calloway commanded his section. In the ranks of the 1st Parachute Squadron, Royal Engineers, was Lance-Corporal Daniel Neville from County Kerry.

These were some of the units that would support and supply the men of the rifle companies contained within the Air-Landing and the two Parachute Brigades. Many would find themselves involved in roles that were totally unexpected, but would without exception adapt and quite often excel.

---

[18] This was the Morris Commercial C8/AT Mk III Artillery Tractor.

1ST PARACHUTE BRIGADE

The 1st Parachute Brigade consisted of the 1st, 2nd and 3rd Parachute Battalions. When veterans talk of their units today they refer to themselves as having been in the 1st Battalion or the 10th, never as 1 PARA or 10 PARA. This is a modern term befitting Northern Ireland or the Falklands; the men of Arnhem do not like it and any serious historian should never use it. Likewise the title of the 156 Battalion is just that, never 156th!

Like the other units in the Division, all the men were volunteers, extremely fit and usually of above average intelligence. Each battalion had three rifle companies as opposed to the four in an ordinary infantry battalion. Within the platoons a sergeant or lance-sergeant instead of a corporal commanded each section. The heaviest weapons carried by the battalion were 3-inch mortars and Vickers machine-guns found in the Support Company. For anti-tank weapons they had to rely on the PIAT or hand-thrown Gammon bombs.[19]

1st Parachute Battalion

By 1944, half of the 1st Parachute Battalion wore the yellow ribbon of the Africa Star, but the remainder of the men had seen little or no active service. Lieutenant-Colonel David Dobie, himself a veteran of North Africa, would lead the Battalion into Arnhem. They would fly from Barkston Heath airfield aboard 37 Dakotas, with their vehicles carried in the Horsa glider.

Among the Irishmen in the Battalion was Lance-Sergeant Frank Bell, from Lisburn, County Antrim, a man strong in both religious faith and professional soldiering. There was also Sergeant John Bermingham from Dublin; he had been a peacetime soldier, serving in the Royal Ulster Rifles in India prior to transferring to Airborne. In India John Bermingham had served with Victor Hughes, who later served in the 3rd Battalion at Arnhem.

'C' Company of the 1st (Airborne) Battalion, Royal Ulster Rifles, 1942. Fourth from the left in the third row is Private 'Billy' Saunders, who would do so much with the 2-inch mortar while serving with the 2nd Parachute Battalion at Arnhem. Fifth from the left in the front row is Lieutenant Mike Dowling from Tipperary, who was killed on 6 June 1944 in Normandy while serving with the 9th Parachute Battalion. *William Saunders*

---

[19] Captain Arthur Gammon of the 1st Parachute Battalion had invented the Gammon Bomb in 1941. It consisted of a stockinet bag filled with plastic explosive and fitted with a screw cap containing the fuse. To arm the bomb the cap was removed and the bomb thrown by hand. An alternative was to leave it lying on the ground as a mine. The PIAT, projectile infantry anti tank, was a shoulder-fired spring-loaded weapon capable of propelling a 2lb bomb some 50 yards.

While John Bermingham was serving with the 1st Airborne, a relation, Sergeant Richard Patrick Bermingham, was serving in the 2nd Royal Tank Regiment with the 7th Armoured Brigade in Italy. He would receive the Military Medal for his actions near Savignano in 1945.[20] The men of the 1st Battalion remembered John Bermingham as a big genial man; they trusted him completely and would have followed him anywhere.

Private Charles Davidson came from Saintfield, County Down, and his was also a military family. His father had served in the 36th (Ulster) Division in the First World War and his brother Johnny was serving in the Durham Light Infantry. Private William John Patrick Devlin was born in Hong Kong; where his father had been a Sergeant Major in an Irish regiment. His cousin, 'Paddy' Devlin, was currently serving with the 6th Airborne Division in the ranks of the 1st (Airborne) Battalion of the Royal Ulster Rifles.

Lance-Sergeant Jack Fryer was another from the Ulster Rifles, and again his was a military family. His father had served in the Royal Marines in the First World War, was awarded the Military Medal and received a commission in the field; an uncle had been killed on the Somme in 1916. In July of 1940, despite being a year under age, Jack enlisted in the 7th (Young Soldiers) Battalion of the Royal Ulster Rifles. A year later he had transferred to Airborne and was posted to the 1st Parachute Battalion.

The Dougan brothers, Norman and Sandy, came from Glenanne, County Armagh. Their father had served during the First World War with the Royal Irish Fusiliers. It was not enough that his two sons served in the Second; he himself saw a further three and a half years service starting in 1939. He was discharged in 1943 due to wounds received while fighting in North Africa.

Robert Alexander, known as 'Sandy', his eldest son, had enlisted in the Home Guard on its formation and then into the ranks of the Royal Inniskilling Fusiliers prior to transferring to Airborne. Here he served in the 1st Parachute Battalion, seeing action in Tunisia, Sicily and Italy before the ill-fated drop at Arnhem. Norman Arthur Dougan lied about his age and, being a well-built lad, was able to enlist at the age of 15 years and 9 months; both brothers served in 'R' Company at Arnhem.

Lieutenant John McFadden commanded 9

Far left The kneeling figure is Private Robert Alexander 'Sandy' Dougan from Glenanne, County Armagh. He was on of two brothers to serve in the 1st Parachute Battalion and one of the first casualties at Arnhem. *Dorothy Hendren*

Left Private Norman Arthur Dougan, brother of 'Sandy'. Like many others who could not escape across the Rhine on 26 September, but went into hiding and in October 1944 swam the Rhine to safety despite wounds, hunger and exhaustion. *Dorothy Hendren*

[20] PRO Kew, WO373/10

Platoon of 'T' Company. The son of Doctor A. J. W. McFadden and grandson of the late Archdeacon Spence DD, he had obtained a scholarship to Campbell College, Belfast, and had played rugby for Northern Ireland. A quiet confident man with natural leadership abilities, he was acknowledged as the best map-reader in the Battalion. Jack Fryer remembers him as

'An absolute gentleman. Very quiet, very polite. He came to us from the Tower Hamlet Rifles; his brother had been killed in a road accident some time during the war. He didn't give orders; he made suggestions, like "I think it would be a good idea if you took your men up ahead Sergeant." That sort of thing. The men loved him. He was the best map-reader in the Battalion. On exercises, especially night marches, the company commander, Perrin-Brown, would say, "Right John, get your boys up to the front", and off we would go, sure we would have the company home in time for breakfast.'[21]

William Magill came from Banbridge in County Down, and joined the 1st Battalion in June 1942, after completing four years service with both the Royal Ulster Rifles and the Royal Irish Fusiliers. He also served in 'R' Company. Sidney Ellis was known as 'Fightin' Sid'; at 37 years of age he was almost a pensioner by Airborne standards. From his home in Sandy Row, Belfast, he had enlisted in the Army as a boy soldier and had later served in India for six years with the Royal Irish Fusiliers. After his term of enlistment was up he returned to civilian life, but maintained his contact with the military by joining the Supplementary Reserve. Finding 'civvy street' too quiet, he went to the Middle East and served for two and a half years with the Palestine Police Force. Returning to Belfast he became a prison warder in the Crumlin Road Gaol. On the outbreak of war he rejoined his old regiment, but a short while later transferred to the Royal Armoured Corps, where he remained until 1943. This time he

'Fightin' Sid' – Private Sidney Ellis of the 1st Parachute Battalion, killed near the St Elizabeth Hospital on Monday 18 September 1944. He was a pre-war soldier and a former member of the Palestine Police.

transferred to Airborne Forces and saw some action in Italy before returning to England to train for 'Market Garden'.

Samuel Hillis was a fellow Belfastman, coming from Donegal Pass. He had enlisted, aged 23, in the Royal Inniskilling Fusiliers in 1940, but had transferred to the 1st Battalion in time for service in North Africa and Sicily, where he had a narrow escape from death when a German mortar bomb exploded on the parapet of his trench. James Usher had joined the battalion from the Ox and Bucks Light Infantry. Usher was also from Belfast and soon made friends with fellow 'townies' Hillis and Ellis. They would serve together until 18 September 1944, when a German bullet changed things for ever.

Peter Markey came from the border town of Newry in County Down. A well-known amateur boxer before the war, he had enlisted in the Army Reserve while working in England. He had gone to France with the Royal Signals and after a successful evacuation from Dunkirk had transferred to the Army Physical Training Corps, a branch of army life dear to his heart. As a Physical Training Instructor he had been one of the first volunteers for

---

21 Major C. Perrin-Brown MC, officer commanding 'T' Company at Arnhem. He was awarded the DSO for his action during 'Market Garden'.

Above Sergeant Peter Markey from Newry, County Down, who served with the 1st Parachute Battalion at Arnhem. Before the war he was a respected and well-known figure in local boxing circles. His maroon beret bears the badge of the Army Physical Training Corps, his previous unit. *David Greeney, New Zealand*

Right James Isaac McMurray from Waringstown, County Down. He first enlisted in the Royal Ulster Rifles before transferring to the London Irish Rifles. *Mr Howard Hamilton*

James Isaac McMurray in the London Irish Rifles, where he gained a fine reputation as a sportsman. *Mr Howard Hamilton*

airborne forces, and in the course of his training he had his arms broken on five occasions, not to mention various other sprains and gashes. As a sergeant at Arnhem he would survive for the first four days without a scratch, but this would change on the Thursday following.

John Towhey came from Eire and had served with the Royal Irish Fusiliers before transferring to Airborne Forces. He was a Bren-gunner in 'R' Company and was to be one of the first casualties of the Battalion during 'Market Garden'. Anthony L. Clarke, another Irishman, came from the Royal Artillery and served in 'T' Company, 1st Battalion, as a Corporal. James Isaac McMurray was born in

Waringstown, County Down, one of four sons born to Thomas and Edith McMurray, three of whom would serve in the British Army during the Second World War. James had been working in Nuneaton, Warwickshire, when war broke out, and he quickly returned home to enlist in the Royal Ulster Rifles. After his initial training he was posted to the London Irish Rifles, where he excelled on the sports field, winning many battalion trophies. Andrew McKee came from Newtownards in County Down. 'Adie', as friends and family knew him, enlisted in the Royal Inniskilling Fusiliers on 14 June 1939. He transferred to Airborne Forces on 9 May 1941, being posted to 'T' Company of the 1st Battalion as a Bren-gunner. He served with the Battalion in North Africa, Sicily, Italy and at Arnhem, where he was one of those captured.

2nd Parachute Battalion

The men of the 1st Battalion had been more than a little aggrieved when 'C' Company of the 2nd Battalion was chosen to take part in the raid that procured vital radar intelligence and equipment in 1942. Operation 'Biting' was carried out on the night of 27 February 1942, when the men of 'C' Company dropped by parachute from 12 Whitley bombers on to landing zones at Bruneval, north of Le Havre in France. The raid was a complete success with the recovery of vital intelligence and equipment at a cost of only a few casualties. By 0330hrs the raiders had been successfully evacuated from a nearby beach by Royal Navy landing craft. The Battalion had both a strong Scots and Irish flavour, and at the time of the raid 'C' Company was known as Jock Company.

Cecil Newell came from Annalong in County Down. Before the war he had been a member of the Ulster Special Constabulary, a force that had been raised in 1920 to assist the Royal Irish Constabulary in its fight against the IRA. When Cecil enlisted in the Royal Artillery in March 1940 the main interest to his recruiters was not the fact that he was fully trained in the use of the .303 rifle and .38 revolver, but that he could ride a motorbike. Apparently this was deemed an essential experience for someone who was to maintain the generators that powered the searchlights. He was sent to Blackburn Heath

to be outfitted for service in Iceland! However, before this could happen it was decided that his skills would be better employed on anti-invasion duties. Cecil was therefore dispatched posthaste to a camp on the Yorkshire coast just north of Hull, where the accommodation consisted of old buses sitting on concrete blocks, having been a pre-war holiday camp. For the next two years Cecil carried out his duties, and the generators continued to work perfectly, which was possibly their only means of defence in the event of invasion; for the first year there was only one rifle between every four men. The garrison reckoned that the barbed wire was as much to keep them in as the enemy out.

Cecil remembered that after the initial panic that invasion was imminent, things settled down to a somewhat boring routine.

Private Cecil Newell from Annalong, County Down. He transferred from the Royal Artillery to Airborne Forces and served in 'A' Company of the 2nd Parachute Battalion in North Africa, Sicily and at Arnhem, where he was taken prisoner. He wears the Royal Artillery cap badge in his maroon beret. Cecil was still serving the Crown in 1971! *Mr Ted Flanagan*

'The CO, he was always looking for something to keep us occupied. One day he took a crowd of men from the battery into the nearest town and we spent the day on the roller-skating rink. Imagine a crowd of soldiers on roller-skates flying about the place. We came home that night with quite a few bruises, probably more than we got on most exercises.'

The officer commanding this unit was not one to allow his men to be idle for long. During the long winter evenings, entertainment was supplied.

'The CO, he was courting the local parson's daughter and he would bring her up to the camp to see the shows. Him and her would sit in the front row, his big bald head shining in the light. When some of us left the cook-house we would lift a handful of dried peas and when you sat down for the show you rolled up your programme into a tube and shot the peas at his head. He took it all in good humour.'

Eventually, after many applications, the Royal Artillery conceded to his demands and he transferred to Airborne Forces.

'It must have been about 2300hrs, the duty NCO came in to the hut, gave me a bump to wake me up, and told me I had to see the OC in his office right away. He said to me, "Newell, you've passed for the paratroopers and you're off tomorrow at 0600hrs. Remember if you are ever near anywhere I'm stationed make sure you call and see me." That was the type of him, a good sort.'

The next morning Cecil found himself on a train bound for a sealed camp situated midway between Chesterfield and Mansfield. Here the training consisted of the trainees jumping off the back of lorries travelling at 30 miles per hour to simulate a parachute landing. This exercise resulted in so many broken arms and legs that it was soon cancelled. When recruits were ready they were taken to an airfield to make their first jump from a tethered balloon.

'At the time I did my first jump they only took two men up at a time. I went up with this corporal; it was very early in the morning, about 0500hrs. Down we came and boy it was great. Not only that but after the jump you got a 24-hour pass, so we asked the RAF instructor if we could have another go. He said to wait and if there were any spare 'chutes we could have another go. About mid-afternoon we were called and up went again. The result was two 24-hour passes, a whole 48 hours away from camp – it was great.'

When it came to jumping from an aircraft Cecil discovered that if you were first out of the door you were usually first on the ground, and therefore among the first to get back to camp to enjoy, among other things, a limited supply of hot water. After one such jump on a rather windy day he had been back to camp, got changed and was waiting at the nearby railway station to go on a well-earned leave when another trainee arrived on the platform.

'Paddy you won't believe it, they had to get the Fire Brigade out, half of the boys are stuck in the trees.'

Apparently the wind had changed suddenly and many men had been blown into the nearby woods.

Reginald Bryan Woods of Malahide, County Dublin, had been studying at Cambridge when war was declared. His was also a military family. His brother Desmond was in the Royal Ulster Rifles and had won the Military Cross serving in Palestine, while their father had served in the Royal Munster Fusiliers in the First World War. Bryan joined the Ulster Rifles at the Regimental Depot at Ballymena, County Antrim, and was shortly commissioned into the 1st (Airborne) Battalion. He later transferred to the 2nd Parachute Battalion and served with them in North Africa and Sicily before Arnhem. Because of his Irish accent he was known as 'Danny Boy' by the other officers, while the enlisted men called him 'Lakari', a Hindustani word meaning 'wood', which shows that the other ranks of the battalion were capable of displaying a little more imagination than their officers. For 'Market Garden' he commanded the Mortar

Platoon in Support Company. James Sims, a Private in the platoon, recalled his first meeting with Lieutenant Woods when he demonstrated a quick method of creating a mortar pit. There was no call for either pick or shovel, just the judicious use of a small quantity of plastic explosive![22]

Captain (Temporary Major) Richard Thomas Henry Lonsdale was described as a 'rumbustious Irishman'. His career was one of near constant movement from unit to unit for behaviour that was described as unconventional. Lonsdale had been commissioned into the 1st Battalion of the Leicestershire Regiment on 27 August 1936. He was a keen rugby player and was one of those responsible for raising the standard of play within the Regiment to such an extent that in 1939 it beat the Welch Regiment in the final of The Calcutta Cup by 6 points to 3.

In the same year Lonsdale was awarded the Military Cross. By this time he was serving with the 1st Battalion in Waziristan on the North West Frontier of India, during one of the innumerable 'imperial policing' duties that the British Army carried out in far-flung corners of the Empire. The

winter of 1938-39 saw the Battalion at Razmak, a vast perimeter camp surrounded by a stone parapet, barbed wire and with massive stone towers at key points. From here troops were able to dominate the surrounding countryside and keep some semblance of law and order. While things were relatively quiet

Lieutenant Reginald Bryan 'Lakari' Woods, the officer commanding the mortars of the 2nd Parachute Battalion at Arnhem Bridge. Injured by shrapnel near the end of the battle for the bridge, he later died of his wounds in prison camp. Here he wears the Royal Ulster Rifles cap badge on his maroon beret. *Desmond Woods*

A patrol of the Leicestershire Regiment prepares to ascend to the piquet post known as 'Dun', near Razmak, North West Frontier, 1938. From left to right they are a Sepoy, Sergeant William Stevens, Lieutenant Richard 'Dickie' Lonsdale, Sergeant A. Horrocks leaning on his rifle, and Lieutenant Hillen standing with hand in pocket. *Ex-Sergeant Bill Stevens, 1st Battalion Leicestershire Regiment*

---

[22] Letter to the author

there was a constant danger from ambushes and snipers. On the night of 14 November 1939 a company was withdrawing its pickets from a position quite close to the main camp when, through no fault of its own, it was left without a reserve while the remaining men made their way back. Suddenly at the end of a long, tiring and uneventful day, there came a burst of fire from the rocks above the trail. As the remaining men dashed for the safety of the main camp it was discovered that there had been casualties. Lieutenant Lonsdale called for volunteers to assist him in bringing in these wounded men, who were lying in the open. With Corporal Vincent and Lance-Corporals Carter and Moore, he successfully brought in all the injured men. As a result of this action Lonsdale and Vincent received the Military Cross and Military Medal respectively.

When the 2nd Battalion was fighting for possession of the Primasole Bridge in Sicily, Lonsdale would be there. When the 11th Parachute Battalion found itself fighting to reinforce the men holding out at Arnhem Bridge and later defending the Oosterbeek perimeter, Lonsdale would be there.

3rd Parachute Battalion

'They left their homes, families and jobs, and came from all over the British Isles – London, Manchester, Glasgow, Cardiff, and Dublin. They came from factories and fields, mines and universities, ships and docks. Some were poor, others comfortably off – but they all knew what a Fascist victory in Spain would mean for the world's future, for everything meant by progress and for everything that makes life worth living. They did the only thing open to them when they learned about the Fascist invasion, and came here, prepared to sacrifice everything if this could stop and push back fascism.

'They came in small groups of ten, twenty or fifty, by various routes. But whichever way they came, their arrival was equally welcome, their spirit and determination were the same.' (Frank Graham, British Battalion, International Brigade, Spain)

'Paddy' Morton had been 'born a socialist' in Belfast in 1920, the son of an ardent supporter of the Trade Union movement. Throughout his boyhood Patrick had been treated to the history of Karl Marx and the Russian Revolution by his father, and the works of Oscar Wilde by his mother; he was also a Catholic. In 1936 he was working in the North of England apprenticed to a small engineering firm, the result of a favour owed to his father by a fellow trade unionist, there being little employment for Catholics in Belfast in the years before the war.

In Spain the first battles against Fascism were being fought in a war that would eventually embroil all of Europe. In the town where Patrick worked men were leaving their jobs and their families to serve in Spain with the British Battalion of the International Brigade. Given his background and the fact that he was 17 years old, Patrick's idealism left him with no choice but to go with them. From Newcastle-upon-Tyne he made his way to London and the short sailing across the Channel to France. There he joined with a group of fellow freedom fighters, men from Dublin, Cardiff, Manchester, Glasgow and London. Travelling by coach they reached the Spanish border, where a representative of the Brigade met them.

Everything in Spain was so different for Patrick. It was a land of outstanding beauty, of vivid colour and strange exotic smells, some of which were even pleasant. As the coach passed through the towns and villages, with their white-washed walls and red-tiled roofs, people came out to cheer, shout 'Salud' and 'No pasaran', all the time giving the clenched-fist salute. In return the men on the bus would sing the 'Internationionale'.[23] Patrick remembers it like it was yesterday.

---

[23] It was during the author's third interview with Patrick – never Paddy – that he was treated to the rousing chorus of this song. We were having lunch in the Europa Hotel, Belfast, infamous for being 'the most bombed hotel in the world outside Beirut'. If you haven't heard the 'Internationale' sung by a very happy 80-year-old veteran of the Spanish Civil War, you haven't lived.

'In Newcastle life had been dull, grey and depressing. Here, despite the raging civil war, everything was so much brighter; the white-washed houses, the rich brown earth and everywhere groves of orange trees. This was where I had my first taste of an orange and I gorged myself on them so much that to this day I cannot bear their smell or taste.'

After a period spent training at the town of Madrigueras, Patrick was attached to a unit of machine-gunners and sent to join the British Battalion on the Jarama Front. The weapon issued to him was a Russian Maxim machine-gun. Patrick noted with some surprise that the weapon he trained on had originally been built in England some 36 years previously. At Jarama Patrick was involved in some of the fiercest fighting of the entire war. After 51 days in the trenches there, Patrick's war came to an end one morning as he waited in a queue for breakfast. An enemy shell landed close to the trench and he was knocked unconscious. When he awoke it was found that his eyesight was badly blurred and when, after several weeks, there was no sign that it was going to improve he was sent home. With a week he was back in Newcastle-upon-Tyne and, by the time his eyesight eventually returned to normal, another war was waiting.[24]

He wanted to enlist in his grandfather's regiment, the Royal Irish Fusiliers, but as he could drive and had experience with machinery he was, like Cecil Newell, sent to the Royal Artillery. With the rank of Bombardier, he accompanied a battery of 25-pounder guns to France as part of the British Expeditionary Force, then spent a miserable winter sitting in another trench. With the commencement of the German Blitzkrieg in May 1940, the battery quickly lost all its transport to air attack. The result was that those guns still surviving had to be abandoned when the withdrawal to the beaches began. Patrick found himself in the role of a machine-gunner once again, and his skills were called into play on many occasions during the long rearguard action on the road to Dunkirk. When his party eventually reached the coast they were directed to one of the lengthy queues stretching out from the beach.

'The thing I remember most about Dunkirk was the silence of the men as we queued up in the water. Long lines of men standing perfectly motionless, no talking, and no unnecessary movement, just waiting. We were cold, tired and hungry, but confident that we would be taken off. The man in front of me had a bad head wound and was unable to see. Holding the man in front of him by the shoulder, they both made their way into deeper water. As we slowly moved along his mate told him, "We both go in the boat and if there is not enough room for both of us, we wait for the next one." With friends like that you can't go far wrong.'

After several hours standing in the cold water a rowing-boat passed along the line of waiting men and gave out life-jackets to some of those that were non-swimmers. Patrick was one of those and he made sure the belt was well secured. Some time later another boat took him and about 20 others aboard and ferried them out to a destroyer. Climbing aboard he collapsed exhausted on the deck. A crewman gave him a mug of hot cocoa and a put a cigarette between his lips. He was so exhausted he was unable to untie the wet cords securing his life-jacket, raise the mug to his lips or even remove the cigarette from his mouth – he was a non-smoker at the time. As the destroyer turned away from the French coast and steered towards the white cliffs of England, Stuka dive-bombers came down out of the sun. A direct hit was scored, the destroyer heeled over and quickly sank.

Patrick was tossed back into the sea, ever thankful that he had been unable to take off his life-

---

[24] It has been estimated that some 132 men fought for the Republican forces, while General Eoin O'Duffy led 700 Irish volunteers of the 15th Bandera of the Spanish Foreign Legion on the Nationalist side; they also fought at Jarama. Source: *An Cosantoir*, February 1984, p39

jacket – his very tiredness had saved his life.[25] For the second time he was hauled aboard a ship and eventually made it back to England on one of the South Coast pleasure-steamers.[26]

After returning to England he spent the next two years on garrison duty in various parts of Wales. Driven almost insane with the boredom of life in the valleys, he volunteered for Airborne Forces and after initial training was posted to the 3rd Parachute Battalion stationed at Bulford in Wiltshire. Here he met one George Albert Fitzpatrick, a Protestant from Limerick and another third-generation Irishman in the ranks of the British Army. His family was not happy with another Fitzpatrick enlisting in the British Army; his grandfather had been killed during 'Black Week' in December 1899 while serving with the Connaught Rangers[27], and his father had died during the German offensive of March 1918. George's mother did not want to hang a third photograph on her parlour wall, or to diligently clean a third set of medals. If George Albert went off to fight she wanted him to come home to clean his own medals. George had worked in England for several years before the war and felt that as the country had given him a job, he should do something in return.

Patrick Morton and George Fitzpatrick, known as 'Fitz', first met in a pub – where else? As they sat outside in the rare spring sunshine a small unit of cavalry rode by.

'Why are your horses so sad?' asked Fitzpatrick. This query was met by blank looks from the troopers. 'Just wondered why all the long faces.'

In the following 5 minutes it was proved that two Irishmen could outrun even thoroughbred cavalry horses, especially if the back gardens of cottages were included in the course, and it was from this time that Patrick realised he had found a friend for life. It was the beginning of a friendship that was well forged by the time the Battalion left for North Africa and would end only in death in September 1944.

Victor Hughes served with the 3rd Battalion at Arnhem as a Lance-Corporal in 'B' Company. He was another ex-Royal Ulster Rifleman who had

Soldiers of the 1st Air-Landing Brigade on air-experience training in a Horsa glider somewhere in England. Note that all the men are carrying a parachute as well. The photograph was published in a Northern Ireland newspaper in 1943.

[25] During the First World War Mr Harry Corry from Dundonald, County Down, was sunk while serving with the Merchant Marine. His life was saved in exactly the same way. At the time of writing Mr Corry is 100 years old.

[26] The future Field Marshal Montgomery was also on the beach waiting to be evacuated. With him was Captain Charles Sweeney of the Royal Ulster Rifles. As they waited to be taken aboard one of the small vessels that would ferry them off the beach, Sweeney was wounded in the head by a piece of shrapnel. This led to an outburst from Montgomery on the foolishness of not wearing a helmet, which was only brought to a halt when Sweeney pointed out that Montgomery was also without a helmet. Charles Sweeney served with Montgomery until the end of the war, when he was tragically killed in a road accident a few days after the surrender had been signed.

[27] British defeats by the Boers at Stormberg, Magersfontein and Colenso came to be known as 'Black Week'.

A group of Royal Ulster Rifles on the North West Frontier in the 1930s. The man fourth from the left is Dubliner John Bermingham, who would later be killed at Arnhem serving with the 1st Parachute Battalion as a sergeant. The man on the right holding the .45-inch revolver is Charles Hughes, who would later serve in the 1st (Airborne) Battalion of the Royal Ulster Rifles in Normandy. The photograph was taken by Charles's brother Victor, who later served in the 3rd Parachute Battalion at Arnhem. *Victor Hughes*

seen service on the North West Frontier of India in the 1930s. One of those with Victor on the Frontier was John Bermingham, later to serve with the 1st Battalion at Arnhem. Victor's twin brother Charles was also on the Frontier at that time and went on to serve with the 6th Airborne Division in Normandy.

Victor remembers the time the 'Rifles' were part of the 1st Air-Landing Brigade and his section was sent to have their familiarisation flight in a Hotspur glider.

'It was in 1942, we were on our way to the airfield when the truck broke down. By the time the driver had it going again we were running late and arrived just as our glider was taking off. The section that was to go after us was taken up instead; I think they were men from the Ox and Bucks. Well, as the glider left the ground it suddenly nose-dived and went straight in. All on board were killed, seven men just like that, six Ox and Bucks and the pilot. Well that did it for me. I decided that these gliders were just too dangerous and I volunteered for the paratroopers.'

These were the men of the 1st Parachute Brigade. Of all the troops sent to Arnhem, these were the most experienced, a story that would be told in the casualty lists of the three battalions, nearly 100 fewer than those suffered by the 4th Brigade.

An Airspeed Hotspur glider in flight in 1942.

4TH PARACHUTE BRIGADE

The 4th Parachute Brigade was originally formed in the Middle East in late 1942 as an independent brigade, then in 1943 it joined the 1st Airborne Division in exchange for 2nd Parachute Brigade. Its CO was Brigadier 'Shan' Hackett DSO, who commanded it from its inception to its destruction in the suburbs of Arnhem in September of 1944.

John Winthrop Hackett had been born in Australia, the only son among the five children of a wealthy Irish family. Hackett's father owned two newspapers in Western Australia and had been the founder of Perth University. Hackett had studied painting at the London Central Art School before taking up an academic career at Oxford to read Greats. His hopes of becoming a don were not to be realised, as his degree was not good enough. Therefore he joined the Army and was commissioned into the 8th (King's Royal Irish) Hussars. 'I never went into the Army,' Hackett insisted. 'I joined my great-grandfather's regiment. There is no such thing as the British Army – there are only regiments. That is the great source of strength in the British endeavour: it's a family thing.'

Hackett did not neglect his studies while in the Army, and his thesis on Saladin and the Third Crusade earned him the degree of Bachelor of Letters. He was Mentioned-in-Despatches twice for his part in anti-terrorist operations in Palestine in 1936 and received two more MIDs while seconded to the Transjordan Frontier Force in 1937. This 'broken-down cavalryman' had been wounded in 1941 while in action against the Vichy French in Syria. By May he was in command of 'C' Squadron of the 8th (King's Royal Irish) Hussars and fighting Rommel's Panzers near Bir Hacheim. On 27 May his squadron was responsible for the destruction of 30 enemy tanks, but with heavy losses to the Hussars' tanks, mostly knocked out by the fire of the dreaded '88'. He was awarded the DSO for action in the Western Desert in 1942, where he had served as GSO1 Raiding Forces, Middle East Land Force. He received another MID while commanding the 4th Parachute Brigade in Italy in 1943. While the Brigade waited at its base at Kabrit, Hackett started a riding school for his officers. It was his belief that infantry officers did not look far enough ahead when moving across country and the view from horseback would teach them to take more advantage of the ground.[28]

Brigadier 'Shan' Hackett, commander of the 4th Parachute Brigade, flanked by his Divisional Commander 'Roy' Urquhart (right) and Field Marshal Montgomery, visiting the 1st Airborne Division in April 1944. Montgomery wears the Parachute wings in his beret, Hackett sports the Staff badge, while Urquhart has the Army Air Corps badge. *Robert Voskuil*

---

[28] A point disputed by Montgomery, who thought the whole idea of officers on horseback was a complete waste of time. However, Montgomery was wrong, and tank losses in the early desert battles proved that commanders were not reading the ground properly.

Within the Brigade Headquarters Defence Platoon were Francis and Thomas Dolaghan, two brothers from Belfast. Francis had served in the Royal Army Service Corps, while Thomas had come from the Inniskilling Fusiliers. The remainder of the Platoon's soldiers were nominally provided by the 1st Battalion Ox and Bucks Light Infantry. The Platoon's role was to provide all-round defence of the Brigade Headquarters; they had their work cut out for them at Arnhem.

After the Battle of El Alamein, the 2nd Battalion of the Royal Sussex Regiment had been selected for conversion to an airborne role. Some 200 men volunteered, the remainder made up with volunteers from the Infantry Base Depot situated at Geneifa. The unit was designated the 10th Parachute Battalion. Two Irishmen who served in the Battalion were Sergeant Jack Bateman, from County Down, one of those that would return in 1945 to help in the making of the film *Theirs Is The Glory*, and Joseph Burke from Cabra in County Dublin. Burke had transferred to the 10th from the Royal Norfolk Regiment.

The 11th Parachute Battalion was the baby of the Brigade. Formed at Kabrit, Palestine, in 1943, many of the men were not of the highest calibre. For the previous three years other units had been recruiting the best that was on offer, including the Commandos, Special Air Service and the other parachute battalions. Nevertheless enough men were eventually found, but the Battalion was still not fully trained when it left the Middle East to join the remainder of 1st Airborne. The only action of the 11th was when 'C' Company was dropped on the Greek island of Cos[29] to capture the local airfield after the Italian surrender. Some bombing by the Luftwaffe was its only action before returning to Britain to join the remainder of the Brigade. Volunteers for the Battalion came from both north and south of the Irish border and from all three Irish Regiments. They included Thomas G. Armstrong, an ex-Royal Irish Fusilier, from Dungiven in County Londonderry; Private Patrick Sullivan from County Wicklow, an ex-Inniskilling Fusilier; and Bill Kerr, an ex-Royal Ulster Rifleman, and future governor of the Crumlin Road Prison in Belfast. Another 'Faugh'[30] with the battalion

Sergeant Jack Bateman from County Down. He served in the 10th Parachute Battalion at Arnhem and was one of those selected to take part in the film *Theirs Is The Glory*.

---

[29] Cos, sometimes spelt Kos, was just one of the many mistakes in the Aegean campaign. This drop was made on the night of 14 September 1943, the DZ for the company having been marked out by members of the Special Boat Squadron. Despite reinforcements from the Durham Light Infantry and RAF Regiment, any thought of defence was quickly dispelled by the incessant and accurate bombing by the Luftwaffe in preparation for its seaborne assault. The company was withdrawn on 25 September. The capture of Cos was supposed to make the defence of Rhodes impossible, and with the fall of Rhodes the invasion of Greece would be feasible.

[30] 'Faugh', pronounced 'Fog', is the nickname given to members of this regiment, taken from their war cry 'Faugh-a-Ballagh', roughly translated as 'Clear the way', although there are several other versions.

was Jim Harkin from County Armagh. Jim had originally enlisted in the Royal Ulster Rifles, but when it was discovered that he was under-age he was returned home under escort of a Battalion Corporal, who suggested he re-enlist in another two years. When that time had elapsed Jim decided to go for the regiment of his home town, so the Royal Irish Fusiliers got the benefit of his services. He accompanied the 'Faughs' to Palestine in 1938, where Arab marksmanship did not impress him in the least, but the constant noise and the smell really got on his nerves.

When the Regiment was sent to Malta Jim went with them and endured the months of bombing from German and Italian aircraft. On Malta Jim was part of the force defending the airfield used by one of the RAF's most famous pilots, 'Screwball' Beurling DSO DFC DFM. 'It was a great day when the Spitfires flew in from the aircraft carrier. They were no sooner on the ground than they were refuelled, re-armed and off again to battle the enemy. Beurling was a man who knew his job, a very conscious worker.'

Shortly after Malta he volunteered for airborne training and was posted to the 11th Battalion. He was one of those who took part in the assault on Cos. His opinion of the enemy was not great. 'There was no fight in the Italians; we completed our mission and were back in our base in ten days.' It must be remembered that the Italians were on the point of surrendering and coming on to the Allied side, so their lack of aggression can be understood.

Among the Battalion's officers was Major Richard 'Dickie' Lonsdale, the 'rumbustious Irishman' already encountered, who moved to the 11th from the 2nd Battalion. At Arnhem he would serve as second-in-command of the Battalion under Lieutenant-Colonel George Lea. Lonsdale's experience in North Africa and Sicily would stand him in good stead during the fighting at Arnhem, where he would command 'Lonsdale Force'.

The third battalion of the Brigade was the 156 Battalion. It had been raised in India as the British Parachute Battalion of the Indian Parachute Brigade and given the number 151. A Colonel Lindsay had formed the Battalion in 1941, and was the first soldier ever to make a parachute jump from the rear of a Whitley bomber. When the Battalion was formed there had been an absolute deluge of volunteers from all over India; this was before Japan had entered the war and most men stationed in India saw little chance of seeing any action. The initial appearance of the men was somewhat strange. They made their jumps wearing solar topees and shorts, a sight to bring fear to any enemy! Later Colonel Lindsay had the topees changed to the more comfortable bush hats. When the Battalion moved to the Middle East its number was changed from 151 to 156 to confuse the Germans into thinking that another parachute battalion had moved into the theatre. In India the men had been issued with bush hats, comfortable to wear and easily stuffed into the front of smocks during jumping. In North Africa they were forced to give these up for the maroon beret, not a popular move – they considered the beret to be a bit effeminate for a military man, more suited to French onion-sellers than soldiers! When first paraded in brand new berets the men looked as though they were wearing pancakes on their heads. The inspecting officer criticised their appearance and told them they would have to learn the proper way of wearing an Airborne beret. A voice from the ranks told him just what the Battalion thought of this headgear, and for once it was not an Irish accent, although one of those who strongly objected to the beret was John Joseph O'Reilly.

Born in Belfast in 1921, 'JJ' had originally enlisted in the Royal Inniskilling Fusiliers. He left them in 1942 while stationed in India to transfer to the then 151 Battalion. This was a fortuitous move for John Joseph. When the Inniskillings left for the campaign in Burma there were more than 600 men in the Battalion. When the 'Skins returned to India there were just over 100 survivors of the original unit. When the 151 became the 156 'JJ' went with it and served in the Middle East, Sicily and Italy. At Arnhem he was serving as a Sergeant in 'C' Company.

Joseph D. Ryan from County Armagh had enlisted in 1935. He was another who had been stationed in India on the outbreak of war. He had volunteered for parachute training and was posted to the 151 Battalion. When the Battalion arrived in North

Left Sergeant John Joseph O'Reilly from Belfast. While serving in India with the Royal Inniskilling Fusiliers he transferred to the newly raised 151 Parachute Battalion (later 156 Battalion). He is wearing the slouch hat that was the preferred headgear of the Battalion before being forced to adopt the more formal maroon beret. *Arnhem Battle Research Group*

Middle Lance-Corporal 'Ernie' Lynas from County Armagh. An ex-'Faugh', he served in 156 Parachute Battalion at Arnhem and was killed on 25 September 1944, at the age of 26. *Lynas family*

Right Private Norman Diffin from County Armagh. He travelled from the port of Larne to Scotland on a coal boat to enlist in the Royal Scots Fusiliers. For operation 'Market Garden' he served in the ranks of the 156 Parachute Battalion. He was severely wounded while aboard the Dakota during the run-in to the drop zone on 18 September 1944. *The Portadown Times*

Africa he served with them until the end of that campaign before he transferred to the Special Air Service. He re-enlisted on the outbreak of the Korean War and served there in the Royal Artillery. Lance-Corporal James Joseph Conway served with his younger brother Edward in the Battalion. From North Africa through to Arnhem they were known as 'the fighting twins', not only because they looked alike, but also from their ability to get themselves into scrapes with consummate ease. 'JJ' and his brother served in 'C' Company. 'Ernie' Lynas came from Portadown, County Armagh. Originally serving in the Royal Irish Fusiliers, he had transferred to the 156 Battalion by the time of Arnhem.

John Mallon Hamilton was the son of John and Margaret Hamilton of Argyle Street, Belfast. He

had originally served with the Warwickshire Regiment and had completed eight years service by September 1944. Norman Diffin had enlisted in the Army on the outbreak of war. He had walked from his home in Tandragee to Gough Barracks in Armagh where he had been recruited into the Royal Scots Fusiliers. A few days later he found himself armed with a travel warrant and on a coal boat bound for Scotland. Within a short time he had transferred to Airborne and found himself in the 156 Battalion.

These were some of the men who would parachute into Arnhem on the first two days of September 1944, but before they would land on that Sunday afternoon the men of the 1st Air-Landing Brigade would be there before them.

1st Air-Landing Brigade

At the time of the Sicily operation the 1st Air-Landing Brigade had consisted of only two Battalions, 1st Battalion Border Regiment and 2nd Battalion South Staffordshire Regiment. In January 1944, after they had returned from Italy, the Brigade was brought up to strength when the 7th Battalion King's Own Scottish Borderers joined it.

The Border Regiment was created in 1881 by the amalgamation of the 34th (Cumberland) and 55th (Westmorland) Regiments of Foot, which became the 1st and 2nd Battalions. During the First World War the Regiment had raised 16 Battalions and served in France and Belgium, Italy, Macedonia, Gallipoli and on the North West Frontier during the First World War; five members of the Regiment won the VC. In 1940 the 1st Battalion went to France with the BEF and again suffered heavy casualties, 250 men killed, wounded and taken prisoner. In October 1941 the Battalion became part of the 1st Air-Landing Brigade, leaving for North Africa in May 1943. The Irish had always been well represented within the Regiment.

William Coffey from Knocklong, County Limerick, was one of four members of the Regiment to win a Victoria Cross during the Crimean War. This happened on 29 March 1855, when Coffey was responsible for throwing a burning shell from his trench, saving the lives of all others present.

The following are some of those Irishmen who served with the Border Regiment in Sicily and at Arnhem. Sergeant John Hunter from Dunmurry, County Antrim, had enlisted in the Regiment in 1932 and soon rose through the ranks. By the time of Arnhem he was a Sergeant in 10 Platoon 'A' Company, and had seen previous service in France, North Africa and Sicily. Edward Hughes had been born in Annahavil, Moneymore, County Down. He had enlisted in 1930 and was married to Sarah. Prior to Arnhem they had moved to Belfast to a small house in Eglinton Street. For the Arnhem operation Edward would serve as a Lance-Corporal in the Scout Section of 14 Platoon of 'B' Company. Corporal Henry Willis, from Lisburn, County Antrim, had enlisted in the Royal Ulster Rifles in 1928. He transferred to the Gordon Highlanders in 1937 and served with them as part of the 8th Army

Bandsmen of the 1st Battalion, Border Regiment, at Woodhall Spa on 25 July 1944. At the extreme right of the rear row is Private 'Paddy' Flynn, a medical orderly in 18 Platoon 'C' Company at Arnhem. He accompanied the wounded into prison camp after the battle, but not before hiding his violin in the thatch of a house in Van Lennepweg. *Border & King's Own Border Regiment Museum*

in North Africa. He joined Airborne Forces in 1942 and was attached to the Border Regiment, taking part in the invasion of Sicily and Italy before going to Arnhem.

Staff-Sergeant Thomas Robinson Deighton was another of the many Irishmen who had served in the ranks of the Regiment over the years. He came from Belfast to enlist and at Arnhem he served as a Staff-Sergeant in the Mortar Platoon of Support Company. H. S. Cousens had been commissioned into the Royal Inniskilling Fusiliers, and at Arnhem he was a Major acting as second-in-command of the Battalion, but due to circumstances both comic and tragic, command of the Battalion would fall on Company Commanders like Major Charles Breese of 'D' Company and Major 'Jock' Neill of 'C' Company.

The South Staffordshire Regiment was formed in 1881 by the amalgamation of the 38th (1st Staffordshire) and the 80th (Staffordshire

Volunteers) Regiments of Foot, and it was the 2nd Battalion of the Regiment that was chosen for the airborne role. The Battalion became part of the 1st Air-Landing Brigade in October 1941 and first saw service in the invasion of Sicily in July 1943, when it provided the 'coup de main' force to capture the Ponte Grande bridge south of Syracuse.

'A pilgrim from the cradle to the grave' is how the Church of Ireland described Alan Alexander Buchanan. Born on 23 March 1907, at Fintona, County Tyrone, he was the son of Hugh Buchanan, a solicitor in the town of Omagh. He attended the Masonic Boys School, Dublin, and later the city's Trinity College. After graduating in 1928, he was ordained as Assistant Missioner in Belfast for the Down Diocese and became Head Missioner in 1933. He remained there for four strenuous years, until being appointed Rector of Inver at Larne, County Antrim. In the meantime he had married Miss Audrey Crone of Knock, Belfast, in 1935, by

Officers of the 1st Battalion Border Regiment at Woodhall Spa on 23 January 1944. On the rear row fifth from the left is Major T. E. Montgomery, officer commanding 'A' Company at Arnhem, who died of wounds received there on 21 November 1944 while a POW. Third from the left in the front row is Major Stuart Cousens. Commissioned into the Royal Inniskilling Fusiliers, he was second-in-command of the Battalion at Arnhem. Sixth from the left is Colin Douglas, the Battalion Adjutant and a well-known television actor after the war. *Border & King's Own Royal Border Regiment Museum*

Left 'A pilgrim from the cradle to the grave' – Captain the Reverend Alan Buchanan, Padre to the 2nd Battalion South Staffords. He was taken prisoner after Arnhem and sent to Fallingbostel. After the war he became Archbishop of Dublin. *The Rt Rev Brian D. A. Hannon MA, Bishop of Clogher*

Middle Private Samuel Montgomery from Belfast. He served as a PIAT gunner in 'A' Company of the South Staffords at Arnhem and was taken prisoner after the battle. *Montgomery family*

Right Private Hugh Flynn from Bangor, County Down. Originally enlisting in the Royal Ulster Rifles, he served in the ranks of the South Staffords on Sicily and at Arnhem, where he was taken prisoner. After the war he emigrated to Canada.

whom he had two daughters. He became Chaplain to the Forces in 1942, being appointed to the 2nd Battalion South Staffords. With them he saw action in North Africa, Sicily, where his glider was doubly lucky in that it was one of the few to make a landfall and stopped just 20 yards from a cliff edge! After Sicily he served for a time in Italy.

Samuel Montgomery from Belfast, another ex-Royal Ulster Rifleman, was a pre-war soldier, having enlisted in 1937. He had seen action in France in 1940, being successfully evacuated from Dunkirk. He transferred to the South Staffords in the winter of 1943 and served in North Africa. At Arnhem this 'ever cheerful soldier' served in 'A' Company as a PIAT gunner.

Hugh Flynn from Bangor in County Down had enlisted in the Royal Ulster Rifles in 1940 and was part of a draft sent to the South Staffords when they became part of the 1st Air-Landing Brigade. He

saw action with them in Sicily and Italy, where he was wounded in the legs. His elder brother was killed serving with the Royal Artillery at Tobruk; their father had served in the Royal Irish Rifles in the First World War.

The King's Own Scottish Borderers was raised on 18 March 1689 as Lord Leven's Regiment. It fought its first engagement the following July at Killiekrankie, a battle of the Jacobite Rising. For the next 250 years the various battalions would serve with distinction in many campaigns.

The 7th Battalion was formed as the duplicate unit of the 5th (Dumfries and Galloway) Battalion in 1939, one of the Regiment's two pre-war Territorial Army Battalions. During 1940-41 the Battalion was situated in various locations in the South of England, ready to combat any threat of invasion. In 1942 it moved to Northumbria, where it went into an intensive period of training. By July

Left Private Samuel Patton Cassidy from Belfast, who served with the 7th Battalion King's Own Scottish Borderers at Arnhem. There is still confusion over the date and manner of his death. *Robert Sigmond*

Middle Private Patrick Browne, a volunteer from 'neutral' Tipperary, served in the 7th Battalion King's Own Scottish Borderers at Arnhem and was taken prisoner after the battle. *Dominic Browne*

Right Captain Brian Devlin, No 3 Section 181 Air-Landing Field Ambulance RAMC, attached to the King's Own Scottish Borderers at Arnhem. Like many Irishmen who were commissioned into the ranks of the British Army, Brian Devlin was an former pupil of Stoneyhurst College, Lancashire, a school that boasts seven Victoria Cross winners, five of whom were Irish. *From 'Off At Last' – An Illustrated History of the 7th (Galloway) Battalion KOSB*

1943 the Battalion was part of the Orkney and Shetland Defence Force. The following November it was sent south once again, this time to Woodhall Spa in Lincolnshire to join the 1st Air-Landing Brigade. Arnhem was to be the Battalion's baptism of fire, and its graveyard.

Among these men was Samuel Patton Cassidy from Belfast; he was 24 years old, married to Mary, and served in the Anti-Tank Platoon of the Support Company. Another was Private Patrick Browne from County Tipperary, who had previously served with the Royal Artillery. The medical officer attached to the Battalion Headquarters was Captain Brian Devlin RAMC. Born in Ireland on 30 June 1919, he was the son of Dr A. J. Devlin, then living in Liverpool. Brian had attended Stoneyhurst College from 1932 to 1935, being commissioned into the Royal Army Medical Corps in 1942. He had seen previous service in North Africa and Italy prior to joining the Borderers just before Arnhem.

At the time of Market Garden each of the Battalions in the Air-Landing Brigade comprised a Headquarters Company, four rifle Companies, 'A', 'B', 'C' and 'D', and a Support Company of two mortar (12 3-inch mortars), two machine-gun (eight Vickers MMGs), and two anti-tank Platoons (eight 6-pounder anti-tank guns). The anti-tank weapon within the rifle companies was the ubiquitous PIAT.

THE GLIDER PILOT REGIMENT

The Glider Pilot Regiment was the force that would carry the 1st Air-Landing Brigade, various headquarter units, RA, RAMC, RE, Royal Signals and the heavy equipment of the parachute battalions to Arnhem. The Regiment was formed on 21 December 1941 and the first commanding officer was Colonel (later Brigadier) George Chatterton. All the men were volunteers and, unlike American glider pilots, were trained to fight as infantrymen after landing. They also had a practical knowledge of all weapons, radios and vehicles used in the British Army and a fair degree of how most enemy weapons performed. Working to Chatterton's rigid standards and under the tutelage of two veteran sergeant-majors from the Brigade of Guards, the Glider Pilot Regiment became an integral part of British Airborne Forces. The first large-scale use of the Regiment was Operation 'Husky', the invasion of Sicily. Initially the operation was not going to include the Air-Landing Brigade, but the decision was reversed. However, there were no gliders immediately available in North Africa, so the bulk of those to be used would be the American Waco, but these were just beginning to arrive by ship in May 1943. It was decided that the operation would require a number of the larger Horsa gliders, which had to be transported to North Africa.

One of the innovators of long-distance glider flying was Major A. J. Cooper.[31] Astley John Cooper was educated at the Nautical College, Pangbourne, Berkshire, from 1925 to 1929 and at the Royal Military College, Sandhurst, where he obtained a half-blue for boxing. He was commissioned from Sandhurst into his father's regiment in August 1931. From his small stature and youthful looks he was immediately nicknamed 'The Babe', a name that followed him throughout his service. After several years he was seconded to the Nigeria Regiment for a tour of duty, rejoining the Cheshires in Palestine during the troubles of 1936-37, and qualifying for the Palestine Medal. 'The Babe' was Adjutant at the Depot on the outbreak of war, and it was due to his unstinting energy and drive coupled with a gift for organisation that saw the Commanding Officer through one of the most difficult times in the history of any regimental depot. After another brief spell with the Nigeria Regiment he returned to England and volunteered for the Glider Pilot

'The Babe', Major Astley John Cooper from County Tipperary, and one of the innovators of long-distance glider-flying. He was killed in action during the invasion of Sicily. *Courtesy of Cheshire Regimental Museum*

Regiment, where he was first a Battalion Adjutant, then a pilot.

In June 1943 the Allies launched Operation 'Beggar', a plan to fly gliders from England to North Africa non-stop to arrive in time for the invasion of Sicily in July. This would involve a distance of 1,400 miles, mostly over water. Major Cooper was one of those selected, and on 3 June, in company with Staff-Sergeant Denis Hall and Staff-Sergeant Antony Antopoulos, he took off from Portreath in Cornwall to fly to Sale in North Africa. At 1000hrs Major Cooper's Horsa glider was forced to ditch in the sea some 200 miles of Cape Finisterre when the towrope to the Halifax tug aircraft broke. The Halifax returned to Portreath after transmitting the location of the downed glider. The Horsa quickly filled with water, but the three-man crew exited through the escape hatch in the roof and into the inflatable life raft. After eight hours floating next to the half-submerged glider, a Royal Navy frigate picked them up, then sank the

---

[31] His father was Major A. S. Cooper of Dundrum, County Tipperary. Austin Cooper had seen service in the South African War of 1899-02 with the 2nd Battalion, the Cheshire Regiment. During the period 1914-18 Major Cooper was Adjutant to Colonel R. J. Cooke OBE DL JP at The Castle, Chester, a position that, according to the regimental history, he performed with exemplary skill.

Horsa with a few bursts of well-aimed gunfire to conceal the wreckage from the eyes of German reconnaissance aircraft. The men were landed at the port of Belfast, and from there it was a short flight back to their base in Cornwall.

On 14 June Sergeants Hall and Antopoulos had another go at flying a glider to North Africa, and again an Irishman made up the third member of the crew, Sergeant 'Paddy' Conway from Belfast. They were over the Bay of Biscay when two German Focke Wolf Condor long-range reconnaissance aircraft attacked the combination of Horsa and Halifax tug. After a ferocious gun battle the Halifax was shot down and the Horsa was forced to cast off to make a crash-landing in the sea. All three crew made a successful escape from the downed aircraft and into their emergency dinghy. After a very cold, wet, miserable night in the open they rigged a sail and headed towards what they reckoned was land. The men estimated that they were about 100 miles from the Spanish coast and reckoned it would take ten days to reach dry land.

Water was rationed to one can between then per day, but this changed after the fourth day when the dinghy overturned in heavy seas, resulting in the loss of half their remaining supply of water and Paddy Conway's harmonica! The water ration was then cut to half a can per day. Steady progress was made, but on the fifth day the dinghy started to leak air and had to be re-inflated using the hand pump, an exhausting effort to men weakened by lack of food and water. On the eighth day Paddy offered to throw himself overboard to give the others a chance. He was told that all would make it or none at all. On the 11th day a Spanish fishing-boat spotted the dinghy. Once safely on board it was found that the three men were badly dehydrated, and luckily for the Glider Pilots the fishermen knew how to deal with them; they were given bowls of hot sugared water and told to sip it slowly. After a week in a Spanish hospital they were returned to England by ship. On return to the United Kingdom Paddy Conway was confined to a psychiatric hospital for a time where he spent his days gambling with the other patients and taking all

their money! Paddy did not take part in the Normandy or Arnhem operations, but did fly on Operation 'Varsity', the crossing of the Rhine in March 1945.

Eric George Wolf Matson was a past pupil of the Masonic Boys School, Dublin. His family came from Bandon, County Cork, where his father had been a member of the local Masonic Lodge. Eric began his studies at the school in September 1933 and continued until 1939. By 1941 he had enlisted in the Royal Inniskilling Fusiliers and remained with them until transferring to the Glider Pilot Regiment in 1943. By February the following year he had gained his wings and was a Sergeant Pilot. For 'Market Garden' he would pilot one of the giant Hamilcar gliders.

Michael Briody and 'Dusty' Miller were another two from the neutral south who served at Arnhem. Briody had come from his home in Kilkenny, joined the Irish Guards in 1929 and saw action with them on the ill-fated expedition to Norway in 1940. That April his battalion had been sent to Norway to help resist the German invasion, but the operation was hampered by both atrocious weather and German dive-bombers, to which the British had no effective reply. Moved from sector to sector as a 'flying column', the Irish Guards' troopship was sunk by air attack on Friday 13 May 1940. The Battalion had been ordered south to reinforce what was described as 'a fragile line' and had embarked on an elderly Polish liner, the *Chobry*. Around midnight the troopship was attacked by a flight of Heinkels, which scored several direct hits with bombs. Severe damage was caused and fires were started, one of which threatened the Guards' ammunition supply stacked on the open deck. The Irish Guards quickly formed a human chain and began to throw the ammunition boxes over the side. The British destroyer HMS *Wolverine* then came alongside, and her Captain, Commander Craske, observed, 'There was no confusion, and no sign of haste or flurry. I never before realised what the discipline of the Guards meant.' Six hundred and ninety-four men were successfully transferred from the sinking liner to the destroyer in just 16 minutes.[32] Despite initial

---

[32] Details taken from the obituary to Major Sir George Fitzgerald Bt, *Daily Telegraph*, 27 April 2001.

Above **Corporal Michael Briody after three years in the Irish Guards. He has the single 'good conduct' stripe on his left sleeve and above it what looks like the crossed flags of a trained signaller. He was born on 29 June 1911 in Thomastown, County Kilkenny, where his father had been a member of the Royal Irish Constabulary.** *Lilian Mann*

successes by British troops on the ground, they were withdrawn the following month.

Two years later Michael Briody, now a Company Sergeant-Major, was seconded to Airborne Forces, one of the two 'veteran sergeant-majors', to instil the highest degree of military discipline in the men of the Glider Pilot Regiment (GPR). The Regiment was in the process of forming and there was a need for a cadre of seasoned officers both on

Above right **Michael Briody after being seconded to the Glider Pilot Regiment. He had recently been promoted from WO2 to Regimental Sergeant-Major and was still to complete his glider pilot training.** *Lilian Mann*

Right **Michael Briody photographed in 1943 in North Africa or Italy.** *Lilian Mann*

the parade-ground and in the barrack hut, to create the 'Total Soldier'. Michael Briody would also become a glider pilot in his own right. Because of his previous experience he was soon promoted to Regimental Sergeant-Major and saw action in North Africa, Sicily, Italy and on D-Day. At Arnhem he was attached to No 2 Wing.

G. R. 'Dusty' Millar, a Corkman, served in 'B' Squadron at Arnhem. Another ex-Irish Guardsman, he had been commissioned into the Royal Inniskilling Fusiliers before transferring to the GPR. When he had left the family home he had told his mother he was off to join the 'guards', and she assumed he meant the police force, as in Ireland the police are known as the Garda Siochana, or Guards for short. He was another veteran of North Africa, Sicily, Italy and Normandy, and would survive Arnhem to fly a glider across the Rhine in March 1945. His peers considered him an outstanding man, and with Wilfred Tallentire, a fellow glider pilot, there existed a friendship that lasted for more than 50 years.

In September 1944 Broadwell Farm was the home of No 2 Wing the Glider Pilot Regiment. From here Lieutenant-Colonel John Place, commander of the Wing, and his co-pilot, Lieutenant Ralph Maltby, were to fly 14 Platoon of 'B' Company 1st Battalion Border Regiment to landing Zone 'S' at Arnhem. John Place was a native of County Dublin, a pre-war regular soldier; his hobby prior to enlisting had been flying. After earning his wings he was appointed as officer commanding No 3 Squadron on its formation. As an officer he was both liked and respected by his men, and had soon formed a happy and efficient unit; the men called him 'the iron fist in the velvet glove'. When he arrived in North Africa, as a major, he became second-in-command to Colonel Chatterton and took charge of the training programme to give the British glider pilots experience on the American-built Waco glider.

On Chatterton's return to England in the summer of 1943, John Place was given command of the 1st Battalion and led it to Italy, before returning to England himself in December of that year. There he was given command of No 2 Wing, and once again he built a first-rate force of glider pilots as efficient on the ground as they were in the air. He served in the Normandy operation, and after receiving those replacements necessary, once again put his Wing into good order for future airborne landings on the continent.

Ralph Maltby, his co-pilot to Arnhem, had been born in the Pacific Islands, where his father, a Belfast doctor, had been practising. Twenty-six-year-old Maltby had seen previous service in Russia as an Air Observer, where his 16-man unit had suffered 50 per cent casualties before being withdrawn. He had received a Mention-in-Despatches, and the Soviet Union had awarded him the Order of the Patriotic War. He had recently married his fiancée, Miss Jean Beath, in Belfast; they had one baby daughter and he was missing them desperately. For Arnhem he would act not only as co-pilot to Colonel Place, but also as the Wing Intelligence Officer.

James Frederick Boyd was the son of Jennie Boyd of Portrush, County Antrim. He had enlisted in the Royal Ulster Rifles on the outbreak of war, but within a short time had transferred to the Glider Pilot Regiment. By the time of 'Market Garden' he had risen to the rank of Squadron Quartermaster. While due to follow on as part of the Regiment's Seaborne Tail, he was one of those that stowed away on the morning of 17 September 1944 and made his way to Arnhem on board a glider of 'B' Squadron.[33]

Wilfred Tallentire came from Tandragee in County Armagh. At Lurgan College he was considered to be somewhat brighter than his fellow students and the headmaster encouraged him to greater things. After leaving school he worked in the family shop in the town and joined the 12th Searchlight Battery, Supplementary Reserve. When war broke out Wilfred went into the Royal Artillery and was one of those sent to France with the BEF. His time in France was just as confused as that of many others, and he soon found himself on the long exhausting retreat to the beaches at Dunkirk. Here

---

[33] The seaborne tail consisted of all the vehicles and personnel of the Division that were not due to fly into Arnhem. These vehicles would advance in the wake of XXX Corps.

he was lifted from the beach by a Margate pleasure-steamer and enjoyed a crowded but comfortable voyage back to England. After two years spent training recruits in Wales, he transferred to Airborne, much against his CO's wishes. He was one of 14 men who applied at that time; four were accepted, and by the end of the war only Wilfred Tallentire was alive! For D-Day he was kept in reserve in England, spending 6 June on Broadwell airfield with a glider full of Ulster Rifles waiting to see if they would be needed; they never were. He flew to France the following day as part of Operation 'Mallard', the landing of the 6th Airborne Division in France.

Prior to Normandy and Arnhem he took part in many of the training exercises where the main problem with the men was airsickness. This was Wilfred Tallentire's answer to the problem:

'As the time approached for the invasion of Europe it was deemed necessary to acquaint all Air Landing Troops with glider transport. How to get in, how to get out and above all to cope with the motion of flight. For weeks troops endured familiarisation, as the exercises were delightfully named in true military style. Airsickness became a problem. By the very nature of the Horsa glider's construction, a claustrophobic feeling was created, even before flying commenced. Added to this impasse, the sensation of rumbling along the runway unable to see what was really taking place induced, if not fear, at least a degree of apprehension. This induction would be followed by a flight of some duration often in turbulent weather causing the glider to lurch and yaw, thus creating untold problems.

'The soldiers with few exceptions were anxious for the excursion to end. Suddenly a snap followed by the dying off of wind noise as the Horsa lost speed, now in free flight. Then horror of horrors, down tilted the nose at an alarming angle. Was this to be the last movement in the wretched machine? Oh no! The approach flight was suddenly apparent, which one felt to be at an angle nearly vertical. At last levelling off and the comforting sound of the wheels rumbling on mother earth.

'It was apparent that troops on landing from a glider were not in tip-top form – indeed, the reverse was evident. Worried minds were at work in high places trying to resolve this thorny problem. Parachutists, on the other hand, came to the scene of action feeling elated and in high spirits. The situation worried officers, for not only was the mental condition weak, many had been actively sick on route. Something had to be done to combat this malady.

'First attempt to control the sickness came in the form of an issue of paper bags, one to each man prior to entering the glider. Dispose of same on landing. In the appropriate place. So stated the order. This scheme was a disaster.

'"What's this for?"

'"Oh, that's to be sick in."

'A good idea, I'll have to be sick. Auto-suggestion – call it what you may. Twenty-four men sat side by side each with a paper bag, waiting. It didn't take long. Mind over matter speeded up the process. Suddenly one bag was used, then sat on the floor and promptly burst. The chain reaction was quick and devastating. In a moment of time every man was sick. So, paper bags were disused – instead four-gallon petrol tins were placed in strategic spots. All went well until suddenly the aircraft lurched, tilting the already used tin. In a flash everyone was sick.

'Now nearly all the pilots chewed gum, available in the canteen. Hence a certain glider pilot thought up an idea – to collect Wrigley 'chicklets', unwrap them and put into a tin. The next training flight with troops was to be a night cross-country to last about two and a quarter hours. As time drew near for take-off, those in charge debated the strength of the wind. Was it too strong, too gusty and so forth? All the while the troops be carried lounged around as servicemen do. The glider pilot made himself known, listened to their questions and doubts. These men of the Royal Ulster Rifles were a little concerned about sickness.

'"Is it going to be rough, Sir?"

"'D'ye think we'll be sick?"

'It was obvious the flight was going to be rough. The pilot knew there was no point in saying otherwise. What he did say was, "Don't worry. It will be bumpy, of that there is no doubt, but you will not be sick." Here he went on to wax lyrical as to the preventative powers of the magical tablets – they taste just like chewing gum, but they are special brand new anti-sick sweets, and so on.

"'Where did ye git them?"

"'Ah! Here's the secret. No one here has ever seen these."

"'They're laxatives," a Belfast doubter said.

"'No they're not – give me yours." He swapped and chewing commenced. They were convinced.

'During flight soldiers sat face to face, rifles between knees, chewing steadily, every one of them, and no one was sick. After such a flight exercise someone of self-importance debriefed the pilots. A lot of stock questions finished with the state of morale and how many were sick.

"'None, Sir."

'The officer looked up. "I don't believe you." The pilot repeated his statement and asked if the officer would like to speak to any that had been on board. The request was refused or his nibs declined.

'Naturally a plan of this sort was impossible to keep secret. It soon got around about the wonder tablets. Questions were asked, vague answers given, but the panacea was soon to fall asunder. The Commanding Officer collared the wonder pilot and wanted to know the ins and outs of the mystery. Two days later there appeared in standing orders for Glider Pilots that they were to ensure that all personnel while in flight were to chew Wrigley's chewing gum. We were back to square one!'

For operation 'Market Garden' Captain Wilfred Tallentire was Officer Commanding No 18 Flight of No 1 Wing, and was charged with a highly important mission. When briefed for the operation he was informed that his glider load was to be 'a special radio that was incapable of being jammed by the Germans.'[34] This was to be flown to Browning's Headquarters near Nijmegen. Because of the importance of the load the trailer was primed with plastic explosive so that it could be detonated in the event of any danger of capture. The load was also to be duplicated in another glider, and Wilfred was detailed to select the pilot! He chose Staff-Sergeant Harris, described as a 'canny Scot' and one of the best pilots in the Regiment. As Wilfred's glider was towed off the runway it carried a jeep, two trailers, four men of the Royal Signals and one American signaller.

Captain John Frederick Smellie, born in Eire, was the son of a prominent family from Holywood, County Down. He had entered Queen's University, Belfast, in 1934 to study Law. On the outbreak of war he had enlisted in the Royal Army Service Corps before transferring to the Glider Pilot Regiment. He acted as second pilot in a Horsa glider during Operation 'Tonga' on the night of 5/6 June 1944, when they carried equipment of 5th Parachute Brigade to Normandy. On 17 September 1944 he would command No 4 Flight. Famous throughout the Regiment for his skill with the bagpipes, John Smellie was the life and soul of the many parties held in the various messes.

Brian Patrick Sheridan Feehily had been born in India in 1918, the son of an Irish military family. After his initial education at Murree and Bangalore, he had enlisted as a Boy Trumpeter in the Royal Artillery when he was 15 years old. He returned with his unit to the United Kingdom just before the outbreak of war and was sent to France with the British Expeditionary Force in 1940. Paddy's unit, the 2nd Field Regiment RA, saw limited action on the continent before being forced back to the Channel coast by overwhelming numbers. He was successfully evacuated from Dunkirk and returned to England where he remained with the Royal Artillery for a further two years.

[34] According the Airborne Forces Museum, this was an American SCR-499 radio set, but it was capable of being jammed!

Brian Patrick Sheridan Feehily – from Boy Soldier in the Royal Artillery to Glider Pilot. He survived a crash-landing during the operation on Sicily and escaped across the Rhine after 'Market Garden'.

In February 1942 he transferred to the Glider Pilot Regiment and was sent to the Depot at Tilshead for his initial training. When his unit went to North Africa, Paddy went with them and from there took part in the invasion of Sicily. For the Sicily operation he flew as co-pilot to Captain Tony Plowman[35] in a Hadrian glider[36], but despite some 7 hours in the air they failed to find their landing zone on the island. For the Arnhem operation he served in 'F' Squadron as a Staff Sergeant.

The Polish Independent Parachute Brigade Group did not include any Irishmen in its order of battle, although there was one American. The Brigade consisted of a Brigade Headquarters, three Infantry Battalions, a Signal Company, Engineer Company, Supply Company, Medical Company, Artillery Battery and an Anti-Tank Battery. In all this was a total of approximately 1,540 men, some of whom would fight north of the Rhine while the majority fought around the small village of Driel. It was here that two 'neutrals' were fated to find themselves fighting alongside men with a different language, but a common cause.

This was the force that would land in Holland in an attempt to take and hold the Arnhem Bridge. However, the Division would first be blooded on other battlefields.

---

[35] Captain Tony Plowman was killed at Arnhem on 24 September, and is interred in the Airborne Cemetery at Oosterbeek, grave 3.C.2.

[36] Hadrian was the British name for the American Waco glider; it was smaller than the Horsa.

3 NORTH AFRICA

The British had been fighting in North Africa since the Italian invasion of Egypt in September 1940. Initial victories by commanders such as Generals Claude Auchinleck and Richard O'Connor had first held, then driven back the Italians before total victory was foiled by the intervention of Winston Churchill. In February 1941 Churchill ordered that the majority of British troops be detached from the Desert Army and sent to Greece. That same month a German officer named Erwin Rommel arrived in North Africa, followed by the vanguard of what was to become the Afrika Corps. The war in the desert was scheduled to last for a long time yet.

The initial deployment of British airborne troops in North Africa came with the invasion of Tunisia in November 1942. The 3rd Parachute Battalion, under the command of Lieutenant Colonel Geoffrey Pine-Coffin landed at Maison Blanche at 0900hrs on 11 November. Here the Battalion was briefed for its first operational jump in North Africa, an attack on Bone airfield, to be made in conjunction with a seaborne landing by No 6 Commando.

The Battalion made a successful drop at 0830hrs on 12 February, the Dakotas flown by American aircrew delivering the sticks accurately on target. Pine-Coffin quickly gathered the Battalion together, the only casualties being several men suffering broken legs from hard landings on the stony ground and one man accidentally shot by his Sten gun as he landed. Unknown to the British was the fact that a battalion of German paratroopers, also making their way towards the airfield, had observed the landing. When the *Fallschirmjaeger*

saw that the British were well in control they returned to their base at Tunis.

Pine-Coffin was later transferred to the 6th Airborne Division, and Lieutenant-Colonel John Fitch, a veteran of Sicily and Italy, commanded the 3rd Battalion at Arnhem. Again Irishmen from both north and south of the border were to be found in the ranks. Kevin Collins came from Chapelzoid, County Dublin. He had originally served in the Devonshire Regiment before transferring to Airborne. A good friend of Kevin Collins was Pat O'Brien, another Dubliner. He was 20 years old in September 1944 and had served in both Sicily and Italy. His father had served with the Connaught Rangers for nearly 30 years and was the Regimental Sergeant-Major when, in 1915, he was commissioned into the Duke of Cornwall's Light Infantry. By the end of his military service he had earned the Distinguished Conduct Medal and the Meritorious Service Medal, together with a host of campaign medals and bars. Pat O'Brien's enlistment in the British Army represented the continuing tradition of the 'family business'.

Mervyn Dennison was born in County Cork, the son of a Methodist minister. He attended Methodist College, Belfast, before going to Queens University, where he read Modern Languages and Law. War broke out before he could sit his finals and he was commissioned in the Royal Ulster Rifles in October 1939. He served with its 1st (Airborne) Battalion and had already done 46 parachute jumps before going to Tunisia to join the 1st Parachute Battalion about Christmas 1943.

He transferred to the 3rd Battalion at the end of the North African campaign. He once recounted to

Barletta, Italy, 1943: from left to right, CQMS Jack Haybourne, Major Mervyn Dennison, who would command 'A' Company of the 3rd Parachute Battalion at Arnhem, and Sergeant-Major Alan 'CB' Watson.

the author the story of the 'Red Devils' and the 'men with tails'. While fighting in the hills at Tamara the weather had been particularly cold and wet, and the men, their uniforms and equipment had become saturated with the red mud peculiar to this theatre. This appearance, combined with the fighting quality of the troops, had led the Germans to call them 'Die Rote Teufeln'. On the other hand, the inability of the parachute smock's crotch strap to stay buttoned and consequently to fall down at the rear of the garment earned them the title of 'the men with tails' from the local Arabs. Mervyn often wondered at the outcome if the German title had not been adopted! When the Germans in turn named themselves 'Green Devils', he thought imitation was the sincerest form of flattery. At Arnhem he would command 'A' Company of the 3rd Battalion.

On 16 November 1942 the 1st Battalion took off from Maison Blanche bound for the town of Beja. Their mission was to persuade the local French troops to join the Allied cause and to carry out aggressive patrolling against the enemy. The drop was unopposed, but some casualties were caused when a Sten gun was discharged accidentally on landing, wounding four men. The only death was

that of Sergeant Desmond Patrick Barnwall from County Wexford, who was killed as a result of a parachuting accident. The French proved most amenable to joining the British, mainly due to the persuasive efforts of Lieutenant Colonel Hill. He informed the French that British tanks were already advancing to assist with the defences. He also doubled the size of his own force by first marching his men through the town wearing steel helmets, then circling around and marching through again this time in berets.

Information was then received from the French that the Germans regularly patrolled from their lines to the railway station at Sidi N'Sir, about 20 miles from Beja, using armoured vehicles. On 17 November 'S' Company, under the command of Major Cleasby-Thompson and with a small detachment of Sappers, made its way to Sidi N'Sir to make contact with the local French commander. One of the platoon sergeants was Joseph Patrick Ryan from Dublin. At Sidi N'Sir they spent a convivial night with the French garrison before setting up the ambush in the early hours of the following morning. The German patrol, consisting of eight vehicles, four large eight-wheeled armoured cars and four lighter armoured cars, was allowed to pass through the ambush spot unopposed. After they had passed, a necklace of Hawkins anti-tank mines was laid across the road.[37] The patrol's weapons were primed and the men settled down to wait for the enemy to return. The ambush was a complete success – the combination of mines, machine-gun and mortar fire destroyed all four armoured vehicles together with two of the reconnaissance cars, and the surviving enemy troops surrendered. Casualties to the 1st Battalion were light, with several men being wounded; these, together with the prisoners and the two remaining German vehicles, were returned to Beja. As a result of his actions at Sidi N'Sir, Sergeant Ryan was awarded the Military Medal.

There have also been several stories of how the airborne war-cry began. One version, told by Mervyn Dennison, concerns a donkey that was 'borrowed' during the time in North Africa and given the name 'Whoa Mohammed'[38], because it proved very difficult to stop once in motion. Another relates to an Arab shepherd who used to pray each evening in front of one of the battalions and yell the name of the prophet. Whatever the

origins of the war-cry, it was heard and recognised by the enemy in the streets of Arnhem and Oosterbeek in September 1944.

On 18 October 1942 Adolf Hitler issued his infamous 'Commando Order'. This required that 'sabotage troops of the British or their hirelings, whether in uniform or not, whether with or without arms, be killed to the last man in battle or flight', and if captured indirectly were to be handed over to the SS. The 'Order' ran to six paragraphs and, among other things, threatened a court-martial for any officer who failed to carry out the instructions or who acted contrary to them.

One particular German soldier also suffered as a result of the 'Order'. Patrick Morton recalled an incident in North Africa in November 1942. Frost's 2nd Battalion had dropped at Depienne in Tunisia. Although the drop was unopposed, again several men had been injured due to bad landings on the sun-baked ground. When the Battalion had to move on, those men unable to march were left behind in the shelter of a nearby building under the care of Corporal Gavin Cadden RAMC. Later in the day they were attacked by elements of 1st

To Airborne soldiers in North Africa, this was 'a bloody great armoured car', to the Germans it was the *Panzerspahwagen (SdKfz 233) mit 7.5cm Stu L/27*. It was a vehicle similar to this that was destroyed by Sergeant Joseph Patrick Ryan of 'S' Company, 1st Parachute Battalion, at Sidi N'Sir, in November 1942.

---

[37] The No 75 (Hawkins) Grenade, named after its designer, was first issued in 1941 and approved for general issue in 1942. It is perhaps inappropriate to call it a grenade; as it was in fact a small anti-tank mine resembling a flat screw-topped talcum powder tin. Designed to be laid flat under the tracks of a tank or, if attached to a piece of cord, pulled across the path of an advancing vehicle, it could also be thrown.

[38] Sometimes rendered as 'Waho Mahomed' or 'Mahomet', depending on who you ask and how long they have been at the bar.

Battalion 5th *Fallschirmjaeger* (paratrooper) Regiment, and after a brief fire-fight the building was stormed under a hail of covering fire. The commander of the attacking force was Oberstleutnant Walther Koch, a veteran of the attack on the fortress of Eben Emael in Belgium in 1940. The surviving paratroopers were taken prisoner and were well treated by the German paratroopers; medical aid was given to those who required it, with food and water being shared out. The prisoners were then handed over to another unit, as Koch's men had to move on. It is not clear if the designated guard unit was German or Italian, but what is certain is what happened next. A German officer issued orders that the prisoners were to be dragged up against a wall and an Italian machine-gun crew was ordered to murder them!

At that moment, as if warned by a premonition, Walther Koch returned to the scene. Jumping down from his vehicle, he kicked over the machine-gun and enforced the release of the paratroopers, ensuring that they were eventually moved to a prisoner-of-war camp in Italy. Koch later suffered a severe head wound in combat and was returned to his home in Germany to convalesce. While out walking near his house one afternoon he was hit by a speeding car and killed – the vehicle did not stop. Surviving members of his regiment attribute this to Gestapo revenge for Koch's refusal to implement the 'Commando Order'.[39]

To most soldiers North Africa was a complete culture shock. To Patrick Morton and Fitzpatrick the experience bore little resemblance to the average soldier's idea of what it would be like. For most men their only experience of the desert and Arabs was going to the cinema and seeing Gary Cooper in *Beau Geste*. One thing quickly learned was that the Arabs would steal anything, and fly sandwiches were not very nice! The men of the 1st Parachute Brigade had a busy time in North Africa, with more time spent in the infantry role than airborne, but nevertheless this experience would stand them in good stead in the battles to come.

On the night of 3 January 1943 the 3rd Battalion was assigned to the 36th Infantry Brigade and took part in an attack on an objective called Green Hill. This was one of a pair of hills that was the Brigade's target for the night, the second being known as Commando Hill. This latter position dominated the main road between Sedjenane and Mateur. The assault was unsuccessful, with only 'A' Company gaining the top of Green Hill, but then being forced to withdraw in the face of overwhelming numbers and firepower. A second attack was launched the following night, and by 10.00hrs the first crest had been taken. The struggle to take and hold the second crest was a bloody affair. The enemy was strongly entrenched behind barbed wire, minefields and gun emplacements. A call by the Battalion for artillery support ended in disaster when some shells fell short, causing 'friendly' casualties. Eventually the hill was taken and the Battalion prepared for the inevitable counter-attack. It was not long in coming. The first German attack was beaten off with heavy casualties, but at the expenditure of almost all small arms ammunition. When a second attack materialised the Battalion was unable to hold and began a steady withdrawal to the base of the hill. As Morton and Fitzpatrick made their way back there was a constant rain of German mortar bombs. As frequently happens on these occasions, sometimes you zig when you should have zagged, and the result was an arm and shoulder full of shrapnel for Patrick.

---

[39] British Airborne troops came into contact with Hitler's Order one month after it was issued. On 19 November 1942 Operation 'Freshman' was launched. A force of two Horsa gliders carrying men of the Royal Engineers and towed by Halifax bombers left RAF Skitten at Caithness in Scotland bound for the Norsk Hydro Electric Plant at Vemork in Norway. This plant was vital to the production of heavy water on which depended the German atomic research programme. Both the gliders and one of the towing aircraft crashed in Norway due to atrocious weather conditions. The Germans murdered those men who survived the crash-landings; they included Lance-Corporal Trevor Louis Masters from Cobh, County Cork, and fellow Irishman Driver Peter Paul Farrell, whose wife Bridget was living in London at the time. Both men were attached to the Royal Engineers. After the war four of those responsible were arrested; three were executed and one committed suicide.

Patrick spent the remainder of January and all of February in hospital. He had several operations to remove the shrapnel, but some of it proved elusive and he would carry enough in his shoulder to set off airport alarms for the rest of his days. Paddy admits he was not a good patient.

'My constant stream of compliments and helpful suggestions to the nurses resulted in the matron, a big strong girl from Mullingar, offering to keep my testicles safely in her office drawer until I was well enough to leave hospital. This caused me to reflect on my value to any future wife. I was a model patient for the last two weeks of my stay.'

When the 16 Parachute Field Ambulance had been serving in North Africa they had lost a fine young doctor killed in action on 10 March 1943. James Gerard Cassidy was the son of James and Ellen Cassidy of Rathfriland, County Down. On the morning of 5 February 1943 Captain Cassidy, together with 20 other volunteers, went up on to Djebel Mansour to collect those wounded left behind when the 1st Parachute Battalion had withdrawn to Tamera. This search lasted from early morning until nightfall, with all the wounded being recovered. On Wednesday 10 March the Brigade area was subjected

The field grave of Captain James Gerard Cassidy RAMC, of Rathfriland, County Down. He was killed in action in North Africa while attached to the 1st Parachute Battalion. *D. Wright via Niall Cherry*

to an intense artillery bombardment, and Captain Cassidy was killed while he treated a wounded soldier who was lying in the open.

William Devlin and Jack Fryer had first met in North Africa. Jack remembered one particular occasion.

'One morning we were having a wash in a mountain stream when Devlin lost his crucifix. I spent two hours up to my elbows in freezing cold water helping him look for it. He was a quiet type, never swore, wasn't the sort to chase after women, didn't drink much, but in action he showed little fear. He knew all the rebel songs. While we were in North Africa there was a lot of fighting in the forests. Out through the trees would come this voice singing *Kelly the Boy from Killanne*. "What's the news? What's the news? O my bold Shelmalier with your long barrelled gun of the sea." This would ring out loud and clear through the trees. The men would shout, "Shut up, for Christ's sake – you'll get us all killed!" He was a really nice fellow.'

At Arnhem both men would serve in 'T' Company. Jack remembered other men for different reasons.

'This was this fellow called Pritchard. He was another Ulster Rifleman, from Belfast – he had an accent you could have cut with a knife. Well, one night he must have knocked off a bicycle in the town to save him the walk back to camp. The following morning I was having a shave when this policeman came in. Pointing at my battledress blouse he asked if it was mine. I said yes. He asked if I had been in the town the night before? Someone with black stripes on their uniform had stolen a bike. That was the problem, then. While we all had the red beret, the riflemen were the only ones with black rank stripes. It took a while for me to convince the law that I was innocent. Pritchard had a good laugh at me for that one.'

Hugh Gordon came from the Woodvale area of Belfast. He was the son of Hugh and Florence and

Members of the Intelligence Platoon of the 1st Parachute Battalion in North Africa. Fourth from the left in the front row is Corporal 'Jack' Fryer; his rank stripes are still 'Royal Ulster Rifle' black. At Arnhem he served in 'T' Company. *Mrs J. Fryer*

had served in the Royal Ulster Rifles prior to Airborne. On 26 February 1943 a mixed force of enemy – Austrian infantry, Italian Alpini and German *Gebirgsjager* – attacked the 1st Battalion together with the remainder of the 1st Parachute Brigade and French troops. Despite the Brigade being spread out over a large area, all attacks by the enemy were beaten off. The 1st Battalion in particular was able to inflict heavy casualties due to a cleverly laid out killing ground devised by their

CO, Lieutenant-Colonel Alistair Pearson. It was during this action that Private Gordon was killed.

Sergeant John Bermingham, the ex-Royal Ulster

Pte. Jas. Pritchard, Army Air Corps, son of Mrs. S. Pritchard, 18 Victor Street, Belfast, missing. A brother is in the Royal Navy. His father died of wounds received in the last war.

Private James Pritchard from Belfast, an ex-Royal Ulster Rifleman He served in the 1st Parachute Battalion at Arnhem.

Private Hugh Gordon from Belfast, who served in the 1st Parachute Battalion and was killed in action in North Africa.

Rifleman from Dublin, had served with Major Vic Coxen during the actions at Sidi Bou Delaa in March 1943. After an attack Coxen's company was returning to its lines in darkness when it ran into a picket line commanded by Sergeant Bermingham. After both sides had identified themselves, Bermingham inquired of Coxen what he should do with the primed grenade he was holding. Coxen told him to get rid of it! With a deft flick of his wrist the Sergeant tossed the grenade to one side of the track. When the blast subsided and the dirt stopped flying it was found that there were no injuries to the company, but nerves were definitely stretched! Despite Coxen's initial anger, he realised that the Sergeant had only obeyed the last order, just as a good soldier should![40]

In North Africa Cecil Newell was attached to the Mortar Platoon of Support Company. On one occasion the Battalion was ordered to take over a stretch of the line previously manned by French Senegalese troops. Support Company moved in just before first light, and as they approached the trenches the Senegalese and their French officers withdrew back through them. As Cecil and the other men jumped into the recently vacated trenches they discovered that British troops with an average height of 5ft 8in were not suited to trenches dug for troops that had an average height of nearly 7 feet! At first light 'stand to' was ordered, and the men had to climb on to ammunition boxes or whatever else was available until picks and shovels were found to partially fill in the trenches.

It is quite often the humour of a situation that the men remember above all else. Cecil Newell recalled the day they all had their hair cut.

'There was this fellow from the south of Ireland called Mulhall. He had a lovely head of bright red hair. Well, one day we all decided to have our heads shaved because of the heat. We reckoned it would keep us cooler. So Mulhall

goes along with it and has his head shaved. Later that day we arranged for one of the Company clerks to present him with a fake leave pass showing him going home the next day for two weeks leave. You should have heard the yells of him. "I can't go home like this – my mother will kill me!" Well, they always said if you can't take a joke you shouldn't have joined.'[41]

While in North Africa Victor Hughes took part in an exercise just prior to the invasion of Sicily. It was a very warm day and Victor was a small wiry man.

'As I left the Dakota, instead of falling after the others in the stick I found myself floating on the thermals. I could only hang there in mid-air as the remaining aircraft flew all around me. I was up there for ages. When I eventually landed it was close to the Brigade Headquarters. This sergeant-major came over and told me that had I stayed up there much longer I would have been posted AWOL.'

Lance-Corporal Victor Hughes from Belfast, who served with the 3rd Parachute Battalion at Arnhem. He was a veteran campaigner of the North West Frontier, where he served in the Royal Ulster Rifles. *Victor Hughes*

[40] In several books written about the 1st Airborne Division in North Africa this story has been told with the suggestion that John Bermingham spoke with a broad Irish accent. The men I interviewed said he spoke in a quiet refined voice, nothing at all like a 'stage' Irishman.

[41] This story was told during a taped interview. Whether the name was Mulhern or Mulhall it is impossible to make out on the tape.

In the Second World War the American Army had a saying 'There are no atheists in foxholes'. Cecil remembered his time at Sedjenane.

'We were attacked there by dive-bombers, Stukas. You never saw them – they came down out of the sun making that terrible screaming noise – all you could do was to get into the bottom of your trench and pray very, very hard.'

German mortar fire seemed to hit his unit at the most advantageous times, and it was assumed that a concealed observer was directing the fire. Cecil experienced this at first hand.

'I was part of a ration party coming back to "A" Company with supplies when we were stopped by mortar fire. I thought we could get in by "C"

Company so we moved towards them. As we came up to the position this guy pops up from a foxhole and shouts, "What the hell are you doing here?" I replied we were trying to get back to "A" company with supplies. "Well, you're not getting in here, you're drawing mortar fire, now bugger off."'

The Arabs were, of course, suspected. The nearest buildings that could be used for cover by an observer were a collection of huts nearby known as the 'woggery'. After several days of this mortaring and some casualties, it was decided that the 'woggery' would have to go. Fair warning was given to the inhabitants both verbally and in writing. Posters were pasted around the buildings and loudspeaker announcements made. A divisional artillery shoot was then directed on to the

General Montgomery speaks to soldiers of the 1st Air-Landing Brigade on 8 July 1943 prior to the Sicily landings. *IWM NA4062*

'woggery'. After a very short time it ceased to be of use to either man or beast and the German mortaring stopped being such a nuisance. Cecil Newell remembered that even without an observer German counter battery fire could be very accurate.

'When we opened up with our mortars on the Germans to our front you only got off three rounds before they had you and the counter battery fire started. On one occasion we had nine bombs arranged around us in a circle without any of them exploding due to the soft sand.'

Cecil remembered the day General Montgomery came along to give one of his famous speeches. He gathered the men around his jeep in his usual manner and told them he was taking the 1st Airborne to Sicily, when an Irish voice shouted out, 'We don't bloody well want to go.' Montgomery then compared their professionalism to the men of his 8th Army, saying that they seemed almost as good. This caused quite a lot of ill feeling among those present. He did not realise that many of these men were ex-8th Army veterans. That was the day he wore a red beret complete with wings – another veteran was heard to remark that Montgomery would have difficulty jumping off the jeep!

On 11 March 1943 Lance-Corporal James Murphy, an ex-Royal Ulster Rifleman from Belfast, was killed during the fighting around Sedjenane. The following April he was posthumously awarded the Military Medal, and on 23 September his widow Annie received word that he had also been Mentioned-in-Despatches.

Some of the deaths incurred by the 21st Independent Parachute Company did not come as a result of enemy action. The first loss to the 21st was that of Private Martin Conboy from Cabra, County Dublin. He died as a result of a swimming accident while the Company was resting in Tunisia in July 1943. The men had been using a half-submerged ship as a makeshift diving platform and on this occasion Private Conboy dived into the harbour and struck his head on part of the ship. He was buried near to where he died.[42]

A postcard showing the Memorial to 1st Parachute Brigade in North Africa. According to the legend it is situated on the roadside between Djebel Aboid and Sejenane in northern Tunisia. It was erected in September 1943. *Georgina Cromie*

---

[42] Enfidaville War Cemetery, Tunisia, Grave II. E. 8.

4 SICILY

The Greeks called it 'Trinacria', to reflect its triangular shape. At 9,926 square miles, Sicily is the largest island in the Mediterranean, situated on the 'toe' of Italy and separated from the mainland by the Strait of Messina. In its past history the island has been colonised by Greeks, Carthaginians, and Phoenicians, and it was conquered by the Romans during the Second Punic War (218-201 BC). During their occupation they treated the islanders in the most awful way imaginable, and the poverty that the Allies found on Sicily in 1943 can be said to have begun with Roman rule. After the Romans came Vandals, Goths, Byzantines and Lombards, followed by an invasion of Saracens in 827, when the island came under Moslem rule. The Saracens were in turn defeated by the Norman crusaders in 1061. For the next 800 years the island was a melting pot of all those who travelled and traded the length and breadth of the Mediterranean.

In 1860 Guiseppe Garibaldi and his thousand 'redshirts' led the Sicilian forces to victory against the army of Naples, and so began the unification of Italy. Prior to 1943 Sicily's mountains and stony ground had probably seen more war, invasion and bloodshed that any other place on earth. Most of its towns and villages were built on the high sides or tops of mountains, making them all the easier to defend. Its people were strong and independent, mistrustful of all outsiders and unforgiving in the case of insult. The island's stony ground and the stone walls that surround the fields would be equally unforgiving when it came to the canvas and plywood of Allied gliders or the flesh and bone of paratroopers' legs.

An Irishman would be involved in the planning for Sicily. Alan Brooke, Chief of the Imperial General Staff, described as a 'hard, moralistic Ulsterman', shared with Churchill the view that a thrust up through the 'soft underbelly' of Italy would be the way to continue the war. It would also keep Russia out of Europe proper as it was hoped that the Allies would get to Berlin first. He had stated at the Casablanca conference that 'We are not strong enough for such an ambitious venture [a cross-Channel attack as proposed by the Americans]. This would only result in disaster if we tried.' Brooke then quoted the terrible slaughter suffered by the Canadians at Dieppe in August of the previous year and added that the vast majority of American troops in North Africa were untested in combat, having seen little action. After the disaster at Kasserine Pass no one could argue with this point.[43] At the end of the day Brooke got his

---

[43] In February 1942 Rommel's Afrika Korps was dug in behind the Mareth Line on the Tunisian-Libyan border, having been defeated by the 8th Army in Libya. On 14 February the 10th and 21st Panzer Divisions made a surprise attack on the US 1st Armoured Division and the US 168 Regimental Combat Team. The Americans were driven back for a distance of 20 miles with more than 2,500 casualties and some 3,000 prisoners. The German advance was only halted when a counter-attack by the British 6th Armoured Division drove Rommel's men back to their positions behind the Mareth Line.

'That hard, moralistic Ulsterman', as Winston Churchill called Alan Brooke.

way and the result was Operation 'Husky', the invasion of Sicily.[44]

Sicily was a nightmare. While those forces landing from the sea on any of the 26 landing beaches had suffered greatly from seasickness, opposition from the shore defences was practically non-existent. However, the men dropping from the sky by parachute or glider faced a different reception.

The invasion, code-named 'Husky', was placed under the supreme command of General Dwight Eisenhower, who in turn gave command of the ground forces to General Harold Alexander, son of an old County Tyrone family. His command was the 15th Army Group, which comprised George Patton's US 7th Army and Bernard Montgomery's British 8th Army. It was here in Sicily that the feud between Montgomery and Patton would begin, a feud that would last throughout the war.

The Airborne element of the invasion embraced four distinct operations, two American and two British. The first British operation, code-named 'Ladbroke', was scheduled for the night of 9 July 1943, the day before D-Day. In this operation the 1st Air-Landing Brigade, under the command of Brigadier 'Pip' Hicks, would land south of Syracuse, its intention being the capture of the Ponte Grande Bridge, the destruction of an enemy coastal battery and the seizure of key points in Syracuse, prior to the main landings on the 10th. The bridge carried Highway 115, the main road from Cassibile to Syracuse across the River Anapo and its accompanying canal.[45]

The immediate capture of the bridge fell to a coup-de-main party consisting of two companies of the 2nd Battalion South Staffords and Engineers of 9th Field Squadron RE, carried in eight Horsa gliders. Their landing zone, designated LZ 3, consisted of two separate strips of land. The first was located half a mile to the south-west of the bridge, while the other was a mile to the north-west. The remainder of the Air-landing Brigade in 136 American Waco gliders would come down on landing zones 1 and 2, located in the area between Punta di Milocca and the Maddalena peninsula, approximately 4 miles south of Syracuse. On LZ 1 would land the remainder of the South Staffords and Brigade Headquarters, while 2 would be that of the Border Regiment.

Once on the ground the Brigade would consolidate a defence around the Ponte Grande Bridge; the South Staffords were to hold it, while the Border Regiment was to proceed into Syracuse and occupy key points. The Brigade was to hold on to these objectives until relieved by elements of the 8th Army. It would also attack and destroy the enemy coastal battery to prevent it bringing down fire on those beaches to be used by the forces landing from the sea.

The second British operation was 'Fustian'. This involved the use of the Brigadier Gerald Lathbury's 1st Parachute Brigade (1st, 2nd and 3rd Battalions), which would land on 12 July to capture the

---

[44] Alan Brooke's diary, published in May 2001 under the title *War Diaries 1939-45: The Diaries of Field Marshal Lord Alanbrooke*, shows just what he actually thought of both Churchill and Eisenhower.

[45] The Ponte Grande Bridge was given the code name 'Waterloo', the same as that given to the main road bridge at Arnhem the following year.

Above An aerial photograph of the Bay of Syracuse taken on 6 May 1943. The City of Syracuse is at the top, with the Ponte Grande Bridge over the canal and river bottom left. *Border & King's Own Royal Border Regiment Museum*

Below Soldiers from the 1st Battalion Border Regiment with their WACO (Hadrian) glider at their airfield around Froha, Algeria, in June 1943. The picture was probably taken prior to most of the 1st Air-Landing Brigade flying to Sousse in Tunisia, their operational base for the invasion of Sicily. *Border & King's Own Royal Border Regiment Museum/IWM NA3842*

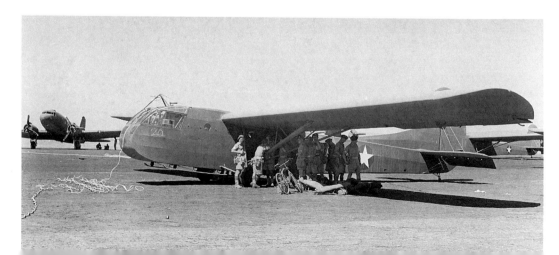

Primasole Bridge. This large steel edifice stretched across the River Simento and carried the road from Syracuse to Catania, Highway 114. The men of the Brigade stood by for the entire day, but at 1745hrs the operation was postponed for 24 hours. Take-off was to be at 1900hrs the following day. That, then, was the plan, but it did not quite work out that way.

OPERATION 'LADBROKE'

The combination of deteriorating weather, the long flight route, inexperienced American aircrew and a lack of communication with the two navies involved resulted in gliders being cast off too early and men being dropped well away from their intended drop zones. Added to this was the hazard of being fired at by the anti-aircraft guns of the invasion fleet, which were inclined to open up on any aircraft that flew within range.

For their flight to Sicily on the night of 9 July, the RAF and American Dakota pilots towing the gliders of the 1st Air-Landing Brigade were ordered to cast off their tows some 3,000 yards from the coast of the island, in order to avoid enemy flak. The inexperienced pilots, unused to flying at night, in adverse weather conditions and being shot at by both enemy and friendly forces, released their charges even further out and the losses to the Air-Landing Brigade were catastrophic. A total of 78 gliders came down in the sea; those lucky enough to reach the island were scattered across some 25 square miles of rocky ground.

Major John Place piloted glider number 55 to Sicily. His co-pilot was Major General Hopkinson, officer commanding the 1st Airborne Division. As they took off Hopkinson remembered his farewell from the commander of the 4th Parachute Brigade. 'Shan' Hackett had introduced him to the American tug pilot who had become a friend. 'With Willie here pulling you, whatever happens to anyone else, you'll get there.' It was to be another case of famous last words.

Also on board the glider was half of 15 Platoon of 'C' Company of the Border Regiment. As the combination neared the coast the Dakota tug aircraft turned off its wing lights and, despite repeated requests from Hopkinson, remained in darkness. Shortly afterwards anti-aircraft fire rose up in front of the tug. Almost immediately the tow-rope was cast off as the American pilot took evasive action, and it was only through the considerable skill of Major Place that the glider stayed in the air. Lieutenant Arthur Springbett of 'C' Company remembered what happened next.

'With great skill Major Place kept the glider airborne long enough for everyone to divest themselves of all equipment and weapons and be ready to carry out the ditching drill that had been rehearsed as soon as we hit the sea.'[46]

All those aboard the glider escaped safely and spent a cold 6 hours hanging on to the wings of the floating craft until picked up by a landing-craft returning from the invasion beaches. One of those Borderers who died on Sicily was Corporal Andrew Eccles from Ballyhalbert, County Down. He had enlisted at the age of 17 in 1931, and had recently married Irene.

An ex-Royal Irish Fusilier, Lieutenant Michael Burke Connell, was also piloting a glider towards

Corporal Andrew Eccles, who was killed while serving with the 1st Battalion Border Regiment during the operation on Sicily. He came from Ballyhalbert, County Down, and was married to Irene.

[46] *When Dragons Flew*, Eastwood, Gray and Green, p67

Lieutenant Michael Burke 'Crow' Connell, Royal Irish Fusiliers, who transferred to the Glider Pilot Regiment and was killed during operations on Sicily in 1943. *Royal Irish Fusiliers Museum*

The view north across the Ponte Grande bridge in July 1993. The southern section of the bridge over the canal is original, but the northern section over the River Anapo has been rebuilt and diverted slightly to the right. There was a pill-box on the bridge just above the wall to the right. *Border and King's Own Royal Border Regiment Museum*

Sicily that day. He was known within the 'Faughs' as 'Crow' because of his rather birdlike nose and habit of shrugging his shoulders 'like an old hoodie flapping', according to his contemporaries. He was born in India to an Irish family, being commissioned into the Regiment in 1939 and promoted to Lieutenant in January 1941. By 1943 he had transferred to the Glider Pilot Regiment, and for Operation 'Ladbroke' he was piloting glider number 58. His co-pilot was Sergeant Herbert Hill, and on board the glider was part of the headquarters of the 1st Battalion Border Regiment. 'Crow' Connell's glider came down in the sea and he and his co-pilot were lost; both of them have no known grave and are commemorated on the Cassino Memorial.[47]

The eight Horsa gliders carrying the South Staffs and Royal Engineers had taken off from Tunisia for the Ponte Grande Bridge, but due to a combination of bad weather and enemy anti-aircraft fire, only two of the eight made it to the Ponte Grande area. One glider blew up on landing when the bangalore torpedoes aboard were hit by enemy fire, which left the remaining glider carrying a platoon of 'D' Company, commanded by Lieutenant Withers, to carry out the operation. Demolition charges were successfully removed, and when reinforced by other South Staffords and men of the Border Regiment, the force at the bridge amounted to approximately 70 men. Apart from their personal weapons, they had one 2-inch mortar and two Bren guns and with these they held the bridge for the next 14 hours. The defenders were only overrun when most of their number were either dead or wounded and they had expended all their ammunition. However, the Italians had possession of the bridge for only a short time before the arrival of the 2nd Battalion Royal Scots Fusiliers, recently landed on the south coast. After a brief fire-fight the bridge returned to British control.[48]

OPERATION 'FUSTIAN'

On the night of 13 July liaison between the Airborne forces, RAF and USAF and both the Royal and US Navies had not improved. As the 113 Dakotas and 16 glider-tug combinations carrying the men of the 1st Parachute Brigade approached the coastline of Sicily it started all over again. Anti-aircraft fire from Allied warships combined with enemy flak began to knock aircraft out of the sky. In some cases the aircrew turned back to North Africa, carrying some very angry and frustrated paratroopers. Those Dakotas that did manage to reach the dropping zones were bathed in enemy searchlights and hammered by flak guns.

Only 39 Dakotas managed to get anywhere near their drop zones. Some 48 dropped their loads up to half a mile away, not a bad effort under the circumstances, while 17 returned to North Africa without any men being able to jump. Eleven Dakotas were brought down by enemy fire, eight of which had already dropped their paratroopers. Almost all aircraft suffered some form of damage. The Brigade's glider element lost the first six into the sea, while a further six crashed on the island. Seven landed safely, albeit some distance away, but four did manage to reach their designated landing zone.

One of the gliders that failed to make a landing was that of Tipperary-born 'Babe' Cooper. Together with co-pilot Sergeant Morgan, he was piloting Horsa glider number 127. As they approached the landing zone the tug aircraft was hit by flak and the glider was forced to cast off at a height of 500 feet. Cooper's glider was carrying Lieutenant-Colonel Crawford, the Royal Artillery commander, and his staff. As the Horsa approached the landing zone it went out of control and, skimming the river, impacted with the bank on the northern side, killing all on board. Astley John Cooper is buried in the cemetery at Catania; he was 31 years old, and

---

47 For further details of Lieutenant Connell's service with the Royal Irish Fusiliers, which was eventful to say the least, see *Say Not The Struggle* by John Horsfall (The Roundwood Press, 1977).

48 The Royal Scots were part of the 5th Division, which had landed near Cassible. Here men of No 3 Commando and the Special Raiding Squadron had captured the coastal batteries. Major Blair Mayne from Newtownards, County Down, was the Squadron's commander; a full account of his military career is now in preparation by this author.

one of the few members of the Glider Pilot Regiment to be awarded the Air Force Cross.

As the men of the 1st Battalion jumped, the enemy flak got their range. Jack Fryer's Dakota was caught in a searchlight beam and quickly became the centre of attention of the gunners on the ground. The aircraft was hit and set on fire; only four men managed to jump clear before the Dakota crashed. Jack was the last of the four. The drop had been made from low level and Jack suffered a back injury on landing. This caused him to become separated from the remainder of his stick and he found cover among some rocks. Suddenly there was a noise to his front. Cocking his Sten gun, Jack issued the challenge 'Red Berets'. The reply should have been 'Kill Italians', but instead a soft, cultured Irish brogue asked, 'Is that you, Corporal Fryer?' Major Mervyn Dennison had arrived in Sicily![49]

When a head count was taken on the ground it was found that the Brigade totalled 12 officers and 283 other ranks, from a total of 1,856 men.

Cecil Newell saw the invasion from the private soldier's point of view.

'The Yanks were firing at us, the British were firing at us, the Italians were firing at us, and

A British Airborne 3-inch mortar team in action. The mortar was the main artillery support for the parachute and air-landing battalions. This particular photograph was taken in Greece in 1945.

---

[49] When Mervyn Dennison told this story to the author, their roles became reversed.

for good measure the Germans joined in. They were also jumping quite close to our drop zones and you didn't know who was who. Somebody asked me how I managed to survive; well, it was simply a matter of looking after number one. Any time I saw a German I knew it was either him or me, and it wasn't going to be me. When I jumped at Sicily I had a rifle and a Sten gun. On the way down you could use the Sten to spray the ground and keep it clear of Germans.'

While at Catania, Cecil's platoon was being bothered by a very accurate sniper.

'One time there was this German sniper annoying us something terrible – every time we moved he had us. I remember this big fellow from the south of Ireland, Frank Lyons you called him. He took the anti-tank rifle and waited. When the German fired, Frank fired at the flash. That night a patrol was sent out, and they found the sniper. Frank had hit the barrel of the German's rifle and had split the barrel and the German in half.'

Cecil survived Sicily and Italy, returning to England to prepare for 'Market Garden'. At Arnhem he would find himself transferred from the mortar platoon to 'A' Company, where he served as a rifleman.

During the battle for the Primasole Bridge on 13/14 July, 'Dickie' Lonsdale commanded 'A' Company, 2nd Battalion, one of the few units to land anywhere near its intended drop zone. On 14 July elements of the Battalion, including Lonsdale's Company, defended the position known as 'Johnny One'. Despite only being armed with their personal weapons, they managed to hold off German attacks until 0900hrs. Then, as another strong enemy attack formed up, Captain Hodge, the Naval Gunfire Forward Observation Officer, made contact with a British cruiser lying offshore. Within minutes a steady stream of 6-inch shells exploded across the landscape, scattering the Germans and preventing any further attempts to concentrate troops for an attack. At 1945hrs Lonsdale became aware of tanks approaching his position from the south. They turned out to be from the 44th Royal Tank Regiment. As the leading tank arrived its hatch opened to reveal its commander to be an officer Lonsdale had played rugby with while at Sandhurst. For his actions at Primasole Bridge 'Dickie' Lonsdale was awarded the Distinguished Service Order.

An incident near 'Johnny One' will also serve to show the calibre of Lieutenant Brian Woods, the former Royal Ulster Rifleman. During the action a large party of the enemy was pursuing Lieutenant Woods and his men as they withdrew up a nearby hillside. On achieving the summit the Lieutenant saw that the nearest cover available to his men was a wood some 200 yards away. Dispatching his men posthaste towards the trees, he turned to face the enemy. Adopting the prone position he opened fire on the pursuing Germans and, with some very accurate shooting with his Colt .45 pistol, managed to cause such casualties that the Germans withdrew.[50]

Billy Saunders was another ex-Royal Ulster Rifleman and a veteran of North Africa before the landing in Sicily. There he served alongside Hugh Adamson from Banbridge, County Down, and they were both wounded during the attack on the position known as 'Johnny Two'. The following year at Arnhem Bill Saunders's work with the 2-inch mortar would prove invaluable during the attack on the railway bridge and the advance into the town.

Boyde Alexander Black had enlisted in June 1938, and was an ex-Royal Ulster Rifleman and veteran of the North West Frontier. He had served in the 1st (Airborne) Battalion of the Royal Ulster Rifles before transferring to the 2nd Parachute Battalion. During the fighting around Primasole Bridge, Boyde was wounded by shrapnel in the leg. He was unlucky in that he was taken prisoner by German troops and shipped off to a prison camp in Poland. He was repatriated the month his brother-in-law, Tommy Scullion, went to Holland.

Landing nowhere near his intended drop zone on

50 Letter to the author

Left Boyde Alexander 'Blackie' Black from Ballymena, County Antrim. A pre-war Royal Ulster Rifleman, he served in the 2nd Parachute Battalion and was wounded during the attack on the Primasole Bridge on Sicily. Subsequently taken prisoner, he was released on the day his brother-in-law, Tommy Scullion of the 21st Independent, took off for Arnhem.

Left 'Blackie' on his retirement as a civilian security guard at St Patrick's Barracks, Ballymena, in May 1985.

Above Private Samuel Garland from Belfast. He served in the Ox and Bucks Light Infantry and was attached to the 1st Parachute Brigade HQ Defence Platoon. He was badly injured during the fighting on Sicily, where he received severe gunshot wounds to both legs and right arm. He is wearing the maroon beret with the Army Air Corps badge. *Georgina Cromie*

the island during the night of 13 July, Patrick Morton of the 3rd Battalion found his Sten gun inoperable due to a broken stock, the result of a bad landing. In the light from an exploding star shell he spotted a half-open supply pannier lying close by. While his mate Fitzpatrick gave him cover, Patrick ran across and quickly grabbed a weapon before dashing back into the cover of a shell hole. As he attempted to assemble the gun, Fitzpatrick heard him say, 'This isn't a Sten gun!' The supply container was German, belonging to the 4th *Fallschirmjaeger* Regiment, which had dropped some time earlier! Nevertheless the German MP40 machine pistol proved to be an excellent weapon, being capable of taking British ammunition, and served him well for the remainder of the battle in Sicily.

When the Dakotas returned to North Africa from Sicily with their cargoes of dead and dying paratroopers, Brigadier 'Shan' Hackett had to

confine those remaining British troops to their camp to prevent a mass lynching of American aircrew. Rumours were circulating that the Americans were being accused of casting off their gliders too far out to sea and scattering the paratroopers all over the island.

During operations on Sicily Montgomery's behaviour swayed from his normal cautious attitude to one of almost reckless abandon. It was not until after the serious reverses suffered during the battles fought on the Catania plain that Montgomery returned to his usual approach to warfare. This recklessness would be repeated again during the planning for Operation 'Market Garden'. By 17 August the battle for Sicily was over. The vast majority of German troops had successfully been evacuated across the Straits of Messina to Italy, but would show in the coming winter that they were far from beaten.

5 ITALY

During the month of August and the beginning of September, the units of 1st Airborne Division that had served on Sicily spent time recovering, and receiving some replacements, and the 4th Parachute Brigade had joined it. For the Border and South Staffords it took weeks before many of those who had landed in the sea managed to return to North Africa. The Division was then selected to land in southern Italy.

On 8 September the Royal Navy's First Cruiser Squadron transported the 1st Airborne Division from Bizerta to the Italian port of Taranto. Danny Gillespie, a veteran of North Africa, well remembered their landing at Taranto.

'We sailed from Bizerta on 8 September 1944 and within 24 hours sailed into Taranto harbour. It was about 5pm, and as a few of us stood about waiting for the gangplank to be lowered a sailor passed by and suggested we stand elsewhere. He was told what to do with his suggestion in no uncertain terms. Shortly after that the ship's siren was sounded, which just happened to be situated above our heads. Three very startled paratroopers leapt several feet straight up in the air!'

The landings at Taranto were largely successful, marred only by the loss of the mine-layer HMS *Abdiel*, when she struck a mine and exploded, resulting in nearly 200 casualties to the 6th (Royal Welsh) Parachute Battalion, among others. After landing, the 1st Brigade took up positions around the port, while the 4th and 1st Air-Landing Brigades moved out towards the north. 'Shan' Hackett's Brigade captured the towns of Massafra and Mottala in quick succession.

When the Brigade went to Italy, Hackett requested the assistance of 'Popski's Private Army'. Hackett had formed this unit while he was

A group of officers from the 1st Air-Landing Light Regiment RA. The figure fourth from left in the front is Lieutenant Gerry Carter from County Londonderry. A veteran of Italy, Lieutenant Carter did not serve with the Regiment at Arnhem. *Lori Woollacott*

stationed in the Middle East, and had been sent from his regiment to GHQ to act as GSO1 Raiding Forces. As well as dealing with such diverse units as the Greek Sacred Squadron, the Special Air Service and the Long Range Desert Group, he had a team of Turkish-speaking assassins and Major Vladimir Peniakoff. Peniakoff, a Belgian national but Russian by birth, was recovering from wounds received in action when Hackett found him and offered him the chance of hitting back at the Germans. The original name for the unit was Number 1 Long Range Demolition Squadron; the War Establishments Committee, which authorised its formation in record time, took that name quite seriously. After quite a lot of discussion between Hackett and Peniakoff, it was decided to rename the unit 'Popski's Private Army'! The army was equipped with American jeeps and trucks that were equally as well armed as those of the Special Air Service.

As well as an innovative thinker, Hackett was also a man who led from the front. On the morning of 11 September 1943, two days after landing from the sea, Hackett's Brigade was making its way north, with the 10th and 156 Battalions advancing on parallel roads. An attack was launched on the town of Castellaneta and 'D' Company of the 10th was held up by a German artillery position supported by a machine-gun nest. The Battalion mortar platoon was firing on the enemy field gun when Hopkinson, the Divisional Commander, and Hackett arrived on a tour of inspection. They reached the mortar observation post just as the enemy gun was destroyed; Hopkinson was watching through binoculars when the enemy machine-gun opened fire, hitting him in the face and head. Hackett and several other officers quickly carried him back to the Dressing Station, but despite treatment he died the following day.[51]

While in Italy some of the men of the 21st Independent Parachute Company had been on what became known as the Santa Agata patrol. The Company had travelled from Foggia and reached the town of San Severo. For the next 24 hours reconnaissance patrols were sent out and roadblocks

established in the immediate vicinity. A platoon was sent to Apricena and from there a ten-man reconnaissance patrol led by Lieutenant Grierson and Sergeant Kent set off across the Fortore River and on to the flat plain beyond. The remainder of the platoon was to maintain a watching brief from a large villa situated on a high hill overlooking the river. In the event of the patrol running into any trouble and needing assistance, a red flare would be fired. Irishmen in the patrol were Jimmy Gamble, Jimmy Cameron, Barney Moore, with the 2-inch mortar, and Danny Gillespie, who was the patrol's Bren-gunner.

After several hours of marching, during which

Four members of the 21st Independent Parachute Company 'resting' in Italy. Back row, John McManus (left) and 'Smokey' London, front row 'Paddy' Gamble (left) and Ron Jeffries. *D. Gillespie*

---

[51] His successor was Major General E. E. 'Dracula' Down.

Private William 'Barney' Moore, who operated the 2-inch mortar in No 1 Platoon of the 21st Independent Parachute Company. *D. Gillespie*

approaches. Lieutenant Grierson ordered the patrol into extended line, and as they began their advance towards the monastery a figure was observed running at high speed towards the building. This was obviously a sentry that had been surprised by the patrol and was heading back to raise the alarm. A member of the patrol fired a hurried shot at the running man only to have it answered by a burst of machine-gun fire from one of the monastery windows. The patrol scattered for whatever cover could be found.

Danny Gillespie dropped to a prone position and returned fire immediately. It was obvious that the machine-gun was shooting from one of the windows, but which one? There was no muzzle-flash or smoke to give away the gunner's position – this was obviously a professional. The only recourse was to fire short accurate bursts of three to five rounds into each window. Sergeant Kent did a quick check and found that Lieutenant Grierson had been seen to fall, hit in the thigh by a burst of fire.

By now resistance from the monastery was growing stronger. The deeper roar from the German MG42[52] overlaid the light chatter of the enemy machine pistols; its distinctive noise, like a ripping cloth, was familiar to those that had heard it before in Tunisia. In danger of losing the fire-fight, Sergeant Kent ordered a withdrawal to be covered by a smokescreen. Barney Moore, using the 2-inch mortar, quickly dropped a high-explosive bomb to allow him to estimate the range – it exploded against the monastery wall. This was followed by a pattern of smoke bombs that exploded with a dull thud between the monastery and the patrol's position. Within a few minutes a dense white cloud blocked the view from the monastery, and the men of the patrol began to withdraw.

As the riflemen withdrew, Danny Gillespie continued to fire bursts at the monastery windows; still unable to identify the exact one from which the machine-gun was shooting, he kept them all under fire. When the patrol had retired to the crest of the

time they questioned some farm workers, information was gleaned that led the patrol towards the high ground on the far side of the valley. Intelligence had indicated a likely enemy position situated in the Santa Agata Monastery. Using the dried-up bed of a mountain stream, the patrol was able to approach quite close to the building. A line of trees provided more cover and the patrol of the 21st was able to close within 200 yards of the objective without being seen. A high wall surrounded the monastery, with the interior building's first floor windows overlooking the

[52] The German MG42 was a belt-fed, air-cooled, general-purpose machine-gun with a calibre of 7.92mm, a range of 2,188 yards (2,000 metres) and a firing rate of 1,200 rounds per minute.

ridge, they in turn laid down covering fire and Danny was able to make his way safely back, all the time being sought out by a steady stream of bullets from the enemy machine-gun. 'They chewed up the ground to my left, to my right and at times seemed to dance in a circle round me, but thankfully I didn't get a scratch.'

When the patrol regrouped in the cover of the ridge, it was found that three men were missing, Lieutenant Grierson, Barney Moore and one other man. Several of the survivors recalled seeing the Lieutenant fire off the red flare as he fell, so it was assumed that assistance was on the way. After a wait of approximately 15 minutes, during which the men called out to indicate a rallying point to the missing men, Sergeant Kent decided to withdraw further back to rendezvous with the remainder of the platoon. Halfway back to their start line they met up with another section of the Company together with the Commanding Officer. Sergeant Kent reported what had happened and that the missing men were in all probability wounded. Later in the day more firing was heard from the direction of the monastery, some of it very heavy. By mid-afternoon several jeeps of 'Popski's Private Army' arrived in the Company position with the three missing men on board. It was discovered that Lieutenant Grierson's wounds were serious and the other two men had stayed with him to lend assistance. The fortuitous arrival of Popski's heavily armed jeeps had provided enough firepower to ensure the safe recovery of the three men. While Barney Moore would continue to serve with the Company to the end of the war, Lieutenant Grierson was destined to spend a long time in hospital, and would not return to the 21st. For his actions at Santa Agata the Lieutenant received a Mention-in-Despatches.

Private 'Paddy' McKnight was a hospital patient while the Company was in Italy. One night, for reasons unknown, he left the ward and wandered out into the countryside. The following day his body was found alongside the local railway line. It was believed a passing train had struck him.

The 1st Air-Landing Light Regiment found that because of its high mobility, light guns and plenty of jeeps, it was often called into action where more conventional artillery would have found the going harder. Service for the Regiment in Italy ranged from the serious to the downright deadly, but it did have its lighter side. One dark night the regimental medical officer, Captain Martin, and Lieutenant Gerry Carter, from County Londonderry, were making their way to a funeral when they were challenged by an English voice from the darkness.

'Jack Hobbs,' came the challenge.

'Is that a password?' asked Carter.

'Sounds like it,' replied Martin.

'Any idea what the reply is?'

'Not a clue.'

At this point a burst of laughter identified the 'sentry' as a fellow member of the Regiment, who was able to inform the two men that they were in the process of marching straight towards the German lines.

After the gruelling Italian campaign of 1943, the 1st Canadian Division paid this tribute to the Regiment. 'The Airborne Light Regiment are a tough, hard-hitting and strong-punching crowd who don't give a bugger for anything.'

At the beginning of October 1943 a small group of volunteers under the command of Captain 'Tim' Timothy parachuted on to a drop zone north of the town of Pescara. It was believed at this time that a large number of allied prisoners of war were wandering the Italian countryside. Captain Timothy's objective was to attempt to make contact with these men and guide them towards various rendezvous points on the coast. Here members of the Special Air Service would provide protection, until evacuation by ships of the Royal Navy. During the landing Captain Timothy became separated from his men and had to make his way alone to the first RV point. Some time later he met a sergeant from the 2nd Parachute Battalion who had been captured in North Africa. Between them the two managed to collect nearly 400 escaped prisoners. Taking them to the RV point with the men of the Special Air Service, they waited for the arrival of the promised transport home. As the Navy boats closed with the shore, firing broke out and in the ensuing mêlée only 40 prisoners managed to make their escape, Captain Timothy among them. Another who was part of this rescue mission was Private James Isaac McMurray, the man from Waringstown, County Down.

Once on the ground, Jim, as he was known to his friends, found himself part of a group consisting of a lieutenant, a sergeant, a corporal and four other paratroopers. Soon they had met up with various groups of escaped POWs, mostly Australian and New Zealanders who had been previously captured at Tobruk. There was great disappointment when they reached their RV point to find that the SAS and Navy had departed. In Jim's own words, 'We were left to hoof it through the German lines with the assistance of an Italian teenage boy who could speak some English. He was also a member of the Underground.' The journey back to the Allied lines in the south proved quite an experience. Food was scarce and any received by the party came from sympathetic villagers, while others, still loyal to Mussolini, refused any comfort. After one such refusal they were trailed by a company of German soldiers for the best part of two days before giving them the slip in one of the many mountain passes. The nuns in a local convent provided much-needed shelter on one occasion. When the Germans came to call, Jim was hidden in what appeared to be a large wooden wardrobe built into the wall of the building.

One morning they spotted the monastery of Monte Cassino rising out of the dawn mist many miles to the south. When they eventually reached the battle area they waited for darkness to make the attempt to cross into the British lines. As they moved off in single file Jim was one of the last to go, with the young Italian boy just in front of him. While crossing no-man's-land the boy stood on a mine and was killed instantly, and Jim received shrapnel in his knee. The flash and bang of the explosion was the signal for the remainder of the paratroopers and escaped prisoners to make a dash for safety, and despite the pain in his knee and blood loss, Jim made it.

The loss of their guide was a great sadness to the men. The boy had led them through nearly 400 miles of enemy territory with the knowledge that, should the soldiers be recaptured they would be returned to prison camp, but he would face a firing squad. All those involved acknowledged that they owed their freedom to him.

In November 1943 the 1st Airborne Division, with the exception of the 2nd Parachute Brigade, was returned to the UK to train for the invasion of Europe. The Division was not used on D-Day or in the following battles in Normandy. While many operations were planned – as many as 16 – all were cancelled; mainly due to the rapid advance of Allied ground troops. Then came Arnhem.

6 INTO THE CAULDRON – ARNHEM

They call it Arnhem. Men talk of being at Arnhem, or are referred to as 'Arnhem men', but the majority of the 1st Airborne Division did not get anywhere near Arnhem. For them the battle was fought in the fields, woods, gardens and streets of the small town of Oosterbeek, some 3 miles to the west of Arnhem. In the Netherlands today the battle is known as the Battle of Arnhem and Oosterbeek.

Before the war the suburbs of Oosterbeek had housed a population of 10,000 people, some of whom formed part of a thriving farming community who lived and worked the fields along the riverbank. Those in the upper part of the village were often retired merchants, many of whom had come home from the Dutch East Indies. Situated in the upper part of the village along the main road were a number of hotels catering for those tourists who came each summer to enjoy walking, boating and swimming in the Neder Rijn (Lower Rhine). The main road from Utrecht towards Arnhem and on towards the German border ran straight through the village, while the railway followed a parallel course just to the north. North of the railway ran the main Amsterdam road, with a new motorway under construction.

To the north of Oosterbeek was Deelen airfield, a large Luftwaffe base. Prior to 'Market Garden', one of Germany's elite night-fighter squadrons, *Nachtjagdgeschwader 1*, had been stationed here, but was subsequently withdrawn due to Allied bombing raids on 15 August and 3 September 1944.

Nevertheless there remained a number of auxiliary ground staff that would be available as infantry if and when the need arose. They might not have made very good infantry, but armed with fully automatic weapons, an ample supply of ammunition and good leadership, their ability to deliver a high volume of fire against a lightly armed enemy would more than compensate for their lack of accuracy.[53] It was the fear of the ack-ack defences around the airfield that prevented the RAF from accepting drop zones closer to Arnhem Bridge, a fear that would turn out to be unfounded.

To the south of Oosterbeek lay the Rhine, the final major obstacle between any Allied advance and the German border. A short distance to the south of the river lay the small village of Driel. To the north of the village a railway bridge and a small ferry crossed the river. This, apart from the pontoon bridge at Arnhem, was the only crossing for the villagers, unless they went to the main road bridge in the town. The area around the village was to be the drop zone for the Polish Parachute Brigade. By September 1944 the village of Driel had existed for 1,000 years. It was situated several hundred yards south of the Neder Rijn, protected from the 400-yard-wide river by a 20-foot-high dyke. As with many other places in Holland, the villagers lived in constant fear of flooding.

Seven miles to the north-east and on the far side of the river stood the town of Arnhem. In the year 1233 a Dutch nobleman by the name of Count Otto of Zupthen and Gelre declared that the city of

---

[53] Kampfgruppe Weber, named after its commander, Captain Willie Weber, consisted of 90 redundant Luftwaffe signallers.

Arnhem was to be the capital of Gelre. Over the next 611 years the city would grow to be one of the most prosperous in Holland before being almost destroyed in one of the great 'what if' battles of the Second World War. Following that initial proclamation Arnhem grew with the passing years. In the days of the horse-drawn stagecoach it became an important way station on the journey from Amsterdam to Cologne in Germany. It was also a route that did not necessitate the crossing of any river.

In time a railway was built, and just before the outbreak of the Second World War a new motorway was nearing completion. In 1935 a major road bridge was constructed, carrying traffic between Arnhem and Nijmegen in the south.[54] Prior to this the only means of crossing the Neder Rijn was via a pontoon bridge, its centre removable to facilitate the frequent barge traffic on the river. Arnhem, like Oosterbeek, also became home to many retired civil servants and merchants who settled there after working in Holland's overseas colonies. Also as in Oosterbeek, tourists played a part in the development of the city. In the flat landscape that prevailed across the rest of Holland, the gentle hills and large areas of forest drew many people to spend their holidays in the village. The pre-war Dutch Army also found a home around Arnhem, with the large open areas of heathland being used for training.

As mentioned previously, fear of enemy anti-aircraft fire led to the allocation of drop and landing zones well away from Arnhem Bridge. The zones to be used by the 1st Airborne Division were situated to the west of Arnhem, the distance from Arnhem Bridge ranging from 4 to 9 miles.[55] It was a considerable distance for troops travelling on foot to effect a surprise attack, but there were compensations. The area chosen was open and flat with few obstacles, was easy to recognise from the air, and only light opposition was expected on the initial landings.

This was the battlefield known as Arnhem, from street fighting around the main road bridge and the St Elizabeth hospital to the fields and gardens of Oosterbeek. Here, in this small village, a perimeter was formed quite early in the action, a perimeter that was constricted by superior German firepower as the battle progressed. In this village, its buildings levelled by shells and bombs, gutted by fire, the Dutch people shared hunger, horror and death with the men of the 1st Airborne Division.

THE PLAN

The war could have finished in 1944 – Montgomery's plan would have made sure of that, had it succeeded. It was a simple plan and for Montgomery unnaturally audacious. The British 2nd Army, under the command of General Miles Dempsey, would make a dash of some 60 miles from the Belgian border to the town of Arnhem. There they would cross the Rhine and outflank the German 'West Wall' to the north and advance down on to the north German plain and into the Ruhr. With British and American troops pouring around the German defences their war production would be destroyed and they would be unable to continue the conflict on the western front.

Between the Belgian border and Arnhem was a series of canals and rivers, including the Waal at Nijmegen, the Maas at Grave and the Neder Rijn at Arnhem. Three Airborne Divisions would be used to capture these crossings and would hold them until relieved by the ground forces. From south to north the 101st US Airborne would capture the bridges over the Wilhelmina and Willems Canals at Son and Veghel. The 82nd US Airborne was responsible for the capture of the bridges over the Maas and Waal at Grave and Nijmegen. The last, and in many ways the most vital bridge, Arnhem, was the responsibility of British 1st Airborne, who would have the assistance of the 1st Polish Independent Parachute Brigade Group.

'Garden', code-name for the ground assault towards Arnhem, would be led by XXX Corps,

---

[54] The Dutch had blown up this bridge in 1940 to deny it to the Germans and its replacement was in turn destroyed by American bombers in October 1944.

[55] *The Devil's Birthday* by Geoffrey Powell, p36

A group of staff officers attending a briefing from Field Marshal Montgomery somewhere in France/Belgium. The officer wearing the black Tank Corps beret is Major Richard Harden MC DSO. Major Harden's family came from County Armagh, and his father was Major J. E. Harden, Royal Irish Fusiliers. Commissioned into the Royal Tank Regiment, 'Dick' Harden had been recalled from service in North Africa and appointed senior liaison officer to Montgomery, a post he would hold until the end of the war. Prior to the Battle of the Reichswald, Montgomery's Tactical Headquarters had to be moved from Zonhoven to Geldorp, just inside the Dutch border. To facilitate the move, an aircraft was supplied to carry Major Harden and Captain Carol Mather (later a Member of Parliament) to Nijmegen, in order to rendezvous with their ground transport. The aircraft, an Auster, piloted by Flight Lieutenant McQueen, flew north towards Nijmegen at 1,000 feet. Out of the blue an enemy FW 190 fighter attacked them. The Auster was peppered with machine-gun and cannon shells, killing the pilot and wounding Mather. Neither Harden nor Mather had any flying experience, but together, and despite Mather's wounds, they managed to glide the aircraft down over a wood and crash-land in a shallow swamp. Both officers survived the impact; Harden only requiring some stitches to a head wound.

The officer in the side cap holding the American M1 Carbine is Major Charles Sweeney MC. Major Sweeney had been commissioned into the Royal Ulster Rifles and had seen previous service in Palestine. He had been ADC to Montgomery since 1940, and during the campaign in France both men had been successfully evacuated from the beach at Dunkirk. They were firm friends despite the difference in age and rank. Major Sweeney was tragically killed in a car accident while escorting a German admiral to prison camp shortly after the surrender in 1945.

under the command of General Brian Horrocks, the half-Irish Presbyterian who had shown such daring and innovation in the Western Desert under Montgomery. XXX Corps was to be led by the Guards Armoured Division, the mailed gauntlet that would punch a hole in the German defences. Within the Division, the 5th Brigade would lead; within the Brigade, the Irish Guards Group would lead; within the Group, Number 3 Squadron would lead; and within the Squadron, Lieutenant Heathcote's troop would lead. Lieutenant Heathcote elected himself to lead the 2nd Army into Holland and towards Arnhem.

In the words of Field Marshal Montgomery, 'The Guards Armoured Division became a byword for professionalism among the Allied units of 1944-45.' Its commander was General Alan Adair, the son of Sir Robert Adair Bt. The Adair family are descended from the Fitzgeralds of Antrim who are mentioned in the Domesday Book, with the baronetcy confirmed at the Battle of the Boyne. Adair was educated at Harrow and was commissioned as a Special Reserve Officer in the Grenadier Guards in 1916. He did not attend Sandhurst, but found himself in France due to the horrific casualties suffered by the Grenadiers, his experience with the Harrow OTC deemed adequate for command. After six months in the trenches he was invalided home with a broken shoulder, the result of an accident. He rejoined his Battalion in 1918, winning a Military Cross and being wounded just seven days before the Armistice.

In 1939 he accompanied his Battalion to France before being posted back to Sandhurst as chief instructor. The following month he was quickly returned to France to command the Battalion. For his actions during a hard-fought rearguard he was awarded a DSO. Back in England he was given command of the 30th Guards Brigade and posted to Salisbury Plain with orders to convert his command into the 6th Guards Armoured Brigade. This became the Guards Armoured Division, and by September 1944 was the spearhead of the thrust that would punch a hole in the German defences and allow the remainder of the 2nd Army to pour through on to the north German plain beyond.

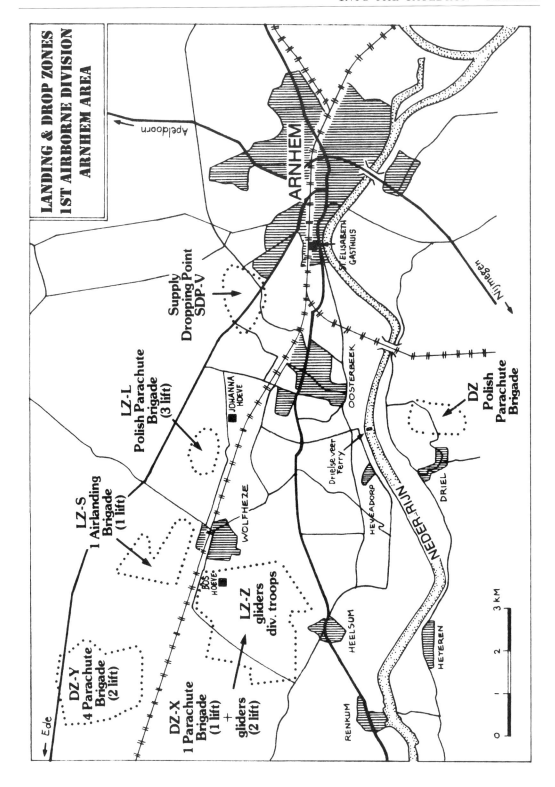

LANDING & DROP ZONES
1ST AIRBORNE DIVISION
ARNHEM AREA

ARNHEM

Apeldoorn

Nijmegen

ST ELISABETH
GASTHUIS

Supply
Dropping Point
SDP-V

LZ-L
Polish Parachute
Brigade
(3 lift)

DZ
Polish
Parachute
Brigade

JOHANNA
HOEVE

OOSTERBEEK

LZ-S
1 Airlanding
Brigade
(1 lift)

Drielse veer
Ferry

HEVEADORP

DRIEL

WOLFHEZE

NEDER-RIJN

BOS
HOEVE

LZ-Z
gliders
div. troops

DZ-Y
4 Parachute
Brigade
(2 lift)

HEELSUM

Ede

DZ-X
1 Parachute
Brigade
(1 lift)
+
gliders
(2 lift)

RENKUM

HETEREN

3 KM

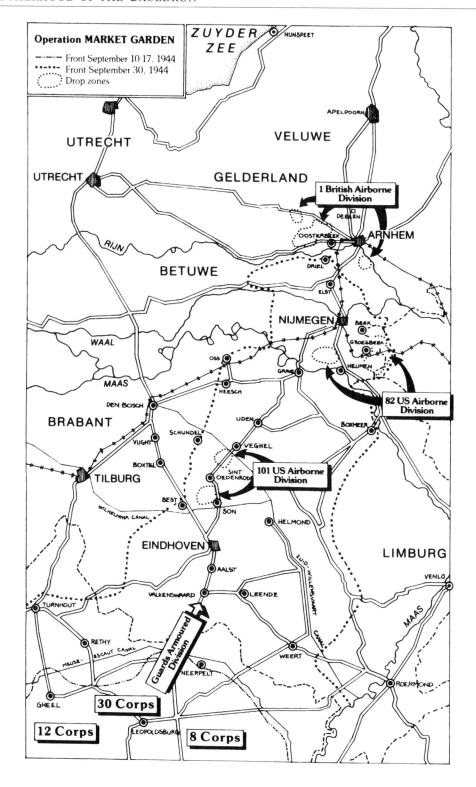

Operation MARKET GARDEN

—·—·— Front September 10-17, 1944
····· Front September 30, 1944
◯ Drop zones

ZUYDER ZEE

NUNSPEET

APELDOORN

UTRECHT

VELUWE

UTRECHT

GELDERLAND

1 British Airborne Division

DEELEN

OOSTERBEEK

ARNHEM

RIJN

BETUWE

DRIEL

ELBT

NIJMEGEN

BEEK

GROESBEEK

HEUMEN

WAAL

OSS

GRAVE

82 US Airborne Division

MAAS

HEESCH

DEN BOSCH

BRABANT

UDEN

BOKMEER

VUGHT

SCHIJNDEL

VEGHEL

BOXTEL

SINT OEDENRODE

101 US Airborne Division

TILBURG

BEST

SON

HELMOND

WILHELMINA CANAL

LIMBURG

EINDHOVEN

AALST

VENLO

TURNHOUT

VALKENSWAARD

LEENDE

RETHY

ZUID-WILLEMSVAART CANAL

MEUSE-ESCAUT CANAL

WEERT

MAAS

NEERPELT

Guards Armoured Division

GHEEL

30 Corps

RDERMOND

12 Corps

LEOPOLDSBURG

8 Corps

Across the axis of advance of XXX Corps lay seven major water obstacles, four canals and three very large rivers. If the worst possible scenario developed and all the bridges were blown, then XXX Corps would be ready. Some 9,000 Royal Engineers and the complete bridging resources of the 21st Army had been gathered, together with approximately 5,000 vehicles to carry it all.

Despite all this, speed was still to be of the essence. As far as the Royal Engineers were concerned, canals were easy – they could span any canal in Holland with a Bailey Bridge. The three rivers, the Maas, Waal and Rhine, were a different matter – these would take just too much time. So it was that on Sunday 17 September 1944, XXX Corps would advance the 64 miles to Arnhem along one road on a one-tank front with ample support from artillery and aircraft, but with no room to manoeuvre if anything went wrong.

THE ENEMY

What was available to the Germans to oppose the airborne landings? The forces can be roughly divided into two commands. To the west of the landing grounds was the Division von Tettau, although describing it as a division is somewhat of an exaggeration. It contained units that ranged from adequate to deplorable, but with some flashes of pure professionalism. To the north-west of Ginkel Heath, soon to be designated Drop Zone Y, was Obersturmfuhrer Laban with his command of 183 men, unfit for full military service and relegated to guarding stores. Nearby was a *Schiffstammabteilung* (Naval Manning Unit), a number of surplus sailors under the command of a Lieutenant, with a few NCOs with practically no idea of infantry tactics. There was a *Fliegerhorst* Battalion, whose men were supernumerary ground-crews from a German airfield, and they were even less useful than the sailors when it came to infantry work.

At the other end of the scale was a German SS Panzer Grenadier Depot and Reserve Battalion 16, under the command of SS Major Krafft[56]; henceforth known as Battalion Krafft, this unit was at full strength and complete in equipment. German armour was available in the shape of Tank Company 224, a number of French Renault tanks that had been captured during the campaign of 1940. Although obsolete by 1944 standards, they could pose a problem to the lightly equipped paratroopers.[57] Unfortunately Tank Company 224 was not destined to meet lightly equipped paratroopers.

To the east and north of Arnhem was II SS Panzer Corps under the command of the redoubtable SS General Willie Bittrich. Both the 9th and 10th SS Panzer Divisions were veterans of the Russian Front and the bocage of the Normandy battlefield. Due to the severe losses incurred in the latter campaign, they were stationed in the Arnhem area for refitting and reinforcements. In Normandy the 9th (Hohenstuafen) had lost all its tanks, most of its heavy weapons and nearly 50 per cent of its personnel. Now in September it was up to its strength of 3,500 men, but still lacked tanks or a full complement of heavy weapons. Those armoured vehicles it did hold were to be passed to the 'Frundsberg', as the Hohenstuafen was to return to Germany for refitting.

The 10th SS (Frundsberg) was stationed on the far side of the River Ijsel, further to the east of Arnhem. At the time of the airborne landing it was described as 'a weak brigade', 3,000 men, 12 anti-tank guns, four motorised, and some Mk. IV tanks.[58] The promised transfer of heavy weapons and vehicles from the Hohenstuafen was interrupted by the arrival of the 1st Airborne Division!

With the announcement of the landings, Bittrich ordered II SS into action. Hohenstuafen was to defeat the airborne forces in and around the area of

---

[56] In *Remember Arnhem* his first name is given as Sepp, in *Arnhem 1944 – The Airborne Battle* he is called Josef, in *The Devil's Birthday* he is called Hans! Pay your money and make your choice!

[57] Some of these vehicles had part of their armament removed and replaced with flame-throwers, the numbers involved ranging from six to 15.

[58] *It Never Snows In September* by Robert Kershaw (Crowood Press, 1990)

Oosterbeek and the landing zones, while Frundsberg was to advance south to defend the bridge at Nijmegen.

Within the Hohenstuafen Division the best-equipped unit was the Reconnaissance Battalion commanded by SS Captain Viktor Graebner. This 500-strong unit had a near full complement of half-tracks and armoured cars. The half-tracks, as well as being used as personnel carriers, also mounted various heavy weapons, such as 20mm anti-aircraft guns, 75mm anti-tank guns and flame-throwers. Because the unit was mobile and would be ready to move within a few hours, it was placed under the command of the 10th SS and ordered towards Nijmegen. It would cross Arnhem Bridge just before the arrival of the British on Sunday evening.

In the woods around Wolfheze, to the west of Oosterbeek, the 2nd Company of Battalion Krafft was carrying out manoeuvres. Krafft's unit was relatively well equipped: together with the usual anti-tank weapons and machine-guns, the Battalion also possessed the *Werferrahmen*, a simple metal frame mounting a number of large-calibre rockets, which was pointed in the general direction of the enemy – not the most accurate of weapons, but deadly when the rockets landed on or near their target. These would soon come into action against the 1st Airborne Division.[59]

SUNDAY 17 SEPTEMBER – THE FIRST DAY

Sunday 17 September was 'Battle of Britain Day', and all over the country church services were being held to give thanks for the victory of the summer of 1940. Then 'the Few' had held back the might of German air power, while today the many were about to return to take part in an operation that was designed to end the war in 1944.

At airfields all over the South of England men were preparing for the battle some of them thought would never come. 'Market Garden' was the 17th operation, and many wondered if even at this late stage it would be cancelled. Several other operations had been cancelled at a late stage, one with the men in the aircraft waiting to take off!

At Barkston Heath, 'Mick' Cox and his section of 'redcaps' were waiting beside their Dakotas for the word to go. The morning went something like this:

1000hrs: tea and sandwiches from the NAAFI wagon
1030hrs: board the aircraft and take your seat
1129hrs: need to go to the toilet
1130hrs: take-off!

Men of the 1st Airborne Provost Company boarding their Dakota. The figure in the centre of the photograph without a helmet is Lance-Corporal 'Mick' Cox from Dublin. He is smiling up at the camera, a smile that will quickly disappear when he realises he is number 13 in the jumping order. *IWM*

[59] This weapon is not to be confused with the *Nebelwerfer*, which was a two-wheeled multi-barrelled rocket-launcher, many of which were also present on the Arnhem battlefield.

An added worry for Mick Cox was the fact that he had drawn position 13 for jumping. Now Mick, a Dubliner, a staunch Roman Catholic and very superstitious, begged his mate 'Jock' Keddie to change places. This was met by a very definite 'No'!

Also on Barkston Heath airfield, Army press photographers were doing the rounds, and captured Sergeant John Bermingham and Private James Usher, among others, enjoying a mug of tea and a bacon sandwich while waiting to board their aircraft. One of those non-combatants who would fly to Arnhem was Jack Smyth, a correspondent with Reuter's News Agency.

Jack had been born in Galway in 1917, one of two sons of an engineer employed by Galway County Council. Jack's father died when he was six and it was left to his mother to support the family by giving music lessons to other children. Jack and his brother Charlie both played the piano, and when older they played in local dance bands. These dances lasted from 10pm until 4am, and they still had to be at university for the first lectures, which started at 9am. Jack was taught shorthand and got a job with the local paper, the *Connaught Tribune*. His first 'scoop' was when the *Atheria* was torpedoed off the Irish coast and the survivors were landed in Galway, just a few days after the outbreak of the war. From the *Tribune* Jack moved to Reuter's, and prior to Arnhem had recently spent some time aboard HMS *Warspite*, where he had witnessed the

largest single naval bombardment of the war when the Royal Navy had shelled German forces at the French port of Brest. Having been told by his employers the day before that he was to accompany the airborne troops to Holland, he had arrived the previous evening:

'It resembled a huge circus preparing to move from one town to another. Long lines of jeeps and motor-cycles were being rubbed down with all the care of prize ring ponies. Engines were being tuned. Steel chains were being attached to the axles so that they could be securely fastened down in the Horsa and Hamilcar gliders that would take them to Holland. The chains were being examined link by link. Machine-guns and PIATs, Sten guns and Bren guns were being dismantled and part lay strewn all over the courtyard like a giant Meccano set. Long cigar-shaped food and ammunition containers were being packed and parachutes being attached to them in readiness for the bombing-up at a nearby airfield. Guns and rifles were being oiled and ammunition pouches filled. Parachute knives and bayonets were being sharpened, and hand grenades lay everywhere in neat piles like a crop of baby pineapples. Plastic explosives were being handled gingerly, and map cases being stuffed with operational maps. Small fires were

Barkston Heath airfield on the morning of 17 September 1944. Men of the 1st Parachute Battalion are enjoying tea and the infamous bacon sandwiches. Second from the left is Private James Usher from Belfast. Next to him is Sergeant John Bermingham from Dublin. James Usher would escape across the Rhine after 'Market Garden', while John Bermingham would be killed on the third day of the operation. *IWM*

burning in odd corners. All identifying personal correspondence was being destroyed. Kit bags were being packed and webbing equipment cleaned. Medical supplies were being checked. Escape kits were being sewn into battle jackets. Everything that might mean the difference between life and death was being scrupulously examined for the last time. Tomorrow would be too late. The officers went back to their quarters in silence.

War Correspondent Jack Smyth, from County Galway, talks to Father Daniel McGowan MC, the padre attached to the RAMC at Arnhem. Father McGowan was awarded the Military Cross for his actions at Arnhem. After the war Jack Smyth wrote a book called *Five Days In Hell*, describing his exploits during the battle. *Jasper Booty*

Each had an all-important postcard to write bearing his new 'address' – it would be posted by the Camp Commandant as soon as the official news of the landing was released. I found the other ranks similarly engaged when I had a last look round before turning in. One man was making his "will" on a piece of copybook paper. Nobody laughed at him.'[60]

At 0930hrs the glider tugs took off from their respective airfields. With a cruising speed of 120mph, they were slower that the paratroop-carrying Dakotas, which could manage 140mph. Due to the huge size of the air armada, it took almost 2 hours to form up over England before flying towards the landing and drop zones in Holland. For men prone to airsickness this was a very uncomfortable 4 hours in the air. The fact that it was a beautiful summer day went unnoticed by those men who spent the flight with their heads buried in brown paper bags or airborne helmets!

As the armada crossed the English coast it split into two streams. The US 101st Airborne was carried on the southern route, while the British 1st and US 82nd took the northern one. On both routes escorting fighters kept enemy aircraft at bay, while below in the Channel rescue boats were strung out almost from coast to coast. As the airborne armada crossed the Dutch coast, rocket-armed Typhoons dived and attacked any German anti-aircraft position that had the temerity to open fire.

These aircraft would eventually fly just under 10,000 men of the 1st Airborne Division to Holland and, despite accidents, loss to enemy fire and errors in navigation, would deliver most of them on to their intended drop and landing zones.[61] The men of the 21st Independent left at 1025hrs, but due to the superior speed of their aircraft, RAF Stirlings, they would of course arrive first.

---

[60] Research indicates that Jack Smyth jumped with the 4th Parachute Brigade on 18 September and was captured the following day during the Brigade's retreat from Johannahoeve Farm. After the war he wrote of his exploits in a book entitled *Five Days In Hell*. He and his wife died in a car accident in Dublin in 1956.

[61] It is impossible to state precisely how many men went to Arnhem. Martin Middlebrook in *Arnhem, The Airborne Battle*, quotes between 8,905 and 8,969.

Men of No 2 Wing Glider Pilot Regiment at Broadwell Farm airfield on the morning of 17 September 1944. Fifth from the left smoking a cigarette is Lieutenant-Colonel John Place from Foxrock, Dublin. Eighth from the left is fellow Irishman Lieutenant Ralph Maltby, his co-pilot to Arnhem and one of the first men to die in operation 'Market Garden'. *Chris van Roekel*

Headquarters Platoon, 21st Independent Parachute Company, on the morning of 17 September 1944. From left to right, the partly hidden figure is Sergeant Jim Crichton, who did not take part in the operation due to a dislocated shoulder, Sergeant Gordon 'Slim' Summerville, unknown, Sergeant Instructor Ken Nutter (attached from APTC), Private Ted Jackson, unknown. Standing with his back to the camera is Major B. A. Wilson, the Company Commander, next to him is CSM Jim Stewart, unknown, and Corporal Fred Weatherley with his perennial cigarette. *Mr Fred Weatherley*

As Wilfred Tallentire's glider bounced along behind the Stirling piloted by his Polish friend 'Uncle' Turno, they crossed the Dutch coast free from any interference so far. Emerging from a 4/10 cloudbank over the coastline, Tallentire found that instead of being 300 feet behind his tug he was flying alongside it! Before he could carry out any manoeuvre to correct this situation, ugly balls of black smoke began to burst around both aircraft and glider.

A few seconds later the Stirling was hit by flak. As bits of the tug aircraft hurtled past the glider, Tallentire quickly cast off the tow-rope. Not wanting to bring his precious cargo down in enemy territory, he swung the glider in a wide arc and flew back out to sea. Coming down in the water just off Walcheren Island, the Horsa made a successful landing and everyone managed to get out of the glider and into the rubber dinghy. As the glider and dinghy floated in a relatively calm sea, its former crew and passengers enjoyed a smoke courtesy of Captain Tallentire and his novel method of keeping tobacco dry.[62]

Suddenly there was a fountain of water just off to the port side; they had come under fire from an enemy gun position. Despite this bombardment

---

[62] When soldiers go into battle they are often issued with items of a personal nature. Think about it.

going on for several hours, all the shells missed their target. On the arrival of the Air Sea Rescue launch, summoned by 'Uncle' Turno, it in turn was shelled with much the same results. Aboard Launch 2687[63] was leading Aircraftsman J. T. Dalkin, who was acting as a Browning machine-gunner. He remembered the incident vividly: the shells came close, but not too close. It only took a matter of seconds to pick up the downed crew and return towards the English coast. Wilfred Tallentire remembered the launch's arrival. 'It came alongside the dinghy like a bus pulling into the stop. Very slick and professional. Within a few minutes we were all aboard.'

The rescue launch safely landed the men at Margate, Wilfred's second visit to this port from the shores of the continent, the voyage made more pleasant by copious amounts of Navy rum! When Wilfred returned to camp he was met be an astonished staff officer who demanded to know what he was doing there. Explaining that he had been shot down, the officer remarked that at least the other radio set would have got through.[64] It was later found out that the gunners manning the coastal battery were Armenian 'volunteers' and pretty much fed up with the war, and had deliberately missed their target. The result of their actions, when the Germans discovered it, was death by firing squad for eight of their number.

The gliders of the Air-Landing Brigade crossed the Dutch coast in perfect formation. John Place was at the controls of Horsa number 161. Most of the German flak batteries had been attacked by the escorting RAF Typhoons, but some had escaped destruction and one of these managed to score a hit on the glider. A shell exploded outside the cockpit window, a piece of shrapnel pierced the fuselage, and Ralph Maltby slumped to one side. Tom Watson, the Border Platoon Sergeant, went forward to give assistance despite having being wounded in the head.

The headstone of Lieutenant Ralph Maltby, the Irishman born in the Pacific Islands and one of the first to die on operation 'Market Garden'. *David Orr*

Lieutenant Maltby died before the medical orderly reached him.

With the sudden realisation that there was only one pilot remaining, the Border men began praying very hard for the survival of Colonel Place. As the Horsa approached the landing zone, machine-gun bullets ripped through the plywood fuselage hitting Private Hughes, the Scout section Bren-gunner in the knee. Apart from this it was a safe and successful landing.

Charles Thomas Brackstone from Dundonald,

---

[63] According to other sources the launch was RML 490, but Dalkin remembers Tallentire and Tallentire remembers Dalkin.

[64] This combination, piloted by the 'canny Scot', was shot down as it came in to land at Groesbeek! The Arnhem Roll of Honour lists S/Sgt Archie A. Harris, aged 23 years, as having died of wounds on 16/11/44 at Apeldoorn. It has not been confirmed if he is the same man.

The headstone of Sergeant Thomas Brackstone of Dundonald in County Down. Sergeant Brackstone was a glider pilot in 'C' Squadron and was killed shortly after landing on LZ-S on 17 September 1944. *David Orr*

County Down, was an ex-Royal Engineer who had preferred flying to marching. On that warm sunny Sunday he, together with Staff-Sergeant Shaw, flew Hamilcar glider number 319 of 'C' Squadron to Landing Zone S near Arnhem. Despite carrying out a successful landing, Brackstone was killed by a burst of machine-gun fire a short time later while helping to unload his glider. Casualties inflicted on the Airborne armada were slight given the size of the target and the number of flak positions to be flown across despite the assistance of the escorting fighters.

As his Dakota crossed the Dutch coast, Lance-Sergeant Jack Fryer of the 1st Battalion looked down on the flooded fields below and noted that the escorting fighters seemed to be doing a great job

against the German flak positions. All in all it was a very relaxing flight.

'Before we took off we had been issued with tablets, two per man. I can't remember what they were called, but they certainly induced a feeling of well-being – everyone appeared relaxed. This was my third operational jump and I should have been more keyed up, but no, I felt totally at ease.'

At 1240hrs the 12 RAF Stirlings carrying the men of the 21st Independent Parachute Company arrived over their drop zones and the men tumbled from the aircraft on to the ground below. 'Doc' Rodgers, now a Bren-gunner in No 2 Platoon of the 21st, always claimed he was the second man in the Company to land on the soil of Holland that warm September day. He quickly dumped his 'chute, unpacked his Bren gun and set of for the RV point. The first man to land is a matter of conjecture; there have been many claims to this, including some from members of the 4th Parachute Brigade, who landed the following day… Private Harry Mitchell, from Belfast, followed 'Doc' down on to the ground, but to a different reception. Landing on top of the outhouse of a nearby farm, thankfully without injury, he was greeted by the farmer's daughter, who promptly presented him with a large cheese. There was even time for a photograph before Harry rushed off to rejoin his platoon. As the remainder of the 21st landed they quickly laid out the white painted panels to mark the drop and landing zones for the following troops.

As the Stirling bombers that had carried the Company to Holland disappeared back towards their base in England, the Pathfinder Company suffered its first casualty. They gathered their equipment from the landing zone and piled it on to a waiting handcart, impounded from a nearby farm. Danny Gillespie heard what happened next. 'A loaded .303 with its safety catch not applied was thrown casually on to one of the handcarts. There was the crack and the rifle went off and Corporal James Jones fell dead, a bullet through the throat.' As the Company gathered itself together, Major Wilson arrived and carrier pigeons were released to

Private Harry Mitchell, 21st Independent Parachute Company, served at Arnhem and received a severe head wound while stalking a German self-propelled gun close to the Oosterbeek crossroads on 23 September 1944. Initially taken prisoner, he was repatriated due to the seriousness of his wound. *D. Gillespie*

take the news of an unopposed landing back to Airborne HQ.[65]

'B' Squadron gliders began to come in to Landing Zone S at Wolfheze at 1255hrs. After making a successful landing, Staff-Sergeant Boyd joined up with other members of the Glider Pilot Regiment who formed ad hoc groups to help defend the landing zones for the second lift due in the next day.

Mary Winkworth waited at her home in Alliance Avenue, Belfast, that September afternoon as her husband Charles flew as co-pilot to Staff-Sergeant

An aerial photograph of LZ-S to the north side of the main Ede-Arnhem railway line (top), and part of LZ-Z and DZ-X on the south side taken on 17 or 18 September 1944 with the gliders of the 1st Air-Landing Brigade on the ground. *Border & King's Own Royal Border Regiment Museum*

[65] This is an interesting point if you consider the newspaper article that appeared in the *Belfast Newsletter* of 2 December 1944: 'William of Orange' '60-mile-an-hour Pigeon was at Arnhem' 'William was dropped with the Airborne Division and flew back to Britain, a distance of over 260 miles, in 4 hours and 15 minutes, carrying an "operational message". He was to be one of many "distinguished service" pigeons at a two-day show in aid of the Royal Signals Memorial Fund in London.' The story that William flew so fast because he was being pursued by the 'Wild Geese' must be considered folklore.

David White aboard their glider to Arnhem. The glider, a Hamilcar, carrying a 17-pounder anti-tank gun, had made an uneventful flight across the North Sea, but things did not go so well as it came in to Landing Zone Z at Jonkershoeve. Colonel Graham Warrack, the Assistant Director of Medical Services, was present on the landing zone as the Hamilcar came in to land.

'I saw one or two Hamilcars coming in. One made a bad landing about 200 yards from the rendezvous point; it appeared to have come down very fast in a potato field and collected a lot of earth under its bows, which acted as a stop and turned it "arse over tip". One pilot was killed and the other injured and pinned down by the load inside.'

Gunner John Winser was aboard the Hamilcar.

'The flight was successful and when we started our landing we congratulated the two pilots, Staff Sergeant White and Sergeant Winkworth. If the pilots flew too fast, I do not know, but as we touched the ground the wheels of the glider dug in to the soft ground and the glider somersaulted. Everything came off the floor, which suddenly became the ceiling and fell down. One of the glider pilots, Sergeant Winkworth, was killed in this landing; Staff Sergeant White was seriously wounded. The cockpit of the Hamilcar was positioned on top of the glider and could be reached by a little ladder in the cargo compartment. Both the gun and the tractor were ripped from their moorings and the Morris truck came down on the little cockpit collapsing on the pilots. The result was terrible.'

Gunner Winser and the remaining gun-crew made a successful escape from the wreckage and only one man, Driver George Cook, required any medical treatment. The gun-crew eventually rescued David White from the wreckage after some 4 hours of very hard work. He was taken to the Dressing Station at the Schoonoord Hotel in Oosterbeek, but sadly, despite all efforts, died later in the evening. Sergeant Charles Winkworth was buried near the crash site, but after the war his body could not be found, just one of the many who have no known grave. He was 22 years old.

As the gliders of the Air-Landing Brigade swept down on Landing Zone S they experienced varying success. Samuel Cassidy landed with the King's Own Scottish Borderers and was helping to unload his anti-tank gun when a shot rang out and he fell dead. The weapon of another Borderer, the safety catch once again not applied, had gone off and a tragic accident started the battle for the Scottish Battalion.[66]

The headstone of an unknown soldier of the 7th Battalion, King's Own Scottish Borderers – possibly the resting place of Samuel Patton Cassidy from Belfast? *David Orr*

---

[66] See also *Off At Last* by Robert Sigmond. There are two versions of how Private Cassidy met his death, and the reader must remember that this was a very confusing battle and it was a long time ago.

Major-General Urquhart's glider had taken off from Fairford approximately 2 hours after the 21st Independent. On board with the General were his batman, a signaller, a jeep, Lance-Corporal 'Paddy' Breen, Private Jackie Mole and two motorcycles. The 'redcaps' had been detailed as escorts to accompany General Urquhart's jeep. However, it was found soon after landing that the motorcycles, Matchless 350ccs, were unable to keep up with the General's jeep on the narrow lanes and sandy tracks. Paddy and Jackie were then allocated to No 4 Section to carry out general duties at Divisional Headquarters.

The aircraft carrying 'Mick' Cox and the other 'redcaps' arrived over its designated drop zone. The flight from Barkston Heath had been without incident – the only sound came from the Dubliner as he sat with fingers crossed and said numerous Hail Marys, enough for the entire Division apparently. A safe landing was made on the soil of Holland, despite Mick nearly being hit on the way down by a field radio that had come loose from someone's leg strap.

As the men of the 1st Parachute Brigade tumbled out of their aircraft the sky seemed to fill with parachutes and look very crowded indeed. Cecil Newell jumped with the 2nd Battalion.

'It seemed that dozens must be killed – there were planes above you, planes below you. I still wonder at the fact that more men were not killed, as they seemed to fall through the aircraft. We were out of the plane at 300 feet – it's not high, but it gave the Germans less time to get a shot at us.'

To Jack Fryer with the 1st Battalion it all seemed slightly unreal.

'We stood up, we hooked up and out we went, just like a training exercise. Coming down I saw an explosion on the dropping zone – possibly someone had dropped a grenade. I don't think it was a mortar shell – there would have been more of them.'

By 1430hrs Frost's 2nd Battalion was on the ground, formed up and prepared to go. Their allocated transport was eight jeeps and two Bren-gun carriers, and into these was loaded all the

Although the landing and drop zones were ideal as far as flatness and size, their distance from intended objectives was just too far for troops moving on foot. This is a recent view of Landing Zone Z near Wolfheze. *David Orr*

Above An aerial view looking roughly north, with the C-47 Dakotas dropping men of 1st Parachute Brigade over DZ-X on 17 September. *Border & King's own Royal Border Regiment Museum*

Below LZ-Z, with Horsa gliders being unloaded, while men of the 1st Parachute Brigade land on 17 September 1944. *Border & King's Own Royal Border Regiment Museum/IWM BU1163*

equipment no one really wanted to carry. As the Battalion made ready to move off, Cecil Newell had just dumped a box of rifle ammunition into one jeep when he came across Sergeant Frank Lyons, the anti-tank rifle marksman from North Africa, lying nursing a broken leg.

'He was mad as anything and cursing all Germans to hell and back. I gave him a bar of chocolate and he was left in the care of the medics. A few days later I really missed that bar of chocolate.'

Sergeant Lyons eventually became a prisoner of war.

Billy Magill from Banbridge, County Down, had served in both the Royal Irish Fusiliers and Royal Ulster Rifles before transferring to the 1st Parachute Battalion. On this sunny Sunday he was in No 8 Section of 3 Platoon of 'R' Company. He remembered that the drop was calm and almost the same as a peacetime exercise. The fact that it was not was brought home to them when Private John Towhey, a volunteer from the south of Ireland, was found dead on the drop zone.

'He was the section Bren-gunner and when we gathered ourselves together we found him lying dead. I don't know if he was shot or what happened to him because we had to quickly move on.'

The first task of the redcaps on the drop zone was to direct all lost troops and vehicles to their rendezvous points and take care of any available prisoners. The various RV points were being marked by coloured smoke, but in the excitement of combat it is easy for men to get confused. When this was completed Sergeant Calloway was to lead his section straight to Arnhem Police Station, while Lieutenant Morley and one lance-corporal went to the main road bridge for duty there.

On the drop zone No 1 Section took charge of a number of German prisoners and fell in behind Frost's 2nd Battalion as it prepared to make its way towards Arnhem Bridge. On the journey into the town the redcaps picked up two stragglers

from the rifle battalions, Private Bob Peatling of the 2nd Battalion and Sergeant Parker of the 3rd. Coming into the town they found themselves at a former girls' school, the cellar of which was being used as Arnhem's Civil Defence Headquarters. Here a police officer named Perdijk offered to lead the section on to the Police Station. After a journey through the dark streets of the town they arrived at the Police Station at 2300hrs and the German prisoners were locked in the cells. After sharing out English cigarettes and chocolate with the Dutch policemen, the redcaps settled down for the night in blankets supplied by the Dutch. All was quiet in the town and as far as 'Mick' Cox was concerned they expected nothing else but relief by XXX Corps the following day, two at the most.

A short time later Billy Magill's platoon suffered its next casualty. The 1st Battalion was making its

Arnhem Police Station, the location of the last stand of Lance-Corporal 'Mick' Cox and the men of No 1 Section, 1st Airborne Divisional Provost Company.
Hans van Wassenberg

way northwards from the landing zone to connect with the main Ede-Arnhem road leading into the town.

> 'We first came under fire about 2 hours after landing. It was on the road into Arnhem – the fellow in front of me, he was from County Armagh, was hit by a sniper. The remainder of the section immediately went towards the house where the shot had come from. On bursting in we found an old Dutch lady in bed in an upstairs room. She told us that the Germans had just left and downstairs we found the remains of a meal on the table.'

These men were probably from KG Weber[67], a unit of 90 men consisting of Luftwaffe signallers under the command of Captain Willie Weber, recently arrived from Deelen airfield. Later they would be taken under the command of Krafft. The man killed was 'Sandy' Dougan; Corporal George Green, his section commander, saw what happened.

> 'There was a burst of machine-gun fire from a house up ahead. As the section crossed a patch of open ground they were fired at from both ahead and the flank. All but two of the section was hit. As the remainder of the Company came forward I went back to check on the men. I found Sandy Dougan lying by the side of the track. He had been killed instantly.'

Billy Magill recalled:

> 'When we were briefed we were told that there would only be German Home Guard troops to oppose us. We were only issued with one 48-hour ration pack as we were to be relieved within 24 hours.'

After that first brush with the enemy, the 1st Battalion continued its way moving northwards towards the Ede-Arnhem road where it was to turn right towards Arnhem.

As it began to get dark the Battalion came under fire from a position to its front. First there was mortar fire; some of the bombs exploded in the treetops, showering the men below with shrapnel and causing casualties. This was followed by machine-gun fire from the flanks that severed branches from the trees, covering the living, dead and dying with a blanket of green. Billy Magill again: 'Then the heavy guns started, there were tanks on the road ahead, the shells screaming through the woods like banshees.' Some of these shells must have been armour-piercing, as men recall seeing mature trees being cut down like ripe corn! Bill Magill well remembers the experience:

> 'My section was sent into a meadow on the left of the track to try and find out where the machine-gun fire was coming from. A shell landed just after we started to move and the entire section was thrown to the ground. Beside me there was a Corporal from Darlington – he had been hit in the face and was dead. I had been hit myself, a piece of shrapnel in the leg. We managed to get back to our company position, but we left six dead men behind. A "medic" jeep came up and I was loaded on to a stretcher and driven with great skill and speed to the Casualty Clearing Station at Oosterbeek.'[68]

With daylight fading and the density of the woods, the only way for members of the Company to stay in contact was to hang on to the tail of the smock of the man in front. By the time Billy Magill rejoined his Battalion it had advanced as far as the St Elisabeth Hospital in Arnhem. As Billy arrived he was detailed to a position and shocked to see 'German tanks all over the place – so much for Home Guard troops! It wasn't long before they started to push us back towards Oosterbeek.'

---

[67] 'KG' (*Kampfgruppe*) means literally 'battle group'. The Germans made great use of this organisation: simply find an officer or NCO, give him some men and sent them off to do battle with the enemy. These battle groups could contain a handful of men or several thousand.

[68] According to information from colleagues in Holland, the CCS at this time was most likely in Wolfheze.

97

Meanwhile 'T' Company was also having problems near the Ede-Arnhem road. By now darkness had fallen and many of the men were feeling sleepy, possibly the after-effects of the tablets with which they had been issued before take-off. Lance-Sergeant Jack Fryer's platoon, which was leading the Company, had stopped by the roadside. Suddenly a figure appeared from the front, and one of the Platoon scouts arrived at the run with a report: 'Paddy, I think I can hear something up in front.' Jack sent him back to inform Lieutenant McFadden, the platoon commander, while alerting the remainder of the men to stand to. Lieutenant McFadden came forward, quickly assessed the situation and ordered the Platoon's 2-inch mortars to fire flares to illuminate the ground ahead, and the platoon Bren guns to be ready to fire. The first flare was a dud, fizzing off impotently into the night, but the second exploded with a dull thump and the area was immediately bathed in a harsh white light.

'In front was a bloody great German armoured car about 50 yards away, a huge great thing. We called for the anti-tank man to come forward. "PIAT! PIAT!" The call went down the platoon. Quickly he came running forward, threw himself flat and took aim at the target. His first shot was too high, hitting the trees that formed an archway across the road. Before he could get off a second shot the Germans reversed away, back up the road going like hell. All this time the Bren-gunner lying beside me was firing on single shot. Yelling at him to put the bloody thing on automatic resulted in a shower of tracer clanging off the armoured car and flying all over the place.'

The condition of the crew buttoned up inside their metal box can only be imagined!

Enemy resistance was increasing in the area between the drop zones and Arnhem at an alarming rate. The 3rd Battalion dropped on Drop Zone X west of Wolfheze; the time was 1353hrs – Major Mervyn Dennison remembered writing the time on his wrist with a copying ink pencil. He recalled:

'The Battalion made a perfect drop, just like a Sunday afternoon on Salisbury Plain. There had been no time for breakfast before leaving the Battalion quarters at Spalding in Lincolnshire. Despite the fact that strict orders were given that all men were to be given a "fat-free" breakfast to lessen the chances of airsickness, nothing deterred the NAAFI ladies from bringing their van on to the airfield. Here they proceeded to distribute a concoction of near cold tea and "sandwiches" consisting of white bread smeared with margarine and containing two slices of cold greasy bacon with the rind still attached. Nevertheless those experienced soldiers in the Company collected all uneaten sandwiches and crammed them into any spare pockets or pouches that were available.'

Corporal Wise, Mervyn's batman, was one of those who ate as many sandwiches as possible as well as stuffing the front of his smock with more of them. He met Major Dennison's perplexed look with the remark, 'We'll get no more food today.'

As the aircraft carrying Major Dennison and Corporal Wise crossed the Channel, Wise became horribly ill, and as no sick bags were carried on this particular Dakota, Major Dennison went to the rear of the Dakota and returned with a brand new steel bucket 'for the Corporal's greater comfort'. He then sacrificed part of his copy of the *Sunday Times* to help clean up the bespattered Corporal. On returning to the open side door of the Dakota to empty the bucket, Mervyn Dennison, in his own words, 'came nearer to death than any time in the war'. As he endeavoured to empty the contents out of the door, the slipstream caught the bucket and him and attempted to drag both of them out of the aircraft. As he says, 'Only the grace of God and the strong arm of the Jumpmaster prevented me from being pulled out.'

For many years afterwards Mervyn often speculated on the surprise of a Dutch farmer finding a new bucket in his field, which would be nothing to the farmer's reaction had a bucket of warm vomit landed anywhere within 12 feet of him! 'The drop had been the best we had ever known –

accurate, a speedy rendezvous – and "A" Company 100 per cent in position.' As he reached his Company rendezvous he found the redoubtable Corporal Wise sitting on a grassy bank, completing his breakfast. The Corporal's invitation of a bacon sandwich was accepted with delight, and the Major sat down and enjoyed 'a handful of crumbs and two greasy rashers of cold bacon.'

They moved off through a crowd of enthusiastic Dutch citizens, who had left their Sunday lunches to see and cheer this great event in their lives. One natty little gentleman in a Norfolk jacket and knickerbockers shook the Major warmly by the hand and said, 'You are very welcome, Tommy, but why have you waited so long?'

It was with great difficulty that the Battalion made its way through the Dutch crowds, but Mervyn led his company as fast as possible waving his blackthorn walking stick in both a threatening and friendly manner. 'The Battalion was almost 100 per cent on parade and "A" Company was its rearguard, so it benefited most from the bounty and kisses of the citizens.'

Patrick Morton and Fitzpatrick came down within 100 yards of each other. As Patrick unbuckled himself from his harness he was surprised to find two Dutch girls helping to collapse his canopy.

'I suppose they were about 17 or 18, very pretty and making a good job of gathering up the parachute. I saw Fitz coming towards me and said something about the day going really well so far and in such pleasant company, when a loud voice yelled out "Oi!" As I turned there was a big clod-hopping RASC Corporal charging towards me. Turning back I saw the two Dutch girls making off with my parachute and the Corporal in hot pursuit. Fitz and I had a smoke and a drink of water while we damned the RASC man for spoiling our potential date, before ambling towards the Battalion rendezvous point that was being marked by red smoke – it was that sort of day, no sense of urgency at all. On the way we met the RASC man coming back, covered in sweat but without the parachute.'[69]

When the Battalion eventually began its march towards Arnhem the crowds of enthusiastic Dutch civilians giving out food and drinks almost caused more delay than enemy action. But things would change the closer they got to Oosterbeek.

On their landing zone the Reconnaissance Squadron waited for the detachment of Sappers from No 3 Platoon 9th Field Company RE to join them for their dash to the bridge. When they failed to turn up, 'C' Troop went on ahead via the railway crossing at Wolfheze. As they crossed the railway and turned right towards Arnhem they ran into the blocking line established a short time earlier by Krafft's Battalion. The ambush was short, sharp and deadly, mortar and machine-gun fire from the railway embankment on their right and from the high ground to their front making short work of the un-armoured jeeps. The troop was practically wiped out and what few survivors there were made their way back to Wolfheze Station. As Gough attempted to re-organise his force there, he received a message that General Urquhart wanted to meet with him. Leaving Captain Allsop, his 2ic, in command, Gough left Wolfheze with one other jeep, to attempt to rendezvous with the divisional commander. It was the last time he would see his Squadron until after the battle.

One of the difficulties encountered by the men of the 2nd Battalion and others as they made their way through Oosterbeek and into Arnhem were the chain-link and metal fences surrounding the Dutch gardens. These fences were made of strong metal mesh, which was too strong to tear down and too high to comfortably leap over. This meant they had to be climbed, an action that not only exposed the climber to enemy fire, but slowed down the rate of advance as the heavily laden men soon became tired after having to do this practically every time they were shot at.

---

[69] The men of the Royal Army Service Corps were charged with the recovery of all parachutes and 'abandoned' equipment left on the landing and drop zones. It is surprising just how much equipment can be 'forgotten' on even the shortest stops.

'The damned fences' – as the men of the 1st Airborne Division advanced towards their various objectives in and around Arnhem on 17 September 1944, units were frequently held up by enemy machine gun-fire. In order to leave the road and seek cover it was necessary to cross these fences. The effort involved while fully laden with weapons, equipment and extra ammunition caused each succeeding delay to become more protracted each time. *David Orr*

As Frost's Battalion reached Oosterbeek, 'C' Company, under Major Victor Dover, was detailed to go south to the Polderweg and capture the railway bridge. As the company advanced down towards the river, No 9 Platoon was out in front, quickly followed by No 8. As the paratroopers closed on the bridge a figure was observed running out into the middle of the structure, bending down, then just as quickly running back. Bren-gun fire was directed towards the German, but he escaped unscathed to the southern bank. Bill Saunders recalled:

'I was carrying the 2-inch mortar in 8 Platoon and my job was to provide cover as the leading Platoon and the Engineers checked the bridge for demolition charges. I was dropping smoke bombs around the enemy positions on the south side of the river when the bridge blew up with some of our men on it!'

Lieutenant Peter Barry, recently serving with the Royal Ulster Rifles, had just led No 9 Platoon on to

the bridge when it was blown up by the enemy; he was badly wounded and was carried to safety by Sergeant Barnbrook. Private Sadler was killed by enemy machine-gun fire during the withdrawal. Peter Barry always maintained that a drop closer to the railway bridge would have resulted in success.

'If we had only landed there, we could have gone in and got it easily – that bridge was there for the taking. Never mind about flak positions. Right there, on those fields between the railway bridge and Oosterbeek, was the place to land. But they landed us at the wrong place, and we carried the can. It was a perfectly sound bridge – you could have got tanks, anything, across. Instead, they had 3 hours warning and were able to blow it.'[70]

The railway bridge was destroyed and a fire-fight developed as the wounded made their way back. Bill Saunders went into action with his mortar again.

'There was one particular machine-gun giving us a fair amount of trouble. I dropped several high-explosive bombs in its general area before the firing stopped.'

This fire may well have come from elements of 10th SS Reconnaissance Battalion as well as the men of the bridge guard squad, who had made a diplomatic withdrawal when the men of 'C' Company had arrived.[71] With no hope of crossing the river, Major Dover led his men towards their second objective, the German Commandant's Office in Arnhem.

Already German resistance was increasing. From the area around Arnhem, Field-Marshal Walther Model, commander of Army Group B, was collecting any men he could lay his hands on – tank crews without vehicles, men waiting to go on leave, men just returned from leave, and anyone else who just happened to be passing through. It was another stroke of bad luck that Model, the commander

---

[70] It was discovered by 'C' Company that the six flak positions defending the bridge were deserted, presumably after being attacked by Allied fighters earlier in the day.

[71] In *Arnhem, The Airborne Battle* by Martin Middlebrook, p148, he claims that these men were from Krafft's command.

responsible for the defence of this part of Germany's Western Front, should have had his headquarters in the village of Oosterbeek. Kampfgruppe 'Harder' consisted of three companies. The first was made up of the above-mentioned tank crews, the second from logistics personnel, while the third was a conscripted naval unit. They were given three Panther tanks as armoured support and thrown into the blocking line forming between Oosterbeek and Arnhem town centre.

Major Dover's 'C' Company had now reached the junction of the river road and Utrechtsestraat and was being held up. A bus loaded with German troops de-bussed in front of Dover's men close to the St Elisabeth Hospital; they were totally unaware of the paratroopers' advance and by the time they realised what was happening the British had opened fire. Eighty men had got off that bus. By the end of the action only three remained to be taken prisoner, and two of those were wounded.

With the enemy dealt with for the time being, 'C' Company continued its advance up Utrechtsestraat towards the Municipal Museum (referred to in many accounts as 'the Monastery'[72]). In darkness at approximately 2130hrs they approached Brugstraat and came up against the main German line of resistance, troops in great number supported by armoured vehicles. This line had been thrown across the axis of advance just after 'A' Company of the 2nd Battalion had made its way through to the bridge.

One of these vehicles, an armoured half-track mounting a 75mm gun, came close to Billy Saunders's position, a ditch on the south side of the road. The half-track joined in the shelling and caused more casualties. When Billy's platoon commander, Lieutenant Russell, inquired if he could drop a few bombs on to the nuisance vehicle, Billy crawled forward to see what he could do.[73]

'I saw at once that the range was too short for conventional firing, so borrowing some extra

shell dressings, I stuffed these under my smock, padding my right shoulder, to cushion the recoil of the mortar. I then lay back against the side of the ditch and, using the mortar as a makeshift anti-tank weapon, fired a bomb straight at the offending vehicle.'[74]

The first bomb was an over, but the second shot hit the armoured cab of the half-track and the crew quickly dismounted from their vehicle with their hands up; for them the war was over, albeit for a little while.[75]

Yet the day's excitement was not over for Billy Saunders.

'Machine-gun fire opened up from one of the dark streets ahead. We dropped to the ground with the tracer going all around us. It stopped – by the sound of it they were changing ammunition belts – and with a shout we were back on our feet and through the window of a nearby building. I was one of the last to cross the road and about half-way through the window when the Germans got reloaded. The tracers were bouncing off the windowsill as I struggled to get inside.'

This building proved to be the PGEM building, headquarters of the Gelderland Electricity Company.

After 'C' Company had left the column, the remainder of Frost's 2nd Battalion advanced along the river road towards Heveadorp when it came under fire from a concealed machine-gun. As several men of the mortar platoon fell wounded, one mortally, 'Danny Boy' Woods ran into the middle of the road firing his pistol in the general direction of the enemy. As this was going on the remainder of his platoon, heavily laden with mortar barrels, base-plates and ammunition boxes, made it to safety.

---

[72] The use of this name appears to have originated from reports from the South Staffords.

[73] Lieutenant I. A. Russell received a Mention-in-Despatches for his action at Arnhem.

[74] This can be done!

[75] Despite the vast of research into what happened during the nine days of Arnhem, it has proved impossible to allocate a unit title to this vehicle. The only indisputable fact is that it was German.

Arnhem. Kussin's bullet-riddled corpse, together with that of the driver, would remain hanging out of the car for a long time, serving as a macabre landmark for those troops passing the spot.

The Germans reacted with speed and vigour to the arrival of 'A' Company, and weapons previously directed at 'B' Company were quickly turned on Dennison's men. The air was soon filled with the scream of 'Moaning Minnies', the German six-barrelled mortar. This would have come from Krafft's positions in the woods to the east of the road running south from Wolfheze. 'A' Company dispersed as far as possible without neglecting its duty to watch the main road and keep it open. Lieutenant Ash's platoon was sent north towards the firing point, and soon the sound of a battle royal was heard. Major Dennison then sent Lieutenant Baxter to reinforce this action, while retaining the third platoon to hold the main road area. The attack north proved to be a model operation; Lieutenant 'Bertie' Ash had spotted and destroyed a German observation post situated on top of a water tower, and between them the two subalterns had accounted for 40 dead, 18 prisoners and the remainder of the enemy dispersed. This ensured a peaceful crossroads for the next 36 hours. Yet as

On the Sunday afternoon, as Major Dennison's Company of the 3rd Battalion made its way from Wolfheze towards Oosterbeek, it came under fire close to the road junction where 'B' Company had previously ambushed a German staff car carrying Major General Kussin, the town commandant of

'Moaning Minnie', the six-barrelled rocket launcher (*Nebelwerfer*) used to great effect by the German Army during the Second World War. Not only did the rockets cause tremendous damage when they landed, but their fearful noise had a debilitating effect on morale.

'Ground Stuka' – 28/32cm rockets that could be ground-mounted or carried in metal racks fitted to the sides of German half-tracks (three per side) – were given the designation *Mittlerer Schuetzenpanzerwagen mit Wurfrahmen, SdKfz 251/1*. The racks could be adjusted for elevation from 5 to 45 degrees, but for traverse the entire vehicle had to be turned. While not the most accurate of weapons, the effect on morale when they landed on or close to your position was considerable.

casualties had been heavy, Major Dennison was concerned.

'Both Lieutenants were wounded and out of the battle. Private Bobby Montgomery, an ex-Inniskilling Fusilier from Innishmore Island on Lough Erne, was badly wounded – he would eventually be taken prisoner. Among far too many casualties was a splendid ex-Ulster Rifleman, Sergeant Rab Grundle. He had been wounded in several places during the attack on the water tower, but with the help of several walking wounded he was able to escort the prisoners to the rear as darkness fell. I found out afterwards that these prisoners gladdened the hearts of the Intelligence Officers at both Battalion and Brigade Headquarters.'

When the 3rd Battalion had found its way blocked near the Bilderberg, Fitch, urged by Lathbury, ordered 'C' Company to try and outflank the enemy

to the north and find an alternative route into Arnhem.

An aspect that seems to have been missed by historians of the Arnhem battle is the one concerning the 'money'. This from Mervyn Dennison:

'Someone at higher levels directed that as all ranks had taken off on Sunday to hold the bridge for 48 hours, there would be a need for cash to be carried so that they could receive their pay later in the week. This would be in good time to enjoy the victory celebrations the following weekend. All company commanders signed for and received great wads of Dutch guilders to be used on a company pay parade, God help us! It was decided in "A" Company that, for security reasons, the money would be divided between all the officers, ready for the great payday in Arnhem. One enterprising young officer was sent into Spalding to buy fleece linings for the boot sizes of all officers. Bank notes were also hidden inside the linings of berets, in the waistbands of trousers, tacked to the inside legs of trousers and beneath the insoles of the boots concerned. There were other ingenious arrangements. What happened in one of the companies illustrates the chaos. As officers were wounded, the company commander still in active service would give his wounded colleague a sympathetic pat on the shoulder and say, for example, "Bad luck, old boy, where have you hidden the money?" One of those who survived would remember the extraordinary case of the very dear friend whose legs were amputated in St Elisabeth's Hospital. A great deal of military effort was devoted to tracing and examining below the linings of his boots.'

'T' Company of the 1st Battalion was again in action with the enemy. Jack Fryer recalled:

'We must have touched the top road, the Ede-Arnhem road, before we moved south again because I remember we were moving fast through the woods when we came under fire again. Down we went into the cover of a garden. A small wall about 2 feet high topped with iron railings surrounded the garden. Every time we lifted our heads we attracted fire. We couldn't spot where it was coming from – dense woods surrounded us. One of the fellows with us shouted, "They're up in that tree over there, the fire is coming from the trees!" I looked to where he was pointing and with the help of a pair of binoculars three Germans were identified, dressed in camouflage suits. We set the Brens on them and they fell out of the trees like birds.'

In Arnhem, Frost's force had reached the bridge and occupied buildings around the north end. The journey had not been without incident. As the Battalion's mortar platoon came into the town it was shot at by a machine-gun situated in one of the side streets. Private James Sims saw what happened next.

'We had moved into the town, Lieutenant Woods in the lead. Suddenly machine-gun tracer began streaming across our front. Lieutenant Woods called up the Platoon Carrier and, manning the Bren gun, ordered an advance straight towards the gunfire. As they closed with the enemy position the Lieutenant kept firing until it was silenced, therefore ensuring the safety of his platoon.'

In situations like this the bravery of the individual concerned cannot be called into question, but sometimes, just sometimes, it would be nice to hear the reaction of the 'bit players', in this case the driver of the Bren-gun carrier.

Cecil Newell remembers when Lieutenant-Colonel John Frost ordered an attack across Arnhem Bridge.

'There was a pill-box in the middle of the bridge with a machine-gun in it. A corporal standing beside me had such a look of horror on his face as the CO gave out his orders, as if to say, "You needn't be sending me out there."'

The pill-box was eventually destroyed, but the volume of fire from the far side of the bridge stopped any further advance by the paratroopers.[76] Instead the Airborne men began to fortify the buildings around the streets leading to the bridge.

'The damned steps' – Cecil Newell's one abiding memory of Arnhem was dashing up these steps carrying boxes of ammunition for the Vickers machine-gun dug in on top of the embankment. The steps are on the west side of the embankment with Arnhem bridge to the right.
David Orr

---

[76] Called a 'pill-box' by many sources, this is in fact another Arnhem 'myth'. On the north end of the bridge were two ornamental stone towers some 50 metres short of the main span. According to information supplied by Dutch historians, Bob Gerritsen and Jaap Korsloot, the Germans had built a wooden emplacement for a 20mm anti-aircraft gun on top of the western tower, and underneath was a wooden hut for the gun-crew. The fire from this gun was supported by fire from enemy armoured cars on the south end of the bridge.

The British presence at the bridge was not great, numbering approximately 750 men. These were mostly from Frost's battalion, 'A' and 'B' Companies, together with 'C' Company of the 3rd Battalion, under Major 'Pongo' Lewis, and five 6-pounder anti-tank guns of the 1st Air-Landing Anti-Tank Battery. Assorted troops from other units included Freddie Gough with two of his Reconnaissance jeeps, a number of men from the 1st Parachute Squadron RE and 9th Field Company RE, the RASC, GPR, REME, RAOC, and MPs and the Brigade Headquarters of the 1st Parachute Brigade. Radio communication was established between the Forward Observation Officer at the bridge and the guns of the Air-Landing Light Regiment at Oosterbeek. As night fell the bridge defenders dug in, confident that they could hold the bridge until relieved within the promised 24 to 36 hours.

South of the Rhine the US 101st Airborne Division had successfully deployed its 501st Regiment and captured the road and rail bridges at Heeswijk and Veghel. The 502nd quickly overran the bridge at St Oedenrode, but the 506th Regiment, attacking at Son, was thwarted by a unit from the 'Herman Goering' Luftwaffe Division, which detonated the bridge spanning the Wilhelmina Canal just before capture. A further attempt by the 2nd Battalion of the 502nd Regiment to capture another bridge at Best failed due to strong resistance from a German parachute battalion.

To the north of the 101st, the 82nd was also experiencing a certain amount of failure. Its 505th and 508th Regiments were deployed to the east of Nijmegen to defend the Groesbeek heights, while the 504th successfully captured the Grave Bridge. Despite some success, XXX Corps was to be delayed.

As the men of the Division became ensconced for the night, the rumour was that Major General Urquhart had been captured and Brigadier Hicks was in command.[77] Urquhart had not been captured, but was trapped 'behind enemy lines' and would not be able to rejoin his HQ until the

Tuesday. Adding to the confusion, Brigadier Lathbury, second in command, had been wounded while with Urquhart and was also out of the battle.

That evening the 21st Independent dug in for the night around Reijers Camp Farm in the middle of Landing Zone S to await the arrival of the second lift the following morning. Apart from a few scattered shots it had been an uneventful day. Attempts by the enemy to make any incursion on to the landing zones had easily been seen off, and only the odd shot whizzing over head reminded many of the men that this was not an exercise. As the men opened their 48-hour ration packs that evening some of them had problems, although they did not know it yet. The said packs had been issued some time before and were quite a temptation to a man after a night out on the beer and a long walk back to barracks. These midnight snacks were to be regretted by some men in the days to come.

On the landing and drop zones the men of the Air-Landing Brigade had moved into position to prepare for Monday's arrivals. The King's Own Scottish Borderers were deployed around Drop Zone Y at Ginkel Heath, even further out to the

George Cunningham, from Belfast, a member of the 21st Independent Parachute Company, served at Arnhem and escaped across the Rhine after the battle. *D. Gillespie*

---

[77] Hicks did not take actual command until the Monday.

west. While the Border Regiment deployed HQ, 'A', 'D' and 'C' Companies between Wolfheze and Heelsum, 'B' Company was positioned to the south-west at the village of Renkum. The HQ Company of the South Staffords had also arrived on the first lift, and dug in for the night at Reijers Camp on LZ-S, sending two platoons into the village of Wolfheze. Their losses on the first day of the operation had been two killed.

To the east of Arnhem, the Frundsberg Division, now unable to use the main road bridge due to Frost's men holding the north end, began to ferry its vehicles across the river for the advance on Nijmegen. This was a slow and laborious process, but eventually enough vehicles would be sent across to cause both the US 82nd and XXX Corps sufficient delay. These would, in due time, include the Tiger II, the most powerful tank in the German Army. It was protected by 6 inches of armour on its front, and its 88mm gun could slice through any Allied tank at nearly a mile range. The Sherman tanks of the Guards Armoured Division did not come close to that sort of firepower or armour. One

Sherman in three within Guards Armoured was a Firefly; a Sherman fitted with a 17-pounder gun. This weapon could penetrate a Tiger, but as they were quite distinctive due to their longer gun barrel they were frequently the first to be knocked out by enemy anti-tank guns. Veterans of tank warfare in Normandy have said that 'if you want to kill a Tiger you have to sacrifice three Shermans.' In the next eight days Guards Armoured would sacrifice a lot more than that!

MONDAY 18 SEPTEMBER – THE SECOND DAY

Monday morning dawned cold and misty in Holland as the men of the 21st Independent moved out to mark the drop zones for the second lift. The zones had been guarded overnight by the men of the Air-Landing Brigade and on the whole it had been a peaceful night. Monday was not to be such a quiet day. As the 21st laid out their markers, aircraft were seen overhead. Thinking these were Allied

Below The much-feared 88mm German anti-aircraft gun, used with deadly effect as an anti-tank gun throughout the Second World War and often referred to by Allied soldiers. The gun was fitted to both the Mark 1 and 2 Tiger tanks. However, the majority of high-explosive shells that fell on Allied soldiers came from more conventional field-guns. Nevertheless the tanks of XXX Corps had good reason to fear the 88! This photograph was taken in Tunisia.

Below right Guardsman William Eccles from Ballywalter, County Down, was killed while serving with the Guards Armoured Division in Holland in September 1944.

fighters escorting the second lift they continued with their tasks. Suddenly with a roar the fighters dived on the landing zones, machine-guns and cannon roaring. At the same time small arms fire from German machine-guns, and shells from anti-aircraft cannon that had been set up in the surrounding woods, began to arc out over the drop zone. As the men of the 21st scattered for cover, the 4th Parachute Brigade arrived.

To the Germans this arrival had not been unexpected. As the air armada had crossed the Dutch coast the enemy had been more vigilant, and this time they had alerted the flak batteries along the route and told the forces around Arnhem. A hail of enemy fire therefore met the parachute drop. Overnight von Tettau had positioned more units near the landing zones, and the attack against elements of the KOSB that had begun as the drop commenced was curtailed only when the Germans realised that paratroopers were landing to their rear. As the Germans withdrew a short distance all their fire was directed skywards.

Down towards the Rhine, 'B' Company of the Border Regiment, on the outskirts of Renkum and dug-in among the brickworks by the river, became involved in a fierce engagement with advancing German forces that would last until the early afternoon.

Hackett's Brigade was coming. Take-off for the second lift had been delayed for 4 hours because of fog at Saltby, Spanhoe and Cottesmore airfields, and the first aircraft did not leave the ground until 1120hrs. At Broadwell Dakota KG 328 of 575 Squadron RAF took off towing a Horsa glider. On board the glider was Lieutenant Colonel Tommy Haddon, officer commanding the 1st Battalion of the Border Regiment, together with Lieutenant Ronald Hope-Jones, the Battalion IO, and nine other members of his immediate staff. Tommy had failed to make it to Arnhem on Sunday when his glider was forced to cast off from its tug shortly after take-off due to bad weather conditions.

The pilot of the Dakota was Flying Officer Edward Henry of the Royal Canadian Air Force. Occupying the co-pilot's seat was Warrant Officer Albert Edward Smith RAF from County Armagh, the navigator was Flying Officer Henry McKinley, born in Belfast but having grown up in America, and the radio operator was another Canadian, WO Bill Fowler.

Albert Smith was the third generation of his family to serve the crown.[78] After leaving school Albert had trained as a radio technician with the Belfast firm of Erskin Mayne, and had enlisted in the RAFVR in 1939 and trained as a navigator. When war was declared he quickly moved up through the ranks, excelling in all positions assigned to him. He was commissioned in 1944, the commission being backdated to June of that year.

He remembers the flight of 17 September as being somewhat of a 'milk run', but not so the second lift. Albert maintained that flying a Dakota/glider combination was a team effort, a job that was made easier if the pilot and co-pilot worked well together, and he found Ed Henry one of the easiest men to work with. When Ed and Albert went to collect their new Dakota prior to Arnhem, Albert had spotted an aircraft bearing the number KG 328 and knew that this was the aircraft for him. Despite Ed Henry's puzzled looks, Albert had insisted that they take this aircraft. When you are a member of a Masonic Lodge and you find an aircraft bearing your Lodge number, you take it as a good omen.

As the Dakota left the airfield they discovered that they had lost the tail of the airborne convoy. Every effort was made to catch up but without success. Crossing the North Sea the combination made landfall at Dunkirk where they turned to port and flew towards Ostend. Here they turned inland and for a while flew beside another glider and tug. Soon this combination turned north and KG 328 was alone again. Approximately 45 minutes later they found themselves over the front line at

---

[78] Albert's grandfather had been a member of the Royal Irish Constabulary, stationed in Caledon. His father was one of the few men to have served six sovereigns. He had rode with the South Irish Horse in the Boer War before transferring to the Royal Engineers for the First World War. He had then been a member of the 'B' Specials, serving in the Ulster Home Guard from 1940 to 1945. After 1945 he continued with his 'B' Special duties until the early 1950s.

Herenthals on the Albert Canal. This placed them between 3 and 4 miles north of their correct course, and immediate steps were taken to correct this, which proved to be a grave mistake. The area around Herenthals was still held by the enemy and very soon German anti-aircraft fire was exploding around the aircraft and glider.

A few moments later the Dakota was hit by flak and Ed Henry, described as one of the best of men, was killed instantly by a piece of shrapnel. Sitting in the co-pilot's seat, Albert Smith was knocked unconscious for a few seconds, and when he regained his senses he found the Dakota climbing at an alarming rate and on the verge of stalling. Quickly pushing the column forward, he brought the aircraft back under control. All the crew of the Dakota had been injured to some extent by the blast from the anti-aircraft shell, and while Bill Fowler provided first aid, Albert tried to keep the aircraft on level flight. The enemy flak had damaged the port engine and the Dakota began to lose height. The glider had also not escaped damage. Sergeant Lester, the co-pilot, reported that the port ailerons had been shot away and were not answering the controls. The glider pilot, Major John Blatch, reacted immediately and cast off from the tug.[79]

After an incredibly steep diving turn, the glider

landed safely, thanks to the skill of Major Blatch, and all on board made a very quick exit. Soon Lieutenant-Colonel Haddon met up with elements of the ground forces and for the third time began to make his way towards his Battalion at Oosterbeek. Back on board the Dakota Henry McKinley had come forward into the pilot's seat to take control. Within a few minutes it became obvious that his flying skills were not up to those of Warrant Officer Smith, and Albert quickly regained control. While Albert had some previous experience of flying a Dakota, this would be the first time he would land one without an experienced pilot sitting beside him.

They spotted Martlesham Heath, an American fighter airfield close to the coast that had quite a long runway, and as the Dakota neared the runway Albert wished it had been longer still. As KG 328 approached the airfield Bill Fowler stood between the pilot and co-pilot's seats and called out the airspeed and height as Albert guided the aircraft towards the ground. When the time came to set the flaps, Bill operated them as if he had been doing it all his life. Albert Smith gives full credit to the survival of all aboard the Dakota to Bill Fowler for his calm and purposeful behaviour on the flight back to England.

The Dakota took the complete length of the

'Bert' Smith DFC RAFVR. His exploits in towing a glider to Arnhem on 18 September 1944 earned him the Distinguished Flying Cross, and he is seen here receiving a gift from the grateful citizens of Richhill, County Armagh, in December 1944. *The Ulster Gazette and Armagh Standard*

---

[79] Major John Blatch received the Distinguished Flying Cross for his actions during 'Market Garden'.

runway and quite a lot of the grass as well before eventually coming to a halt. It was more by good luck than judgement that they managed to pass between a row of parked American fighters. When the ground-crew examined the aircraft it was discovered that the damage was such that it was deemed unfit to fly again without a major overhaul. The result of this exploit was the immediate award of the Distinguished Flying Cross to Albert Smith. Henry McKinley was also decorated. It still makes Albert angry that Bill Fowler did not receive any award, and in some books about 'Market Garden' he is not even mentioned as having been on board. On 20 September Albert was taken to London to make a broadcast for the BBC on the Arnhem operation. Arriving in the capital he was treated to a slap-up lunch before being taken to the studio where he was handed a script. He was requested to read this into a microphone during a broadcast that was to go out just after the 9 o'clock news. When Albert examined the script he refused, accusing it of being incorrect and sensationalist. It was his opinion that descriptions of aircraft breaking apart in mid-air and men falling in flames would only cause unnecessary suffering to those people listening to the radio and knowing that their son/husband/father was away on active service. He then offered to write his own script, and this was accepted; when finished it was taken away for typing. In his own version he mentioned that he had never landed a Dakota before 'without an experienced pilot being on board', and it was only after he had read the script live on air that he realised the BBC had removed that phrase – it was obvious that the BBC were going to have their 'hero' whether he liked it or not.

Tommy Scullion, on the drop zone with the remainder of the 21st Independent, remembered that the first parachutes tumbled from the aircraft at 1430hrs.

'We had been holding off German attacks since before midday and had been able to pin them down. As the gliders came in the enemy fired on them and we had to call down mortar fire on one particular machine-gun position in a farm nearby, but not before this had set some gliders on fire.'

Private Tommy Scullion from Ballymena, County Antrim. An ex-Young Soldier with the Royal Inniskilling Fusiliers, he served with the 21st Independent Parachute Company from North Africa to Palestine, and was one of those selected to return to Holland in 1945 to make the film *Theirs Is The Glory*. *D. Gillespie*

Dakota No 43-15180 of 314 Troop Carrier Group USAF was the one carrying the Machine-Gun Platoon of the 156 Battalion. On board was Private Richard Killingworth, an ex-Royal Ulster Rifleman, who had transferred to the 156 Battalion in North Africa. As his aircraft approached the drop zone it received a direct hit from a German anti-aircraft gun and crashed near the village of Ochten, about 20 kilometres to the south-east of Oosterbeek. There were no survivors. Due to the fire that followed the crash it was impossible to identify any individuals and they were buried in a mass grave close to the crash site.

The 156 Battalion lost more men when the Dakota carrying Private Norman Diffin was hit by

The memorial on Ginkel Heath. As the men of the 4th Parachute Brigade jumped on to the open ground to the front of the memorial, German troops fired from the tree-line to the right of the photograph. *David Orr*

flak. Cannon shells peppered the fuselage of the aircraft and it also crashed, but thankfully did not burn. Norman Diffin would not become a prisoner of war; his injuries were so severe that he was repatriated almost immediately and was destined to spend a long time in hospital as a result. One of those men of the Battalion that did manage to get on to the ground in one piece was Sergeant 'Bertie' White. As he called for the men of his section to take cover, his Irish brogue was cut short by a burst of German machine-gun fire.[80]

Major 'Dickie' Lonsdale was waiting with the remainder of his stick for the green light when a lump of shrapnel came through the fuselage and wounded him in the hand. Nevertheless when the light changed from red to green he was off with the rest of them.

All over Drop Zone Y confusion reigned. On the ground Danny Gillespie and 'Doc' Rogers of the 21st had their Bren guns in action almost continually and ammunition was being expended at a prodigious rate. The return fire from German mortars and machine-guns seemed to indicate that the enemy was suffering no such shortage. On seeing the green light, Bill Kerr jumped with the remainder of the 11th Battalion. As his parachute canopy blossomed above his head his problems began.

'I had attached some spare Bren-gun magazines to my waist webbing, not as securely as I should have, and the slipstream kept these flapping up against my face. By the time I landed I was bleeding from my nose and mouth and feeling slightly fuzzy.'

Another man owed his life to the small pack secured across his chest when a bullet fired from the ground embedded itself in it without passing through or detonating the hand grenades inside. Less lucky, Private Joseph Burke, from Cabra, County Dublin, was killed as he made his way to the 10th Battalion rendezvous point.

As the men of the 4th Parachute Brigade prepared to move out to their respective objectives, the plan was changed. According to an interview featured in the *Sunday Telegraph* on 15 September 1974, 'Shan' Hackett lay to rest the myth that there was disagreement over who should command the 1st Airborne Division in the absence of both Urquhart and Lathbury.

Shortly after landing, Hackett was met by the chief staff officer of the Division, Lieutenant Colonel Charles Mackenzie, who informed him that as both the Commander and 2ic of the Division were missing, Brigadier Hicks had taken command.

---

[80] Sergeant White was buried in the temporary cemetery on Ginkel Heath.

The Zuid Ginkel Café, to the north of Drop Zone Y. The wood close to the café was the rendezvous of the men of the 10th Parachute Battalion on 18 September 1944. The Germans occupied the surrounding woods, and the café became the German commander's headquarters. Fierce fire-fights developed around this area, and on one occasion German anti-aircraft guns fired on their own positions in the café as it was surrounded by the attacking Airborne men. This action hastened the withdrawal of the local German commander, who was subsequently relieved of his command. *David Orr*

Hackett was to detach his 11th Battalion and sent it immediately to Arnhem to reinforce the men at the bridge. Hackett maintained that he did not resent this order, but did feel that the choice of battalion to be detached should have been his, in view of the possible non-arrival of troops or of casualties sustained.

Later on Monday evening Hackett received what he described as 'incomplete and unclear orders' for the following day. He immediately went to Divisional Headquarters situated in the Hartenstein Hotel at Oosterbeek. Despite reports in several books, 'Shan' Hackett maintained that there was no dispute between Brigadier Hicks and himself with regard to who should command the Division. Hackett described Hicks as a fine commander of infantry whom he also found likeable and honest. Despite the fact that Hackett was the senior man, he realised that Hicks had been on the ground that little bit longer and had a somewhat clearer idea of what was going on.

Monday was a different story for the 'redcaps' in Arnhem Police Station. The men had awakened to the sound of a tumultuous battle outside, and the crump of exploding shells and the ripping roar of machine-gun fire echoed around the building. The Dutch police informed them that only the north end of the bridge was in British hands, and no Airborne troops had advanced further than the St Elisabeth Hospital. At 0800hrs the Police released all the Dutch prisoners before retreating to the air raid shelter across the road from the station.

The garrison of the building now consisted of one sergeant with most of his section, and Peatling and Parker of the 1st and 2nd Battalions. They had adequate ammunition, but little food. Sergeant Calloway detailed the men to defensive positions and by 0830hrs they were ready for whatever was going to happen. By midday the redcaps had still not been discovered. German soldiers swarmed all around the building and vehicles of all kinds roared up and down the street, but their attention was on other things. Some Dutch policemen called at the station but could tell them little other than that there was heavy fighting around the bridge. For the remainder of that Monday German troops and vehicles passed the station, all heading for the bridge.

In the early hours of the morning things were also hotting up at the 2nd Battalion's mortar platoon position. Lieutenant Woods and Private James Sims made their way to the house occupied by elements of the Machine-Gun Platoon on the Rijnkade to set up an observation post for the Battalion mortars. The two 3-inch mortars had been well dug in on a grass patch, known as the 'island', just outside Brigade HQ. As the Battery Commander of the 3rd Light Regiment[81] had made contact with his guns situated near the church at Oosterbeek, a fair amount of high-explosive support was available to the bridge defenders. Private Sims was taking the place of Lieutenant Wood's batman who had been wounded some time previously. The journey took quite a while as the entire area was being swept by enemy fire. On entering the selected house it was discovered that no contact could be made with the mortars using the radio. The result of this was that the two men then made their way to another building, known as the 'White House', on the corner of Markstraat and Kadestraat. Once again it was found that the radio was inoperable, and the highly technical approach of hurling it against the wall did not effect any better reception. Therefore there remained only one way to communicate with the mortars: Private Sims would stick his head out of the rear window, risk the bullets passing by in a steady stream, and shout the Lieutenant's fire control orders across the gap to the mortar crews! This worked exceptionally well.

On Sunday, just before Frost and his force had arrived at the bridge, the Reconnaissance unit of the 9th SS Panzer had sped south across it towards Nijmegen. Now it was coming back. This unit, under the command of Hauptsturmfuhrer Viktor Graebner, consisted of a mixture of 22 armoured cars and half-track armoured personnel carriers, each vehicle loaded with first-class soldiers. On 17

The grave of Sergeant Sydney Power from County Armagh, killed while serving at Arnhem in the 2nd Parachute Battalion some time between 21 and 25 September 1944. Such was the confusion of the fighting around Oosterbeek/Arnhem that it was sometimes several days before an individual was 'missed' by his comrades. *David Orr*

September Graebner had been decorated by his divisional commander with the Knight's Cross for his actions in Normandy, before being dispatched south to make a reconnaissance with regard to reported enemy troops. With no enemy found, Graebner was returning to his Headquarters in Arnhem. Well aware that the British held the north end of the bridge, he decided that his best weapon was speed and ordered what could best be described as a good old-fashioned cavalry charge across Arnhem Bridge and into the centre of the town.

The first resistance came from the guns of the

---

[81] Major Denis Munford was awarded the Dutch Bronze Lion for his actions at Arnhem.

Aerial photographs taken on 19 September 1944 showing Arnhem Bridge and the wrecked armoured vehicles of the 9th SS Panzer's Reconnaissance Unit commanded by Hauptsturmfuhrer Victor Graebner, who was killed in the attempt to take the northern end of the Bridge. *Border & King's Own Royal Border Regiment Museum*

Light Regiment positioned around Oosterbeek. The Forward Observation Officer, Major Denis Munford, stationed with Frost's men, called down fire on the approaching column and caused some casualties before Graebner's vehicles reached the bridge.[82] As the German vehicles closed with the occupied houses on the north bank, they were met by a storm of rifle and machine-gun fire.

From the schoolhouse overlooking the northern approach ramp, Lance-Corporal Daniel Neville from County Kerry, serving with the 1st Parachute Squadron Royal Engineers, was fighting against German attacks from the town. Dug in on the ramp itself was Private William Roberts, an ex-Royal Ulster Rifleman from Belfast. He would eventually be taken prisoner. Graebner's command was shattered in the attack, with few vehicles making it into the town, mostly the heavy 'Puma' armoured cars that had led the charge. The slower open-topped half-tracks and trucks protected only by sandbags suffered the most. With their vehicles stopped by mines and PIAT fire, the crews were shot down as they abandoned the damaged vehicles. With the bridge blocked by burning and destroyed vehicles, no further attempts could be made by the Germans to cross. Graebner himself was killed and it is believed his body fell into the river; it was never found.[83]

Later that day Cecil Newell was sitting comfortably in his foxhole on the western side of the embankment when

'An officer said to me, "Paddy, come on and we'll see if there are any tanks about." We took a PIAT each, a couple of bombs in our pockets, and went under the bridge among the concrete pillars supporting the approach ramp. He went around one side of a pillar and I went round the other side. Well! There were about 20 tanks, or so it seemed, all lined up facing us with their crews standing waiting. I thought to

myself I don't know what you're going to do, but I know what I'm doing! I sneaked back round the pillar and there he was coming back on his side. He smiled at me and said, "Paddy, that's tough."'

Immediately thereafter both men made a hasty retreat back to their foxholes.

The fire the Germans poured into the Airborne enclave on the north side of Arnhem Bridge intensified by the hour as more and more units arrived. Cecil Newell:

'You could not hear your mate shout in your ear, they were firing that hard. They didn't have to use sights – they were firing point-blank into the houses. Then we heard and saw our shells falling on the Germans and we thought it was from XXX Corps and that we would be out that night.'

This shell-fire came from the Air-Landing Light Regiment at Oosterbeek, which was supplying some much-needed support.

The pillars supporting the modern-day bridge at Arnhem. It was among supports such as this that Private Cecil Newell of the 2nd Parachute Battalion and the unnamed officer went on their unsuccessful 'tank hunt'. *David Orr*

[82] The British artillery stopped firing when the German vehicles reached the bridge as they did not want to cause damage to the structure, but as the shells of the guns had little effect on the enemy armoured vehicles, damage to the bridge would have been negligible.

[83] Recent research suggests that his remains may have been recovered and are currently resting in the German Military Cemetery in Ysselstein. See Kershaw, p350.

Officers of the Royal Regiment of Artillery who served at Arnhem. Back row, extreme left, is Lieutenant P. P. R. de Burg. 'Paddy' de Burg served as a Staff Lieutenant in the Headquarters of the Royal Artillery at Arnhem and received a Mention-in-Despatches for his gallantry during the battle.
Lori Woollacott

Back at the PGEM building, Billy Saunders was going without breakfast. Having spent the night holding off attacks from an increasing number of enemy units, 'C' Company was forced away from its objective, Arnhem Bridge.

'They drove us back into the houses around the Museum on Utrechtsestraat, where we lost a lot of men crossing Nachtengaalstraat, a narrow street with high fences on both sides.'

Once again those particular Dutch metal fences were causing trouble to the Airborne men. In desperation the last of the much-needed PIAT bombs were fired against the fence to allow the paratroopers to cross. Billy Saunders used his mortar to fire smoke bombs into the street to help conceal the men of 'C' Company as they ran across the road. Then out of the smoke came German armoured vehicles. Sergeant Campbell of 'C' Company took up a position in house number 34 and proceeded to hurl hand grenades at the advancing vehicles. They in turn began lobbing shells in the direction of the paratroopers, and to add to the confusion set some of the houses on fire. Despite the spirited resistance of what few men remained, the enemy was just too strong and the survivors of 'C' Company continued to withdraw back towards the Museum.

Billy Saunders, now out of ammunition for his mortar, was fighting as a rifleman.

'I occupied the first floor of a house that looked straight down the road. I put my head over the windowsill and saw a self-propelled gun aimed directly at the room with the balcony where some of our fellows were. I shouted for them to get out and this was no sooner done than the SPG fired and the shell totally destroyed the room. Then I saw a paratrooper getting ready to drop a grenade on some Germans below his window – just as he was about to throw, a German stick grenade came sailing up and hit him on the chest. Both grenades exploded at once and he was killed.'

Later the remnants of 'C' Company found themselves surrounded by a mixed force of infantry and tanks. The majority of the men had been wounded, including the Company Commander. Bill Saunders, like the remainder of those men still on their feet, was down to his last few rounds of ammunition for his rifle. The position was hopeless – few men remained unwounded, the enemy surrounded them and many of the adjoining buildings were burning. Major Dover had no option but to surrender. Billy Saunders remembers these last few minutes.

'After the CO ordered us to surrender the Germans brought up civilian cars and the wounded were carried outside. As the vehicles took away the wounded those of us who were able-bodied were marched away.'

115

'Airborne House', the PGEM building on Utrechtsestraat, the last stand of 'C' Company of the 2nd Parachute Battalion. Private Billy Saunders was in the first-floot room on the extreme right-hand side with the balcony rail (see also the picture on page 102). From here he saw the barrel of a self-propelled gun aim directly into the room, and it was evacuated just before being destroyed by a shell. It was from this building that the remnants of 'C' Company surrendered to the Germans. *David Orr*

The 3rd Battalion had moved that morning at about 0430hrs. 'A' Company was again acting as rearguard. Now the skirmishes with the enemy were becoming serious. As the Battalion continued its advance it was ceaselessly mortared and machine-gunned. At one point Major Dennison sent an ex-Royal Ulster Rifles corporal armed with a Bren gun to the upstairs window of a nearby house to try and offer some retaliation across the parkland. Within a few seconds there was the clatter of army boots on the parquet staircase and the gallant corporal was heard to exclaim, 'Sure, I daren't go in. There's an oul doll in bed up there, with her teeth out and screaming her head off!'

The advance became more and more disjointed. This was mainly due to the arrival of the German armour, constant attacks by which, combined with the interference of enemy snipers, caused an inordinate number of hold-ups. Mervyn Dennison then met with Lieutenant Colonel Dobie and agreed a plan to try a flanking move to the north, while the remnants of the 1st Parachute Battalion pressed on to the south-east towards the bridge. During this attack Major Dennison was blown unconscious by the blast from a mortar bomb. He had just recovered from this when he received bayonet wounds to both hands in close combat with an enemy rifleman, who was swiftly dispatched by a member of the Company. Lieutenant Burwash of 'B' Company had become separated from his platoon and he was detailed by Major Dennison to take over those men still present in 'A' Company. With the remaining Company Bren-carrier loaded with ammunition and other supplies, he was to lead them towards the remains of the 3rd Battalion near the St Elisabeth Hospital. Here the reserve ammunition on board the carrier was welcomed and distributed. At this stage the survivors of the 3rd were under constant attack.

As the 11th Battalion advanced into Arnhem, Bill Kerr's platoon came under machine-gun fire and he dived into a nearby ditch, losing his helmet in the process. (During the retreat towards Oosterbeek on Tuesday, he again came under fire and again dived into a nearby ditch, where he found an abandoned helmet. Picking it up he saw his name stencilled on the sweatband inside the rim – it was the same ditch and the same helmet.)

In the darkness of Monday night Patrick and Fitz lay in a ditch close to the roadway just short of the town. The German fire was near constant, the rattle of machine-guns overlaid with the deeper thump of anti-aircraft guns being fired horizontally along the streets, their 20mm shells bouncing from building to building like demented fireworks. Fitzpatrick remarked, 'As gutters go, I've known better. Do you remember the night we had in that pub at the village, what was its name, Shipton Bellinger, that was it.' Patrick replied, 'Ah Fitz, we are all in the gutter, but some of us are looking at the star shells.'

By now the 1st Battalion, having fought a running battle with elements of the 9th SS throughout the night, had made its way through Oosterbeek and was following Frost's original route as far as the junction of Kingelbeeksweg and Utrechtseweg, close to the St Elisabeth Hospital. The Battalion was again under fire, including numerous snipers operating from the buildings around the hospital. It was just such a shot that killed 'Fighting' Sidney Ellis. As usual Sidney was with his two friends, Samuel Hillis and Jimmy Usher. Samuel Hillis saw what happened.

'The three of us were fighting our way up past the big hospital. The fire was very heavy, lots of machine-guns and sniper fire. It was a single shot that hit Sid. The bullet smacked him on the chin and deflected down and into his heart. At first we thought he was only wounded and proceeded to give him first aid. We then turned him over and found he was dead. We three were the only Belfastmen in our Battalion and we were in many a tight corner together. Strictly speaking Sid should not have been in the paratroopers at all. He was 38 and too old, but a little thing like that didn't bother Sid. He liked to be where there

was trouble and he certainly was in plenty of trouble at the last. He died fighting like a lion.'

Sergeant Jack Fryer was having his own problems on the lower road.

'We couldn't get past them because it was like daylight with all the tracer fire. It was near where the bottom road meets the top road below the Hospital and the Museum. The fire was coming from the hospital and from across the Rhine where there was a brickfield and factory. Every move we made the Germans had us under fire.'

The shooting from the south of the river was particularly vicious, with several 20mm and 37mm anti-aircraft guns situated there liberally hosing the north bank with shells. This bottleneck can best be described as the butts of a firing range. Those Germans shooting from the south bank of the river had a clear view of any troops attempting to use the lower or upper road, and any shell or bullets that missed their target buried themselves into the embankment. The Germans firing from the north down towards the river road saw any of their fire

Where the roads divide. The high road, on the right of the photograph, goes up past the St Elizabeth Hospital, while the lower road to the left runs parallel to the Rhine. Attempts to use either road to get to Arnhem Bridge ended in disaster. *David Orr*

that was high splash into the Rhine. Men that did manage to run this gauntlet were met by fire coming from those German units stationed to the east between the advancing Airborne and Arnhem Bridge. Any move forward by the relieving force simply put their heads into a noose of firepower, but nevertheless the attempts were made.

Jack Fryer's Platoon had reached the area directly opposite the brickworks situated on the southern bank, and they came under fire from 20mm anti-aircraft guns shooting from south of the river. Sergeant 'Porky' Collis was wounded, falling on open ground in full view of the German gunners. On being told of this Jack, dumped all his unnecessary equipment, ran out and, despite 'Porky' living up to his name by being a well-built man, managed to get him on to his shoulders and run back to cover. All this time the enemy guns were silent. Whether the gunners were changing magazines or were being charitable, Jack didn't stop to find out – he just considered himself very lucky to have got away with it.[84]

At the Hartenstein in Oosterbeek, Major Haig took Paddy Breen and Jackie Mole to carry out a search in a nearby turnip field for something to eat for both the redcaps and their prisoners. They only managed to recover a small amount from abandoned ration packs, but these helped to alleviate the hunger for a few hours. Some time later a supply container dropped close to the tennis courts being used as the POW cage, and some of the redcaps managed to drag it into the Company position. When it was opened it contained a supply of plastic cap badges and the previous Sunday's newspapers. Now at least there was something to read and an adequate supply of toilet paper.[85]

At Renkum, to the west of Oosterbeek, 'B' Company of the Border Regiment had been in action for much of the day in and around the Renkum brickworks against superior enemy forces. By early afternoon, with all the company vehicles badly damaged by shell and mortar fire, the Company withdrew to the east, taking with it one battered jeep and the two Vickers machine-guns. The two mortars and two anti-tanks guns were spiked and left behind. Near Heelsum Private Joseph Walker, 20 Platoon 'D' Company, from County Down, was killed at this time.

Near midnight the redcaps in Arnhem Police Station prepared to make their move, either to get

The Airborne Museum in the former Hartenstein Hotel at Oosterbeek. In September 1944 the present front entrance was the rear of the building. *David Orr*

---

[84] This incident, like several others in the battle, went unnoticed by any commissioned rank and therefore, no matter how well deserved, no award was forthcoming.

[85] See *The Pegasus Patrol* by Turnbull & Hamblett

The headstone of Private Joseph Walker, aged 22 years. He came from Moira, County Down, and was killed on 18 September 1944 near the village of Renkum while serving in 'D' Company of 1st Battalion, Border Regiment. *David Orr*

to the bridge or to rendezvous with those Airborne troops advancing into the town. Mick Cox tore his blanket into strips to bind round his steel-shod boots and ensured he had all his equipment. although they waited most of the night the order did not come. Sergeant Calloway was missing for a time, possibly attempting to get through to the bridge; when he returned daylight was breaking and the opportunity was lost.

Monday had seen the US 101st launch a successful attack against Eindhoven, its 506th Regiment driving out the defenders and securing the bridge over the River Dommel situated to the

east of the town. At Son bridging equipment had come forward and Engineers were constructing a Bailey bridge. The 2nd and 3rd Battalions of the 502nd had failed to capture the bridge at Best and it was blown at 1100hrs that morning. XXX Corps was being delayed, again.

At the small village of Driel, south of the Rhine, an Irishman named Cooney of the 2nd Parachute Battalion was hiding from the Germans. He had arrived that morning at about 8am with another soldier, having come from north of the river, crossing via the ferry.[86] They had a German prisoner with them and told the villagers they were looking for the Second Army. Informed that there was no sign of any relieving British troops and that the country between the village and Nijmegen was in enemy hands, the two paratroopers settled down to wait for darkness. That evening Arnoldus Baltussen, one of the villagers, took the men and their prisoner to the Driel ferry so they could cross north and join up with the forces in Oosterbeek. Some two and a half hours later the party returned to the village, this time with two British officers, the prisoner having been left at Oosterbeek. Just after midnight the four men left for Nijmegen with Arnoldus Baltussen acting as guide. They had only gone a short distance when a German motorcycle driving along the road without lights surprised them. Immediately the party jumped into the ditch at the side of the road and hid while the danger passed. When the German had disappeared it was found that Private Cooney had twisted his ankle and was unable to carry on with the journey, so while the three British soldiers continued towards Nijmegen, Arnoldus Baltussen took the injured Irishman back to the village. Here he was offered a place to hide in the Baltussen home, but refused, instead hiding in a woodshed in a nearby orchard. The other men managed to reach Nijmegen and returned to Driel on the morning of the 19th. They made the same trips over the next three nights, staying each time with the Baltussen family.

'Paddy' Cooney was not the only stranger hiding in Driel at this time. Polish conscripts on the run

---

[86] It is believed that the second soldier was Sergeant Eric Matson of the Glider Pilot Regiment, but this has not been confirmed. See under his entry in the appendix.

from the Wehrmacht were hiding in the Protestant church. Some wounded aircrew from a crashed Stirling bomber were also concealed in the village, together with some Jews who had previously been hiding in Oosterbeek.

TUESDAY 19 SEPTEMBER –
THE THIRD DAY

The dawn of Tuesday 19 September brought little alleviation to the men in Arnhem Police Station. They were sharing a meagre breakfast of some tea and soup with their German prisoners when news arrived in the shape of two Dutch police officers. They informed the redcaps that the British advance had been stopped at the St Elisabeth Hospital and that the forces at the bridge were completely surrounded. Later in the afternoon a burst of Sten-gun fire from the Police Station rooftop into an unwary group of German soldiers standing across the street alerted the enemy to the redcaps' position. Within a short time the Police Station, for so long ignored, now became the centre of attention to those enemy in the immediate vicinity. The German assault when it came was launched from all sides, supported by intense machine-gun fire and the lavish use of hand grenades. The German prisoners in the cell began shouting to the attackers to attract their attention. In the hope of creating a diversion the redcaps released them from their cell and they streamed outside. In the resulting chaos Sergeant Calloway was killed, but three of the defenders managed to get away; Sergeant Parker and Lance-Corporal Whitmill ran off into the maze of side streets, while Bob Peatling made his way up into the attic of the Station and hid there until 31 October! 'Mick' Cox was taken prisoner and eventually ended up in a prison camp.[87]

Back at the St Elisabeth Hospital the battle continued to rage. Close by at the junction of the upper and lower roads, 'T' Company was having its share of surprises. Jack Fryer remembered one such occasion.

'I came round a corner and there was a Jerry appearing to throw something. I quickly realised he was dead. Then a wee Welsh fellow came up, saw the same thing and shouted in an excited voice, "Shoot him, shoot him!" I said, "He's dead." "No he's not!" he yelled. "Well, you shoot him then." And he did.'

At 0630hrs the South Staffs reached the Museum, where they ran into even stronger opposition. There was just no room for manoeuvre. Four battalions were trying to fight their way through two small gaps and there was no co-ordinated command. Survivors of the 1st Battalion, some 30 men, pushed through to within 800 yards of the bridge, while the 3rd Battalion had made about the same distance earlier. The 11th Battalion was caught in the process of forming up to attack and was sent reeling back in confusion.[88]

All four Commanding Officers had been killed, wounded or taken prisoner during the morning and it proved impossible to instil any cohesion into further attacks. 'A' Company of the South Staffs was at the Museum and the ever-cheerful Bobby Montgomery was doing his bit with the PIAT. With the discharge of his last bomb, the enemy armour began to close in and serious damage was caused to the building by shell-fire.

'Heavy fire had forced us from the upper floors of the Museum down into the cellar. Here the floor was covered in dead and wounded. Outside in the street we could hear a Jerry voice shout "Fire!", so we got our heads down while the tanks tried to bring the roof down. The wounded were getting the worst of it. Still on their feet along with me were Sergeant Brown, Corporal Maynard, two men of the Support Group and Captain Buchanan, the Padre.'

---

87 There are three men of this name listed in the POW records, but none has the initial 'M'. The author feels that in this case the name 'Mick' is used in a similar fashion to 'Paddy'.

88 It is this part of the Arnhem battle that causes the most confusion and argument among historians. It has probably been explained best by Middlebrook in his book *Arnhem, the Airborne Battle* (Viking, 1994).

In almost all accounts of the fighting at Arnhem the Museum building is referred to as 'the Monastery'. The building was originally a gentlemen's private club, but it went bankrupt in 1903 and lay derelict for some 15 years before being taken over as the Arnhem Municipal Museum, which it remains to this day. In September 1944 Private Samuel Montgomery of the South Staffords was one of those that held out here until he ran out of ammunition for his PIAT. He was eventually taken prisoner. *David Orr*

There was some discussion as to whether they should stand or flee. Sergeant Brown and Padre Buchanan decided to try and make the river and work their way back towards Oosterbeek, while the remainder elected to fight on.

'After the Sergeant and Padre left we continued to fire on the Jerries from time to time. Unfortunately the fire returned was twice as much as we put out and the wounded shouted things like "Leave the bastards alone!"'

When their ammunition was nearly exhausted Samuel and the other three decided that it was time to give up.

'There were just the four of us left, Corporal Maynard, the two Support Group and myself. We decided that the wounded would be better off with the Jerries so we busted up all the weapons we could find and signalled Jerry with a dirty towel. About 10 minutes later I had my hands on the back of my head and was following a Jerry who was my escort. He turned and yelled at me "Schnell!" – "Faster!" – and walked straight in front of a Jerry tank that was driving past. I grabbed him by his shoulder strap and pulled him back towards me. He must have "caught on" very quickly otherwise he might have belted me. I remember thinking at the time, "What the hell am I doing?", but on reflection I'm glad I did it. A short time later when we were locked in a compound I saw Padre Buchanan being marched passed with a Jerry escort. It was here that I met a Merchant Navy man captured at Arnhem. He told me he had volunteered to throw supplies from RAF planes and was shot down.'[89]

Lance-Corporal Fred Budd was a medic with the 181st Air-Landing Field Ambulance and he remembered that the very presence of Padre Buchanan was a great boost to the morale of the wounded. 'He was one of the finest men you could ever hope to meet.' Fred Budd also lays to rest a myth that all medics were conscientious objectors and went into battle unarmed. The author has a photograph of Fred and another medic taken prior to Arnhem, showing each of them armed with a Browning pistol.

'With all due respect to conscientious objectors who had their reasons for being so, there were none in the 181st Air-Landing

[89] Letter to the author

Field Ambulance. We had only one thing in mind during the battle, to treat and protect our wounded. We were also trained on and used Sten and Bren guns on Sicily.'[90]

Some survivors of these four battalions, approximately 500 men, began to drift back towards Oosterbeek where they were rallied by 'Sheriff' Thompson and placed into defensive positions on the eastern side of the perimeter.

At Arnhem Bridge James Sims saw the end of the 'White House', Lieutenant Woods's observation post.

'I had been ordered out of the "island" in the middle of the road where the mortars had been dug in, as by this time the roof of the "White House" was on fire. The Germans fired a burst of tracer at the house as if to warn the men inside that they were going to shell it. No men emerged, but a burst of machine-gun fire answered the Germans. A self-propelled gun opened fire on the house from about 100 yards and continued to shell it until the roof collapsed on the men inside. Lieutenant

Woods was badly wounded by shrapnel and was removed to the Aid Post. I was wounded myself by shell-fire a short time later while digging a slit trench at one of the houses on the corner of Markstraat. The vehicle then moved up to Brigade HQ and from a range of 200 yards quickly reduced the building to a heap of rubble. We got our own back – the self-propelled gun was finally dealt with by the 3-inch mortars when one of the bombs landed close to it, exploding some stored ammunition.'

On Landing Zone L the gliders carrying the guns of the Polish Anti-Tank Battery were coming in. The men of No 1 Platoon of the 21st had guided them on to the ground using smoke markers and marker panels. The gliders came down on to a landing zone that was under a constant storm of German machine-gun and mortar fire. As the last glider came to a standstill the Germans launched a strong counter-attack from the north, working their way down through the trees towards the Independent Company's position, but they were met by a barrage of fire from the Platoon, with assistance from some of the recently landed glider pilots. The Platoon

The railway line was an obstacle between the 4th Parachute Brigade and the remainder of the 1st Airborne Division. In some places it was on a high embankment while in others in a deep cutting. In either case it was swept my enemy machine-gun fire that made crossing almost impossible.
Courtesy of David Orr

---

[90] Edwin Heath, a well-known Northern Ireland hypnotist, served in both the 1st and 6th Airborne Divisions. He remembered that their platoon medic in Normandy was also a conscious objector. In the evening, while the men in the barrack-room played cards, the medic would come in and get ready for bed. As he knelt to pray the men stopped playing until he had finished. The medic was killed in action in Normandy. A little-known point concerning these men is that they were denied any promotion or awards, despite many of them performing deeds worthy of the Victoria Cross.

Commander, Lieutenant Eastwood, realised his position could not be held for long without reinforcements. Observing British troops moving away from the suburbs of Arnhem and making their way towards the west, he dispatched Sergeant Kent with Jimmy Gamble to go and round up some men to assist with a counter-attack. Down at the railway they found an officer and what was described as 'a rather defeated-looking shambles', none of whom showed any interest in lending a hand. The officer quoted vague orders with regards to a withdrawal to the railway station at Wolfheze and swiftly disappeared, taking his 'shambles' with him. When Kent and Gamble informed Lieutenant Eastwood that no assistance was forthcoming, the Lieutenant decided that it was time to go.[91]

At his headquarters along the north side of the railway line south-east of Johannahoeve, Hackett was striving to fulfil his Brigade's task of forming a defensive perimeter north of Arnhem. His plan was for the 156 Battalion to capture the high ground at Koepel, while the 10th was to establish a strong base on the Ede-Arnhem road some 1,000 yards to the north-east of Johannahoeve. Later in the day he met with Urquhart, a meeting that was interrupted by strafing Me109s. Urquhart, unaware of the failure of the 11th Battalion to capture the Mariendaal, discussed with Hackett the withdrawal of his two battalions south of the railway in preparation for an advance on Arnhem. As the two battalions left their positions they lost many casualties from intense machine-gun fire from both flanks and the rear, the Germans snapping at their heels all the way.

Francis Dolaghan was killed shortly after the 4th Parachute Brigade Headquarters crossed the railway via a tunnel. His brother Thomas was forced to leave his body as the Brigade continued on towards the east.

What was left of the 1st Battalion was still attempting to get towards the bridge. Some men had reached a factory overlooking the river when they came under strong cannon fire from the far bank. Sergeant John Bermingham was wounded,

together with Private Frank Dobrozyski and Sergeant Millburn. They were taken to the Casualty Clearing Station at the St Elisabeth Hospital, where despite treatment from British medical staff both Sergeant Bermingham and Private Dobrozyski died of their wounds. Frank was a Cockney from the East End of London, and when the bodies were exhumed after the war for reburial in the Airborne Cemetery, confusion over his name caused him to be buried alongside men of the Polish Parachute Brigade. When his family found out about the mistake, they refused the offer from the War Graves Commission to move the body, electing to let him lie among fallen comrades.[92]

At the bridge Frost was preparing for the arrival of the Polish Brigade, due to drop on DZ-K, just south of the bridge. Frost had formed a 'flying

The culvert under the railway line close to Wolfheze. Originally designed as a means of taking storm water from the land north of the railway embankment down towards the Rhine, it proved wide enough to accommodate the Airborne jeep. Vehicles belonging to the 4th Parachute Brigade Headquarters and the 156 Battalion used this route as a means of safely crossing the railway embankment. Any attempt to go over the top exposed men and vehicles to enemy machine-gun fire, although two of the huge 17-pounder anti-tank guns were successfully driven over the top.

91 See *First In* by Ron Kent (Batsford, 1979)
92 Since then his body has been moved and is today in Oosterbeek 25.B.9.

The headstone of Francis Dolaghan, one of three sets of Irish brothers to serve at Arnhem. His brother Thomas survived the battle and became a prisoner of war. *David Orr*

column' using Gough's two jeeps and a Bren-carrier to sally out and meet the Brigade. This force would dash south across the bridge and hopefully cause enough of a distraction to allow the Poles to establish a defensive perimeter and send some reinforcements across to Frost. Volunteers to man these vehicles from the spare officers at Brigade HQ were described as 'unenthusiastic'. Frost told Gough, 'Now is the chance to earn your family's fifth VC.' In fact it would have been the fourth, and Freddy Gough believed it would have been a posthumous award. Fortunately the chance did not arise – the Polish drop was postponed due to their airfield in England being fog-bound.[93]

That afternoon the RAF again attempted a re-

supply drop, and Dakota call-sign FZ-626 of 271 Squadron left Down Ampney bound for the supply-dropping zone north of Oosterbeek. One of those on board was Lance-Corporal James Grace, an Air Dispatcher with the RASC. James had been born in Dublin in the year of the great Somme battle, and was married to Bertha, a girl he had met while on leave in Gloucester.

As the aircraft came in over the battlefield at approximately 1630hrs, it was met by heavy ground fire. Despite sustaining severe damage from the flak the Dispatchers continued to push the heavy containers from the Dakota as it flew steadily across the dropping zone. However, the anti-aircraft fire proved too much and the Dakota crashed into the ground; of the eight crew-members, three survived. James Grace was not one of them.

Another aircraft of 271 Squadron attempting a re-supply run earned the respect of every man that saw its effort. David Samuel Anthony Lord DFC piloted that Dakota. 'Lummy' Lord had been born in Cork in 1913, where his father, a Warrant Officer in a Welsh regiment, had married Mary Ellen, a local girl. Lord had seen earlier service in India and Burma, where he had been awarded a DFC.

Now on this sunny afternoon his Dakota flew at 1,500 feet through a hail of flak to reach the dropping zone. Two hits were made on the starboard wing and it began to burn. Despite being fully justified in abandoning the mission, Lord took his aircraft down to 900 feet to ensure an accurate drop on the supply zone. On completing the first run he was informed by the crew that two supply panniers remained. With the wing now well on fire he turned to make another approach. After successfully dropping the last of the containers he ordered the crew to bail out. By now the Dakota was down to 500 feet and as Lord struggled to hold the aircraft steady the wing collapsed and folded back as the Dakota went into a turning dive and plunged into a ploughed field below. There was only one survivor, Flight Lieutenant Harry King, the navigator; who was thrown clear as he attempted to assist the other dispatchers with their parachutes.

[93] *Remember Arnhem* by John Fairly (Peaton Press, 1978)

Above The memorial to the Air Dispatchers of the Royal Army Service Corps, one of whom was Lance-Corporal James Grace from Dublin. He died when his Dakota crashed on 19 September 1944, the same supply drop in which David Lord earned his Victoria Cross. *David Orr*

Right Flight Lieutenant David Lord was born in County Cork to an Irish mother and Welsh father. He was awarded the Victoria Cross for his gallantry on 19 September 1944 when he remained at the controls of his Dakota, which had been hit, and attempted to drop much-needed supplies to the troops of the 1st Airborne Division at Arnhem. *David Orr*

An added tragedy was that those supplies that David Lord and his crew died to deliver fell into German hands.

At Oosterbeek 'Dickie' Lonsdale was appointed to command the 11th Battalion together with those men of the 1st Parachute Brigade who were withdrawing from Arnhem, and to form them into a defensive perimeter on the eastern side of Oosterbeek Church. This began on the Tuesday the evening and would eventually become 'Lonsdale Force'.

WEDNESDAY 20 SEPTEMBER – THE FOURTH DAY

It was now Wednesday, the fourth day of the 'two-day' operation. At the Independent Company's position the men heard the noise of aircraft overhead. It was a re-supply drop by Dakotas and Stirling bombers, escorted by numerous Allied fighters. The barrage of flak put up by the Germans was described as awesome; so much metal was flying up towards the aircraft that the 21st Company War Diary reported several men being injured by falling shrapnel as they looked up in the air. Sergeant 'Paddy' Cockings and his section were captured on this day.

'Lonsdale Force' came into existence on the Wednesday, consisting of those men who had withdrawn from the suburbs of Arnhem the previous day. A picket was formed across the river road leading out of Arnhem and incorporated any stragglers that managed to escape from the tightening cordon between Oosterbeek and the bridge. Lonsdale made his headquarters near the church. This building was over a thousand years old, one of the oldest churches in Europe. Next door to the church was the parsonage, home of the Ter Horst family. Around the area the Light Regiment had deployed its batteries in order to supply support fire to the battalions advancing on the bridge, while the Ter Horst home was used as a First Aid Post to treat minor wounds. This changed very quickly and soon the house was overflowing with wounded. Kate ter Horst assisted the British medical orderlies on a near constant basis, yet still had time for her own family sheltering in the cellar. On one particular night she made her way from stretcher to stretcher reading a passage from the Bible by the light of a torch. 'You shalt not be afraid for the terror by night, nor for the arrow that flieth by day.' Even nearly 60 years later men cannot remember that psalm without a tear coming to their eye.

Oosterbeek Church still bears the scars of battle. The walls are covered with strike marks of bullets and shrapnel, giving some idea of the severity of the fighting around this area. *David Orr*

Oosterbeek Church today. It is still used for services and is a focal point for anyone paying a visit to the Arnhem battlefield. *David Orr*

Every man who fought at Oosterbeek would remember Kate ter Horst, 'the Angel of Arnhem', and her tragic death, the result of a road accident in 1992, would leave the survivors stunned.

Jack Fryer was one of those who made their way back.

'I remember seeing one of our officers lying in the bottom of the ditch beside the road – I can't remember his name, but he was dead. What a waste – all that training just to end up dead in the bottom of a ditch. There may have been few of us left, but we were still the 1st Battalion, still "T" Company!'

The first attack against Lonsdale's command came at dawn, a mixed force of infantry and tanks. The infantry were held off with ease, appearing reluctant to expose themselves to fire. The tanks were a different matter. With a shortage of anti-tank weapons some units were forced to give ground.

This was especially true of a group of about 40 South Staffords who fled in panic when faced with an attack by German flame-throwers. This weapon was fearsome in the extreme and even experienced troops were wary of it. Thankfully it was limited by its range and fuel capacity. Those men that ran were quickly rallied by an officer and, under the control of their own NCOs, returned to their former positions. The attacks continued throughout the day with enemy armour making an appearance with greater regularity.

'Lonsdale Force' was badly weakened by these attacks and Brigadier Hicks ordered 'Sheriff' Thompson to withdraw his outer defence line, under command of Lonsdale, to the area closer to the guns near the church. It was near here that Lonsdale made his headquarters and here he delivered a speech worthy of Henry V. Over the years this speech has attained an element of myth, but the men I interviewed said it did happen and it did do a lot to raise the morale of those present,

The headstone of Private Kevin Collins of Chapelzoid, Dublin, killed in action at Arnhem some time between 18 and 25 September 1944 while serving in the 3rd Parachute Battalion. *David Orr*

although one man admitted he slept through the whole thing. An officer, just escaped from the enclosing German perimeter, arrived at the Church at this time and noted 'men who were dirty, hungry and obviously exhausted, yet taking time to clean their weapons before attending to anything else.'

Hunger was always on their minds. Jack Fryer can't remember what particular day it was, but his section had become part of 'Lonsdale Force' and it was after the speech in the Church. It was dark and it was raining when one of the men spotted a supply pannier hanging from a nearby tree some 50 yards in front of them. Despite not knowing what the pannier might contain, perhaps more red berets, Jack made a dash across the open ground towards the tree.[94] They were in luck! A full box of compo rations was removed from the container and quickly hoisted on to his shoulder, followed by an equally quick dash back to the section slit trench. A little later in the evening Sergeant Peter O'Leary, a friend of Jack, came calling. On inquiring where all the food had come from, the section, as a man, pointed to the relevant tree and container. As O'Leary observed the volume of fire falling on the ground between the trench and the tree he remarked 'Bugger that', before going elsewhere in search of supper.

Morton and Fitzpatrick were settled in their trench when they had a visitor. A small shower of earth announced the arrival of one of the company officers as his head appeared over the edge of the trench.

'Got any pepper?' he enquired.

'No, Sir, but there is some compo salt,' replied Fitzpatrick.

'Salt! No – pepper! Toilet pepper!'

'Sorry, Sir, but you're welcome to borrow my New Testament,' said Fitzpatrick.

Billy Magill was sharing a room in one of the houses on the perimeter with three other men. The room, on the first floor, was proving to be very uncomfortable, full of wrecked furniture and broken bricks. Part of the roof was missing and the interior was soaking wet.

'We were trying to make a brew and found the place too crowded for the four of us so decided to move next door. As the last man went through the door a shell came through the wall, completely demolishing the vacated room.'

---

[94] If all the stories of men finding supply containers stuffed with red berets are true, someone back in England had a strange idea of what was needed in an Airborne battle. Most historians agree that possibly some berets were used as packing and the legend has grown from this. Nevertheless, on 14 February 2001 the author attended a lecture given by Brigadier M. N. S. McCord regarding his experiences in Korea with the Royal Ulster Rifles. As a junior subaltern he once led a patrol north across the Yalu River. Cut off by the river when it flooded, it was necessary for the patrol to be re-supplied by air. When the supply canister was opened it contained boots!

Hackett's Brigade decamped from their positions in the woods to the south-east of Wolfheze and advanced towards the perimeter at Oosterbeek. The 156 Battalion was in the van, and as they turned into the Breedelaan they came under concentrated machine-gun and mortar fire. Each attempt to outflank the German position was met with strong resistance. One company of the 156 Battalion got as far as the houses on the forward slope leading down to the Wolfhezerweg, but was fired on by patrolling self-propelled guns and pinned down. To Hackett it appeared that they had run into a major enemy force advancing towards Oosterbeek, therefore the axis of advance was changed and the 10th Battalion was directed towards the Valkenburglaan. As the Brigade moved through the woods, enemy tanks appeared along the rides and tracks, their machine-guns firing near continuously, cutting down the running paratroopers and forcing some smaller groups to surrender. The Brigade took very heavy casualties during this time; the commanding officer and second-in-command of the 156 Battalion were both killed and the Battalion became separated from the 10th.

'C' Company of the 156 Battalion attacked and cleared out a tree-ringed depression next to the Valkenburglaan (forever after called 'Hackett's Hollow'). It was here that the Brigadier rallied some 100 men and seven officers of the 156 Battalion and his Brigade Headquarters, about 150 men in total. The remainder of the day was spent in holding off enemy attacks from the surrounding woods. Later that evening, under increasing enemy pressure, Hackett realised that to remain in the hollow would only lead to eventual surrender. Therefore he gathered the survivors together and Major Geoffrey Powell, officer commanding 'C' Company, led them in a bayonet charge straight through the German lines and on into the perimeter. Such was the unexpected ferocity of this charge that casualties were light and success attained. When they arrived they found that Colonel Smyth's 10th Battalion, now reduced to 60 men, had arrived some hours before.

The Border Regiment was dug in on the western side of the perimeter with 'A' Company in the area of Sonnenberg, just north of the main Utrecht-

Above **The headstone of John Mallon Hamilton of Argyle Street, Belfast. He served in the 156 Parachute Battalion at Arnhem and died of wounds in St Joseph's Hospital on 21 September 1944.** *David Orr*

Below **William Maltman from Belfast served in the 156 Battalion at Arnhem as a Company Sergeant-Major and was taken prisoner after the battle.**

Arnhem road. There was the sound of enemy armour coming from the wood to the west and the Scout section of 10 Platoon deployed a PIAT to deal with any encroachment. At 1000hrs a self-

129

'Hackett's Hollow' – even today, so many years later, the marks of bullet strikes and shrapnel can clearly be seen on the tree trunks. The two figures in the background are the redoubtable Adrian Groeneweg and a very pregnant Barbara Orr, wife of the photographer. *David Orr*

propelled gun together with a tank and supporting infantry advanced towards the Border position. At the same time Lieutenant Scrivner, the Platoon commander, and Sergeant Hunter left Platoon headquarters on a tour of inspection. As the noise of the vehicles came closer, the PIAT team moved into the cover of a nearby cottage and prepared to fire. Then everything appeared to happen at once – the German tank moved out from the trees into the open, and Lieutenant Scrivner and Sergeant Hunter came round the corner of the path and found themselves in full view of the tank. It immediately opened fire with its machine-guns, killing Sergeant Hunter. Scrivner dived for cover as the Scout section Bren gun fired in return, killing the tank commander. The Bren gun continued to give covering fire as the Lieutenant and PIAT team made their way to safety.

Patrick Harrington from Durrus, County Cork, a former Royal Irish Fusilier serving in the 11th Battalion, was killed in the fighting to the east of

Oosterbeek Church. Tommy Allen, from Belfast, another ex-Irish Fusilier, was manning a Vickers machine-gun in the Support Company of the 11th Battalion. Largely unaffected by the daily and nightly shelling, he claimed that he had got used to it during the air raids while serving with the Royal Irish Fusiliers on Malta. His machine-gun kept a steady stream of bullets directed towards the enemy. During one attack he was hit in the chest by a well-directed burst of fire from a similarly armed German. Taken to the dressing station at Kate ter Horst's house, his wound proved serious and after the evacuation he became a prisoner of war. William John Patrick Devlin, the Hong Kong-born Irishman, was also killed this day, being one of the many buried in the Ter Horst's garden.

At the bridge the 1st Parachute Squadron RE was still fighting and holding its own small patch of territory against frequent enemy attacks. At approximately 1500hrs the schoolhouse occupied by the Engineers was attacked by a Tiger tank and a self-propelled gun. Both these vehicles stood off a little way and proceeded to shell the schoolhouse to bits. Within a short time the building was on fire and the interior began to collapse. With nothing to combat the armoured vehicles the men were forced to evacuate. The wounded were brought out into the open ground to save them from the burning building, while unwounded men tried to make their escape through the streets to the east of the bridge. It was during this frantic mêlée that Lance-Corporal Daniel Nevill from County Kerry was killed.[95]

Cecil Newell's war came to an end on the night of the fourth day.

'Me, I was shot, I think on the Wednesday night. This Scots sergeant and I came across two Bren guns still with full magazines. We took them to the windows and started to fire on the infantry below. There was a big bang and the next thing I knew I was sitting on the stairs with some fellow giving me a cigarette. You could see the hole where the shell had come through the wall; it was where the Scots sergeant had been standing. That was the end for me – there weren't many of us left by then.'

Some men, as yet unwounded, tried to make a run for it. Private Edward Tucker, an ex-Royal Ulster Rifleman from Belfast serving in Frost's battalion, was a member of the machine-gun platoon. As their house burned down around them they moved out into the garden and dug a new position. When it became obvious that further resistance was useless, Tucker and a sergeant named Cloves decided to break out of the perimeter around the bridge. As they made their way through the narrow streets a German patrol came in sight. Ducking into cover Sergeant Cloves immediately fell asleep and his snoring almost attracted the attention of the passing patrol. They split up and Tucker made his way to the St Walburgis Church, where he found

some other Airborne men hiding. Some German troops came into the church and an unknown private ran out in an attempt to draw their fire, but was quickly shot down. In the resulting confusion Tucker again made his way out into the streets of Arnhem. A short distance further on he met another group of Airborne men standing in one of the side streets. Approaching them he realised too late that the men were prisoners. Before he could turn and run he was forced to surrender his weapons and for him the war was definitely over!

At Driel the villagers gave shelter to several more Allied soldiers found in the surrounding fields. That evening the 'regular' messenger service between the river and Nijmegen stopped at the village and informed those soldiers hiding that they were better off in Driel than inside the perimeter at Oosterbeek. Prior to 1400hrs that afternoon a warning was received that the Germans were on their way. The Airborne men quickly left the Baltussen house and hid in the fields nearby. As the Germans surrounded the house, Cora Baltussen went outside and with great courage and conviction managed to persuade the Germans that there were no Allied soldiers present in the village. As she was doing this Arnoldus telephoned several of his neighbours and warned them that the Germans were searching for British paratroopers. As a result of the action taken by both Arnoldus and Cora, all those hiding in Driel were saved from the Germans.

Private Edward Tucker, an ex-Royal Ulster Rifleman, served in the 2nd Parachute Battalion at Arnhem. Even in extreme old age he maintained he would have done it all over again.

Paratrooper Edward Tucker, Airborne Forces.

---

[95] In his book *Arnhem: the Battle Remembered*, author Robert Jackson states that the self-propelled gun involved in this action was a Ferdinand armed with a 105mm gun. It is more likely that the SPG was a Wespe or Stug III, as both the 9th and 10th SS had been equipped with these vehicles in Normandy and would therefore by re-issued with the same vehicles, if available.

THURSDAY 21 SEPTEMBER – THE FIFTH DAY

At about 0500hrs on Thursday morning all resistance ceased in Arnhem town centre. As the bridge returned to German ownership, Nijmegen Bridge was captured by the combined operation involving paratroopers of the US 82nd Airborne Division and the tanks of the Guards Armoured Division. Described as one of the 'most audacious actions of the war', men of Colonel Reuben H. Tucker's 504th Parachute Infantry Regiment crossed the river at Nijmegen using British-supplied assault boats. At the same time Sherman tanks of the 2nd Grenadier Guards stormed across the bridge, both attacks being made against strong opposition.

Despite this success, the capture of Arnhem Bridge by the Germans now meant that it was open for traffic, and Field Marshal Model was able to send more forces towards the remaining elements of the 1st Airborne at Oosterbeek, while more units could also be sent south to oppose the advance by XXX Corps.

When the force at Arnhem Bridge surrendered, the wounded Lieutenant Woods was carried to the railway station and sent to Stalag XIB, where he died of his wounds on 14 October and is today buried in Becklingen War Cemetery, plot 8 row C grave 3.

At about this time the 1st Airborne in Oosterbeek made contact with the 64th Medium Regiment of XXX Corps deployed at Nijmegen. From a distance of 12½ miles, the 4.5 and 5.5-inch guns of the 64th provided much-needed support to the men defending the 'cauldron'.

At approximately 1600hrs German forces around Dunkirk caught sight of the aircraft of the Polish Brigade as they crossed the French coast. Flak batteries along the route were alerted and more than 100 German aircraft took to the air. Despite the ferocity of these attacks, escorting fighters were able to deal with most of them, while Typhoons suppressed the anti-aircraft guns with well-directed rockets and cannon. At Driel the Poles jumped on to a drop zone swept by machine-gun and mortar fire and casualties were sustained. Thirteen Dakotas were shot down, the majority after their loads of paratroopers had jumped. When General Sosabowski called for a head count, he found he had just over 950 men.[96]

Meanwhile those units of the 10th SS that had been defeated at Nijmegen were falling back towards Arnhem, fighting every inch of the way. Bittrich ordered Lieutenant Colonel Harzer, commander of the Hohenstaufen, to attack the Poles at Driel. He was also responsible for the formation of the *Sperrverband* Harzer.[97] They also had orders to keep the road from Arnhem to Nijmegen open. Bittrich was concerned that the Poles might cut the road and launch an attack against the south end of Arnhem Bridge. One effect of the Poles' arrival was a general easing of the attacks on the remainder of the 1st Airborne, albeit for a short time.

Within the Oosterbeek perimeter the Reconnaissance Squadron was occupying houses to the north of the MDS crossroads. Here they received orders from Division to assist the men of 'B' Company of The Border Regiment who were being hard pressed at Westerbouwing. It was decided to send the 3-inch Mortar Platoon of Support Troop. As Lieutenant Christie, the troop commander, had been killed the day before, Newtownards man Sergeant Leslie McCreedie took command, and shortly after 0900hrs he and two mortars with crews arrived at the Border position on the western side of the perimeter. There were several ex-Border men in the Reconnaissance crews and they soon settled down into their new homes.[98] Almost at the same time the Germans launched a heavy attack with tanks and infantry on the positions, and after desperate fighting the survivors were forced off the heights and withdrew towards the Van Borsselenweg-Benedendorpsweg

---

[96] See *Poles Apart* by George F. Cholewczynski (Greenhill Books, 1993), p146

[97] *Sperrverband* translates as 'blocking group', a variation on the designation battle group.

[98] *Remember Arnhem* by John Fairley

Within the image: Vital Holland Bridge FRES DRI

Above A photograph of the Nijmegen Bridge taken from a Dublin newspaper of 19 September 1944. The caption reads, 'The bridge at Nijmegen over the River Waal, described as the "most important piece of masonry in the world at the present time."' While Eire papers did not report the names of 'neutrals' serving in the British Army, their reporting of events was both fast and accurate.

Below Nijmegen Bridge looking east in 2001. *Stuart Eastwood*

crossroads and the gasworks. Those mortars supplied the day previously by the Reconnaissance Squadron had been destroyed by enemy shell-fire, and there were casualties among the crews. Sergeant McCreedie escaped serious injury and managed to return to his unit to report the loss.

By now the small village of Oosterbeek resembled a scene from Hell. Houses were burning, tracer fire and shells rained down on a near constant basis and the fighting was at extremely close range. In several places British troops held the upper floors of buildings while the Germans were in residence on the ground floor. Hand grenades were exchanged up and down flights of stairs while bullets ripped through floorboards trying to find a target. Those German tanks and self-propelled guns brave enough to risk coming into the narrow streets were met with raw courage as men ran out from between houses or the cover of once neat hedges and lobbed hand grenades and Hawkins mines at them. The Germans called it *Der Hexenkessel* – 'the witches' cauldron' – and 24 hours a day the cauldron boiled with fire and smoke and blood as German and British guns turned buildings into red dust and men into red gore.

Peter Markey, now fighting with 'Lonsdale Force' south of the village, was caught in the blast from a German shell. The result of this was a piece of shrapnel lodged in his neck. Together with three other injured men, he was ordered back to seek medical aid at one of the Dressing Stations. In order to get there it was necessary to crawl through a culvert, but as they emerged on the other side another shell landed and Peter's companions were all killed, while he received further wounds to his legs, shoulder and again in the neck. He lay in agony bleeding profusely for some time when helpful hands began to pull him towards the First Aid Post. Looking up he saw a Dutch woman pulling him along the ground. With great effort and with no help from Peter she dragged him the remainder of the way to the Dressing Station. To his regret he was never able to find out who she was.

Patrick and Fitzpatrick were sharing a slit trench on the eastern side of the perimeter; it was late afternoon.

Fitz asked, 'Got a match?'

Patrick passed over the box of Swan Vestas.

A few seconds later, 'Got any cigarette papers?' The packet of papers was duly passed over.

'Got any tobacco?' With a weary sigh Patrick handed over a tin of Gold Flake, with the following observation. 'My granny once said to me, wee son, when you go out into the world you will meet all kinds of people. Some you will like and some you will not, but just remember this – a friend in need is a fucking nuisance!' Banter[99] such as this was, despite its initial impression, the sign of true friendship. Those that have 'taken the shilling' will understand. The time spent in the slit trenches and buildings around and within the Oosterbeek perimeter was exhausting, hungry, frightening and confused, but never boring.

Patrick and Fitz had just finished a meagre supper and were resting at the bottom of their trench; the sound of firing had receded slightly, and it could almost have been described as quiet.

'He did not wear his scarlet coat, for blood and wine are red, and blood and wine were on his hands. When they found him with the dead, the poor dead woman whom he loved, and murdered in her bed.'

Fitz, who had been snoring in the bottom of the trench, sat up and asked, 'Is that *The Ballad of Reading Gaol*? I'm trying to sleep and you're going to go on for another hundred and eight verses, God save us.'

Some time later a shout came from the same slit trench directed towards the section sergeant's position.

'Sergeant, Sergeant!' shouted Fitzpatrick. 'Can I be moved to another position? Morton is quoting poetry again!' As he slumped back in the bottom of the trench, Patrick asked, 'What did he say?'

'Couldn't make it out properly – sounded like not giving something to a duck.'

A Tiger tank approached the Light Regiment's 'B' Troop situated down near the Church in Oosterbeek. Major Robert Cain of the South

---

[99] Banter is an Irish term meaning jesting, teasing, mockery, derision or repartee. The only rule involved in banter is that if you give it out you must be prepared to take it back.

Staffords at once set out and stalked the vehicle. This was not his first tank hunt, and over the past few days he had racked up quite a score of enemy vehicles using a PIAT. As the Tiger approached the gun position Major Cain, accompanied by Sergeant John Daly, made a successful attack and the tank was destroyed, while German infantry following up behind the vehicle was put to flight by accurate fire from Sergeant Daly's Bren gun. This was just one incident from an action-packed and very confusing day, during which the battery was credited with knocking out at least three enemy armoured vehicles in that particular sector. Major Cain was later awarded the Victoria Cross for his actions during the battle, the only such award during the operation that was not posthumous. Sergeant John Daly was awarded the Distinguished Conduct Medal.

The King's Own Scottish Borderers were now dug in around the Dreyeroord Hotel, known to the men as the 'White House' (not to be confused with the building also known as the 'White House' in Arnhem), in an area to the north of the Oosterbeek crossroads and close to the village railway station. Sometime during the day the machine-gun platoon lost Private William Middleweek, a former Irish Fusilier, who was killed during an artillery bombardment.

It was also on this date that Danny Gillespie and other members of the 21st Independent were ordered by Major Wilson to form a line just behind the KOSB positions and fix bayonets! The reason for this was that a number of survivors of that Battalion, including an officer and several NCOs, had abandoned their trenches and weapons at the sound of an attack by tanks. As the men reached Major Wilson's line he ordered them back, saying that if necessary he would put his own NCOs in charge and drive them back at bayonet point. At this they returned to their own lines and nothing more was said about the incident. Such timely action was necessary as the flank of the entire position had been laid wide open. As a result of the threat of more tank attacks, the 21st received one 6-pounder anti-tank gun to bolster its defences. To be fair to these men of the KOSB, they had seen little or no action before the operation. There were several such incidents at Arnhem, and usually the

firm hand of an officer or NCO was enough to rectify the situation. In the case of individual men who refused to fight, and these were few, their conscience would bear witness to their behaviour. In the case of one particular officer the stony silence that greeted his arrival in the post-war Officer's Mess or other social functions for many years after the battle was a constant reminder that with rank comes not only privilege, but responsibility.

Later in the afternoon, at approximately 1630hrs, a strong German attack was again launched against the Borderers' positions at the 'White House'. This time the men stood and the attack was beaten off, but it took a bayonet charge led personally by Lieutenant Colonel Payton-Reid to re-establish the position. When it was relatively calm it was

It is a brave man, or woman, who will attempt to fell a tree in Oosterbeek with a chainsaw today. Each mark on the bark represents a bullet or piece of shrapnel. When trees have to be taken down for whatever reason, an axe is the better option. *David Orr*

discovered that 50 per cent of the 300 surviving men had become casualties. With the number of men remaining, Payton-Reid decided that the position could no longer be held and therefor a withdrawal was ordered. Those men severely wounded were evacuated by jeep, with the walking wounded following shortly after. The Battalion's second-in-command, Belfast-born Major John Coke, who had been wounded previously, was assisted by Brian Devlin. They had only gone a short distance when they were ambushed by a party of Germans and taken prisoner.[100]

Patrick Sullivan, fighting with the 11th Battalion, was killed around the area known as Hoofdlaan to the west of the Hartenstein. Bill Kerr, also of the 11th Battalion, was situated just south of this position and was out patrolling with his section when they came across an anti-tank gun with its dead crew lying around it.

'We manned the 6-pounder until the fire from a German machine-gun forced us into a

'Scots steel tempered wi' Irish fire is the weapon I desire.' So spoke the poet Hugh MacDiarmid, and it was a phrase that could have been coined for Belfast-born Major John S. A'D. Coke, second-in-command of the 7th Battalion King's Own Scottish Borderers at Arnhem. The Coke family has supplied soldiers to the Crown for generations: John's brother had been killed serving with the 6th Battalion KOSB near St Oedenrode, Holland, on 14 August 1944. At the request of the family he was also buried in the Airborne Cemetery, Oosterbeek. John Coke was killed on 18 October 1944, during the ill-fated operation known as 'Pegasus II'. He was awarded a posthumous MID for his part in Operation 'Market Garden'. *From* Off At Last: An Illustrated History of the 7th (Galloway) Battalion KOSB

A 'neutral' from County Wicklow, 26-year-old Private Patrick Sullivan of the 11th Parachute Battalion was killed at Arnhem on 21 September 1944. *David Orr*

---

100 Brian Devlin was allowed to continue working in the St Elisabeth Hospital.

nearby slit trench. We called to a Bren-gunner to come forward and lay down some counter-fire. As he approached our position a "Moaning Minnie" landed between him and us and I was knocked unconscious by the explosion. When I woke up I was half buried in the trench and the only one left alive. When I had managed to burrow myself out I crawled back to where the platoon were dug in. I couldn't move my jaw and as I attempted to remove my helmet my Platoon Commander made me lie still. He lifted the helmet and slid a shell dressing over a gash in my head. My "found" helmet had saved me.'

That evening around the positions of the 21st Independent there fell what was described as an uneasy silence, a strange sensation after nearly three days of continuous noise. Then suddenly from the

The carving in the bark of this tree reads '1st Airborne Div. Sept '44'. *David Orr*

woods came the sound of American dance-band music, emanating from a truck fitted with loud-speakers. When the music stopped a voice, speaking in good English, called on the Airborne men to surrender. This invitation was replied to by a collection of catcalls and disparaging remarks with regard to the parenthood of the speaker. A further invitation to come forward waving a white handkerchief was greeted with total disbelief – who had a white handkerchief after all this time? Further broadcasts were cut short when Tommy Scullion crawled forward to the edge of the wood and let fly at the truck with a PIAT. The direct hit scored ensured no further interference.

A shortage of cigarettes and tobacco caused problems for many men after the first few days. In the case of Danny Gillespie it was hunger that started him smoking. Just before take-off Danny had bought a carton of American Lucky Strike cigarettes with the idea that they might come in useful for trading; on the third day of Arnhem he had his first smoke.

FRIDAY 22 SEPTEMBER – THE SIXTH DAY

Friday dawned misty, and drizzle continued throughout the day until nightfall. It was the sixth day, and despite the shortage of food and sleep most men were still able to keep their spirits up. Now occupying a house on the perimeter, Morton and Fitz were scraping together a meagre meal.

'And Gentlemen abed in England this day will think it accursed they were not here,' quoted Fitz.

'They might think themselves accursed, but at least they'll have had a decent breakfast,' replied Morton.

By now all ranks within the Division were feeling the pangs of hunger and many men regretted passing up the offer of sandwiches from the NAAFI ladies the previous Sunday morning.

In the darkness of early Friday morning approximately 50 men of the Polish Brigade managed to cross the river into the perimeter. The crossing was made using a small number of two-man rubber boats and under fire from enemy

Looking north from the Oosterbeek crossroads towards Stationsweg and the houses held by the men of the 21st Independent Parachute Company. The white building on the left is 'Quatre Bras'. *David Orr*

mortars and machine-guns. At 0400hrs the operation had to be abandoned as the crossing had become too dangerous.

The 21st Independent Company was moved back from its position at Ommershof and took up new defences running from Stationsweg to Pietersbergseweg and Paasberg, south of the crossroads. Major Wilson made his Headquarters in a house on Paasberg, while men of No 1 Platoon took up positions in a house called 'Quatre Bras' at the crossroads.

It was this Friday morning that one of the outstanding images of 'Market Garden' was taken. In front of the house of the Kremer family several defenders lined up to get their photograph taken. The group included two glider pilots, and seven members of the Company, including Jimmy Cameron, Harry Mitchell and John Rodley. Within the next two days Jimmy Cameron and John Rodley would be dead and Harry Mitchell gravely wounded.

German attacks penetrated the battery positions of the Light Regiment situated around the Church

and were only ejected after bitter hand-to-hand fighting. Meanwhile, south of the Neder Rijn, by mid-morning some armoured cars of the Household Cavalry had arrived at Driel. They had crossed the newly captured road bridge at Nijmegen at dawn and driven to Driel via back roads without encountering any enemy. Among them was Lieutenant David Corbett, a Fermanagh man who would later rise in the ranks of the Royal Ulster Constabulary. That morning also saw Private Cooney doing his bit for the defence of Driel. At about 1100hrs he went out into the surrounding countryside to try and recover some weapons from the drop zone. On several occasions during this time he was almost spotted by the enemy and was forced to hide in some very unattractive and odoriferous places. He returned to the village later in the day soaking wet, covered in mud, smelling like a pigsty, and without any weapons. Nevertheless he received a great welcome from the villagers. Cora Baltussen referred to him as 'The cheerful Irishman'.

That evening, as darkness was falling, some tanks

approached Driel from the south. Unsure of where the enemy was, the Poles readied their weapons and waited for the tanks to come closer. As the tanks approached a string of mines that had been placed across the road earlier, they were identified as British Shermans. Henk te Dorsthorst, a young Dutchman living in Driel, tried to warn the tanks of the danger, but the driver of the leading tank misunderstood his waving and drove over one of the mines. In the ensuing confusion casualties were caused before order could be restored. The tanks from the 4th/7th Dragoon Guards, part of the spearhead of the 43rd Wessex Division, were supported by infantry from the 5th Duke of Cornwall's Light Infantry and two DUKWs loaded with supplies for the 1st Airborne Division.

Back within the 'cauldron' the medical services were stretched to their limit, yet all men received some form of treatment. After three nights under medical care in various places Mervyn Dennison found himself and another comrade loaded on stretchers, which were then strapped on to a Bren-gun carrier and driven at both great speed and with great skill westwards towards the crossroads at Oosterbeek. Here three hotels had become the Main Dressing Stations for the Division. Major Dennison was taken into the Vreewijk Hotel, being run by Corporal 'Chirpy' Couling of the RAMC with the assistance of a dozen or so medical orderlies. Mervyn said this about Corporal Couling: 'He was a man without equal when it came to caring for the wounded. Quite a few men survived that battle because of his unstinting care and devotion to his patients. He deserved so much more.'[101]

The hotel was situated on the Arnhem side of Stationsweg and was visited several times a day by the few doctors available. They were assisted in their duties by the divisional padres and Dutch Red Cross workers. The divisional Roman Catholic padre[102] had earlier been severely wounded by shellfire, and some of the soldiers from Northern Ireland were amused by one commendable result. A Dutch Roman Catholic civilian padre voluntarily

undertook the work of helping the wounded and wore an orange sash, orange being the colour of the Dutch Resistance movement. Even today there remain Ulstermen who say that it did them good to have received the last rites from a priest wearing an orange sash – although one man claims he never had a day's luck since! One day the medics carried in an SS Obersturmbahnfuehrer, who had been badly wounded in the legs and feet. He refused the offer of morphine on the grounds that the British were trying to poison him. Mervyn Dennison, who was the patient lying next to him, recalled:

'He turned out to be a very agreeable companion, speaking good English, and as a result received his fair share of what food and cigarettes the Dutch were able to smuggle in to us. When the sad news arrived that the remnants of the Division were to retire across the Rhine, the Germans moved into the hotel. They threatened us with their shouts and curses and told us to get up and get out. We owe something to our friend the SS Colonel who sat up on his blanket, gave them hell and told them to mind their manner to these British, who were both soldiers and gentlemen!'

While the Dressing Stations were doing their best to care for the wounded, the battle continued to rage outside. Attacks were made and driven back, and positions taken and lost, sometimes with monotonous regularity. When the actual fighting calmed, both sides still kept up intensive and aggressive patrolling. The Germans searching for weak spots in the perimeter defences, while the Airborne men hunted down enemy snipers and stalked the German armour.

At 1600hrs the 21st launched another patrol from its positions at Pietersbergseweg, sending it out towards the east to try and establish contact with the 10th Battalion. This patrol was made up of four men, Sergeant Philipson, Corporal Gibson, Private Brown and Private James Vincent Fiely

---

[101] Corporal Harold Roy Couling, 16 Parachute Field Ambulance, was awarded the Distinguished Conduct Medal.
[102] Rev Bernard Joseph Benson RACD, who had his arm amputated and later died of his wounds.

Above **The woods surrounding the village of Oosterbeek show the close nature of the fighting. Those who have experienced combat in the hours of darkness will understand how easy it is for trees and bushes to take on a life of their own.** *David Orr*

from Dublin. Tommy Scullion's Bren gun had been hit in the gas block by a German bullet and was only capable of firing single shots. Nevertheless a regular stream of bullets gave covering fire to the patrol as it made its way through the alleyways and gardens towards Annastraat, which they reached without suffering any casualties. Here they gained access to a house, and while Philipson and Brown went upstairs for a look around, Fiely and Gibson remained outside. From the upstairs bedroom window Sergeant Philipson spotted a bare-headed figure in the window opposite – a man casually munching on an apple. Philipson called out, 'Are you 10th Battalion?' This query was answered by a burst of machine-gun fire, which was quickly joined by an assortment of other German automatic weapons and a shower of hand grenades from other windows – never was a reply more in the negative! Private Fiely, crouching at the corner of the house, was hit by one of the first bursts of fire and died immediately. The two men now trapped inside the house returned the fire as best they could, paying specific attention to the apple-eating German. When the enemy fire slackened somewhat, they made good their escape, taking Corporal Gibson with them. They were unable to recover Jim Fiely's body.

Below **The headstone of Private James Vincent Fiely of Fairview, Dublin. Private Fiely was killed while on patrol with other members of the 21st Independent Parachute Company on 22 September 1944; he was 23 years old.** *Steven Nicholls*

Above Annastraat in Oosterbeek: it was here that the 'Fiely' patrol of the 21st Independent Parachute Company came under fire from the apple-eating German and his friends. *David Orr*

Below The view from the rear first-floor window of No 34 Pietersbergseweg, Oosterbeek, the one-time Bren-gun position of Private Tommy Scullion, 21st Independent Parachute Company, during the battle, and the regular room of the author on his many battlefield trips. No 34 was ideally suited for anyone doing a tour of the Oosterbeek area, but sadly the building is no longer used as a hotel.

When the patrol had arrived at the corner of the house, two other members of the 21st, who were in a house further along the street, had seen them arrive. They knew of the German presence in the houses opposite and attempted to call out a warning, but were too far away to be heard. While the fire-fight was in progress one of these men fired a phosphorus grenade at the closest of the machine-gun teams; it exploded in the branches of a tree and showered the gun team lying below.

In 'Lonsdale Force' Jack Fryer was ensconced in the back garden of a house in Benedendorpsweg.

'Near my trench was a bird-bath and close by the door to the cellar of the house. Down in this cellar were Dick Whittingham and his mortar crew, with the mortar sitting just outside the door. Every now and again they would dash out of the cellar, let fly a few bombs and be back down again before the Germans could retaliate. Each time Dick fired, the garden was peppered with German bombs in return.'

This enemy fire could sometimes be useful. After one particularly close hit from a shell, a crack in a nearby wall opened to reveal a hidden hoard of food.

'Inside we found a cupboard full of tinned food, some Dutchman's secret store. There were tins of hot-pot, strawberries and condensed milk. Now at about this time a Polish anti-tank gun crew had set up just outside the garden. Our medic collected all available rations and made a big pot of stew, but just as he finished, a shell meant for the Poles hit the wall of the house and bricks and stew went everywhere. You should have heard the language. Still, the strawberries and condensed milk tasted delicious.'

One of the men who served as part of Dick Whittingham's crew was Private Frank McCormick from Dublin.[103]

Private Frank McCormick, the Irishman who may have served under the name McClusky.

On Friday night the rain came down in torrents and everyone suffered a miserable time, the only consolation being that it helped a little to alleviate the water shortage. Morton and Fitzgerald spread a ground sheet over a small bush and funnelled water into a helmet before transferring it to a waiting water-bottle. Fitzgerald was a romantic soul at heart:

'The last time I kissed a girl it was raining. We were coming home from a dance; it was somewhere in Connemara, walking along in the soft rain hardly noticing it. We stopped to buy chips from a van and stood talking for what seemed like hours. When we kissed for the first time her lips tasted of salt and vinegar. She was a very special girl. I've never been able to eat chips since without thinking of her.'

Morton was more pragmatic. 'Pity she wasn't here now. We've no salt left.'

SATURDAY 23 SEPTEMBER – THE SEVENTH DAY

At the crossroads in the middle of Oosterbeek encroaching enemy armour coming up from the town was making life difficult for the defenders. Some action was called for, and Harry Mitchell with his PIAT moved out from one of the houses on Utrechtseweg occupied by the Independent Company and waited for a target. Within a short time a self-propelled gun clanked up the main road towards the junction. Before the vehicle came

---

[103] He may have served under the name McCluskey.

within PIAT range a shell exploded from its 75mm main gun, striking close to Harry's position. The result was a blow to the head that put Harry out of the battle and out of the war! So severe was his wound that he was repatriated. Private Jimmy Cameron was hit in the leg some time in the afternoon; it was a serious wound and he was taken to the Casualty Clearing Station.

'Paddy' Boyd's group of glider pilots was positioned in the area south of the Tafelberg Hotel. That evening a patrol was sent our to harass the Germans, something the glider pilots did on a regular basis. Approximately an hour into the patrol it came under fire. There were prolonged bursts from the enemy guns, bringing down tree branches and throwing up fountains of dirt. As 'Paddy'

peered around the corner of a wall, the brickwork exploded as enemy bullets impacted and he was hit in the head. Staff-Sergeant Briggs, a fellow glider pilot, ran forward to help him and received a burst in the back. With streams of bullets seeming to come from all directions the remainder of the patrol were forced to withdraw to their own lines, the bodies of the two fallen men having to be left behind.[104]

That day the bagpipes that had brightened up many a glider pilot party and had sounded not a few mournful laments would be heard no more when Captain John Smellie fell in the fighting around the Polderweg. In 'Lonsdale Force', John Joseph O'Neill, an ex-'Faugh' serving in the 11th Battalion, was also killed. He was buried nearby in a field

The Oosterbeek crossroads in May 2000. The white structure on the right of the photograph is the modern-day Schoonoord Hotel. In 1944 it served as one of the Main Dressing Stations during the battle, and both the 181 Air-Landing Field Ambulance and 133 Parachute Field Ambulance operated there. Down the road to the right is the Tafelberg Hotel, while on the left is the Vreewijk Hotel, completing the trio of medical establishments. Today the Schoonoord is a restaurant and the Vreewijk an office. The Tafelberg is in the process of being converted into apartments. *David Orr*

<hr>

[104] After the battle their field graves were found 150 yards south of the Tafelberg.

The Tafelberg Hotel, one of the medical posts during the fighting around the town of Oosterbeek in September 1944. *David Orr*

The grave of Staff-Sergeant James Frederick Boyd, Glider Pilot Regiment. He 'stowed away' on 17 September, only to be killed six days later. *David Orr*

grave, but in the confusion of battle its location was lost.[105]

In a shell-damaged house about 300 yards from the Church, Patrick Morton and Fitzgerald had a Bren gun pointing out through what remained of a ground-floor window in the general direction of Arnhem. The carpet, damp from the previous day's rain, had a liberal covering of spent brass cartridge cases mixed with brick dust and feathers from a burst pillow. In the fireplace Paddy was attempting to make a 'brew' from what remained of the 24 ration packs. Glancing up through a hole in the ceiling he said to his companion, 'Fitz, go and ask our upstairs neighbours if they can spare a cup of sugar?'

Fitzpatrick in turn looked up through the said hole where another Bren gun team lay on the floor. 'Not a chance, they're a couple of Tykes – more chance of borrowing from the Jerries.'

Patrick replied, 'Well, you know what they say – "Shake a bridle over a Yorkshireman's grave and he will arise and steal a horse".'

The half-brick that came down through the hole in the ceiling and bounced on the top of Morton's helmet proved that whatever their equine skills, there was nothing wrong with the Yorkshiremen's hearing.

At the crossroads in Oosterbeek the Dressing Station in the Schoonoord Hotel had fallen into enemy hands, and the Germans prepared to evacuate

---

[105] It is the view of Dutch historians that many graves were lost due to shelling during the winter months. Today he is remembered, like all those who have no known grave, on the Groesbeek memorial at Nijmegen.

A memorial sculpture in the garden of 'Quatre Bras' at Oosterbeek. The 21st Independent Parachute Company had a Bren gun position in a slit trench in this garden during the battle for the crossroads, and the sculpture represents swords beaten into ploughshares. *David Orr*

the wounded in various vehicles, including captured Airborne jeeps. Those capable of walking were marched away towards the St Elisabeth Hospital.

Into this small haven of quietness rode an unwary German motorcyclist. Danny Gillespie saw what happened next.

'We had a Bren gun behind a tree in the garden of "Quatre Bras", just by the roadside. A German dispatch rider came up the main road and calmly stopped his machine and began to consult a map. A quick burst from the Bren resulted in him being carried into the Casualty Clearing Station at the Schoonoord, and the Company added one Zundapp motorbike to its order of battle.'

The motorbike was used to great effect by the 21st Independent until the luckless rider was shot and the bike became inoperable.

This Saturday was also the day the Germans moved some of those captured at Arnhem Bridge to prison camp in Germany. 'Paddy' Tucker and another Irishman named Fitzpatrick were in the same lorry as Major J. A. Hibbert of the 1st Parachute Brigade Headquarters, Major Anthony Cotterill, a war correspondent, and Major Denis Munford of the 3rd Air-Landing Light Battery. As Hibbert and Cotterill made an escape attempt by jumping from the truck, the German guard fired indiscriminately into the crowded prisoners. Eight men were killed, including Private George McCracken, a 29-year-old ex-Royal Ulster Rifleman who had been serving in Frost's battalion. Tucker and Fitzpatrick were two of the men subsequently lined up against a wall to be shot. It was only the intervention of Major 'Freddy' Gough, who explained to the confused guards that the men were British and not Russians, that saved their lives.

SUNDAY 24 SEPTEMBER – THE EIGHTH DAY

It was now Sunday 24 September, the seventh day of an operation that had been expected to last some 48 hours.

Having been given command of the eastern side of the perimeter by Major General Urquhart, 'Shan' Hackett was on a tour of inspection when his battle came to an abrupt end. As he moved from position to position a mortar bomb fell close by and lacerated his leg and stomach with splinters that caused severe internal injuries. Hackett always maintained, despite the risk of being called paranoid, that the shells seemed to follow him as he moved around the perimeter, a phenomenon noticed by several other men in this battle and others. Hackett was taken to the St Elisabeth Hospital where he recovered consciousness lying on the floor being prodded by a German boot. Turning Hackett's body with his toecap, a German surgeon pronounced him well beyond help. Nevertheless, a British surgeon decided that there was a chance and had Hackett moved into the operating theatre. Lying on the table, Hackett was once again the subject of the German surgeon's conversation; his view being that it was a waste of time to operate and suggesting euthanasia. 'With a head or stomach wound just give an injection and leave them.' Thankfully a British doctor proceeded to treat Hackett, and in the ensuing operation removed the piece of shrapnel from Hackett's stomach.[106] The operation was a success and Hackett settled down to a slow recovery. With Hackett out of the battle, command of the Brigade fell to Lieutenant Colonel Ian Murray of the Glider Pilot Regiment.

Lance-Sergeant Jack Fryer's platoon was by now defending a house in Benedendorpsweg.

'This was the day Corporal Clarke found a box of Dutch cigars. Now he didn't smoke and when we asked him what he intended doing with them, he said he was taking them home for his father. He was told in no uncertain terms that his chances of seeing his father again were as remote as a snowman celebrating the New Year in Hell! Thereafter the section enjoyed a very good smoke.'

A little later in the afternoon there was a call for volunteers to search the buildings for unused field dressings or even bed sheets to use as bandages. Corporal Clarke volunteered to go. 'I told "Nobby" to be careful and to make sure he was back within the hour.'

A short time later a sergeant from another platoon came by. Jack described what followed. 'This

The headstone of Corporal Anthony Clarke, 1st Parachute Battalion, killed in action as a member of 'Lonsdale Force' while attempting to collect medical supplies on 24 September 1944. *David Orr*

---

[106] The British surgeon was Captain A. W. Lippman-Kessel, a South African Jew; he received the Military Cross and an MBE for his actions at Arnhem.

Sergeant-Major, he was a black Belfastman[107] and he demanded to know where Corporal Clarke was. I told him he was away scavenging for bandages. "No he's not," he replied, "he's outside lying dead", and with that he stormed off.'

Jack led the section out and recovered the body. Anthony Clark was buried in a field grave behind the schoolhouse; he was 22 years old.

And so the battle went on. Jack Fryer again:

'The noise, it was the bloody noise I remember the most. It just seemed to go on and on all the bloody time. Once when we were moving to another position we passed a man hit by an anti-tank shell – he was cut in half as neatly as with a bandsaw.'[108]

Trooper Harry Kerr was with the Reconnaissance men in the streets to the north of the MDS crossroads in Oosterbeek. His position was in a garden in Oranjeweg. A German sniper was causing the Reconnaissance men severe trouble and as Trooper Kerr crawled through a hole in the hedge to recover ammunition from one of the parked jeeps a shot from the sniper wounded him. It was only with great difficulty that he was pulled back into cover.

Belfastman John McClune, a Lance-Corporal with the 11th Battalion, was killed during an attack on the west side of the perimeter near the Hartenstein Hotel; he was 25 years old.

At 1700hrs a truce had been declared to evacuate more of the wounded from the Casualty Clearing Stations. Billy Magill was unfortunate enough to be

Lance-Corporal John McClune from Belfast. He was an ex-Royal Inniskilling Fusilier who served in the 11th Parachute Battalion at Arnhem.

in one of them, the Tafelberg Hotel, when that truce was called, and the Germans arrived to evacuate the wounded.

'I was sitting there getting my bandages changed when the Germans came in and I was told I was a prisoner. I remember this German officer coming in and he was immaculate, his uniform covered in badges and him overflowing with confidence and arrogance. We sat and stood about the place, tired, hungry and dirty. To them we must have looked pathetic, but to us they were the pathetic ones. For the last seven days, despite their artillery and tanks, they hadn't beaten us, we were still in control, and all I wanted was a cup of tea.'

The walking wounded were formed up outside and marched in a weary column towards Arnhem; to Billy Magill the sights along the road were sombre.

'So we walked down the road towards the town. All along the route were dead Germans and dead Airborne. We came to the hospital and saw men wearing red berets and red crosses driving jeeps carrying the wounded. German soldiers were driving some of the jeeps. Inside the St Elisabeth Hospital I never saw such a sight. Everywhere, even on the stairs, lay wounded men both British and German – it was a sad end to what was supposed to have been a short sharp action.'

Within the hospital British and German doctors treated the wounded in order of seriousness – no favouritism was shown to one side or the other. On Pietersbergseweg, Tommy Scullion and the men of the Independent Company watched as the wounded made their weary way up towards the crossroads.

After the truce ended and firing had broken out from both sides, a German ambulance drove up and stopped outside one of the houses occupied by the 21st. A few minutes later it drove away and there

---

[107] In this case the term 'black' is used to describe personality, temperament and possibly religion as opposed to colour.
[108] Possibly Corporal Albert Osborne, 1st Parachute Battalion

standing in front of the house were three fully armed Germans, who stood about seemingly unaware that there was any enemy present. One of

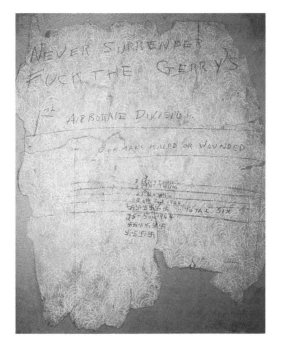

the 21st stuck his head out of the window and shouted 'Boo!' The Germans were completely surprised and did nothing, just stood staring at the window. As the men inside called for their surrender, two RASC men with a Bren gun in the next house let fly with a long burst and all three Germans fell into the ditch at the side of the road. One was still alive, and when searched was found to be a member of the Vienna Water Police. The enemy was coming from far and wide. The German's haversack contained packets of Player's and Grey's cigarettes and several bars of Cadbury's chocolate, obviously taken from a re-supply container that had fallen outside the perimeter.

The battle had now been raging for eight days. No one had had a change of clothes or even taken their boots off. There had been little food and even less sleep. The threat of death and injury was constant, as was the noise. Yet in this place, this cauldron of Hell, there was still time for the little things in life, the things that made these men just that little bit special. As Sergeant Summerville was making his rounds of the platoon positions he met up with Ron Kent, a habitual pipe-smoker. Kent had arrived on the first day of the operation with three pipes and half a pound of tobacco crammed into his helmet. He still had plenty of tobacco and matches but was left with only the stub of his remaining pipe. As Sergeant Summerville came into the room he was able to present Kent with a brand new briar pipe that he had found elsewhere. Kent was overjoyed with the gift, and when he crossed the river at the end of the battle the pipe was still firmly clamped between his teeth.

Above left **The daily British sniper score recorded on a piece of Dutch wallpaper, now on display in the Airborne Museum, Hartenstein.** *David Orr, with the permission of the Curator*

Left **Sergeant Gordon 'Slim' Summerville from Belfast and Private James Cameron from Carrickfergus, County Antrim, and Danny Gillespie, all members of the 21st Independent Parachute Company. They are seen feeding the pigeons in Trafalgar Square, London, just before 'Market Garden'. Several days into the operation those birds would have made a most welcome meal!** *D. Gillespie*

MONDAY 25 SEPTEMBER – THE NINTH DAY

It was 0100hrs on Monday 25 September, the ninth day of the operation. Elements of the 4th Battalion of the Dorsets crossed the river. The Dorsets had landed in Normandy as part of the 43rd (Wessex) Division shortly after D-Day, and during the fighting across France had suffered heavy casualties, but by September had been brought back up to strength.

As the time approached for the crossing there was still no sign of the promised boats. The Dorsets and Polish paratroopers waited in silence, while across the river the cauldron continued to boil. When the boats eventually arrived there were fewer of them than expected, so all were given to the Dorsets and the planned Polish crossing was cancelled. The infantrymen manhandled the boats across the mud towards the river bank while German machine-gun fire splattered into the mud,

causing some casualties. The actual crossing began at 0100hrs, 3 hours behind schedule. As the boats set out from the south bank they were supported by XXX Corps artillery fire. This barrage was intended to keep the Germans quiet, but some shells fell on two houses in the nearby village of Heveadorp, the resulting fire illuminating the river with an eerie glow. When the boats reached mid-stream enemy machine-guns opened fire and more casualties were caused, with at least one boat being sunk.

A total of 17 officers and 298 men of a total of four companies and a headquarters group made landfall. While the landing on the north bank was not strongly opposed, the men, now broken up into small parties, met fierce resistance as they attempted to make their way through the woods towards the perimeter at Oosterbeek. Only a handful of men of 'A' Company and some signallers made it into the perimeter, coming in to the positions held by 'Breeseforce'[109] of the Border Regiment.

A memorial on the wall of the Westerbouwing Restaurant to the Dorsets' attempt to cross the Rhine into the perimeter in aid of the 1st Airborne Division. One of those that made the attempt was Lieutenant D. Eccles from Navan, County Meath; he was taken prisoner shortly after landing on the north bank of the river. The restaurant is located to the west of the village of Oosterbeek and is on the high ground that was defended by 'B' Company of the 1st Battalion Border Regiment. *David Orr*

---

[109] 'Breeseforce' consisted of two depleted platoons of 'A' Company, a few remaining men of 'B' Company and some paratroopers, all commanded by Major C. F. O. Breese, OC 'D' Company, 1st Battalion The Border Regiment, who received the American DSM for his actions at Arnhem.

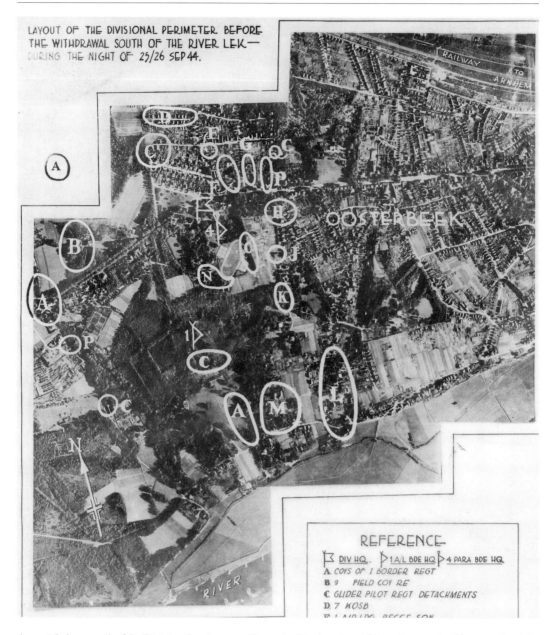

An aerial photograph of the Divisional perimeter at Oosterbeek before the withdrawal across the Rhine on the night of 25 September 1944. Flag: Divisional HQ at the Hartenstein; Flag 1: 1st Air-Landing Brigade HQ; Flag 4: 4th Parachute Brigade HQ; A (left edge): 'C' Company, 1st Border; A (lower centre): 'Breeseforce'; B: 'A' Company, 1st Border, 9th Field Company RE, 4th Parachute Squadron RE and 261 Field Park Company RE; C (lower left): D Company, 1st Border; C (centre and upper right): Glider Pilots; D: 7th KOSB; E: 1st Air-Landing Recce Squadron.; F: 156 Parachute Battalion; G: 10th Parachute Battalion.; H: 21st Independent Parachute Company; J: 4th Parachute Brigade Composite Platoon; K: RASC; L: 'Lonsdale Force' (elements of 1st, 3rd and 11th Parachute Battalions; M: Divisional Artillery; N: Divisional HQ troops; P: units of 1st Polish Parachute Brigade. *Border & King's Own Royal Border Regiment Museum*

Lieutenant Daniel Eccles of County Meath was on of those that crossed that night.[110] An attempt to get six DUKWs loaded with medical supplies across failed. Three of the vehicles bogged down in the soft bank as they made their way towards the river, while the three that manage to cross stuck in the mud on the northern bank and it proved impossible to unload them.

Lieutenant-Colonel Tommy Haddon and his HQ party, who had successfully made their way up the line of advance after his forced landing at Herenthals, also crossed the river this night. After landing on the northern bank they quickly made off towards Oosterbeek and the Battalion. Lieutenant-Colonel Haddon quickly became separated from his party and with many others found himself a prisoner. Never can an officer have tried harder to carry out his duty towards the men under his command.

The 156 Battalion was fighting for its existence in the Paul Krugerstraat area to the north of the Hartenstein. 26-year-old Portadown man Private Ernie Lynas was killed during an enemy artillery barrage. Private George Tansley, the ex-Inniskilling Fusilier, was also killed. The Germans managed to set up a machine-gun only 300 yards south of the Hartenstein. The guns of the Medium Regiment firing from 15,000 yards to the south knocked out this position, and the fire brought down an observation post situated on a rooftop close by.

At Driel the Poles were holding off German attacks from the east. From the embankment carrying the main Arnhem-Nijmegen road, self-propelled guns and tanks shelled the Polish positions around the village. One of the men helping to defend these trenches was Sergeant Eric Matson of the Glider Pilot Regiment, who was believed to have come south of the river with Private Cooney. Matson was a former pupil of the Masonic School, Dublin, and had enlisted in the Glider Pilot Regiment from the Royal Inniskilling Fusiliers. Despite being wounded in the face he remained with the Poles until they were withdrawn

on 7 October. Why he did not return to his unit with the survivors of the Division when they came back across the river on 26 September is not known. Perhaps this says something about the qualities of both this 21-year-old Dubliner and the Polish Brigade more than anything else.[111]

The Poles, without their anti-tank guns, which had landed north of the river, managed to hold off the enemy tanks using just PIATs and some land mines. This was made a little easier by the fact that the roads leading into Driel were raised on the top of dykes, making manoeuvre impossible. Nevertheless it took vast reserves of courage to lie waiting for the approach of a tank, while you had nothing more than a small 2-pound bomb perched on the end of a spring.

OPERATION 'BERLIN'

Just after 0800hrs on Monday 25 September Major General Urquhart decided that the position of the 1st Airborne within the Oosterbeek perimeter was no longer tenable. A message was passed to XXX Corps that evacuation would begin at 2200hrs that night. General Urquhart suggested to Lieutenant Colonel McKenzie, one of his staff officers, that what they needed were some of the tricks as used by the British during their withdrawal from Gallipoli, where mechanical devices were designed to fire weapons at various times. Instead of this it was decided that those wounded incapable of walking would remain behind to expend the remaining ammunition and deceive the Germans into thinking the perimeter was still intact.

The operation duly began at 2200hrs on the Monday evening. A heavy barrage from the guns of XXX Corps landed all around the perimeter, while glider pilots acted as guides on the various routes down to the Neder Rijn. Long human snakes of men slowly made their way towards the river bank, each man holding on to the unbuttoned tail of the airborne smock of the soldier in front.

It was the last night of being in the cauldron and

---

[110] He is not listed as a POW or casualty, so it is presumed he was one of those that escaped at the end of the battle.

[111] Details of how Sergeant Matson ended up in Driel are taken from a report in the *Belfast Telegraph* of 12 October 1944. The Masonic Boys School, Dublin, was founded to educate the orphaned sons of Freemasons.

An aerial photograph taken in 1944 of the River Rhine from the west of Heveadorp (bottom) to the eastern side of Oosterbeek just beyond the Church; the Driel Ferry is in the centre. On the night of 25 September soldiers of the Division withdrew from the perimeter down across the open ground to the north bank of the Rhine (left) and the boats during Operation 'Berlin'. *Border & King's Own Royal Border Regimental Museum*

Private G. J. Marshall of the South Staffords, one of the fortunate few to escape across the Rhine after Arnhem. Private Marshall lives in Holywood, County Down, and is seen here in October 1944 receiving a wallet of notes from the chairman of Holywood British Legion, Captain G. H. Creighton. Presentations such as this were a frequent and most welcome occurrence to returning servicemen.

it was raining hard. 'Paddy' Breen was making his way down to the river and, meeting up with an unknown Lance-Corporal, they approached a road junction and were shot at from the darkness. Diving into a ditch at the side of the road the pair waited until the firing stopped. When all was silent but for the noise of the pouring rain, they continued down the road for a few hundred yards when a shell exploded close by. 'Paddy' was hit in the face and the Lance-Corporal was mortally wounded – he died screaming abuse at the Germans. 'Paddy' lay in the road for the remainder of the night before being found by a German patrol early the next morning. After a kick in the ribs from one member of the patrol, then a welcome drink of something alcoholic from another, he was taken to the hospital in Apeldoorn where the wounds to his face and head were treated. From here it was a train journey across the border into Germany and another spell in a military hospital. After his recovery he was sent to the POW camp at Muhlhausen.

'JJ' O' Reilly was stumbling along holding on to the tail of the smock of the man in front when a salvo of mortar bombs sent the line reeling in confusion. When he had recovered his senses he was unable to catch up with the column of men who had moved on ahead, but by the time he approached the river bank it was getting light and the operation to evacuate had finished. There was nothing for him to do but make his way back inland and find somewhere to lie up and wait for another chance.[112]

As the long columns of men wended their way down towards the river, German mortar and artillery fire fell around them, the noise almost drowned out by the roar of the XXX Corps guns firing, their shells falling all around the shrinking perimeter. Corporal Willis, the Lisburn man, made his way down to the river, and behind him followed a single file of 14 men. Arriving at the Rhine they were greeted by a hail from the river. A Canadian accent called out instructions and the Border men climbed aboard a Canadian storm boat, with a crew of two Engineers and fitted with a powerful outboard motor. It had come across the river at a speed of 20 knots; on its return journey, with a load of between 13 and 15 men, it was reduced to 6 knots. Nevertheless this was a lot quicker than the British assault boat, which was rowed by a crew of two men. As the night wore on this rowing crew had to be increased as men tired, first to four men and eventually eight. With each increase in the number of rowers, the number of men who could be rescued was in turn reduced.

Sergeant Peter Quinn of the Reconnaissance Squadron was also making his way towards the river, and German mortar barrages were coming down at irregular intervals and making movement difficult.

---

[112] Sergeant O'Reilly went into hiding with the Dutch Resistance and was able to escape during 'Pegasus I' in October – see Appendix.

Above The memorial to the Royal Engineers and Royal Canadian Engineers who manned the boats that evacuated the survivors of the 1st Airborne Division across the River Rhine during Operation 'Berlin'. The memorial is placed close to the point on the southern bank of the Rhine where the majority of the boats landed. *David Orr*

'About 2130hrs a clatter of mortar bombs came down, lighting the woods and road with a queer blue light. The men scattered like demons in a pantomime. I was lifted off my feet with the blast of one bomb, and recovered consciousness lying against the trunk of a tree. There was no one about, so I pushed on quickly and eventually contacted two of my section. A machine-gun was firing at us, so we dashed pretty fast towards a clearing on the right where we found some much-needed cover. Everything went all right until we came to a T-junction. Here we saw several figures standing in the darkness of some houses opposite and slightly to our left. Having our previous experience in our minds, we went as quickly as possible to the right, which proved to be the correct way.'

Two hours later Sergeant Quinn had moved much closer to the river when the blast of a mortar bomb sent him sprawling for the second time that night. Struggling to his feet he saw Captain Allsop, the second-in-command of the Squadron, felled by a burst of machine-gun fire. Lifting the helpless officer on to his shoulder he made his way down to the river bank, some 200 yards away. Here both men were lucky enough to find a waiting boat, and soon willing Canadian hands helped them aboard.

Having got aboard a boat did not necessarily mean that the men were safe – there was still a very wide river to cross, a river that was being illuminated by star shells and laced with machine-gun bullets and shrapnel and boiled by German mortar bombs. Most boats were so full of men that there were only a few inches of clearance between the gunwales and the water; the risk of being swamped was great, and many men drowned when their boats turned over due to shells exploding close by.

Jack Fryer had received his orders from the Platoon commander and was waiting in his slit trench for the word to go.

Left Sergeant Peter Quinn from Athlone. He served in the Airborne Reconnaissance Squadron at Arnhem and escaped across the Rhine after the battle. He is seen here in October 1944, demonstrating items of Airborne equipment to the cadets of the Royal Ulster Rifles during their weekly parade in Victoria Barracks, Belfast.

'Mortar bombs were falling all around the area; you could hear them coming closer and closer. Suddenly I heard this voice calling "Paddy! Paddy!", and without thinking I jumped out of the trench and saw this body lying on the ground. As I pulled him to his feet a mortar bomb landed quite close, blew off my smock and knocked me back into my trench, my left arm and side full of shrapnel. Almost immediately I was back out and found it was my mate, Peter O'Leary, lying as if he were dead. As I tried to lift him an officer came out of a nearby house and between us we carried him into cover. That's the last I remember as I collapsed with loss of blood and shock. When I next saw Peter it was just before we went to prison camp – he didn't have a mark on him!'

Paddy Feehily finished his job of acting as guide to the other survivors of the 1st Airborne Division just before dawn broke. With a final look back towards what remained of the 'cauldron' he made his way to the river's edge and made a successful crossing.

Hugh Flynn was one of those who would not cross to safety. With bullets in both legs he lay with the other wounded and waited for the inevitable. Meanwhile an officer came by and told him that the Division was pulling out. He was asked if he could make his way down to the river, and when he said no he was given a weapon and asked to fire the occasional shot towards the German positions to create the impression that the Airborne men were still in position.

Private Charles Davidson of the 1st Parachute Battalion was another unable to cross the river on the night of 25 September, but he was able to evade capture for the next three days before being discovered. Sent to prison camp, he was one of those that endured the long march as the Russians encroached on German territory. When he eventually arrived home his sister Mary described him as a walking skeleton. Despite all the fine words written about the men of Arnhem, Charles Davidson maintained that 'the war stole our youth and no one cares'.[113]

Norman Dougan had been wounded in the thigh by a burst from an enemy machine-gun. Unable to make his way down to the river, he was given a Sten gun and told to fire off his remaining ammunition until first light. With dawn breaking and all ammunition expended, Norman made his way into the woods and hid. For the next few days he managed to evade capture and eventually make contact with the Dutch Resistance. A man called Willie Tiemens took him to the cellar of a farm near the river together with an unknown sergeant. The sergeant died during the night and Norman had to stay with the body for the next 12 hours, as it was too dangerous to risk moving in daylight. That night Willie Tiemens, with other members of the Resistance, came and removed the body, burying it in the vegetable patch to conceal from the Germans the fact that earth had been freshly dug.[114]

Bill Kerr of the 11th Battalion made a successful crossing despite missing the Canadian rescue boats.

'On arriving at the river we found all the boats had gone and the order was given "Every man for himself". As I approached the bank an officer inquired if I was going to swim across. I said no, but added that I intended to go into the water and proceed along the bank below the German guns towards the west. Here I hoped to find another way to cross the river. He offered to come with me despite a leg wound – he had been using a rifle as a crutch. After a considerable walk along the river bank we found a rowing boat. Leaving the officer there I returned to the original crossing place and there met six Polish paratroopers. I

---

[113] Quoted in the *Lisburn Star*, 24 September 1999

[114] On the night of 22 October, Norman was one of 123 men to escape across the Rhine in Operation 'Pegasus'. Led down to the river bank through the darkness of a cold autumn night, Norman missed the rendezvous with the rescue boats and decided to swim across. It says something for his constitution that after nine days of combat, nearly a month hiding in various cellars and barns, and still with two bullets in his leg, he was able to cross a 300-yard-wide, swiftly flowing river in the darkness. Nevertheless that is what he did. After the war he emigrated to Australia.

brought them back with me and the eight of us managed to row across the river. When we reached the southern bank, the Poles departed in a group while the officer and I made our way towards the British lines, taking great care as we knew we were still in enemy territory. Eventually we came to a road junction manned by members of the Military Police. They directed us towards Nijmegen and assured us that the road was safe. The officer collapsed at this point and as I went to his aid my legs gave out and I couldn't move. It must have been a reaction to the news from the Military Police. If they hadn't told us it was safe we would have marched all the way to Nijmegen, but once we were told, our bodies just gave out.'[115]

Danny Gillespie had a similar experience.

'I reached Nijmegen safely and was met by the Seaborne Tail. They brought me into a large barn and I was supplied with a dixie of tea and a beef sandwich. Immediately I finished I smoked a cigarette, something I rarely did, walked outside, threw up the lot and immediately fell asleep.'[116]

Paddy Morton and Fitz were packed up and ready to go. Not that there was a lot to pack. Paddy had his Sten gun with one spare magazine, while Fitz had a rifle and two phosphorus grenades. Just before they left there was a terrible wailing from close by.

'That sounded like a banshee,' whispered Fitzpatrick. 'You know what that means – someone is going to die.'

'And just what the hell do you think people have been doing for the last bloody week and a half?' shouted a very tired, hungry and frightened Morton. But that shout would be regretted for the remainder of his life.

They moved out and joined the long snaking line of men making their way down to the river. After nearly 2 hours of inching along in the pouring rain they were within a few hundred yards of the river bank. Then the mortaring started. The line dissolved as men scattered for cover. Patrick and Fitz found themselves crouching in a recently made shellhole. After a few minutes discussion they decided to make a run for the river. When a slight easing of the mortar barrage was sensed they sprinted towards the river, Fitz out in front by about 10 yards. Too late Patrick saw the tracer coming from the left. It appeared to consist of a solid line of fire and was about chest high, and even as he shouted a warning it seemed to cut Fitz in half. He stopped as if he had run into a brick wall, then the bullets found the smoke grenades in his ammunition pouches and he started to burn. As he fell to his knees he screamed, then another, merciful, burst came from the German machine-gun and he fell silent. Patrick leapt over his friend's body and continued to run for the river. He knew it was useless to stop – he had seen enough bodies in Spain to recognise that Fitz was dead and he didn't want to see what was lying in the pathway. But there was nothing he could do about the stench of burning flesh that caught in his throat and made him want to vomit. Patrick doesn't remember crossing the river or the march to meet the Seaborne Tail. He does remember that after drinking a large mug of strong sweet tea he slept for nearly 24 dreamless hours. The nightmare of what happened to his friend that night did not start for another two years.

At the end of it all there was the destruction of the 1st Airborne Division, the Dutch population of Arnhem and Oosterbeek were made to suffer a terrible winter, careers were stifled, reputations ruined, but most of all there were the deaths of good men.

---

[115] Bill Kerr was awarded the Dutch Bronze Lion by the Netherlands Government after the battle.

[116] Of the 186 men of the 21st who went into the Arnhem battle, 20 were killed and 46 became prisoners of war, while 120 escaped across the river. This is a much greater percentage than many other units, which can probably be attributed to the following. Throughout the battle the Company constantly fought as an intact unit; despite having to move positions on several occasions, the loss through stragglers was practically nil. The behaviour of officers and NCOs meant that the men were constantly 'under command' and never felt themselves left out on their own.

7 AFTERMATH

On Wednesday 27 September the wounded that had been left inside the perimeter were taken to Apeldoorn where they were kept in a transit camp for the next four days. Private James Cameron of the 21st Independent had died the day before.

Some men went to prison camp and, weakened by wounds, hunger and exhaustion, patiently waited for liberation from the advancing Allied armies. Others in turn waited for the chance to escape and in the chaos of the following few months got their chance and took it. Some were impatient and took any opportunity to escape, even on the journey to the camp. Several such stories have been told to the author over the years, and some are repeated here.

The walking wounded and other prisoners were marched from Apeldoorn for a distance of 7 kilometres to a railway station, where they were loaded on to cattle trucks, between 40 and 60 men to each truck. One medical orderly was allowed to travel in each wagon, but the only medical supplies available were those remaining from the battle, and these were few. The food ration was one loaf of bread per man, with the instruction to make it last for the next five days. After several days, in which the train made its slow way towards Germany, Peter Markey, together with a glider pilot and Sergeant Michael Kiely from Dundalk, decided to attempt an escape. Ripping up some of the floorboards they made a run for it when the train stopped after being strafed by an Allied fighter. Unfortunately some other prisoners tried to run out through the wagon doors and alerted the Germans. One of the officers was shot dead by the

guards and the remainder forced to surrender in the face of having two further prisoners executed for each one that failed to return.

After a total of seven days on the train they arrived at Fallingbostel, not one of the worst camps, but food was very scarce. Despite this the prisoners were expected to put in a full day's work, which usually involved a long march both to and from the workplace. After four weeks Peter and some of his Arnhem comrades were transferred to Sagan, a totally different camp. Here living conditions were terrible and food practically non-existent. His friend Michael Kiely looked like a walking skeleton, having lost 6 stone in the previous few months. In January 1945 the Germans marched those men fit enough to walk out of the camp towards the west. Those too ill to move were left to their fate – these included Peter Markey and Michael Kiely. On 16 January the sound of Russian artillery was heard, and Markey and Kiely decide to make their way out of the camp towards the advancing Russians. After only a few miles they met up with a Soviet reconnaissance unit and, recognised immediately by their maroon berets, were showered with vodka and their first English cigarettes since Arnhem.

The Russians sent them to Odessa, on the Black Sea. This involved a train journey of some 300 miles and took quite a time, with conditions being marginally better than the train that had taken them to prison camp. By 17 March, St Patrick's Day, they were still only halfway to their destination when a halt was made at a small railway station. Here they met an Irish Lieutenant Colonel, whose name Peter can't recall but who organised such a party that it was remembered for many a long year.[117] When they eventually reached Odessa they were put aboard a Red Cross ship where they were well looked after, arriving back in England on 18 April 1945.

A few days after the Division had withdrawn across the Rhine, Major Dennison and the remainder of the wounded in his party were herded into a variety of trucks and driven to the area of the summer palace of the Dutch Royal Family at Apeldoorn. Some were fortunate enough to sleep in the palace, but most of the wounded were in a large military hospital nearby. Mervyn Dennison contradicts once again the common belief about the brutality of the enemy.

'Most of the survivors would confirm the chivalry of one brand of good soldiers to another. The Divisional Director of Medical Services had spent many hours during the battle driving to and from the German headquarters organising cease-fires to permit the removal of our wounded, or, on several occasions, to permit the exchange of wounded prisoners. And so the wounded began their journey to prison camp. A few evaded their guards and hid up in the homes of those wonderful Dutch families. Most went into Germany in great discomfort in those "40 hommes, 8 cheveaux" (40 men or 8 horses) bare wooden wagons. Stalags for other ranks ranged from bad to tolerable. Officers did much better in Oflags, but wherever it might have been, one has to remember that it was within five or six months of the end of the war and the Germans were as short of food and necessities as the prisoners.'

Of the 588 men of the 3rd Battalion who parachuted into Arnhem, only one officer and 27 other ranks escaped across the river. Although Mervyn Dennison was not that officer, he was one of only two officers of the 1st Airborne Division to escape from the heart of Germany back to Allied lines.

Mervyn Dennison was one of those imprisoned in Spangenburg Castle, a moated fortress on top of a rock to the east of the German town of Kassel. He was a prisoner for six months, during which time he sat his Bar finals with the assistance of the Red Cross. He had just finished this when the Germans decided to move the prisoners west, away from the advancing Russians. As the column of men marched out of the castle Dennison and one of his subalterns, Lieutenant Tony Baxter, slipped away while their comrades confused the guard dogs by blowing cigarette smoke in their faces. They managed to reach American Army lines and were soon repatriated to Britain, where Major Dennison ended the war serving with the Parachute Regiment in Dorset. He was awarded the Military Cross for his actions at Arnhem.

Having been called to the Bar in Northern Ireland in 1945, he elected to join the colonial legal service in 1947 and left to become a Crown Counsel in Northern Rhodesia. He was appointed a QC in 1960 and became a High Court Judge in Zambia in 1961. He held various other posts before returning home in 1967. He worked as a clerk for Fermanagh County Council until 1973 when he retired for the second time. He was President of the Northern Ireland Branch of the Parachute Regimental Association and served as a part-time member of the Royal Ulster Constabulary Reserve, where even the Chief Constable was once heard to address him as 'Reserve Constable Dennison Sir'! Mervyn Dennison died on 12 January 1992 after a short illness; he was 78 years old.

Jack Fryer's prison camp was at Sagan near the Polish border. Medical care was rudimentary and Jack developed TB, an illness that would return in later life. When Soviet forces were reported to be closing in from the east, the Germans prepared to march the prisoners towards the west. This march lasted for two months in cold conditions and with very little food.

---

117 In the early 1950s a British officer whose duty included visits to Spandau Prison clearly remembers one of the Russian guards whistling 'The Minstrel Boy'.

Mervyn Dennison in later life as a High Court Judge.

Lieutenant John McFadden, Jack's platoon commander in the battle, was also wounded and became a prisoner of war. He contracted polio while in Fallingbostel and died in November 1944. He is buried in Germany.

Cecil Newell remembered his time in prison camp.

'We had to shift railway lines and sleepers. It took four of us to lift one sleeper, then along would come this Russian and lift one all by himself, despite the fact that they got very little to eat – but then again, they would eat anything!'

James McMurray had been captured while being treated for a serious hand wound and had also spent a long cold winter as a guest of the Germans. During his time in the prison camp his hand had become infected. A French doctor performed surgery and removed from the wound a small-calibre bullet, which James believed had come from a German officer's pistol during the confused fighting in Arnhem. As the Russians closed in on the prison camp, James became another of those who took part on the long march towards the west, and like many others suffered from the cold and hunger. When eventually released by American troops, he was in agony from dysentery and had lost 3 stone in weight.

'We thought they would leave us for the Russians, but no, we were marched towards the west. We started at the beginning of February and reached Hanover at the end of March. The first day we were put to work filling in the bomb craters made by the RAF the previous night. We had no sooner started than the Americans arrived. The Germans were scared stiff of the bombers – at the first sound of the air raid sirens both guards and civilians scattered to the shelters, leaving us prisoners to our own devices.'

Jack remembers standing in the middle of the railway marshalling yards waving his arms and yelling up at the B17s, 'Send it down on these bastards, send it down!' Jack's freedom came with the arrival of the American Army.

In the St Elisabeth Hospital 'Shan' Hackett had recovered enough to be smuggled out by the Dutch Resistance, and was put in a home only a short distance from a German military police billet! As the days passed he got stronger, spending his time reading the New Testament in Greek and writing a report on the battle as he had seen it. On his return to England after his escape from Holland, Hackett found 'My beloved brigade was dead and buried; I had been its midwife and its sexton.' He was happy to drop a rank, becoming GSO1 of an armoured division serving in Italy, and not sorry to leave behind his Airborne experience. For his actions at Arnhem he was awarded a Bar to his DSO in May 1945. The citation uses words like inspiring, tireless, excellence and outstanding. After 1945 Hackett was in command of the Transjordan Frontier Force, a position he held until 1956. From

TWICE POSTED AS MISSING

WARINGSTOWN SOLDIER NOW PRISONER IN GERMANY

Local listeners to the German Radio may have heard it announced recently that Corporal James McMurray, Waringstown, Lurgan, who was with an Airborne Division at Arnhem, is now a prisoner of war in German hands.

A number of people who heard the announcement were kind enough to write to his mother — Mrs. Edith McMurray, Waringstown—who has since been informed by the War Dept. that they also "lifted" the message.

This is the second occasion that Corporal McMurray has been posted as missing. for from September, 1943, till he arrived home in March, 1944, his family knew nothing concerning him except that he had been reported missing.

Corporal McMurray joined the Royal Ulster Rifles in 1940, and later volunteered for service with an Airborne Division. He served through the North African campaign and in Italy, being wounded twice. In September, 1943, he was one of a number of paratroops dropped behind the Italian lines, and it was in that operation that he was wounded and missing for six months.

Two of Corporal McMurray's brothers are also in the Services.

FIVE MORE ULSTER REPATRIATES

ARRIVE IN LARNE.

Among five repatriated prisoners arriving in Northern Ireland this morning were a Gortin (Mid-Tyrone) man returning after five years in captivity since Dunkirk days; a Waringstown man captured at Arnhem, and an officer of a South African unit taken prisoner at Tobruk.

They were Captain R. T. Pyne-Mercier. Imperial Light Horse. Union Defence Force, captured at Tobruk in June, 1942; Sapper J. H. Campbell, R.E., Colvahillion, Gortin, Omagh (Dunkirk, May, 1940); Cpl. L. Thomas, South Wales Borderers, 4 North Edward Street, Derry (Belgium, September, 1944); C. S. M. C. Laurie, Seaforth Highlanders, 57 Nevis Avenue, Belfast (France, June, 1944), and Cpl. M'Murray, 1st Paratroop Battalion, Waringstown, Co. Down (Arnhem, September, 1944). Captain Pyne-Mercier is staying with relations at 6 Knocktern Gardens, Belfast.

At Larne the men were met by the Mayoress (Mrs. J. Burton) and Major J. N. G. Stewart, M.C., Base Commandant, and provided with tea, cigarettes and chocolate by the Y.M.C.A.

Two newspaper cuttings regarding James Isaac McMurray of Waringstown, County Armagh. William Joyce, the traitor known as 'Lord Haw-Haw', made the radio broadcast regarding his capture. Joyce, born in America of an Irish father and English mother, was captured at the end of the war by two British officers, one of whom was Captain 'Bertie' Lickerish, who had served with the Reconnaissance Squadron at Arnhem. Joyce was hanged at Wandsworth Jail in January 1946.

Mr Howard Hamilton

there he moved to the British Army of the Rhine, where he commanded the 7th Armoured Division, the 'Desert Rats' with whom he had previously served in the Western Desert! In later years he served as Commandant of the Royal Military College of Science at Shrivenham, GOC Northern Ireland, Deputy Chief of the Imperial General Staff, and Deputy Chief of the General Staff, MOD.

His account of his time in Holland after 'Market Garden' was published as *I Was A Stranger* in 1977; the title comes from St Matthew's Gospel. In 1978 Hackett wrote his second book, *The Third World War, August 1985*; printed in ten languages, some three million copies were sold. The book was updated in 1982 as *The Third World War, The Untold Story*, and proved every bit as popular. Several other publications followed, and during the Falklands War he was frequently seen on television as a specialist commentator. Honour followed honour over the years and, despite his position and appointments, the humble student or private soldier was treated with the same respect as heads of state. He relished his long life and once remarked, 'Life begins at 70 – you have had your lot and every day after it is one for free, to use and to be enjoyed.' General Sir John Hackett died in September 1997 at the age of 86.

OPERATION 'PEGASUS'

After the withdrawal of the 1st Airborne Division on the night of 25/26 September 1944, a large number of men managed to avoid capture and go into hiding. Many of these 'evaders', as they became known, owe their lives to members of the Dutch

Resistance. The men of the Resistance based in the town of Ede, with the assistance of several British officers, devised a plan that would enable some 150 evaders to cross the Rhine to the Allied front line at Nijmegen.

After a reconnaissance of the northern bank it was decided that the village of Renkum offered the best location for a crossing. It was initially decided that those men making the crossing would gather at Renkum on the night of 23 October. However, the Germans issued an order that the civilian population of Bennekom, a nearby village, had to evacuate their homes by 22 October. This provided the Resistance with a golden opportunity to profit from the resulting upheaval on the roads. The operation, given the code name 'Pegasus', was brought forward to the night of 22 October, a Sunday.

On the Saturday, the roads crowded with evacuees, the Airborne men made their way to the rendezvous point. Dressed in civilian clothes and accompanied by members of the Resistance they made their way along the various roads to the woods north of the hotel Nol in t'Bosch, situated to the north-west of the village of Bennekom. By late Sunday afternoon there were 138 British soldiers

'Paddy', believed to be either Sergeant or Corporal William Ryan from Eire. He escaped after the battle and hid with the Dutch Resistance until he was able to escape across the Rhine during Operation 'Pegasus'.
Paul Vroemen

gathered in what became known as the 'English Grove'. Here they changed back into uniform and were issued with weapons collected by the Resistance. Two Russian prisoners that had escaped from Deelen Airfield and ten Dutchmen who had been given permission to join the Allied forces then joined the party. With the arrival of darkness a mist fell, making an ideal environment in which to make the crossing.

At 2300hrs the men began to move south towards the river. A column was formed, each man holding on to the man in front. The column slowly made its way towards the Rhine in a far from silent procession. Major Digby Tatam Warter, one of the British officers in charge of the evacuation, described it thus: 'It was as if a whole herd of elephants came thundering down through the woods.'

South of the river waited the men of the 2nd Battalion, 506th US Parachute Infantry Regiment. There they had assembled lorries and ambulances to transport the survivors to Nijmegen. The crossing began just after midnight, and by 0200hrs on Monday 23 October had been successfully completed.

An attempt to mount a similar operation in November was not so successful. Due to the widespread publicity surrounding 'Pegasus I' the Germans were more alert, and both the Airborne and Dutch Resistance suffered considerable losses.

NORWEGIAN INTERLUDE

The 1st Airborne Division, less the two Parachute Brigades, was chosen to fly to Norway to supervise the surrender of German forces in the country. 'Boy' Wilson led the 21st Independent Parachute Company to Norway on 9 May 1945, the day after VE Day. Once again they flew in Stirling bombers, the same aircraft that had taken them to Arnhem. This time the reception was a little more welcoming, with the Germans surrendering with all due formality.

The 21st Independent was one of the units tasked with disarming and recovering the weapons that had been issued to the Norwegian Resistance. This involved a great deal of walking up and down

A patrol of the 21st Independent Parachute Company engaged in the recovery of weapons from Resistance fighters in the mountains of Norway during the summer of 1945. The man sitting on the extreme left is Private 'Paddy' Redmond, a volunteer from the 'neutral' south. *D. Gillespie*

Norwegian mountains, as the various Resistance groups had been very careful not to hide all their weapons in one spot.

Another task was to assist in the rousing of sleeping German POWs early in the morning and having them parade in the search for members of the Gestapo, who on the surrender had changed into ordinary German uniforms to avoid detection; however, as Danny Gillespie pointed out, 'Despite being dressed in ordinary German uniforms, you could tell the Gestapo by the arrogant look in their eyes.' On these occasions members of the Norwegian population who had suffered at the Gestapo's hands came to the camp and identified many of these war criminals.

Still the weather was good and the hospitality even better. One afternoon Danny Gillespie's platoon was tasked with providing a display of the Company equipment to the local population. This display took place in a large car park in the centre of

Oslo. There were other units present, including Reconnaissance troops and some Americans who were showing off the merits of their famous Jeep.

It was a sunny afternoon, and Danny noticed some children climbing about on one of the Recce jeeps. Two small boys of approximately 12 years of age were engrossed in the workings of the PIAT, which was pintle-mounted on the bonnet of the Jeep. As one boy peered down the 'barrel', the other pulled the trigger. As always happens on these occasions, someone had left the weapon cocked – but thankfully unloaded! As the propulsion for a PIAT bomb is a very strong spring-loaded metal bolt, the potential result can be well imagined. Danny remembers the horrific scream that came from the boy as the firing bolt removed his nose. His face covered in blood, he fled with a turn of speed that surprised all present, and was never seen again. Despite widespread inquiries, no trace of the boy was ever found.

Above 'Danny' Gillespie of the 21st Independent Parachute Company always maintained that you could tell those SS troops who attempted to evade detection by wearing regular German uniform by the arrogant look in their eyes. Here British Airborne troops assisted by American soldiers round up German prisoners of war in Norway. *D. Gillespie*

Below Duty for most Allied units in Norway consisted of an endless round of parades, demonstrations and the occasional party. Here men of the 2nd Battalion South Staffordshire Regiment take part in the ceremonial parade in Oslo for the return of Crown Prince Olaf from exile in Britain on 20 May 1945. They are carrying the No 5 Rifle, commonly referred to as the Jungle Carbine. *D. Gillespie*

Above Reconnaissance Squadron jeeps on parade in Norway. *D. Gillespie*

Below Members of the 21st Independent Parachute Company relaxing in Norway. The man in the white vest is 'Curly' Cowan. *D. Gillespie*

Above A children's party courtesy of British Airborne troops in Norway, 1945. *D. Gillespie*

Below A Vickers 'K' machine-gun fitted to the bonnet of a Reconnaissance Squadron jeep in Norway. This photograph was taken on the same day that the young Norwegian boy lost his nose to the PIAT. *D. Gillespie*

Left The 'mascot' of the 21st Independent Parachute Company while it was in Norway – today he is in his early 60s. *D. Gillespie*

Below Men of the 21st Independent Parachute Company relaxing in Norway in 1945. Alf 'Ginger' Jones is sitting on the step; the others are, from left to right, Idris Ball, Ken Lockett and Tommy McMann. *D. Gillespie*

The certificate presented in 1945 by the King of Norway to all those servicemen who took part in the liberation of his country. *D. Gillespie*

GOING HOME

Wilfred Tallentire was sent to the Far East for the remainder of the war. There was little for the glider pilots to do, and Wilfred spent much of his time hitching lifts on various supply drops just to put the time in. When Wilfred arrived in camp there was no accommodation available and the men were supplied with tents, with a ratio of two men per tent. As it was the wet season it was necessary to build an earthen platform on which to pitch the tent to stop it being washed away in the torrential rain. However, there were no spare hands available, so when Wilfred arrived he set to, but the English

officer with whom he was to share the tent was away on a flight, so Wilfred built the platform himself. He had just finished putting up the tent when his new partner arrived. He was most upset that a fellow officer had been reduced to manual labour, but as Wilfred remembers, 'I preferred to get my hands dirty and sleep dry than wake up the next morning in the middle of a lake.'

Wilfred also remembers the incident of the Indian wedding.

'A few weeks after we arrived there was a wedding between two of the Indian camp workers. It lasted for two days, two days of continual noise, music and the beating of drums. My fellow camper complained about it at great length. He then remarked that this commotion seemed to have little effect on myself. I informed him that he had obviously never had the pleasure of experiencing the 13th of July in Scarva.'[118]

Wilfred returned home and today lives in happy retirement in a small cottage overlooking the sea.

Jack Smyth also went to the Far East. He was attached to the American forces in the Pacific, where he covered the dropping of the atom bomb on Nagasaki, and was with the US Task Force that entered Tokyo Bay to receive the Japanese surrender. After the war he returned to Ireland, married Eileen Gallagher in 1946 and went on to become the Managing Editor of the Irish Press. In 1956 he published *Five Days In Hell*, the story of his time spent with the 1st Airborne Division at Arnhem. On 2 December that year he and his wife were both killed in a car accident in Dublin when their vehicle left the quay and fell into the River Liffey; they left a son and daughter.

Norman Dougan returned to Glenanne in County Armagh. He knew his brother was dead, but was forced to keep it to himself until the arrival of official notification from the War Office. When

---

[118] For those readers not familiar with this facet of Irish history, the following may help explain. On 13 July each year in Northern Ireland a section of the population celebrates the victory of King William over King James at the Battle of the Boyne in 1690. A 'sham' battle is fought near the village of Scarva, County Down, involving a lot of noise, music and the beating of drums.

York Street Railway Station, Belfast, on the morning of 21 April 1945. These returning prisoners of war include, from the left, Sergeant Jimmy Black, a Belfast man who served with the 156 Battalion and was taken prisoner at Arnhem, and Lance-Corporal J. O'B. McWilliams of Bangor, County Down, who served in the 6th Airborne Division and received a Mention-in-Despatches for his actions on D-Day. The man fourth from the left holding the kit-bag is Corporal J. Atkinson of the Royal Army Medical Corps. He has the Pegasus badge on the right sleeve of his battledress blouse, but efforts to trace his Airborne unit have proved unsuccessful. The man next to him is Corporal John McCleave from Belfast, who served in the 156 Battalion and was also taken prisoner at Arnhem. The lady on the extreme right is Mrs H. P. Gilbert of the Red Cross, who, judging by photographs that appeared in the local press, seems to have welcomed every train carrying returning prisoners of war.

he saw the telegram boy arrive a few days later he went off into the nearby woods for a long walk. After the experience of Arnhem he was never able to settle down and decided to make a new home in Australia.

After the war General Alan Adair formed the 13th Infantry Division and commanded it in Greece from the end of 1945, in which year he was also appointed CB. After the end of his tour he resigned his commission and took up farming in England. Alan Adair was described as 'a Grenadier to the last drop of his marrow'. In 1961 he was appointed Colonel of the Regiment, only the second man since 1681 not to have been a Duke or an Earl. He succeeded his father to become the 6th Baronet in 1949 and was Deputy Lieutenant for County Antrim. Alan Adair died in August 1988.

Albert Smith left the squadron on 13 March 1945, and from that day he lost his interest in flying. 'I realised that throughout the war my absence from home had caused endless worry to both my parents and wife. I realised that home and family had become more important than flying.' Albert was demobbed in July 1946. He returned to County Armagh and, after a brief flirtation with starting his own radio business, decided to go into teaching, a

profession he followed until his retirement. Today, at 83 years of age, he spends a lot of his time supporting the RAF Association and playing golf.

Cecil Newell first went back to Arnhem in 1984.

'The Dutch people were great. They asked me why I hadn't been back before. I told them I was ashamed. When we had last seen Arnhem it was a total wreck. They were great people; I stayed with a man who took me around the battlefield visiting the places I had been. On the way down from Amsterdam I didn't recognise anyone on the train – I was looking for young faces, lads of 19 and 20, not old men. I was looking for men from 40 years ago.'

After the war Padre Buchanan returned to Northern Ireland and was appointed Rector of St Mary's in Belfast, moving to a parish in Bangor, County Down, in 1955. He was canon of St Patrick's Cathedral, Dublin, in 1957, before returning to Clogher in 1958 as Bishop. He was enthroned as Archbishop of Dublin in Christ Church Cathedral on 20 November 1969, and was Primate of Ireland from 1969 until he retired in 1977. Alan Alexander Buchanan, described by those who served in the 1st Airborne Division as 'a saint among men', died in 1984.

Interviewed by the writer Charles Whiting some 40 years after the battle, 'Paddy' Tucker maintained that after all that happened and despite eight months in a German prison camp, he would have done it all again.[119]

Paddy Feehily finished the war as a Squadron Sergeant-Major with the Glider Pilot Regiment, but was quick to recognise that the day of the glider had come and gone. He transferred to the Parachute Regiment and after several promotions was commissioned in 1955, and awarded the MBE in 1962. Paddy retired from the Army in 1972 with the rank of Lieutenant Colonel, but continued with the military connection by becoming the full-time Adjutant of the Worcester and Sherwood Foresters Regiment, which post he held until forced to retire due to ill health in 1982.

Jack Fryer was demobbed in 1945 and came home to marry Janet. Shortly afterwards he was found to have TB and spent two years in hospital seriously ill. After leaving hospital he was unable to return to joinery and worked for a time in the 'dole' office[120] in Corporation Street, Belfast. This was an awkward time for Jack: post-war Belfast had few jobs for returning servicemen and many of those that came in to see Jack were Catholic and there was little work to be found if you were not the 'right sort'. Jack always found these meetings embarrassing, as he was unable to give his friends and former comrades a job. Jack would find himself in Army uniform again just over 25 years later; with the advent of 'the troubles' he joined the Ulster Defence Regiment, where his experience and skills quickly turned shambling civilians into something resembling soldiers. When he retired again, as CQMS, he was happy to spend his time playing golf at his local club. He returned to Arnhem on many occasions, both renewing and keeping alive the friendships he had made over the years. His last visit was for the 50th anniversary in 1994. Jack Fryer died in November 1996, after a short illness.

Billy Magill was demobbed in England in 1945

'The best of men' – Jack Fryer was one of the finest people you could hope to spend a social evening with.

with the offer of a job with the Rover Car Company in Birmingham. He remained there for the next ten years, and when he came home to Northern Ireland he got a job with the then Down County Health & Welfare Board. In 1971 this became the Southern Health Board and Billy continued to work with them as head of transport; for his services to the Board he was awarded the British Empire Medal. He returned to Arnhem in 1984 and again in 1994, on that occasion together with Billy Saunders, Hugh Adamson and Jack Fryer.

Tommy Scullion had met and married Peggy, a local girl, while stationed at Newark prior to Arnhem, and after the war he decided to settle down locally. He worked for British Gypsum until he retired at the age of 61, suffering from severe

---

[119] '44 In Combat On The Western Front From Normandy To The Ardennes by C. Whiting (Century Publishing, 1984)
[120] Unemployment office

'Not a patch on the old .303' – Billy Saunders today, happily retired and still a good shot.

arthritis. He became a stalwart member of the 21st Independent Parachute Company Club and attended practically all meetings and functions and making many pilgrimages back to Arnhem. He died in January 1990.

Andrew 'Adie' McKee continued to serve after the war, going to Palestine from October 1945 to May 1948. He served in the BAOR from July 1948 until his discharge in August 1949, with the rank of CQMS.

After returning to the UK, Brian Horrocks was selected as GOC Western Command, where he remained until medically discharged. He was appointed Black Rod to the House of Lords and successfully presented a television programme called *Men in Battle*.

For Field Marshal Montgomery, 'Market Garden' would forever be the stain on an otherwise impeccable military career. His reasons for the failure were fivefold. First, the strength of German forces in the Arnhem area was completely underestimated. Allied Intelligence was well aware that II SS Panzer Corps was refitting at Arnhem,

and despite the severe losses suffered in Normandy, it was a short distance from Germany with reinforcements close at hand. Montgomery, having fought the enemy in North Africa, Sicily and in Normandy, was well aware of the enemy's ability to regroup and react with complete professionalism. Second, there was his own failure to insist on the Air Force doing a 'double shift' on 17 September, to ensure the complete delivery of the 1st Airborne Division north of the Rhine. Third was his failure to impart to those under his command the need for the utmost urgency in the land advance, not only by those directly involved in the push up the single highway from the Belgian border, but also those on the flanks and elsewhere. The fourth reason for the failure was the weather, an element over which no one had any control, and fifth was his believed failure of Eisenhower to give full logistical support to the efforts of Second Army. Montgomery fully accepted responsibility for the first three reasons.

At home the Airborne Forces Security Fund was set up and throughout Northern Ireland there were many fund-raising activities – dances, variety

Above 'Had the pious, teetotalling Montgomery wobbled into SHAEF with a hangover, I could not have been more astonished than I was by the daring adventure he proposed… [Although] I never reconciled myself to the venture, I nevertheless concede that Montgomery's plan for Arnhem was one of the most imaginative of the war.' So said US General Omar Bradley. This photograph of Montgomery was taken at his son's fifth birthday party.

Above right A cutting from a Northern Ireland newspaper advertising a dance in aid of the Airborne Forces Security Fund, just one of the many functions held throughout Britain in the months after Arnhem. *Ulster Gazette and Armagh Standard, 8 December 1944*

Right Private John Joseph Butler from Belfast. 'JJ', as he was known, was one of the founder members of the Northern Ireland Branch of the Parachute Regimental Association, which despite its name is open to all who served in Airborne Forces. Early meetings of the Branch were held in the Lifeboat Bar, Customs House Square, in the city.

Airborne Forces Security Fund. A depot shop for the Flag Day scheme was opened at Donegall Place yesterday. From left are Lieut.-Colonel D. C. Lindsay (chairman of the Ulster Committee), Mr. S. Sides, Mr. B. Horan, Mr. N. Goorwitch, Mr. J. O. Wilson, Lieut. L. Burke, Major F. R. Hynds, M.C., and Mr. J. W. Morgan, F.R.G.S. (hon. secretary).

(On left) Members of the Royal Ulster Rifles (Airborne), who were wounded in Normandy on D-Day, attended the opening of the depot shop.

RESIDENCE PERMITS

Ulster People Who Mus Have Them

The opening of a shop in Donegal Place, Belfast, to support the Airborne Forces Security Fund, October 1944.

shows, book sales, concerts. The flag-day held in Belfast on 27 October 1944 raised £3,302 for the Fund.

There was also the 'Arnhem Cup', a trophy raced for at Dunmore Stadium, Belfast's home of greyhound racing. James Beattie had been born in Klondyke Street, off the Shankill Road in Belfast. As a boy he had suffered from rheumatic fever and a severe slipped vertebrae condition that left him barely able to walk. After release from hospital his doctor recommended long walks in the open air. To encourage this his father bought him a greyhound and soon both boy and dog were enjoying the then reasonably fresh air in the parks around Belfast. As a result of this James developed a great interest in greyhound racing and soon his dog, now named 'Border Keeper', was entered for the Arnhem Cup

on 10 October 1944. It was a six-dog race and from the beginning 'Border Keeper', a black 18-month-old, led the field. This was a one-off race for the Arnhem Cup, and Lord Londonderry presented the trophy to James. James died in a few years ago and his widow, Joan, keeps the Cup in pristine condition, in memory not only of her husband, but to show another way in which local people supported the veterans of 'Market Garden'.

On 21 October 1944 the postman delivered a telegram to 'Lindifarm', Demesne Road, Holywood, County Down, officially notifying Mrs I. M. Wood that her son, Captain Jack Smellie of the Glider Pilot Regiment, previously missing in action, was now a prisoner of war. It would be the end of the year before she would find out that Jack had been killed in action.

Above James Beattie's 'Border Keeper', the first and only winner of the Arnhem Cup, was an 18-month-old 'black' greyhound. *David Orr*

Above 'Border Keeper' successfully sired several other winners – this is his stud card. *David Orr*

Below left James Beattie receiving the Arnhem Cup from Lord Londonderry at Dunmore Park, Belfast, on 28 October 1944. *David Orr*

Below The Arnhem Cup. The inscription reads 'In aid of the Royal National Lifeboat Institution and The Airborne Forces Security Fund 28 October 1944'. *David Orr*

PALESTINE

Patrick Morton, now serving with the 6th Airborne Division, found the situation in Palestine puzzling to say the least. There were many Jews serving in the Division, men who had fought valiantly throughout the last six years of war to rid Europe of Nazism, and here in the new Jewish homeland those same men were being spat at and called 'Storm Troopers'.

It is generally accepted that the 'Palestine problem' had its roots in the Balfour Declaration of 1917. This statement proclaimed that Britain would look with sympathy on the concept of a national homeland for the Jews. The declaration was made in the fourth year of a war in which Britain was fast running out of manpower and the will to fight. There was a need to ensure the continuing support of American Jews and their financial support for the war effort against the Central Powers.

Up to 1939 the number of Jews arriving in Palestine had not been any great problem. Now,

Above Danny Gillespie and Joan, recently married and enjoying a brief holiday in London just before Danny left for service in Palestine. *D. Gillespie*

Left Airborne troops wrapped up as much against the stinging sand as the unexpected cold spell at Beirut in August 1946. Second from the left is Danny Gillespie of the 21st Independent Parachute Company, demobbed shortly after this photograph was taken. *D. Gillespie*

with the war in Europe over and a huge number of displaced Jews looking for a new home and a fresh start, things were very different. The Arabs, not unnaturally, took great exception to this sudden influx, and soon British troops were needed to try and maintain order between the two sides.

One hot afternoon Patrick was part of a patrol called to an incident during which some local people had been hurt in a grenade attack. As Patrick bent over to help an injured woman, a figure stepped out of the surrounding crowd and shot him twice in the back. These were the days before flak jackets or body armour, and it was only as a result of prompt first aid on the spot, followed by some very skilful surgery, that his life was saved. His injuries meant the end of his military career and he returned to England to spend a very long time in hospital.

On a hot, dusty Friday afternoon in Palestine, Danny Gillespie was a Platoon Sergeant responsible for 30 men. The following Monday he was a hospital porter pushing a trolley full of dirty laundry along the corridors of the Royal Victoria Hospital in Belfast. 'For me the war ended in 1945 – I just wanted to get on with living a normal life.' Danny has since retired after many years as a joiner, and today he is a grandfather and happy to take care of his extensive garden and occasionally sit and talk about his army days. He is firmly convinced that someone or something kept a careful eye on him during combat. Five years of war and not a scratch while serving in all the campaigns of the 1st Airborne and throughout the nine days of Arnhem must be something of a record.

At the same time that Danny was working as a porter, Gordon Summerville was driving an ambulance for the same hospital. He stayed for a few years before going off to find a new life in Australia.

A TRAITOR?

Soon after the Battle of Arnhem stories began to circulate regarding the actions of a traitor on whom the disaster at Arnhem was blamed. Christian Lindemans, known as 'King Kong' because of his physique, was regarded as one of the bravest members of the Dutch Resistance. He had begun to

work for the Germans in 1944, in exchange for the release of his brother and girlfriend from jail. Both were also members of the Resistance. In September 1944 he passed information to his German handlers that an airborne invasion of Holland was imminent. This was not exactly news to the Germans – they were aware that both the 82nd and 101st American Airborne Divisions had been withdrawn from Normandy and that the 1st British Airborne had not been used on D-Day and was still waiting to see action. They also knew that the only target within range of Allied transport aircraft was Holland. Lindemans's information placed the landings at Eindhoven, 30 miles south of Arnhem, and was only passed to the Germans two days before the operation started. Lindemans was arrested the following October and sent to Britain for interrogation. In 1946, while awaiting sentence by a Dutch court, he died; it was believed that he committed suicide, but some others believe persons unknown killed him.

This penchant for laying the blame for the Arnhem disaster at the foot of a traitor can also be extended to the Irish. In the book *Neutral Ireland and the Third Reich*, John P. Duggan describes the following. During the summer of 1944 a man called Russell returned to Ireland after working in England. He was the cousin of Dr Liam Grogan, a veteran of the 1916 Rising, and a friend of Eduard Hempel. Hempel was the Minister Plenipotentiary for the Third Reich to Eire from 1937 to 1945. Russell informed Grogan that there were strong indications in England of a proposed airborne invasion of Holland. Grogan at once took Russell to see Hempel and Hempel in turn was supposed to have forwarded the information to Germany. In the absence of a German radio transmitter in Dublin, which had been seized by the Irish Government prior to D-Day, it is difficult to see how this could have been done, but it is possible that a message was sent via one of the other neutral countries.

Even if either or both of the above stories are true, they made no difference to the deployment of German forces in Holland. Despite Duggan's claim that II SS Panzer Corps was 'poised in a high state of combat readiness', this was simply not so. Their combat readiness consisted of troops resting and refitting after the horrendous battles in Normandy and the long haul back towards the German border.

Added to this is information supplied by professor Eunan O'Halpin, who rightly points out that any report other than one coming from a trained observer would carry little if any weight in Berlin.[121] Nor is there any mention in German intelligence reports of anything about Arnhem coming from Ireland. Likewise, post-war British reports contain no reference to any such leak.

It would be mischievous to add to the conspiracy theory, but what if the above story is true and the relevant information did indeed reach Berlin before the launch of 'Market Garden'? Why was Model not told? Did he have enemies in the high command who hoped for something sinister to befall the Field Marshal? Model came from a humble background, he was not a Junker, and he was an ardent Nazi. Perhaps a surviving supporter of the 'July plot' held back the information to give the Allies a chance. A case of 'get yourself out of this one, Walther!'

The betrayal theory persists to this day, and as late as April 2000 the story was still being reported in the press.[122]

THE FILMS

In August 1945 the Rank Organisation made the film *Theirs Is The Glory*. Direction was put in the hands of Brian Desmond Hurst, an Irishman with quite a success in the film industry. He had gone to Hollywood in the 1920s as an assistant to John Ford, returning to Britain in 1934 to begin his own career. Prior to 1945 he had worked on other war films, including *The Lion Has Wings*, *Dangerous Moonlight* and *The Malta Story*.

In the beginning Rank had wanted to make a cheap film using archive footage with some specially shot scenes of a light-hearted nature and starring one of its then leading men. Thankfully this did not happen, and it was decided that no stars or actors would appear and the men of the 1st

Airborne Division would portray all the roles themselves. Those selected were mostly men from the 21st Independent Parachute Company, then in Norway and Denmark. Among those chosen were Tommy Scullion, John Daly and Jack Bateman. Tommy Scullion remembered that the Irishmen seemed to get on very well with Hurst, and Tommy particularly enjoyed being chauffeured around London in a Rolls-Royce! 'Dickie' Lonsdale was another Irishman to become a film star. His recreation of his famous speech in Oosterbeek Church is one of the highlights of the film.

For the privilege of using British soldiers the Rank Organisation had to pay the army £3 per day per man, but this money was not passed on to the men involved. The Arnhem Film Unit was formed at a mushroom farm at Braintree, Essex, and when all personnel had been gathered together they flew to Holland on 6 August 1945, the day the Allies dropped the atomic bomb on Hiroshima! Conditions around Arnhem/Oosterbeek were primitive to say the least. The accommodation offered to the men in Nijmegen was described as 'indifferent', and the Unit had to be totally self-sufficient, which meant bringing its own generators for power, lighting and heat, and supplying interpreters and some 20 jeeps to operate a messenger service as the telephone system was still inoperable.

Both Arnhem and Oosterbeek were still in ruins, and in addition to the damage caused during the battle the Germans had indulged in widespread looting. All the houses in Oosterbeek had their doors removed to supply roofing for German slit trenches. When Hurst had to use shots of the fighting around Arnhem Bridge; the bridge had to be painted on to a sheet of glass to create the effect that it was still standing, when in fact it had been destroyed by air raids by the American Air Force on 6 and 7 October 1944.

The film covers the actions around the bridge, the fighting in the suburbs of Oosterbeek and the eventual withdrawal across the Rhine. No blank

---

[121] Professor Eunan O'Halpin is the author of *Defending Ireland: The Irish State and its enemies since 1922* (Oxford, 1999). Also, in preparation, *British Intelligence and Ireland in the Second World War* (Oxford, 2003).

[122] *Daily Telegraph*, 20 April 2000; article by Neil Tweedie

Shooting a scene from *Theirs Is The Glory*. **The figure in the slit trench applying the camouflage cream is Tommy Scullion from Ballymena, County Antrim. The figure in the light trench-coat is believed to be the Irish director, Brian Desmond Hurst. Hurst had quite a distinguished career as a film director, his films including** *The Malta Story*, *Dangerous Moonlight*, *Tom Brown's Schooldays* **and** *The Black Tent*. *Airborne Museum, Hartenstein*

ammunition was used; every shot fired and grenade thrown was real, as were the enemy tanks, although when the tanks are seen firing, a 'special effect' courtesy of Brocks, the fireworks-makers, was used, as was also the case with some of the shell bursts. Possibly it was felt that enough damage had been done to the locality. Practically all of the film was made in Holland. The exception was the evacuation across the Rhine, and the location for this part of the film is usually given as a gravel pit at Wraybury, just outside London. The actions of the American Divisions were referred to but not portrayed. While surviving stills show that filming was done to show the Polish Brigade in action, their part was cut from the final version; one can only assume some political reason for doing this.

The film opens with ten men preparing for their last night in camp in England before the operation. Its poignant ending shows only two men returning to the barrack hut. Possibly this is to represent the 2,000 men who returned from the 'cauldron'. All in all, despite its age, it remains one of the best accounts of the battle that has been committed to film.

In 1975 the Hollywood producer Joe Levine decided to make his 492nd film, and engaged Richard Attenborough to direct *A Bridge Too Far*, based on the book of the same name by Dublin-born historian Cornelius Ryan. With a budget of $25,000,000 and a plethora of Hollywood's biggest stars playing the leading and some smaller roles, shooting began in the Dutch town of Deventer in the summer of 1976. This was not Attenborough's first association with Arnhem; in *Theirs Is The Glory* he had provided a voice-over during one of the opening scenes.

Despite the money and some top-class performers the film is a mess. While several small cameos stand out, overall what comes across is a film that was made for an American audience with US 'kick ass let's go!' pitted against British 'stick in the mud do it by the book' attitudes.

Film-makers have a moral responsibility to their audience to show to their best endeavours the truth of what happened when they portray historical fact as entertainment. In *A Bridge Too Far* we have a film that is too far from the truth.

A series of photographs taken during the making of the film *Theirs Is The Glory*. The men shown are from the 2nd and 10th Parachute Battalions. *Mr Ken Kirkam*

Above Tickets for the première of *Theirs Is The Glory* were made from metal taken from British gliders. The film was shown in Belfast in the Ritz cinema. *David Orr via Mr Tom Wylie*

Below A photograph showing two scenes from the film *Theirs Is The Glory*. In the right-hand photograph Kate ter Horst prepares to read from her Bible, an incident recalled by every man who was in her house during this time. The photograph has been autographed by the film's Irish director, Brian Desmond Hurst. *D. Gillespie*

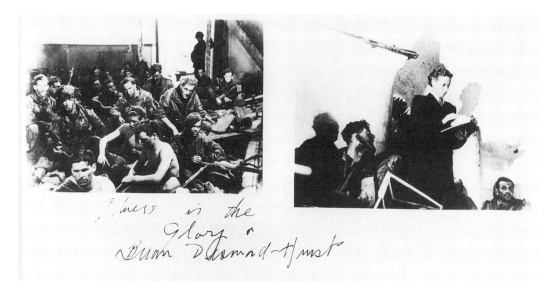

8 THE LAST WORD

Patrick Morton would for the rest of his life walk with the aid of a stick, the legacy of that hot afternoon in Palestine. He bears no animosity towards those responsible for his wounds, nor for those he had fought from the hills of North Africa to the suburbs of Arnhem. He realises that there is no profit in hatred – you just have to get on with living. So many of those with whom he had served had been denied that chance – he had a future, but theirs, like that of his friend Fitzpatrick, had ended in September 1944.

But there was personal disappointment after all he had experienced during six years of war, fighting for what he believed was a better world. He came back to Northern Ireland in the summer of 1956 to the same old antagonism and bitterness he had left more than ten years before, nowhere more so than within his own family. Apart from his wife, now deceased, and his two children, no one in his family is aware of the part Patrick played in the war, and never will. When his son and daughter, both active members in the Republican movement, discovered in the early 1970s that he had served in the British Army, they never spoke to him again, their silence as much to protect themselves as other members of the family. They have refused to agree to his funeral arrangements, so when he dies an undertaker will transport his body south to Limerick where another family will accept the coffin and arrange burial beside a memorial stone in the hills above a small village. There is a brass plaque fixed to the stone and on it is inscribed a poem written by Christina Rossetti. Over the past few years Patrick has found himself visiting the hill with increasing regularity, almost anxious to be with his friend again. With each passing visit the climb gets a little harder, but nothing will put Patrick off these visits. Home has become a strange land and these hills seem friendlier as the years go by.

Remember me when I am gone away,
Gone far away into the silent land;
When you can no longer hold me by the hand,
Nor I half turn to go, yet turning stay.
Remember me when no more, day by day,
You tell me of our future that you planned;
Only remember me; you understand
It will be late to counsel then or pray.
Yet if you should forget me for a while
And afterwards remember, do not grieve;
For if the darkness and corruption leave
A vestige of the thoughts that once I had,
Better by far that you should forget and smile
Than that you should remember and be sad.

At the top of the hill he sits and talks to his friend.

'There was never much silence where we were lads, not during those last nine days. I hope it's quiet where you are now – you deserve it. You and all the rest of the generation that made "the supreme sacrifice" – did we waste our time, your lives, was it worth bothering about? They say the soil of Holland is soft and the bodies are well preserved, even after all this time. I don't know about that, but whatever their state it has to be better than the peace we had hoped for – we failed to preserve that. They called it VE Day – Victory in Europe. What a joke – even as it was being celebrated

181

For many years two giant cranes displaying the 'Krupp' logo have dominated the Belfast skyline. For the workforce they were saviours, allowing Harland & Wolff to compete in the modern shipbuilding world, but to others they resurrected memories best forgotten. Industrialist Gustav Krupp enthusiastically supported Adolf Hitler after be became Chancellor of Germany in 1933. Under the management of his son Alfried, the firm prospered further during the Third Reich. The Krupp factories were often sited close to 'known sources of labour', ie concentration camps. Alfried Krupp was appointed Minister of War Economy in 1943, a position he performed with diligence and professionalism. He was arrested at the end of the war, stood trial for war crimes, and was sentenced to 12 years imprisonment and the confiscation of all his property. He was nevertheless released from prison in 1951 and had most of his vast fortune returned. Such is the power of big business. *David Orr*

the fighting was going on. And what happened the following summer? We, the civilised people of the West, we destroyed two cities full of civilians in the name of peace. The future – what future? It's the same old hatred, the same old fear, and the same old hypocrisy.

'The peace we fought for became a "cold war", and now it's warming up at a fast rate, breaking out all over the world like a rash. I'm an old man and my only happiness is the memories of when I was young and had friends who were young and who like me were so naive as to believe we could make a difference, that we could change things for the better. My grandson took me to his home for dinner last Sunday. He drove me there in a Japanese car, his wife cooked Italian food, and on the way home, the supreme indignity. We were coming back to my house. Passing the shipyard he told me he had a job there now. I looked up at those two big yellow cranes – "Samson" and "Goliath" they call them. Do you know what is stamped on the side of them? Krupp, bloody Krupp. I have shrapnel in my shoulder supplied courtesy of bloody Krupp. And what about you – who made the bullets that killed you, the bullets, shells and mines that did for the rest of them?

'Perhaps the only hope for mankind is that a future generation will believe what we once believed and that there will be such numbers that a difference will be achieved, but I doubt it.'

On particular days, when something terrible has happened in Northern Ireland, or elsewhere, Patrick repeats, almost as a personal mantra, a quotation told to him by Sergi, a Russian volunteer with whom he had served in Spain:

'Je voudrais, et ce sera le dernier et le plus ardent de mes souhaits, je voudrais que le dernier des rois fut etrangle avec les boyaux du dernier pretre'.[123]

Patrick considers that this would give the world a chance.

---

[123] 'I should like to see, and this will be the last and the most ardent of my desires, I should like to see the last king strangled with the guts of the last priest.'

POSTSCRIPT

None are forgotten. In May 1999 the author was paying another visit to the Airborne Cemetery at Oosterbeek, and at the headstone of Private Ernest Lynas was a wreath that had been laid the previous day by the pupils of Millington Primary School, County Armagh.

While walking back into the village he was stopped by an elderly couple carrying fresh flowers. They asked for directions to the Airborne Cemetery, and the question was asked in an Irish accent.

APPENDIX 1

ROLL OF IRISHMEN WHO SERVED IN OR WITH THE 1ST AIRBORNE DIVISION 1942-45

This roll has been compiled from various sources. These include local newspaper reports, *Pegasus* Magazine, the Commonwealth War Graves Commission Cemetery & Memorial Registers, the Arnhem Roll of Honour by Jan Hey, and interviews with veterans of the Division. The Airborne Forces Museum, Aldershot, and the Airborne Museum at Oosterbeek have been invaluable in adding to and correcting this roll. The information listed here and in the main text is not all that is available, but is all that is felt to be relevant to this book. Certain information such as full home

The main entrance to the Airborne Cemetery at Oosterbeek. The design and architecture is a familiar sight when visiting Commonwealth War Graves Commission cemeteries anywhere in the world. *David Orr*

addresses, both present and wartime, and in some cases details of death are not given for obvious reasons.

It has been noted that many of those taken prisoner at Arnhem, while listed as prisoners, have no camp or POW details. This has been attributed to the conditions that existed in the final months of the war.

Readers will also note that in some instances members of the Royal Irish and Royal Inniskilling Fusiliers seem to share similar numbers. From 1922 to 1937 there existed a joint corps of the Royal Inniskilling Fusiliers and Royal Irish Fusiliers, with their Depot being in the town of Omagh, County Tyrone. This joint corps came about as a result of the proposed disbandment of the Royal Irish Fusiliers in 1922, together with the five other southern Irish Regiments. This was despite their Depot being in Armagh and approximately 85 per cent of their recruits coming from the local area. However, due to the friendship that existed between the colonels of the 'Faughs' and 'Skins' and the influence exerted by many others, the 'Faughs' survived when the Royal Inniskilling Fusiliers voluntarily reduced to one Battalion, and the two Regiments amalgamated as a joint corps.

One of those who worked hard on behalf of the 'Faughs' was the CIGS, Field Marshal Sir Henry Wilson, himself an Irishman, and murdered by the IRA on the doorstep of his London home in 1922. Training for the joint corps was carried out at Omagh. In many cases soldiers joined one regiment and were given army numbers identifiable to that regiment, eg 704... for Royal Irish Fusiliers, but on completing their training found themselves transferred to the Royal Inniskilling Fusiliers, whose numbers were 697.... From 1922 army numbers had been issued on an individual basis, not regimental, and as a result 'Faughs' and 'Skins' quite often shared similar numbers.

It must also be pointed out that this list is incomplete. It is doubtful if there will ever be a 'definitive' list of all the Irishmen who served in the 1st Airborne Division. The fact that some men served under assumed names is just the beginning of the problem of carrying out research after so many years. There have also been attempts in the past to draw up a complete list of all the men who took part in Operation 'Market Garden'. With the exception of the dead, it has again been impossible to do so. The cemetery references, eg 9.C.5, indicate Plot, Row and Grave number in the respective cemetery.

The Airborne Memorial at the village of Heelsum, photographed in 1945 and 2001. The arch is constructed of drop-canisters and the centrepiece is an Airborne 6-pounder anti-tank gun. *Border & King's Own Royal Border Regiment Museum*

Name: Adamson, Hugh
Rank: Private
No: 7019397
Unit: 2nd Parachute Battalion
Hugh Adamson came from Banbridge, County Down. He originally enlisted in the Royal Ulster Rifles before transferring to Airborne Forces. He was posted to the 2nd Parachute Battalion and saw service in North Africa, Sicily and at Arnhem, being wounded on all three occasions. He became a prisoner of war after Arnhem, but the POW register holds no camp details. He is now living in America and has not been shot since. His father served in both World Wars. A good friend of Billy Magill and Bill Saunders, he returned to Holland for the 50th Anniversary of the battle in 1994.

Name: Adamson, Stanley
Rank: Captain
No: 327110
Unit: 9th (Airborne) Squadron Royal Engineers
Stanley Adamson came from Belfast, the son of Henry and Margaret Adamson. He served as a Sergeant with 591 (Antrim) Parachute Squadron RE on D-Day and later in the campaign in France. He was commissioned in late 1944 and was posted as a Second Lieutenant to the 9th, then serving in Norway. When the 9th was transferred to the Sixth Airborne Division and sent to Palestine, Stanley Adamson went with them as a Captain. On the morning of Monday 18 November 1946, while inspecting a stretch of railway line, he was killed by a terrorist land mine; he was 27 years old. Buried in Ramleh War Cemetery, Israel, 9.C.5.

Name: Addley, T.
Rank: Unknown
No: Unknown
Unit: 16 Parachute Field Ambulance RAMC
From Belfast, County Antrim, he served in North Africa with the 1st Parachute Brigade in 1942. His name was mentioned in conversation with other Airborne veterans, but according to information received from Niall Cherry, author of *Red Berets and Red Crosses*, he may only have lived in Belfast. This could have been the result of marrying a local girl, not an uncommon occurrence and one that continues to this day. Reported as being taken prisoner after Arnhem, he is not listed in POW records, which is unusual as most medical orderlies remained with the wounded.

Name: Allen, Thomas W.
Rank: Lance-Corporal
No: 7013043
Unit: 11th Parachute Battalion
Born in Belfast, County Antrim, on 1 July 1914, he was the eldest of three children. After service with the 2nd Battalion Royal Irish Fusiliers on Malta, he transferred to the 1st Airborne Division in July 1943. Wounded at Arnhem on Wednesday 20 September, he was taken prisoner of war and sent to Stalag XIB. Repatriated on 21 April 1945. A sister and two brothers also served, one of whom was killed at Dunkirk in 1940. Thomas Allen died on 10 June 1991.

Name: Armstrong, Frederick (known as Fred)
Rank: Private
No: 6977461
Unit: 1st Parachute Battalion
An ex-Royal Inniskilling Fusilier, he was the son of Mr and Mrs J. Armstrong of Benburb Street, Belfast. He transferred to Airborne Forces and served in North Africa and Sicily, where he was batman to Lt-Colonel 'Jock' Pearson, who commanded the Battalion at that time. At Arnhem he again acted as batman, on this occasion to Major J. C. Bune, 2ic of the Battalion, who was killed in action on 18 September 1944. Armstrong was taken prisoner at the end of the battle and sent to Stalag XIB at Fallingbostel, POW number 117365. His brother John was killed in action while serving with the Royal Ulster Rifles (London Irish Rifles) in February 1945, in Italy.

Name: Armstrong, Thomas G.
Rank: Private
No: 6998464
Unit: 11th Parachute Battalion
An ex-Royal Irish Fusilier from Owenbeg, Dungiven, County Londonderry, he had served with elements of the 11th Parachute Battalion on Kos. Bill Kerr, also of the 11th Battalion, mentioned serving with this man at Arnhem, so possibly he was in 'A' Company or the Machine-Gun Platoon. He was taken prisoner after Arnhem and sent to Camp IVB at Muhlberg, POW number 075436. Conversation with veterans at various PRA dinners suggested that he may have escaped, but there is no confirmation of this.

Name: Atkinson, J. R.
Rank: Corporal
No: 555346
Unit: Royal Army Medical Corps
From Belfast, County Antrim, he is seen in a newspaper photograph of returning prisoners of war taken at York Street railway station on 21 April 1945. Also in the photograph are several Arnhem prisoners. He is listed in the POW register as being at Camp IIB, Fallingbostel, POW number 118650. Corporal Atkinson has the Pegasus badge on his battledress tunic, but as yet no information is available on his unit. He is listed in *Red Berets and Red Crosses* by Niall Cherry, but again no unit is listed.

Name: Bankhead, Henry James
Rank: Corporal
No: 4614108
Unit: 156 Parachute Battalion
Born in Ballymena, County Antrim, he was a former member of the Duke of Wellington's Regiment. Henry Bankhead transferred from the Regiment's 2nd Battalion to Airborne Forces in December 1941 and served in 'C' Company of the 156 Battalion, seeing action in Italy. Taken prisoner after Arnhem, where he was Major Powell's signaller, he was sent to Camp XIIA, Limburg, SD Lahn, POW number 075329. Demobbed in June 1946. He is the author of *Salute to the Steadfast*, a personal history of the 151/156 Parachute Battalion.

Name: Barnett, Bryan Anderson
Rank: Sergeant
No: Unknown
Unit: Glider Pilot Regiment
He entered Queen's University, Belfast, in 1942, on a War Office Pre Entry Course. Originally he served with the Royal Engineers before transferring to the Glider Pilot Regiment. He is not listed in the prisoner of war records, and is believed to have served in all theatres until the end of the war.

Name: Barnett, F.
Rank: Sergeant
No: Unknown
Unit: No. 6 Section Airborne Provost Company
From Ireland, he was part of the Provost Company's Seaborne Tail during 'Market Garden'.

Name: Barnwall, Desmond Patrick
Rank: Sergeant
No: 408765
Unit: 1st Parachute Battalion
The son of Major John and Jannie Barnwall of Campile, County Wexford, he enlisted in the Monmouthshire Regiment on the outbreak of war. He transferred to Airborne Forces and served in North Africa with the 1st Parachute Battalion. Sergeant Barnwall was killed during the drop at Mateur on 16 November 1942, as the result of a parachuting accident; he was 25 years old. He is buried in Medjez-el-Bab War Cemetery, 4.D.12.

Name: Barrett, Francis
Rank: Sergeant
No: Unknown
Unit: No. 6 Section Airborne Provost Company
Believed to have come from Collon, Drogheda, County Louth, he was reported as having been taken prisoner after Arnhem, but is not listed in the POW records.

Name: Bateman, Jack
Rank: Sergeant
No: Unknown
Unit: 10th Parachute Battalion
A native of County Down, he served at Arnhem and escaped across the Rhine at the end of the battle. He was one of those selected to take part in the film *Theirs Is The Glory*. He is believed to have served with the 1st Parachute Battalion after the war.

Name: Beare, Kenneth Robert
Rank: Lance-Sergeant
No: 7022780
Unit: 4th Parachute Battalion
From County Londonderry, he entered Queen's University, Belfast, in 1941 to study Science and Medicine. He enlisted in the Royal Ulster Rifles on 23 February 1942, and transferred to the 1st Airborne Division in February 1943, serving with them in North Africa. He was later posted to the 4th Battalion, Independent Brigade, and served in 'C' Company in Italy, where he was wounded in December 1943. He took part in Operation 'Anvil' in August 1944, received a Mention-in-Despatches for his actions in Italy dated 29 November 1945, and served in India from February 1945 to July 1946.

Name: Bell, Cecil
Rank: Private
No: 7021431
Unit: 2nd Parachute Battalion
An ex-Royal Ulster Rifleman from Belfast, County Antrim, he was the son of Mr and Mrs Alexander Bell of Pitt Street, Belfast. Three of his brothers also saw service, James in the Royal Navy, and Thomas and Alexander in the Army, both of whom were discharged due to wounds received in action. Private Bell served in the 2nd Parachute Battalion at Arnhem. On 20 October 1944 Dr S. Rodgers, local Unionist candidate for Pottinger Ward, Belfast, presented Cecil Bell with a wallet of notes on behalf of the local people after his return from prison camp, stated in the newspaper report to have been Stalag II, although no such camp is listed in the POW records. It is possible he was in Stalag XIB, Fallingbostel, but how he was able to return home within one month of being captured remains to be explained.

Private Cecil Bell

Name: Bell, R. F. 'Frank'
Rank: Lance-Sergeant
No: 6984171
Unit: 1st Parachute Battalion
From Lisburn, County Antrim, he may have served in either the Royal Irish Fusiliers or Inniskillings; he is listed in various newspaper reports as being in both regiments (see the introduction to the nominal roll). He was taken prisoner after Arnhem and sent to Rez Laz Lingen. After the war he was a staunch member of the Plymouth Brethren.

Name: Bell, Robert
Rank: Private
No: Unknown
Unit: Unknown
Well known in Northern Ireland boxing circles before the war, Private Bell did a demonstration parachute jump for the King in June 1941 at an unknown location. Prior to Airborne Forces he served with the British Expeditionary Force in France, being successfully evacuated from the beach-head at Dunkirk. This information is taken from a well-worn and undated, but probably contemporary, newspaper cutting.

Name: Bermingham, John
Rank: Sergeant
No: 7012746
Unit: 1st Parachute Battalion
The son of Catherine Bermingham from Dublin, he had been a pre-war soldier in the Royal Ulster Rifles, serving in India (see Hughes, Victor). He served in the ranks of the 1st Parachute Battalion in North Africa and Sicily, and was killed in action at Arnhem on 19 September while serving in 'T' Company. he is buried in the Airborne Cemetery at Oosterbeek, 20.A.18.

Name: Black, Boyde Alexander
Rank: Private
No: 7013844
Unit: 2nd Parachute Battalion
Following in the footsteps of his father (who had been an 'Old Contemptible' of 1914), Boyde travelled from his home in Ballymena, County Antrim, and enlisted in the Royal Ulster Rifles on his 18th birthday in June 1938. In 1939 his battalion was posted to Palestine and from there to the North West Frontier in India. This was followed by a mini world tour of Gibraltar, Malta, Sierra Leone and Durban, then a return to England and a camp on the Isle of Wight. In 1940 he transferred to the 1st (Airborne) Battalion of the Ulster Rifles. From there he again transferred, this time to the 2nd Parachute Battalion. He was with the 2nd Battalion on Operation 'Husky' on 13 July 1943, being wounded in action at Primasole Bridge, where he was taken prisoner. He was sent to Stalag VIIIB, Upper Silesia, Poland, and Stalag 344, Lamsdorf, Germany.

Due to his wounds he was repatriated to Sweden in September 1944, before eventually returning to England. In January 1945 he married Beatrice Scullion, the sister of Tommy of the 21st Independent Parachute Company and a veteran of Arnhem. Boyde had great respect for the Red Cross and often stated that without the Red Cross parcels received while in prison camp things would have been so much worse. From 1962 he worked as a civilian security guard at St Patrick's Barracks in Ballymena, County Antrim. He was to stay there for some 23 years before retiring in May 1985. At the time of his retirement the Colonel of the Regiment was his old platoon commander of 1939!

Name: Black, James A.
Rank: Sergeant
No: 4614109
Unit: 156 Parachute Battalion
From Belfast, he enlisted in the Duke of Wellington's Regiment prior to transferring to the 1st Airborne Division. He served in 'C' Company of the 156 Parachute Battalion at Arnhem, was taken prisoner after the battle, and sent to Camp XIB, Fallingbostel, POW number 147376.

Name: Blake, C. A. H. B.
Rank: Major
No: Unknown
Unit: 1st Air-Landing Brigade Headquarters
Born in County Wicklow, 'Tony' Blake attended Sandhurst and joined the Royal Ulster Rifles in 1931. The majority of his pre-war years were spent with the 1st Battalion in Egypt, Hong Kong, Shanghai and India. In 1938 he went to Russia on a course, and during the German attack on Poland was completing his studies in Warsaw. He escaped and after many adventures made his way to Rumania. During the war he spent little time with his Regiment, but held many important Staff appointments. He was an instructor at OCTU, and served as an Intelligence Officer at the War Office and in the Middle East. He also served in the Russian Liaison Group, and was attached for a time to the Polish Brigade. During 'Market Garden' he served as Brigade Major with the 1st Air-Landing HQ and was one of those to escape across the river at the end of the battle, being awarded the Distinguished Service Cross for his actions during the operation. After Arnhem he moved to the Far East and by the end of the war was 2i/c of the 1st Battalion, Royal Inniskilling Fusiliers. In 1948-49 he became PA to General Sir James Steele during his tour as C-in-C and High Commissioner of Austria, but was killed in action in Korea on the night of 3/4 January 1951 while in temporary command of the 1st Battalion, Royal Ulster Rifles. At the time of his death he had gone forward to the scene of battle where two companies of the Battalion were surrounded. He was last seen directing the remaining troops and transport out of the battle area.

Name: Bowden, James H.
Rank: Lance-Corporal
No: Unknown
Unit: No 3 Troop 591 (Antrim) Parachute Squadron RE
Bowden first enlisted in the Antrim Fortress Company RE (TA), but transferred to Airborne Forces and served in the 591 Parachute Squadron on D-Day and on Operation 'Varsity', the crossing of the Rhine in March 1945. When elements of the 1st Airborne Division were sent to Norway in May 1945, 591 Parachute Squadron went with them.

Name: Boyd, James Frederick
Rank: Staff-Sergeant
No: 7013328
Unit: Glider Pilot Regiment
An ex-Royal Ulster Rifleman, he was the son of Jennie Boyd of Portstewart, County Londonderry. He served at Arnhem as Squadron Quartermaster in 'B' Squadron, one of those who 'stowed away' on 17 September. Killed in action on 23rd September 1944, he was first buried some 150 yards south of the Hotel Tafelberg, but is now in the Airborne Cemetery at Oosterbeek, 3.D.11.

Name: Brackstone, Charles Thomas
Rank: Sergeant
No: 2083005
Unit: Glider Pilot Regiment
Son of Rupert and Lily Brackstone of Dundonald, County Down, and husband of Winifred Ethine, he flew to Arnhem as a co-pilot to Staff-Sergeant Shaw in glider number CN319, of 'C' Squadron. The tug aircraft was a Stirling from 644 Squadron flown by Pilot Officer McConville. Charles Brackstone was killed in action at Arnhem on 17 September 1944, aged 23 years, and is buried in the Airborne Cemetery, Oosterbeek, 3.C.12

Name: Breen, Tom 'Paddy'
Rank: Lance-Corporal
No: 1917769
Unit: 1st Airborne Provost Company, Corps of Military Police
From Eire, an ex-Royal Engineer, he had seen previous service in Iceland, North Africa, Sicily and Italy. At Arnhem he served in the Divisional Headquarter Detail and was wounded before being taken prisoner after the battle. No POW camp details are listed.

ANTRIM (FORTRESS) Coy, R.E.(T.A.)

The Antrim Fortress Company, Royal Engineers (TA), attending their annual camp at Grey Point Fort, County Down, in 1938. Tenth from the left on the second row from the rear is Jim Bowden, who would serve as a Lance-Corporal in the 591 (Antrim) Parachute Squadron RE, when it was attached to the 1st Airborne Division in Norway. *J. Bowden*

Name: Briody, Michael
Rank: Regimental Sergeant Major (WO1)
No: 2727183
Unit: Glider Pilot Regiment
Born in County Kilkenny, he served in the Norwegian campaign with the Irish Guards, and in North Africa, Sicily, Italy and Arnhem with the Glider Pilot Regiment. He is not listed in POW records and is presumed to have escaped across the Rhine. He was awarded the Dutch Bronze Lion for his actions at Arnhem. Commissioned in the RASC, after the war he was awarded the MBE – see main text. He died on 6 April 1991, aged 80 years.

Name: Browne, Patrick
Rank: Private
No: 1711838
Unit: 7th Battalion King's Own Scottish Borderers
From Kilnamack, Clonmel, County Tipperary, he originally served in the Royal Artillery, and was taken prisoner of war after Arnhem. At the time of writing Pat is over 80 years old and the above information came from his brother, who obviously knows few details of Pat's war service. According to prisoner-of-war records, the only P. Browne captured at Arnhem was serving with the King's Own Scottish Borderers. No POW camp is listed, which is again relevant for someone who was at Arnhem.

Lieutenant Michael Briody MBE in 1945 after being commissioned; he wears the medal ribbons of the MBE, 1939-45 Star, Italy Star, France and Germany Star, Defence Medal and the Dutch Bronze Lion. After the war he continued to serve in the Army and transferred first to the Royal Army Service Corps and later to the Army Pay Corps. He was posted to the Airborne Forces Depot as Paymaster, where he raised and trained the Depot shooting team, taking them to Bisley on many occasions. He died in April 1991.

Name: Bryans, 'Paddy'
Rank: Sergeant
No: Unknown
Unit: Glider Pilot Regiment
This Irishman served with Wilfred Tallentire in the Glider Pilot Regiment, but is believed not to have returned to Ireland after the war.

Name: Buchanan, Alan Alexander
Rank: Captain/Reverend
No: 218713
Unit: 2nd Battalion South Staffordshire Regiment
From County Tyrone, he served as Padre to the South Staffords, having seen previous service in Sicily before 'Market Garden'. He was taken prisoner after Arnhem and sent to Stalag XIB, Fallingbostel. He received a Mention-in-Despatches for 'Market Garden', and after the war he was Archbishop of Dublin. A memorial window was unveiled to him at Clogher Cathedral on 4 June 2000.

Name: Burke, Joseph
Rank: Private
No: 5781130
Unit: 10th Parachute Battalion
Formally with the Royal Norfolk Regiment, he was the foster son of James Bergin, from Cabra, County Dublin. He was killed in action at Arnhem on 18 September 1944, one of approximately 19 deaths suffered by the Battalion that day. He has no known grave, but is commemorated on the Groesbeek Memorial, panel 9.

Name: Butler, John Joseph
Rank: Private
No: 6979090
Unit: 156 Parachute Battalion
'JJ' Butler came from Belfast and enlisted in the Royal Inniskilling Fusiliers in 1940. He transferred to Airborne Forces and was posted to the 156 Battalion. (He was reported as having been wounded during the action on Sicily, but the 156 Battalion did not serve there.) Again wounded at Arnhem, he was taken prisoner and sent to Stalag IVF, Hartmansdorf, Chemnitz, POW number 267855. He was a founder-member of the Northern Ireland Branch of the Parachute Regimental Association, the inaugural meeting of which was held in a small room above the Lifeboat Bar in Belfast in the early 1950s.

Name: Cameron, Alan
Rank: Unknown
No: Unknown
Unit: 4th Parachute Brigade Headquarters
He was from Ireland, but there are no further details. (An Alan Cameron is listed as a deserter from the Irish Defence Force; his date of birth, 1921, would be right for a member of the 1st Airborne Division at Arnhem.)

Name: Cameron, James
Rank: Private
No: 6982743
Unit: 21st Independent Parachute Company
From Carrickfergus, County Antrim, he was an ex-Young Soldier in the Royal Inniskilling Fusiliers, and one of the original members of the 21st. He served in North Africa

The Battalion Headquarters and Signal Section of the 2nd Battalion South Staffords in 1943. Padre Alan Buchanan can be seen in the front row, seventh from the left. *Alex Junier*

Gale & Polden Ltd., Aldershot & London.

and Italy, and died of wounds received at Arnhem on 26 September 1944 while serving in No 1 Platoon. He is buried in the Airborne Cemetery at Oosterbeek, 18.C.4.

Name: Campbell, Jack
Rank: Sergeant
No: 875151
Unit: 591 (Antrim) Parachute Squadron RE
He enlisted in the Antrim Fortress Company RE (TA) in 1937, and transferred to 591 Squadron in April 1943. He served with the 6th Airborne Division in Normandy, and the 1st Airborne Division in Norway in 1945.

Name: Carter, Gerald S.
Rank: Lieutenant
No: Unknown
Unit: 1st Air-Landing Light Regiment, Royal Artillery
From Castlerock, County Londonderry, he served with the Regiment in Italy, but did not go to Arnhem.

Name: Carter, Robert
Rank: Private
No: Unknown
Unit: Unknown
A photograph from his nephew is inscribed 'Uncle Bob at Arnhem'. The photograph shows a man with wings on his beret, so he probably belonged to one of the parachute battalions. An R. C. Carter, No 5725548, is listed in the POW records, but no camp details are given, which again would fit in with someone taken prisoner at Arnhem, but it is impossible to be certain. The regimental number identifies the holder as ex-Dorset Regiment, a fact that cannot be confirmed by the family.

Name: Cassidy, James Gerard
Rank: Captain
No: 114828
Unit: 16 Parachute Field Ambulance RAMC
He was the son of James and Ellen Cassidy of Rathfriland, County Down, and was killed in action on 10 March 1943 while attached to the 1st Parachute Brigade in North Africa. On the morning of 5 February 1943, Captain Cassidy, together with 20 other volunteers, went up on to Djebel Mansour to collect those wounded left behind when the 1st Parachute Battalion withdrew to Tamera. This search lasted from early morning until nightfall, with all wounded being recovered. On Wednesday 10 March the Brigade area was subjected to an intense German artillery bombardment and Captain Cassidy was killed while he treated a wounded soldier who was lying in the open. He was Mentioned-in-Despatches for this action, the award being dated 23rd September 1943. He is buried in Tabarka Ras Rajel War Cemetery, Tunisia, 3.C.7.

'A plain and simple testimonial' – the War Memorial in the village of Rathfriland, County Down, showing the names of eight men who died in the 1939-45 war. The first is that of Captain James Gerard Cassidy, RAMC, killed in action aged 28 in Tunisia while attached to the 1st Parachute Brigade. There are 72 names for those killed in the Great War. *David Orr*

'Uncle Bob at Arnhem' – so reads the caption on this photograph of Private Robert Carter from Dublin. The ground would appear to be incorrect for Holland, being much too stony. It was more likely taken in North Africa, Sicily or possibly 'Somewhere in England'. Private Carter's Airborne unit is unknown. *Tom Carter*

Name: Cassidy, Samuel Patton
Rank: Private
No: 14207764
Unit: 7th Battalion King's Own Scottish Borderers
From Belfast, Northern Ireland, husband of Mary, he served at Arnhem in the Anti-Tank Platoon of Support Company. There is confusion over his date of death – he was killed in action at Arnhem on either 17 or 25 September 1944. He has no known grave and is commemorated on the Groesbeek Memorial, panel 4.

Name: Catterson, R. J.
Rank: Gunner
No: 961900
Unit: 1st Air-Landing Light Regiment, Royal Artillery
From Coleraine, County Londonderry, he was reported to have served at Arnhem. Gunner Catterson is not listed in POW records, so may have escaped across the Rhine after the battle.

Name: Caves, John. J.
Rank: Sergeant
No: 7020145
Unit: Glider Pilot Regiment
An ex-Royal Ulster Rifleman, he was taken prisoner at Arnhem while serving with 'B' Squadron. He died from illness on 31 March 1945 while a prisoner of war in Camp XIB, Fallingbostel. He is buried in Berlin War Cemetery, 10.A.14 (not listed on the CWGC website).

Name: Chapman, David
Rank: Private
No: 7013441
Unit: 1st Air-Landing Brigade
An ex-Royal Ulster Rifleman from Lisburn, County Antrim, he was listed as missing in action, then as a prisoner of war after Arnhem, being sent to Camp 4G, Oschatz, POW number 84782. According to information received from Victor Hughes, ex-3rd Battalion, he may have served in the 1st Parachute Battalion.

Name: Clarke, Anthony Leslie
Rank: Corporal
No: 1086655
Unit: 1st Parachute Battalion
Originally from Northern Ireland, he transferred from the Royal Artillery and was killed in action while serving in 'T' Company at Arnhem on 24 September 1944, age 22 years. He is buried in the Airborne Cemetery at Oosterbeek, 1.B.14.

Private David Chapman

Name: Cockings, E. G. J.
Rank: Sergeant
No: 845368
Unit: 21st Independent Parachute Company
A volunteer from Eire, he transferred from the Royal Horse Artillery to Airborne Forces. He served in Italy and was taken prisoner of war after Arnhem and sent to Camp IIB, Fallingbostel, POW number 118241.

Name: Coghlan, Edward
Rank: Private
No: 2933459
Unit: 1st Parachute Battalion
The son of Richard and Elizabeth Coghlan, who resided at Liverpool in 1944, Private Coghlan had originally enlisted in the Cameron Highlanders. He was killed in action at Arnhem on 18 September when the Battalion was fighting around the area of the St Elizabeth Hospital, and he was first buried nearby, but is now in the Airborne Cemetery at Oosterbeek, 20.A.18.

Name: Collins, Francis
Rank: Lance-Corporal
No: 7021134
Unit: 2nd Parachute Brigade Headquarters
From Glasnevin, County Dublin, he was the son of Mary Collins. Lance-Corporal Collins died on Thursday 20 January 1944 in Italy, having originally served with the 1st Airborne Division in North Africa. He is buried in Sangro River War Cemetery, XI.A.23.

Name: Collins, Kevin
Rank: Private
No: 5630527
Unit: 3rd Parachute Battalion
From Chapelzoid, Dublin, he was the son of Charles and Briget Collins. A former member of the Devonshire Regiment, he was killed at Arnhem between 18 and 25

September 1944. He is buried in the Airborne Cemetery at Oosterbeek, 5.D.15.

Name: Conboy, Martin Francis
Rank: Private
No: 14407718
Unit: 21st Independent Parachute Company
From Cabra, County Dublin, Eire, the son of Patrick Joseph and Julia (née Folan), he was killed in a swimming accident on 15 July 1943 and interred in Enfidaville War Cemetery, Tunisia, II. E.18.

Name: Connell, Michael Burke 'Crow'
Rank: Lieutenant
No: 95534
Unit: Glider Pilot Regiment
An ex-Royal Irish Fusilier, he was killed in action on 10 July 1943 during the attack on Sicily. 'Crow' Connell was born in India of Irish parents and lived in Surrey before the war. Commissioned into the Royal Irish Fusiliers on 1 September 1939, he was promoted to Lieutenant on 1 January 1941. He performed well with his Battalion during the fighting in France in 1940, and was successfully evacuated from Dunkirk. He came down in the sea during the attack on Sicily and has no known grave, but is commemorated on the Cassino Memorial, panel 11. During the Sicily operation many men were drowned when their gliders came down in the sea, all of whom are commemorated on the Cassino Memorial.

Name: Conway, E. M.
Rank: Private
No: 7264685
Unit: Royal Army Medical Corps attached to 156 Battalion
From County Dublin, Eire, brother of John Joseph, he served as a medic attached to the 156 Parachute Battalion. He was taken prisoner after the battle and sent to Camp IIB, Hammerstein, POW number 118398.

Name: Conway, John Joseph
Rank: Lance-Corporal
No: 7043131
Unit: 156 Parachute Battalion
The brother of E. M. Conway, he served in 'C' Company. Taken prisoner after Arnhem, he was sent to Camp IIB, Hammerstein, POW number 117320.

Name: Cooney, M.
Rank: Gunner
No: 3714297
Unit: 1st Air-Landing Light Regiment, Royal Artillery
From Dublin, he is believed to have served at Arnhem. He is not listed in POW records so may have escaped across the Rhine at the end of the battle.

Name: Cooney, W.
Rank: Private
No: 7606009
Unit: 2nd Parachute Battalion
From Ireland, he served in the Royal Army Ordnance Corps before transferring to Airborne Forces. He fought with distinction alongside the Polish Brigade at Driel, but was captured and sent to Camp 334, Lamsdorf, POW number 27852.

Name: Cooper, Astley John AFC
Rank: Major
No: 52601
Unit: No 1 Wing Glider Pilot Regiment
From Dundrum, County Tipperary, the son of Major A. S. and Evelyn E. Cooper, he was commissioned into the Cheshire Regiment, but transferred to the Glider Pilot Regiment and was killed in action on 10 July 1943 while attempting to land his glider during the invasion of Sicily. He was one of the instigators of long-distance glider flying and had survived at least one crash-landing in the sea. He is buried in Catania War Cemetery, II.J.22.

Name: Corbett, David
Rank: Lieutenant
No: Unknown
Unit: 2nd Household Cavalry
From County Fermanagh, he led a unit of armoured cars into Driel. He later joined the Royal Ulster Constabulary.

Name: Cousens, H. S.
Rank: Major
No: 63589
Unit: 1st Battalion Border Regiment
He was commissioned into the Royal Inniskilling Fusiliers as a 2nd Lieutenant on 30 August 1937, being promoted to Lieutenant in 1939. By October 1940 he was a Captain serving as a Temporary Major with the 2nd Battalion. For operation 'Market Garden' he served as 2ic of the 1st Battalion, Border Regiment, and escaped across the Rhine after the battle.

Name: Cowan, 'Curley'
Rank: Private
No: Unknown
Unit: 21st Independent Parachute Company
He served with the Royal Inniskilling Fusiliers in India, then transferred to Airborne Forces, possibly serving in the 156 Battalion for a time. He served with the 21st Independent until Norway.

Name: Cox, 'Mick'
Rank: Lance-Corporal
No: 7690750
Unit: 1st Airborne Provost Company, No 1 Section
From Dublin, he was at Arnhem Police Station when it was captured. He is not listed in POW records under M, but may be one of three other CMP listed. The author believes that in this case 'Mick' is not short for Michael, but is a nickname on a par with 'Paddy'.

Name: Craigie, D. J.
Rank: Captain
No: Unknown
Unit: 1st Air-Landing Light Regiment, Royal Artillery
From Finglass, County Dublin, he served with the Regiment in Italy, but is not listed as having served at Arnhem.

Name: Crandles, Austin
Rank: Private
No: 14340452
Unit: 2nd Battalion South Staffordshire Regiment
From Carrickfergus, County Antrim, he enlisted at the age of 19 years and served in Sicily, where he was reputed to be the third man out of his glider. A prisoner of war after Arnhem, he was sent to Stalag IVB, Muhlberg, POW No 89261. His two brothers also served – Billy in the Royal Air Force as a Corporal, and Jim as a QMS in the REME.

Private Austin Crandles

Name: Crothers, R.
Rank: Gunner
No: 14413830
Unit: 1st Air-Landing Light Regiment, Royal Artillery
From Lisburn, County Antrim, he is reported to have served at Arnhem, but no POW details are listed, so he may have escaped across the Rhine after the battle.

Name: Cunningham, George
Rank: Private
No: Unknown
Unit: 21st Independent Parachute Company
From Belfast, County Antrim, he served with Danny Gillespie throughout his time in the Company. He escaped across the Rhine after Arnhem.

Name: Currie, E. G.
Rank: Private
No: 6984939
Unit: Unknown
From Dungannon, County Tyrone, he had previously served with the Royal Inniskilling Fusiliers before transferring to Airborne Forces. He was reported as a returning prisoner of war from Arnhem in the local press in an un-dated cutting, having been held in Camp XIIA, Limburg, SD Lahn, POW number 90370.

Name: Daly, John Joseph
Rank: Sergeant
No: 6210701
Unit: 1st Air-Landing Light Regiment, Royal Artillery
From County Waterford, he served at Arnhem with 'B' Troop, No 1 Battery, and gave covering fire to Major Robert Cain VC when he attacked enemy tanks at Arnhem. For this action he was awarded the Distinguished Conduct Medal, and later returned to Arnhem to take part in the film *Theirs Is The Glory*.

Name: Davidson, Charles McLain
Rank: Private
No: 7048033
Unit: 1st Parachute Battalion
From Saintfield, County Down, he was the son of John Davidson, a sack merchant. He had previously served in the Royal Irish Fusiliers before transferring to Airborne Forces. Taken prisoner at Arnhem while serving in 'R' Company, he was sent to Stalag XIB, Fallingbostel. His father served in both World Wars and his brother Johnny served in the Durham Light Infantry during the Second.

'The war stole our youth and nobody cares.' The opinion of Private Charles McLain Davidson.

Name: Davies, Eric John MC
Rank: Lieutenant
No: 207782
Unit: 2nd Battalion South Staffordshire Regiment
From Arklow, County Wicklow, he was captured when his glider crashed in the sea during the invasion of Sicily. He escaped from a German POW camp in September 1943 and brought back information valuable to the Allies, for which he was awarded the Military Cross. He may also have served at Arnhem as commander of No 10 Platoon, 'T' Company, 1st Parachute Battalion.

Name: De Burgh, P. P. R.
Rank: Lieutenant
No: 273178
Unit: Headquarters, Royal Artillery
The De Burgh name is well known in Irish history; in the 19th century the family held estates of some 56,000 acres in East Galway. 'Paddy' De Burg served on operation 'Market Garden' as a Staff Lieutenant in the Headquarters of the Royal Artillery. On Monday 26 September, the last day that the 1st Airborne Division would spend in the 'cauldron', Lieutenant De Burg and Major Philip Tower spent a long, wearing 6 hours preparing an artillery plan to cover the withdrawal of the Division across the Rhine. For his actions at Arnhem 'Paddy' De Burg was awarded a Mention-in-Despatches.

Name: Deighton, Thomas Robinson
Rank: Staff-Sergeant
No: 3597017
Unit: 1st Battalion Border Regiment
From Belfast, County Antrim, he was taken prisoner at Arnhem while serving in 24 (Mortar) Platoon of Support Company and sent to Stalag VB, POW No 18676.

Name: Dempsey, Edward D.
Rank: Private
No: 14403795
Unit: 1st Battalion Border Regiment
From Dublin, he was taken prisoner at Arnhem and sent to Stalag XIB, POW No 118011.

Name: Dennison, Mervyn William MC
Rank: Major
No: 100018
Unit: 3rd Parachute Battalion
Born in County Cork, he was commissioned into the Royal Ulster Rifles, then transferred to Airborne Forces and served in North Africa, Sicily and Italy with the 1st Battalion. He was wounded in action at Arnhem while commanding 'A' Company, 3rd Battalion. Taken prisoner, he was sent to Camp 09A/H, Spangenburg, Bel Kassel, from where he escaped. He was awarded the Military Cross for his actions at Arnhem.

Name: Devlin, Brian
Rank: Captain
No: 252477
Unit: 181 Air-Landing Field Ambulance RAMC
A former pupil of Stoneyhurst College, Brian Devlin was the son of Dr F. J. Devlin of Liverpool. Born in Ireland in 1919, he was at Stoneyhurst from 1932 to 1935. Commissioned into the Royal Army Medical Corps, he served in North Africa and Italy prior to Arnhem. For 'Market Garden' he was attached to the 7th Battalion, King's Own Scottish Borderers. He served with the KOSB in Norway, ended his career with the rank of Lieutenant Colonel and was awarded the OBE.

Name: Devlin, William James Patrick
Rank: Private
No: 2931426
Unit: 1st Parachute Battalion
Born in Hong Kong, the son of an Irish soldier, he first enlisted in the Cameron Highlanders. He was killed in action at Arnhem on 20 September 1944 while serving in 9 Platoon, 'T' Company, and was buried in the Airborne Cemetery at Oosterbeek, 2.A.10. He was a cousin of 'Paddy' Devlin, 1st Battalion Royal Ulster Rifles, 6th Airborne Division.

Name: Diffin, Norman
Rank: Private
No: 3130880
Unit: 156 Parachute Battalion
From County Armagh, he first enlisted in the Royal Highland Fusiliers. He was seriously wounded while still on board his Dakota on the run-in to the drop zone at Arnhem, and was repatriated. His brother was killed while held as a prisoner of war by the Japanese.

Name: Dillon, Joseph Francis
Rank: Private
No: 4409524
Unit: 2nd Parachute Battalion
The son of Denis and Mary Dillon, of Dublin, he was a former member of the Royal Sussex Regiment. He transferred to Airborne Forces and took part in Operation 'Fustian', the paratrooper landings in Sicily on 14 July 1943. He was killed during the fighting around the hills known as 'Johnny One' and 'Johnny Two', and is buried in Catania War Cemetery, IV.C.23.

Name: Diver, Patrick MM
Rank: Corporal (Acting Sergeant)
No: 6976789
Unit: 4th Parachute Battalion
Born in Gweedore, County Donegal, he won the Military Medal as an acting sergeant with one of the parachute battalions in North Africa. His number indicates that he was an ex-Royal Inniskilling Fusilier. The citation to his Military Medal reads as follows. 'During a raid on a bridge Sgt Diver was a Bren-gun commander in the leading section of the assault platoon. They came under fire from enemy mortars and machine-gun fire and the Bren-gunner was wounded. Sgt Diver not only took over the gun but also assisted in the control of the section during the assault. When the platoon was ordered to withdraw Sgt Diver was the last man to leave the position. He also continued to give covering fire to the platoon until it reached reasonable cover. His coolness and courage throughout the action was an inspiration to all present.'

Name: Dolaghan, Francis G.
Rank: Private
No: 64880 (incomplete number)
Unit: 4th Parachute Brigade Headquarters
From Northern Ireland, and brother of Thomas, he was Hackett's batman at Arnhem and was killed in action there as a member of the Brigade Defence Platoon on 18 September 1944. He is buried in the Airborne Cemetery at Oosterbeek, 29.C.10.

Name: Dolaghan, Thomas
Rank: Private
No: 6977906
Unit: 4th Parachute Brigade Headquarters
An ex-Royal Inniskilling Fusilier, he was the brother of Francis G., and also served in the Brigade Defence Platoon. Captured after the battle, he was sent to Camp XIIA, Limburg, SD Lahn, POW number 89826.

Name: Doran, Joseph
Rank: Gunner
No: 14414451
Unit: 1st Air-Landing Light Regiment, Royal Artillery
He was from County Donegal, and according to a list compiled by the Irish Defence Force in 1945 he was one of 5,000 men who deserted from the Irish Army during the Second World War. He was dismissed from the IDF on 8 August 1945. He is not listed in POW records so may have escaped across the Rhine after the battle.

Name: Dougan, Norman Arthur
Rank: Private
No: 69855?8 (incomplete number)
Unit: 1st Parachute Battalion
From County Armagh, he enlisted under-age at 15 years and 9 months and served in the Royal Inniskilling Fusiliers prior to transferring to Airborne Forces. After Arnhem he was one of the few men to escape across the river on Operation 'Pegasus II' in November; he was the brother of Robert Alexander.

Name: Dougan, Robert Alexander (Sandy)
Rank: Private
No: 6985006
Unit: 1st Parachute Battalion
The brother of Norman Arthur Dougan, he was killed in action as a member of No 8 Section, 3 Platoon, 'R' Company, at Arnhem on 17 September 1944, and is buried in the Airborne Cemetery at Oosterbeek, 17.C.13.

Name: Dowds, A. E.
Rank: Gunner
No: 1115784
Unit: 1st Air-Landing Light Regiment, Royal Artillery
From County Wicklow, he is believed to have served at Arnhem. He is not listed on POW records, so may have escaped across the Rhine after the battle.

Right A type-written letter from Lance-Corporal George Green to Norman Dougan explaining the manner of his brother's death on 17 September 1944. *Dorothy Hendren*

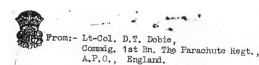

4913437, L/C. GREEN, G.W.,
"R" Coy,
1st.Bn.The Parachute Regt,
A.P.O. ENGLAND.

1-10-44.

Dear Chum,

    I tried my hardest to see you before but my luck was out every time, however I take this opportunity of writing to you and telling you how your brother Robert met his death.

    He was a member of my section and we were ordered to attack a German machine gun-post, as we went into the open we were fired on both from a position forward and to our left. All except 2 of the section were either wounded or killed, and we were forced to crawl back into a wood.

    Eventually, the m.g's were silenced, and I made it my business to check up on my section, I came across your brother lying on the side of the road, he had been killed instantly.

    This took place on the main road, North of the railway towards Arnhem, I must apologize for not knowing the exact name of the place.

    That's all I can tell you about Robert's death, but I can tell you that he was a very good kid, brave and well-liked by all his fellow members of the platoon, and it came as a terrific blow to all his most intimate pals.

    We must now pray that God will keep him as one of his own, until the day arrives that we shall meet again.

Faithfully Yours,

(Sgd) George Green.

Please give my sympathy to all your people in their sad loss.

Below A letter to Mrs Dougan from Padre Watkins on the death of her son Robert Alexander. *Dorothy Hendren*

Below right A later letter from Lieutenant Colonel Dobie, officer commanding the 1st Parachute Battalion. *Dorothy Hendren*

From:- The Chaplain,
1st Bn. The Parachute Regt.,
A.P.O., England.

22nd October, 1944.

Dear Mrs. Dougan,

    You will by now have received officially the painful news that your son was killed in action at Arnhem on September 17th. May I express to you my own very deep sympathy in your great loss, and the sincere respect of those of us in this Battalion who have returned from that terrible, yet historic battle.

    Your son was killed in our first engagement with the enemy, in wooded country, to the west of the town towards mid-night on the first day. I think you may be assured that he did not suffer.

    Your loss of a son is our loss of a good soldier and a comrade held in high regard by all of us. Will you please accept our simple tribute of respect for him, and sympathy for you.

Yours very sincerely,

(Sgd) R.T. Watkins.

From:- Lt-Col. D.T. Dobie,
Commdg. 1st Bn. The Parachute Regt.,
A.P.O., England.

14/11/1944.

Dear Mrs. Dougan,

    Words are completely inadequate in such tragic occasions and I can but say how deeply I sympathise with you in your loss.

    Your son fought a great battle with the rest of this magnificent battalion in the worst fighting in Arnhem, and he died bravely. I cannot say enough for such men as he; you may justly feel proud of him - as we are.

    I have been unable to write before now as I have only just returned from behind enemy lines.

    My battalion joins me in paying tribute to your son and expressing their deepest sympathy.

Yours sincerely,

(Sgd) D.T. Dobie.

6985006 PRIVATE
R. A. DOUGAN
PARACHUTE REGIMENT
ARMY AIR CORPS
17TH SEPTEMBER 1944 AGE 20

"THEM ALSO
WHICH SLEEP IN JESUS
GOD BRING WITH HIM"
I. THESS. 4.14

'You are my sunshine' – the headstone of 'Sandy' Dougan from Glenanne, County Armagh. Sandy's sister Dorothy still remembers the song he used to sing to her when she was a little girl.

Name: Dunbar, Thomas Mitchell
Rank: Lance-Corporal
No: 10565391
Unit: 21st Independent Parachute Company
From Ireland, he was killed in action at Arnhem on 23 September 1944; he has no known grave and is commemorated on the Groesbeek Memorial, panel 8.

Name: Earls, Richard
Rank: Private
No: 4867509
Unit: 2nd Parachute Battalion
From County Carlow, he may have served in either the 2nd or 156 Battalions at Arnhem. No prisoners of this name are listed, so he may have escaped across the Rhine after the battle.

Name: Eccles, Andrew
Rank: Corporal
No: 3709614
Unit: 1st Battalion Border Regiment
Husband of Irene, he came from the Ards peninsula in County Down and was killed in action on 10 July 1943 on Sicily, aged 28 years. He has no known grave and is commemorated on the Cassino Memorial, panel 7.

Name: Eccles, D. L.
Rank: Unknown
No: 132275
Unit: 4th Battalion Dorset Regiment
From County Meath, he was reported as captured during his Battalion's attempt to cross the Rhine and reinforce the Oosterbeek perimeter. There are no details in the POW records.

Name: Edwards, George Henry Horton
Rank: Sergeant
No: 588664
Unit: Glider Pilot Regiment
From Newcastle, County Down, he enlisted in the Northamptonshire Regiment on 31 August 1939 and transferred to the Glider Pilot Regiment on 31 May 1944. According to information provided by his son, he served at Arnhem and escaped across the river at the end of the battle.

Name: Ellis, Sidney
Rank: Private
No: 6974976
Unit: 1st Parachute Battalion
From Belfast, he was the son of William and Clara Ellis of Sandy Row, Belfast. An ex-Royal Inniskilling Fusilier, he was killed in action at Arnhem on 18 September 1944, and is buried in the Airborne Cemetery at Oosterbeek, 20.A.12.

Name: Feehily, Brian Patrick Sheridan
Rank: Staff-Sergeant
No: Unknown
Unit: Glider Pilot Regiment
'Paddy' Feehily was born to an old Irish family in India in 1918. He joined the Royal Artillery in 1933 and served with the BEF in France in 1940. In 1942 he transferred to the Glider Pilot Regiment and saw service in Sicily, Italy and at Arnhem. After 'Market Garden' he escaped across the Rhine. He served a total of 49 years in the Army, finally retiring due to ill health as a Lieutenant Colonel in 1982; he was awarded the MBE in 1962.

Name: Feely, Jack
Rank: Private
No: 7019398
Unit: 2nd Parachute Battalion
From County Down, he was an ex-Royal Ulster Rifleman. From information gained from another Arnhem veteran, he is reported to have escaped across the Rhine at the end of 'Market Garden'.

Name: Ferguson, Samuel
Rank: Unknown
No: Unknown
Unit: 4th Parachute Brigade
From Belfast, County Antrim, he was the brother of Mrs Amelia Rafferty. he served in the Ox and Bucks in the 6th Airborne Division during the Normandy invasion, and was attached to the Brigade Defence Platoon of 4th Parachute Brigade for 'Market Garden'. He was wounded in action, but not listed in POW records, so may have escaped at the end of the battle.

Name: Fiely, James Vincent
Rank: Private
No: 5338078
Unit: 21st Independent Parachute Company
From Dublin, the son of Thomas and Mary Fiely, he had previously served in the Royal Berkshire Regiment. He was killed in action at Arnhem on 22 September 1944 serving with No 2 Platoon, and is buried in the Airborne Cemetery at Oosterbeek, 30.A.4.

Name: Finn, James 'Jimmy'
Rank: Private
No: Unknown
Unit: 10th Parachute Battalion
Born in Dundalk in 1917, he served in the Irish Army until the outbreak of war when he travelled to England to enlist. He subsequently joined the 10th and at some point returned to Ireland. He was arrested as a deserter, but treated with sympathy and given an immediate discharge. An Irish officer told him, 'I don't blame you for going – if I had been 20 years younger I'd go myself.' Jimmy served at Arnhem and was taken prisoner and badly beaten when captured (no POW details). After the war he settled in Leicestershire with his wife Doris. Jimmy died in 2001 and Doris in June 2002.

Name: Finnegan, H. 'Paddy'
Rank: Private
No: 7364938
Unit: Royal Army Medical Corps
From Ireland, he was Colonel Warrack's batman at Arnhem and was attached to the Headquarters Regimental Aid Post. After the battle he was at the field hospital at Apeldoorn. (Name sometimes spelled as Finnigan)

Name: Fitzpatrick
Rank: Unknown
No: Unknown
Unit: Unknown
This was the Irishman who was with Private Tucker at Arnhem Bridge. See main text.

Name: Fitzpatrick, Nicholas
Rank: Private
No: 3535515
Unit: 1st Battalion Border Regiment
From Eire, the son of Nicholas and Elizabeth Fitzpatrick, he was killed in action on 9 July 1943 when his glider came down in the sea during Operation 'Ladbroke', the airborne assault on Sicily. He has no known grave and is commemorated on the Cassino Memorial, panel 7.

Name: Flynn, Hugh
Rank: Private
No: 7021326
Unit: 2nd Battalion South Staffordshire Regiment.
From County Down, he was an ex-Royal Ulster Rifleman. A prisoner of war after Arnhem, we was sent to Camp IVB, Muhlberg. His brother Edward was killed in action at Tobruk, while his father had served in the Royal Irish Rifles in the Great War. Hugh Flynn emigrated to Canada after the war.

Name: Flynn, James 'Paddy'
Rank: Private
No: 3595670
Unit: 1st Battalion Border Regiment
He served as a medical orderly in No 18 Platoon, 'C' Company, at Arnhem, was taken prisoner and sent to Camp VIIA, POW number 140070.

Name: Forsyth, William
Rank: Private
No: 7018862
Unit: 2nd Parachute Battalion
He was the adopted son of Mr and Mrs A. Patterson of Belfast, County Antrim, and had previously served in the Royal Ulster Rifles. He was listed as missing in action, then a prisoner of war after Arnhem, but no camp details are available.

Private William Forsyth

Name: Fryer, John (Jack)
Rank: Lance-Sergeant
No: 7018830
Unit: 1st Parachute Battalion
He enlisted in the Royal Ulster Rifles on 11 July 1940, and transferred to Airborne Forces on 7 May 1942. He served in North Africa, Sicily and Italy, and was wounded in action at Arnhem, taken prisoner and sent to Camp XIIA, Limburg, SD Lahn, POW number 92040. Post war he served in the Ulster Defence Regiment.

Name: Gamble, James
Rank: Private
No: 6985403
Unit: 21st Independent Parachute Company
An ex-Royal Inniskilling Fusilier from Coleraine, County Londonderry, he was one of the original members of the Company. He escaped across the Rhine after Arnhem.

Name: Gamley
Rank: Unknown
No: Unknown
Unit: 2nd Parachute Battalion
According to the records of the Somme Hospital, Belfast, this man served at Arnhem, but no further details are known, and he is not listed in POW records.

Name: Garland, Samuel
Rank: Private
No: 5382425
Unit: Ox and Bucks Light Infantry
From Belfast, County Antrim, he enlisted on 28 September 1936 and served in India. He joined the Defence Platoon of the 1st Parachute Brigade while in North Africa in 1942, and was seriously wounded during the fighting in Sicily. He was demobbed on 15 February 1946.

Name: Gedye, William Harry
Rank: Private
No: 3602825
Unit: 1st Battalion Border Regiment
From Northern Ireland, he was the son of Samuel and Mary Ann Gedye. He was killed in action when his glider came down in the sea during the invasion of Sicily. He has no known grave and is commemorated on the Cassino Memorial, panel 7. He is not listed on the CWGC website.

Name: Gillespie, Dennis Ivan
Rank: Private
No: 6985847
Unit: 21st Independent Parachute Company
He enlisted in the Ulster Home Guard despite being under-age, then went to the Royal Inniskilling Fusiliers, Young Soldiers Battalion. He was one of the original members of the 21st Independent, served at Arnhem with No 1 Platoon, and escaped across the Rhine after the battle. He went on to serve in Norway and Palestine.

Name: Girvin, Robert
Rank: Staff-Sergeant
No: 7022767
Unit: Glider Pilot Regiment
An ex-Royal Ulster Rifleman from Belfast, he served with the GPR at Arnhem, flying from Manston to LZ-Z. His co-pilot was Sergeant Gault, their glider being towed by Flight Lieutenant Scott of 296 Squadron. he was listed as missing in action and prisoner of war after Arnhem, but no camp details are available. His late father served in the Great War. (His name is sometimes spelled as Girven or Girvan.)

Name: Gordon, Hugh
Rank: Lance-Corporal
No: 7012623
Unit: 1st Parachute Battalion
An ex-Royal Ulster Rifleman, he was the son of Hugh and Florence Gordon and the stepson of Charles S. Frost

Above **Private Samuel Garland, Ox and Bucks Light Infantry, attached to the 1st Parachute Brigade Defence Platoon. After being wounded in Sicily, he spent a considerable time in hospital in England. He is wearing the ribbon of the Africa Star on his battledress, awarded to members of the 1st Parachute Brigade for their service in Tunisia.** *Georgina Cromie*

Below **Mrs Georgina Cromie with the Airborne smock belonging to her late brother, Private Samuel Garland. On his death the family presented the smock to the author.**

of Belfast, Northern Ireland. He was killed in action on 26 February 1943 during the fighting in 'Happy Valley', Tunisia, aged 23 years. He is buried in Medjez-el-Bab War Cemetery, Tunisia, 2.H.11.

Name: Gough, C. F. H. 'Freddy' MC
Rank: Major
No: 31420
Unit: 1st Airborne Reconnaissance Squadron
One of a long line of famous Irish soldiers, he had served during the Great War in the Royal Navy. Major Gough commanded the Recce Squadron at Arnhem; he was captured when Arnhem Bridge was returned to German hands and sent to Oflag XIIB, POW number 595. He was awarded the Military Cross for his actions in Italy.

Name: Gough, Samuel
Rank: Gunner
No: 961355
Unit: 1st Air-Landing Light Regiment, Royal Artillery
From Coleraine, County Londonderry, the son of Mrs H. Gough, he enlisted in the Royal Artillery in 1940, then transferred to the 1st Airborne Division. He was a prisoner of war after Arnhem, held in Camp IV D, Torgau, POW No 89226.

Name: Grace, James
Rank: Lance-Corporal
No: T843117
Unit: Royal Army Service Corps
From Dublin, the son of Mr and Mrs J. Grace, and husband of Elsia Bertha Grace of Gloucester, he was killed in action as an Air Dispatcher at Arnhem on 19 September 1944 while aboard Dakota FZ-626 of 271 Squadron. Until the spring of 1990 he was listed as having no known grave and was commemorated on the Groesbeek Memorial, panel 9, but he is now buried in the Airborne Cemetery at Oosterbeek, 4.B.15.

Name: Gray, Frederick J.
Rank: Private
No: 6980488
Unit: 11th Parachute Battalion
An ex-Royal Inniskilling Fusilier from Belfast, he was taken prisoner of war after Arnhem, but no camp details are available. According to local press reports his brother-in-law, name unknown, also served in Airborne Forces. (His name is sometimes spelled as Grey.)

Private Frederick Gray, Army Air Corps, son of Mr. and Mrs. J. Gray, 18 Lawnmount Street, Belfast, missing at Arnhem. He was formerly with the Royal Inniskilling Fusiliers. A brother-in-law is with the airborne

Private Frederick Gray from Belfast, an ex-Royal Inniskilling Fusilier, who served in the 11th Parachute Battalion at Arnhem and was taken prisoner.

Name: Green, Joseph
Rank: Private
No: Unknown
Unit: 1st Parachute Battalion
From Newtownards, County Down, he served in the 1st Battalion of the 1st Airborne Division in North Africa, then transferred to the 6th Airborne Division, serving in the 8th Battalion during the Battle of the Bulge. He saw post-war service in Palestine.

Name: Greenall, John
Rank: Private
No: 3606248
Unit: 1st Battalion Border Regiment
From County Antrim, he served in No 14 Platoon, 'B' Company, and was missing in action and taken prisoner of war at Arnhem. He was held in Stalag XIIA, Limburg, and Stalag IVB, Muhlberg, POW No 075398.

Name: Grey, W. D.
Rank: Private
No: 3961771
Unit: 11th Parachute Battalion
From Northern Ireland, formerly of the Welch Regiment, he was taken prisoner after Arnhem and sent to Camp XIB, Fallingbostel, POW No 117769.

Name: Grundle, Robert
Rank: Sergeant
No: 7010116
Unit: 3rd Parachute Battalion
An ex-Royal Ulster Rifleman from County Londonderry, he served in 'A' Company at Arnhem and was wounded in action. Taken prisoner at Arnhem, he was sent to Camp VIII C at Kunau, Kz Sprottau/Sagan, POW number 118007.

Name: Hackett, John Winthrop 'Shan' DSO MBE MC
Rank: Brigadier
No: 52752
Unit: 4th Parachute Brigade
The commander of the 4th Parachute Brigade at Arnhem, he was seriously wounded during the battle. He escaped from hospital and eventually made a successful return to Allied lines. After the war he was a successful author.

Name: Hamilton, John Mallon
Rank: Private
No: 5109896
Unit: 156 Parachute Battalion
From Belfast, the son of John and Margaret Hamilton, he had originally enlisted in the Royal Warwickshire Regiment and had eight years service by the time of 'Market Garden'. His date of transfer to Airborne Forces is unknown. He died of wounds at St Joseph's Mental Hospital, Apeldoorn, on 21 September 1944, and is buried in the Airborne Cemetery at Oosterbeek, 23.B.5.

Private John Mallon Hamilton

Name: Hamilton, Thomas L.
Rank: Gunner
No: Unknown
Unit: 1st Air-Landing Light Regiment, Royal Artillery
From Dollingstown, County Armagh, he worked as a weaver prior to enlisting at the outbreak of the war. He served in North Africa, Sicily and Italy prior to Arnhem, then after the war he returned to his trade for a time before going to work for the Government at Stormont, where he stayed until his retirement. (According to the files of the Airborne Battle Study Group, he was taken prisoner after Arnhem and sent to Camp III A, Luckenwalde. On cross-checking the POW register, the man listed has the initials T. I.. The author holds a

Gunner Thomas Hamilton from Dollingstown, County Armagh, who served with the 1st Air-Landing Light Regiment RA at Arnhem and escaped across the Rhine after the battle. *Hamilton family*

newspaper cutting describing Gunner Hamilton receiving a presentation from the people of his home town – it is dated 18 October 1944!)

Name: Harden, Richard. DSO
Rank: Major
No: 71219
Unit: Royal Tank Regiment, attached to 1st Airborne Division
He was the son of Major J. E. Harden, Royal Irish Fusiliers, of Harrybrook, County Armagh. Richard Harden was a Staff Officer to Field Marshal Montgomery during 'Market Garden', and was awarded the DSO (see *London Gazette*, 11 October 1945).

Name: Harkin, James 'Jim'
Rank: Private
No: Unknown
Unit: 11th Parachute Battalion
From The Rocks, Armagh, he served in 'C' Company at Arnhem, escaping across the Rhine after the battle.

Name: Harrington, Patrick
Rank: Lance-Corporal
No: 6978585
Unit: 11th Parachute Battalion
From County Cork, he was the son of John and Ellen Harrington. An ex-Royal Irish Fusilier, he was killed in action on 20 September at Arnhem, and is buried in the Airborne Cemetery at Oosterbeek, 6.A.7.

Name: Herron, D. M.
Rank: Sergeant
No: 7015309
Unit: 2nd Parachute Battalion
A native of Belfast, County Antrim, he enlisted in the Royal Ulster Rifles in September 1939, transferring to Airborne Forces in late 1941. He was wounded and taken prisoner of war while serving with the 2nd Battalion in North Africa, having fought at Sfax and Sousse. Reported by the Red Cross to be in hospital at Caserta near Naples in December of 1942, he was sent to Camp IIIA, Luckenwalde, POW No 140298.

Name: Hillis, Samuel
Rank: Lance-Corporal
No: 6984400
Unit: 1st Parachute Battalion
The son of James Hillis, a linesman, of Donegal Pass, Belfast, he served at Arnhem, escaping across the Rhine after the battle.

Name: Hills, Alfred William
Rank: Private
No: 3596885
Unit: 1st Battalion Border Regiment
From Belfast, he was missing in action at Arnhem on 26 September 1944. Possibly wounded and captured after the evacuation of the perimeter, he was sent to Stalag XIB, POW No 117920.

Name: Hourigan, David Francis
Rank: Captain/Chaplain 4th Class
No: 102157
Unit: Royal Army Chaplains Department
The son of Thomas and Mary Hourigan of Eire, he was killed in action on Sicily on 10 July 1943 while attached to the 1st Air-Landing Brigade; he was 36 years old. He is buried in Syracuse War Cemetery, 1.E.11.

Name: Houston, James I.
Rank: Major
No: 53748
Unit: 3rd Parachute Battalion
Born and resident in Londonderry, James Houston was originally commissioned into the Essex Regiment. For operation 'Market Garden' he commanded HQ Company of the 3rd Parachute Battalion. He was killed on 20 September 1944; with no known grave he is commemorated on the Groesbeek Memorial.

Name: Hughes, Edward
Rank: Lance-Corporal
No: 3596264
Unit: 1st Battalion Border Regiment
From Moneymore, County Down, his wife lived in Belfast. A veteran of 14 years service, at Arnhem he was listed as missing in action, then prisoner of war, and sent to Stalag XIIA, POW No 075689. He is reported to have died in prison camp of wounds received during the battle.

Lance-Corporal Edward Hughes

Name: Hughes, Victor T.
Rank: Lance-Corporal
No: 7012356
Unit: 3rd Parachute Battalion
Formerly of the Royal Ulster Rifles, from Belfast, Victor served on the North West Frontier in 1939 with his twin brother Charles and John Bermingham, from Dublin.

Charles was wounded serving with the 6th Airborne Division in Normandy; another brother also served. Victor was reported as wounded, then missing in action at Arnhem, before his family was informed that he was a prisoner of war. He was sent to Camp XIIA Limburg, SD Lahn, POW number unknown.

Name: Hume
Rank: Unknown
No: Unknown
Unit: 4th Parachute Brigade HQ
This name was mentioned in conversation by other Arnhem veterans as someone who came from Ireland.

Name: Hunter, Alan George
Rank: Staff-Sergeant
No: 6153101
Unit: Glider Pilot Regiment
From County Antrim, he first enlisted in the East Surrey Regiment before transferring to the Glider Pilot Regiment in 1942, being posted to 'C' Squadron. He carried the 1st Airborne Division during the Sicily operation. During Operation 'Tonga' on the night of 5/6 June 1944, he and his co-pilot Sergeant Terrence Collins fought alongside ground troops in Normandy, until betrayed by French collaborators on 3 July. Taken prisoner of war, they were sent to Stalag 8C. Liberated by advancing American troops on 2 April 1945, he later served in Palestine until leaving the Army in December 1945. He then settled in the Waddington area where he was President of the local branch of the Royal British Legion. He was awarded the MBE (civil) in 1986 for his work with the local Youth Training Agency.

Name: Hunter, John
Rank: Sergeant
No: 3596799
Unit: 1st Battalion Border Regiment
Born in County Antrim, he was the son of George and Elizabeth Hunter and husband of Lily, who lived in Prudhoe-on-Fyille. He enlisted in 1932 and served with the Battalion in France and Sicily. Platoon Sergeant of 10 Platoon, 'A' Company, he was killed in action at Arnhem on 20 September, and is buried in the Airborne Cemetery at Oosterbeek, 28.A.3.

Sergeant John Hunter

Private Alexander James

Name: Hurley, Patrick
Rank: Private
No: 3450725
Unit: 1st Battalion Border Regiment
From Eire, he was killed in action at Arnhem on 22 September 1944, age 24 years, and is buried in the Airborne Cemetery at Oosterbeek, 16.B.3

Name: Hynes, William G. 'Billy'
Rank: Corporal
No: Unknown
Unit: 1st Parachute Battalion
From County Antrim, he enlisted with Billy Magill, and after service in North Africa he transferred to the Independent Parachute Brigade and served in the South of France, Italy and Greece, where he was wounded. He was still going strong in 2001. His father served in both World Wars and his brother served in the Royal Artillery during the Second.

Name: James, Alexander
Rank: Private
No: 7021875
Unit: 2nd Parachute Battalion
Ex-Royal Ulster Rifles from Belfast, he was taken prisoner at Arnhem while serving with the 2nd Parachute Battalion, and sent to Camp XIIA, Limburg. His brother Robert was wounded in action while serving with the Highland Light Infantry.

Name: James, Alexander B.
Rank: Private
No: 7022645
Unit: Unknown
From Cosgrove Street, Belfast, he was reported in the local press as having been taken prisoner at Arnhem and sent to Camp XIIA, Limburg, POW number 075364. he was possibly the brother of Alexander James listed above.

Name: Jamison, Robert
Rank: Sergeant
No: Unknown
Unit: Glider Pilot Regiment
He entered Queen's University, Belfast, in 1942 on a Royal Air Force Pre-Entry Course, and qualified as a Flight Sergeant prior to transferring to the GPR. He is believed to have served in all theatres.

Name: Johnstone, T. K.
Rank: Private
No: 3194665
Unit: 7th Battalion Kings Own Scottish Borderers
From Ireland, he was taken prisoner at Arnhem while serving in 'A' Company HQ, and was sent to Camp XII A, Limburg

Name: Kavanagh, Desmond T.
Rank: Captain
No: 204081
Unit: 250 (Airborne) Light Composite Company, Royal Army Service Corps
Born in Eire, he commanded No 2 Para Platoon and the 2nd Para Jeep Section on Operation 'Market Garden'. On Tuesday 19 September Captain Kavanagh led a force of four jeeps and trailers with approximately 24 men out of the British positions towards the supply-dropping zone about a mile distant and certainly in enemy hands. The

convoy had just crossed the railway bridge at Oosterbeek Halt when it came under fire from a German tank concealed in the trees lining the Dreijenseweg. The convoy, travelling at speed, lost its lead vehicle to an enemy tank shell and the following jeeps piled into the back of each other. Casualties were caused, some fatal, and as the survivors made their way back to British lines, Captain Kavanagh gave covering fire with a Bren gun. As the last of the RASC men left the ambush site, Captain Kavanagh was killed; he was 25 years old. he is buried in the Airborne Cemetery at Oosterbeek, 6.B.1.

Name: Kendrick, Samuel John
Rank: Private
No: 14439768
Unit: 1st Parachute Battalion
From County Wexford, he enlisted in the Royal Irish Fusiliers and was posted to its 6th (Young Soldiers) Battalion. He was 18 in 1944 when he transferred to Airborne Forces. He did his initial training at Hardwick Hall, with parachute jumps at Ringway, and further training at Clay Cross, Derbyshire. When posted to the 1st Battalion he was attached to the Assault Pioneer Platoon and trained on the use of the flame-thrower. Considered too young to go to Arnhem, he was detailed to carry out various fatigues around the camp. The day before the operation started, a member of the Support Company went AWOL and Private Kendrick was drafted in at the last minute to fill the vacancy. At Arnhem he was equipped with a flame-thrower, and during the fighting around the Laundry van Hofwegen at Oosterbeek his unit suffered heavy casualties in its command structure. The platoon commander, Lieutenant Sutton, was badly wounded, and Sergeant McKnight and Corporal Osborne were killed, the latter after being hit in the back by a 'friendly' 6-pounder anti-tank shell. Private Kendrick was taken prisoner at the end of the battle, but no prison camp details are listed.

Name: Kerr, H. A.
Rank: Trooper
No: 7020098
Unit: 1st Airborne Reconnaissance Squadron
From County Down, he was shot by a sniper in Orangestraat, Oosterbeek, and subsequently captured and sent to POW Camp XIB, Fallingbostel, POW No 118345. Trooper Kerr was the nephew of Miss Kerr of Badentoy, Newry, County Down.

Name: Kerr, William
Rank: Private
No: 6985438
Unit: 11th Parachute Battalion
From Belfast, he had enlisted in the Royal Ulster Rifles before transferring to Airborne. He was wounded in action during 'Market Garden' and escaped across the Rhine after the battle. When released from hospital he was informed that he was going to Japan! Thankfully the war ended soon after. Following the war he was Governor of the Crumlin Road Gaol in Belfast.

Name: Kiely, Michael
Rank: Unknown
No: Unknown
Unit: Unknown
From Dundalk, County Louth, he was a prisoner of war after Arnhem and escaped to the Russian lines with Peter Markey. He is not listed in POW records.

Name: Killingworth, Richard
Rank: Private
No: 7014183
Unit: 156 Parachute Battalion
From Northern Ireland and formerly with the Royal Ulster Rifles, he served in the Machine-Gun Platoon of Support Company and was killed in action on 18 September 1944 when his Dakota (43-15180) of 314 Troop Carrier Group, 50 Troop Carrier Squadron USAAF, crashed after being hit by flak near Ochen, 20 kilometres south-west of Oosterbeek; there were no survivors. He is buried in Jonkerbosch War Cemetery, 8.B.1.

Name: Kilmartin, Michael, G.
Rank: Lieutenant
No: 217467
Unit: 1st Parachute Battalion
Born in Eire, Michael Kilmartin was living in Sussex just before the outbreak of war. For Operation 'Market Garden' he commanded No 2 Platoon in 'R' Company of the 1st Battalion. He was killed in action on Tuesday 19 September 1944 and, having no known grave, is commemorated on the Groesbeek Memorial.

Name: Lamont, David
Rank: Private
No: 6983731
Unit: 4th Parachute Brigade
An ex-Royal Inniskilling Fusilier from Ballymena, County Antrim, he was the son of Mr and Mrs David Lamont. His wife and child were residing in Manchester

in September 1944. he was reported missing at Arnhem, then a prisoner of war at Camp VI C, Munster.

Name: Lavelle, J.
Rank: Private
No: 6978609
Unit: 11th Parachute Battalion
An ex-Royal Inniskilling Fusilier from Augher, County Tyrone, he was reported in the local press as being taken prisoner at Arnhem, but there are no prison camp details listed.

Name: Leese, M.
Rank: Unknown
No: Unknown
Unit: 156 Parachute Battalion
From Coutnacsherry, County Cork, he served at Arnhem, but is not listed in POW records, so may have escaped across the Rhine at the end of the battle.

Name: Lennon, Norman
Rank: Private
No: 14993889
Unit: Unknown
From Belfast, he transferred from the Buffs to the 1st Airborne Division as a much-needed reinforcement in early 1945.

Name: Lewis, M. 'Paddy'
Rank: Staff-Sergeant
Number: Unknown
Unit: Unknown
The only clue that this man was Irish is that other veterans remarked that he had pro-IRA opinions!

Name: Lismore, Patrick
Rank: Private
No: Unknown
Unit: 11th Parachute Battalion
In an undated local press cutting he is reported to have escaped across the Rhine after Arnhem; the cutting was donated to the author together with a red beret by his nephew. He may have served in No 6 Platoon, 'B' Company.

Name: Logan, Thomas D.
Rank: Private
No: 1433668
Unit: Unknown
From Belfast, he had originally enlisted in the General Service Corps and had five years service prior to 'Market

Private Norman Lennon from Belfast was one of the much-needed reinforcements for the 1st Airborne Division after the debacle that was 'Market Garden'. He is seen here in the uniform of his previous Regiment, the Buffs. *Mrs Sadie Lennon*

Garden'. Taken prisoner after Arnhem, he was sent to Camp Oflag 79, Braunschweig, POW No 118681. Oflag 79 was an officers' camp, so it is possible he was a batman. Records show him wounded in action and a patient in the German hospital at Apeldoorn on 23 September 1944. If this is correct he may have been in the 2nd Battalion.

Name: Lonsdale, Richard Thomas Henry DSO MC
Rank: Captain (T/Major)
No: 69129
Unit: 11th Parachute Battalion
Commissioned into the Leicester Regiment (later Royal Leicestershire) on 27 August 1936, he served with its 1st Battalion in Waziristan, where he won the Military Cross. He commanded 'A' Company of the 2nd Parachute Battalion on Sicily and was awarded the DSO. He served as 2i/c of the 11th Battalion at Arnhem and was given command of 'Lonsdale Force'. He escaped across the Rhine at the end of the battle, and returned to Holland in 1945 to assist in the making of *Theirs Is The Glory*.

Name: Lord, David Samuel Anthony VC DFC
Rank: Flight Lieutenant
No: 49149
Unit: 271 Squadron Transport Command RAF
Born in County Cork of a Welsh father and Irish mother, he was killed in action at Arnhem on 19 September 1944 and posthumously awarded the Victoria Cross. He had previously been awarded the Distinguished Flying Cross for service in Burma. He is buried in the Airborne Cemetery at Oosterbeek, 4.B.5.

Name: Lowe, G. M.
Rank: Sergeant
No: Unknown
Unit: Unknown
His name is mentioned in conversation with other Arnhem veterans as having escaped across the Rhine after Arnhem; he not listed in POW records.

Name: Lundy, J.
Rank: Gunner
No: 988102
Unit: 1st Air-Landing Light Regiment, Royal Artillery
From County Londonderry, he served at Arnhem and is not listed as a prisoner of war, so may have escaped across the Rhine at the end of the battle.

Name: Lynas, Ernest
Rank: Lance-Corporal
No: 7043594
Unit: 156 Parachute Battalion
From County Armagh and husband of Violet, he had originally enlisted in the Royal Irish Fusiliers. He was killed in action at Arnhem on 25 September 1944, age 26 years, and is buried in the Airborne Cemetery at Oosterbeek, 28.B.2.

Name: Lynas, Frank
Rank: Sergeant
No: Unknown
Unit: 2nd Parachute Battalion
From Eire, he served in North Africa and Sicily prior to Arnhem, where he served in the Mortar Platoon of Support Company. He was taken prisoner of war after the battle, but there are no prison camp details.

This scroll commemorates
Lance-Corporal E. Lynas
Army Air Corps

held in honour as one who served King and Country in the world war of 1939-1945 and gave his life to save mankind from tyranny. May his sacrifice help to bring the peace and freedom for which he died.

The Memorial Scroll sent to the next-of-kin of Lance-Corporal E. Lynas, 156 Parachute Battalion, killed at Arnhem on 25 September 1944.

Name: Lyons, F.
Rank: Private
No: Unknown
Unit: 2nd Parachute Battalion
His name was mentioned in conversation with other Arnhem veterans. He is reported to have escaped across the Rhine after the battle.

Name: Magee, James Patrick 'Red'
Rank: See below
No: 7014381/323030
Unit: 21st Independent Parachute Company
Originally from County Wicklow, he enlisted in the London Irish Rifles (TA) in March 1939. He transferred to Airborne Forces in February 1942, serving in the HQ Section of the 21st as a clerk and later as a platoon commander. He served in Tunisia from May to September 1943 and the Ardennes from December 1944 to February 1945; from September 1945 to May 1946 he served with the 5th Independent Company of 5 Commando in action against the Japanese and

Indonesian terrorists in Java. Commissioned from the ranks, he ended his career at Lt-Colonel. 'I never made an operational parachute jump, but received two very interesting briefings for drops on Rome and in Malaya, both of which were thankfully cancelled.'

Name: Magill, Robert
Rank: Private
No: Unknown
Unit: 1st or 2nd Parachute Battalion
From Ravenhill Road, Belfast, he lost part of his leg while serving in North Africa.

Name: Magill, William 'Billy'
Rank: Private
No: 7013863
Unit: 1st Parachute Battalion
From County Down, he served with the Royal Irish Fusiliers before transferring to Airborne Forces. He served in North Africa, Sicily and Italy, and at Arnhem he served in No 8 Section, 3 Platoon, 'B' Company. He was taken prisoner of war and sent to Stalag XIB, Fallingbostel, POW No 11736. He was awarded the OBE after the war.

Name: Maltby, Ralph Alexander
Rank: Lieutenant
No: 73034
Unit: Glider Pilot Regiment
The son of Francis Brough Maltby and Enid Rosamond Maltby of Belfast, he was commissioned into the Royal Artillery. Awarded the 'Order of the Patriotic War' by the Soviet Government for service in Russia, and a Mention-in-Despatches while attached to the RAF, he was killed in action with No 2 Wing GPR on 17 September 1944, aged 26, and is buried in the Airborne Cemetery at Oosterbeek, 3.C.18.

Name: Maltman, William H.
Rank: Company Sergeant-Major
No: 6341462
Unit: 156 Parachute Battalion
From Belfast, he was a survivor of the Dunkirk campaign, where he had served with the Royal West Kent Regiment. He had also seen previous service in India, where he transferred to the 151 Battalion. He served in the Middle East, where 151 became 156, and at Arnhem, where he was captured after the battle and sent to Camp XIIA, Limburg, SD Lahn, POW number 92052. His father served in the First World War, while three brothers served in the Second.

Name: Marken, Robert 'Bob'
Rank: Unknown
No: Unknown
Unit: 1st Parachute Battalion
Born in Belfast on 13 March 1924, he enlisted in November 1940 and is believed to have served at Arnhem. After the war he served with the Middle East Land Forces from 1951 to 1954. He also saw action during the Suez operation and did a second tour of the Middle East from 1958 to 1959. After retirement he worked as a civilian driver with the British Embassy in Washington DC.

Name: Markey, Peter
Rank: Sergeant/Instructor
No: 2338631
Unit: 1st Parachute Battalion
From County Down, husband of Elizabeth, he originally served with the Royal Signals. He was wounded and taken prisoner of war after Arnhem and sent to Camp XIIB, Fallingbostel, POW number 118009.

Name: Marshall, Gordon. J.
Rank: Private
No: Unknown
Unit: 2nd Battalion South Staffordshire Regiment
The son of a Great War veteran, Gordon Marshall came from Holywood, County Down. According to a local newspaper report he served at Arnhem and escaped across the Rhine after the battle – see the photograph on page 153.

Name: Matson, Eric George Wolf
Rank: Sergeant
No: Unknown
Unit: Glider Pilot Regiment
An ex-Inniskilling Fusilier from Bandon, County Cork, he enlisted in 1941 and transferred to the Glider Pilot Regiment in 1943, qualifying in 1944. On Operation 'Market Garden' he was 2nd Pilot to Staff-Sergeant R. Garnett in a Hamilcar glider, chalk number 323, of 'C' Squadron. The glider was towed from Tarrant Rushton to LZ-Z at Arnhem by a Stirling bomber flown by Pilot Officer Herman of 644 Squadron. A local newspaper reported that Matson had fought with the Poles at Driel. After the war he was commissioned into the RAOC.

Name: Mawhinney, Herbert
Rank: Sergeant
No: 5109805
Unit: Unknown
From Moltke Street, Belfast, he enlisted in the Royal Warwickshire Regiment in 1935. He was taken prisoner at Arnhem, but no prison camp details are listed.

Sergeant Herbert Mawhinney from Belfast, a former member of the Royal Warwickshire Regiment. According to local newspaper reports he served at Arnhem, but his Airborne unit is as yet unknown.

Name: McArthur, Don
Rank: Private
No: Unknown
Unit: 21st Independent Parachute Company
He is reported to have come from Ireland, but lived in Scotland. He served with the Company in North Africa and Italy, then transferred to the Independent Platoon and saw service during Operation 'Anvil' in the South of France and in Greece.

Name: McCleave, John
Rank: Corporal
No: 6984197
Unit: Unknown
According to newspaper reports he was an ex-Royal Inniskilling Fusilier from Belfast. Missing in action, then a prisoner of war after Arnhem, he was sent to Camp XIB, Fallingbostel, POW No 118395. A brother also served.

Name: McClune, John
Rank: Lance-Corporal
No: 6979069
Unit: 11th Parachute Battalion
The son of Mr and Mrs James McClune of Fourth Street, Belfast, he enlisted in the Royal Irish Fusiliers in 1937. His father was a First World War veteran and also served

Corporal John McCleave

in the Second. he was killed in action on 24 September 1944 at Arnhem and is buried in the Airborne Cemetery at Oosterbeek, 26.A.11.

Name: McCormick, Frank
Rank: Private
No: Unknown
Unit: 1st Parachute Battalion
From Dublin, he may have served under the name of McCluskey. At Arnhem he was a member of Dick Whittingham's mortar crew in the garden at Benedendorpsweg in Oosterbeek.

Name: McCracken, George Ernest
Rank: Private
No: 7017277
Unit: 2nd Parachute Battalion
The son of William and Emiline McCracken of Northern Ireland, and husband of Irene Florence, who resided at Stoke Newington, London, during the war, he was an ex-Royal Ulster Rifleman. Taken prisoner after the recapture of Arnhem Bridge, he was one of a number of men murdered while a prisoner of war at Brummen on 23 September 1944; he was 29 years old. He is buried in Eastern General Cemetery, Enschede, Holland, grave No 196.

Name: McCreedie, Leslie
Rank: Sergeant
No: 7019665
Unit: 1st Airborne Reconnaissance Squadron
An ex-GPO engineer from Newtownards, County Down, he enlisted in the Royal Ulster Rifles on the outbreak of war. Transferring to Airborne Forces, he served in North Africa and Italy prior to 'Market Garden'. At Arnhem he served in the Mortar Platoon and escaped across the Rhine after the battle.

Name: McCullough, Samuel C.
Rank: Private
No: 7021325
Unit: Unknown
An ex-Royal Ulster Rifleman from County Down, he was one of three brothers to serve in the war, having previously worked in Messrs Short & Harland, a local aircraft factory. He was taken prisoner at Arnhem and sent to Camp IV B, Muhlberg, POW number 89330. His brother Joseph died of wounds while serving with the 1st (Airborne) Battalion of the Royal Ulster Rifles, 6th Airborne Division, on Operation 'Varsity', the crossing of the Rhine in March 1945, while his other brother, John, served in the Merchant Navy. Their father had served with the Royal Inniskilling Fusiliers and Machine Gun Corps in the First World War and the Royal Warwickshire Regiment in the Second.

Private Samuel McCullough from Bangor, County Down. An ex-Royal Ulster Rifleman, he served in 'C' Company of the 2nd Parachute Battalion during 'Market Garden'.

Name: McFadden, James
Rank: Private
No: 7046886
Unit: 1st Parachute Battalion
This ex-Royal Irish Fusilier came from Dungannon, County Tyrone, and was the son of John and Florence McFadden, and husband of Elizabeth. He was killed in action between 13 and 20 July 1943, during the fighting on Sicily; he was 23 years old. He is buried in Catania War Cemetery, III.J.39.

Name: McFadden, John Terence M.
Rank: Lieutenant
No: Unknown
Unit: 1st Parachute Battalion
From Belfast, he was the son of Dr and Mrs. A. W. J. McFadden CB. An ex-pupil of Campbell College, Belfast, he had played rugby for Northern Ireland. After leaving school he was employed by Prudential Insurance. Commissioned into the Artists Rifles, he served as a Lieutenant with the Royal Ulster Rifles, and transferred to Airborne Forces. He saw service in Sicily, then served at Arnhem as OC 9 Platoon, 'T' Company. Taken prisoner on the recapture of Arnhem Bridge, he died of illness in Camp XIB, Fallingbostel.

Name: McGeough, J. O.
Rank: Staff-Sergeant
No: 6030074
Unit: Glider Pilot Regiment
He originally served in the Essex Regiment, then transferred to the Glider Pilot Regiment, date unknown. For 'Market Garden' he served in 'C' Squadron No 2 Wing, was captured at Arnhem and sent to Camp XIB, Fallingbostel, POW number 117374.

Name: McGinty, J.
Rank: Private
No: 2826218
Unit: 156 Parachute Battalion
Born in Ireland, he moved to Paisley in Scotland. Enlisting in the Seaforth Highlanders, he served with the 1st Battalion at Agra in India, where he transferred to the 151 Parachute Battalion, moving with the battalion to the Middle East where it changed to the 156 Battalion. He served at Arnhem in 5 Platoon of 'A' Company, was wounded in action and taken to Apeldoorn, then to Camp XIB, Fallingbostel, POW number 118380. The wounds he received at Arnhem troubled him until he died.

Name: McGlone, John
Rank: Private
No: 2760448
UNIT; 4th Parachute Brigade
From somewhere in Ireland, he was killed in action while serving at Arnhem on 20 September 1944, age 24 years. He is buried in the Airborne Cemetery at Oosterbeek, 28.A.1, and is listed in the Commonwealth War Graves Register as having been in the 4th Parachute Battalion, which is probably an error.

Name: McGowan, Daniel MC
Rank: Captain/Father
No: 287572
Unit: Royal Army Chaplains Department
Continuing the tradition of Irish priests serving as padres to British regiments, Daniel McGowan served as Padre to the 16th Parachute Field Ambulance at Arnhem. For his actions during 'Market Garden' he was awarded the Military Cross.

Name: McGrath, William John
Rank: Unknown
No: 5781548
Unit: Unknown
The son of Mr and Mrs James McGrath of Coleraine, County Londonderry, he first enlisted in the Royal Norfolk Regiment. His Airborne unit is unknown, but he was taken prisoner of war after Arnhem and sent to Camp XII A, Limburg, POW No 89830.

Name: McKee, Andrew
Rank: Private
No: 6980327
Unit: 1st Parachute Battalion
From Newtownards, County Down, he enlisted in the Royal Inniskilling Fusiliers in 1939 and transferred to the 1st Parachute Battalion in May 1941, serving in 'T' Company as a Bren-gunner. He saw action in North Africa, Sicily and Italy, and was taken prisoner at Arnhem, but no camp details are listed. He continued with his Army career until August 1949, serving in Palestine and with the BAOR. He retired with the rank of CQMS.

Name: McKernan
Rank: Private
No: Unknown
Unit: 2nd Parachute Battalion
From Northern Ireland, he was mentioned in conversation with other Arnhem veterans. There is no McKernan listed in British POW records, so if he was there he possibly escaped at the end of the battle.

Name: McKinley
Rank: Warrant Officer
No: Unknown
Unit: Royal Air Force
Born in Belfast and taken to the United States by his mother when he was 12 years old, he was in the same aircraft as Bert Smith on 18 September 1944.

Name: McKnight, J.
Rank: Private
No: Unknown
Unit: 21st Independent Parachute Company
He was killed in an accident in Italy in 1943, somewhere between Foggia and Barletta. He is not listed on the CWGC website.

Name: McLoughlin, David
Rank: Private
No: 7047407
Unit: 2nd Parachute Battalion
Born in Belfast in 1924, he enlisted in the Royal Irish Fusiliers at the age of 17. Transferring to the 2nd Parachute Battalion, he served in North Africa, Sicily, Italy and at Arnhem, where he was taken prisoner, possibly when Arnhem Bridge fell back into German hands. No POW camp details are listed

Name: McMurray, James Isaac
Rank: Corporal
No: 7016765
Unit: 1st Parachute Battalion
From County Armagh, he first served with the Royal Ulster Rifles and London Irish Rifles, and was recommended for the MM. he was taken prisoner at Arnhem and sent to Camp XIIB, Fallingbostel, POW number 117362.

Name: McNeice, Leslie
Rank: Private
No: 7046985
Unit: 1st Parachute Battalion
An ex-Royal Irish Fusilier from Whitehouse, County Antrim, his father had served in both World Wars. At Arnhem Private McNeice served in 'R' Company and was listed as missing in action and later prisoner-of-war. He was sent to Camp 079, POW number 117377. He died in 1982.

Private David McLoughlin from Belfast. He was an ex-Royal Irish Fusilier and a veteran of North Africa, Sicily and Italy before being taken prisoner at Arnhem while serving with the 2nd Parachute Battalion.

In his third and final unit of the war, James McMurray qualified as a parachutist and served in the 1st Parachute Battalion. He was captured at Arnhem. *Courtesy of Mr Howard Hamilton*

Taken prisoner after the battle, he was sent to Camp XIB, Fallingbostel, POW number 89843. His father Samuel also served in the war, as did two brothers.

Private Leslie McNeice

Name: McWilliams, Samuel
Rank: Private
No: 7021652
Unit: 2nd Parachute Battalion
An ex-Royal Ulster Rifleman from Medway Street, Belfast, he served in 7 Platoon, 'C' Company, at Arnhem.

Private Samuel McWilliams was an ex-Royal Ulster Rifleman from Belfast. He served in the 2nd Parachute Battalion during operation 'Market Garden'.

215

Name: Millar, G. R. 'Dusty'
Rank: Lieutenant
No: 176150
Unit: Glider Pilot Regiment
An ex-Irish Guardsman from County Cork, he served in 20 Flight, 'B' Squadron, No 1 Wing at Sicily, Normandy and Arnhem. He escaped across the Rhine after the battle and went on to serve on Operation 'Varsity', the crossing of the Rhine in 1945, for which he was awarded a Mention-in-Despatches.

Name: Miller, 'Dusty'
Rank: Private
No: Unknown
Unit: Unknown
He was mentioned in conversation with other veterans of 'Market Garden'. Born in Eire, but raised in Manchester, he was reported taken prisoner after Arnhem and sent to Stalag IIIA, Luckenwalde.

Name: Mitchell, Harry
Rank: Private
No: 6986281
Unit: 21st Independent Parachute Company
From Northern Ireland, he first enlisted in the Royal Inniskilling Fusiliers in 1941. Transferring to the 21st Independent in 1942, he served in No 1 Platoon and was wounded by a shell from an enemy self-propelled gun at Oosterbeek on 23 September 1944, and repatriated due to the seriousness of his wound.

Name: Mollan, Thomas William
Rank: Private
No: 3602982
Unit: 1st Battalion Border Regiment
From County Monaghan, he was the son of Walter E. and Margaret M. Mollan of Selloo. He was killed in action on 10 July 1943 in Sicily, aged 28 years. he is buried in Syracuse War Cemetery, IV.D.7.

Name: Montgomery, Robert V.
Rank: Private
No: 6986106
Unit: 3rd Parachute Battalion
An ex-Royal Inniskilling Fusilier from Lough Erne, County Fermanagh, he was wounded in action serving at Arnhem with 'A' Company, taken prisoner and sent to Camp XIB, Fallingbostel, POW number 118766.

The grave of Private Thomas Mollan, 1st Battalion Border Regiment, in Syracuse War Cemetery, Sicily.
Border & King's Own Royal Border Regiment Museum

Name: Montgomery, Samuel
Rank: Private
No: 7013157
Unit: 2nd Battalion South Staffordshire Regiment
An ex-Royal Ulster Rifleman from Runnymede Drive, Belfast, he was a veteran of France in 1940 and North Africa in 1943. He served at Arnhem in 'A' Company as a PIAT gunner and was taken prisoner and sent to Stalag III, POW number 90005. He was liberated by American troops on 23 April 1945. He died in 1992.

Name: Montgomery, Terence 'Terry'
Rank: Private
No: 7013242
Unit: 1st Parachute Battalion
The son of Mrs Campbell, of Benburb Street, Belfast, he was married to Jane who lived in Oxford. This ex-Royal Ulster Rifleman had eight years service prior to Arnhem, and was wounded in action there, taken prisoner and sent

to Camp XIIA, Limburg, POW number 92037. His father had served in the First World War.

Private Terence Montgomery

Name: Montgomery, Thomas Everard
Rank: Major
No: 160794
Unit: 1st Battalion Border Regiment
Born in the Pacific Islands, the son of Thomas Alexander and Gladys Montgomery and husband of Lavender Montgomery of Kilshannig, Co Cork, he served at Arnhem as OC 'A' Company. He died in hospital of wounds received on 21 November 1944, aged 36, and was buried by the Germans in the New Cemetery at Lingen/Ems, 13.11. The grave was not located after the war and he is commemorated by a special memorial in the Airborne Cemetery at Oosterbeek.

Name: Moore, William 'Barney'
Rank: Private
No: 6984259
Unit: 21st Independent Parachute Company
Born in McMaster Street, Belfast, Barney was a shipyard apprentice with Harland & Wolff prior to enlisting in the Royal Inniskilling Fusiliers. He transferred to Airborne Forces and was one of the original members of the 21st Independent. A veteran of North Africa and Sicily, where he was a member of the 'Santa Agata' patrol, he was wounded in action at Arnhem, later taken prisoner, and sent to Camp XIB, Fallingbostel, POW number 118742. After the war he settled in Stratford-upon-Avon.

Name: Morgan, 'Paddy'
Rank: Private
No: Unknown
Unit: 10th Parachute Battalion
He was mentioned in conversation with several Airborne veterans as having been captured at Arnhem. There are four men of this name listed in the POW records.

Name: Morgan
Rank: Gunner
No: Unknown
Unit: 1st Air-Landing Anti-Tank Battery, Royal Artillery
From County Clare, he was at Arnhem, but none of the men listed as POWs has the rank of Gunner, so he may therefore have escaped at the end of the battle.

Name: Mount, James
Rank: Sergeant
No: 6976696
Unit: 1st Parachute Battalion
An ex-Royal Inniskilling Fusilier from Belfast, he served with the 1st Airborne Division in North Africa, Sicily and Arnhem. He had a total of 15 years service, and during 'Market Garden' he served in 5 Platoon, 'S' Company. Taken prisoner of war after Arnhem, he was held at Frankfurt-on-Main, POW number 118392. He described the camp as filthy in the extreme, and during his time of imprisonment he lost 5 stone in weight. Liberated by the American Army under General Patch on 2 April 1945, he came home to Belfast on the same train as Major Mervyn Dennison.

Name: Mulhall
Rank: Sergeant
No: Unknown
Unit: 2nd Parachute Battalion
From Eire, he served with Cecil Newell at Arnhem.

Name: Mulligan, James
Rank: Private
No: Unknown
Unit: Unknown
From Pollyarnon, Castlederg, County Tyrone, he had seven years service prior to being captured at Arnhem. He is not listed as a prisoner of war under AAC, but may have served with another unit. (His name is also spelled as Milligan in some sources.)

Name: Murphy, Andrew Joseph
Rank: Flight Sergeant
No: 628480
Unit: 196 Squadron RAF
The son of James and Brigid Murphy of Flagmount, Clifden, County Kilkenny, Flight Sergeant Murphy was killed on 20 September 1944 while on a re-supply flight to Arnhem. The aircraft was a Stirling (LJ-988) flying from Keevil, and it crashed at Natuurbad, Doorwerth, west of Oosterbeek at 1430hrs on 20 September. The cause of the crash is at present unknown, and there were

no survivors. He is buried in a collective grave in the Airborne Cemetery at Oosterbeek, 4.A.11-13.

Name: Murphy, James MM
Rank: Lance-Corporal
No: 7012729
Unit: 3rd Parachute Battalion
From Belfast, ex-Royal Ulster Rifles, he was the son of Hugh and Ellen Murphy, and was married to Annie. he was killed in action on 11 March 1943 at Sedjenane, aged 30, and is buried in Medjez-el-Bab Cemetery, 4.A.18. He was awarded the Military Medal (*LG* 22 April 1943) and a Mention-in-Despatches (*LG* 23 September 1943).

Name: Neville, Daniel
Rank: Lance-Corporal
No: 1911650
Unit: 1st Parachute Squadron Royal Engineers
An ex-Royal Engineer from Listowel, County Kerry, he was the son of Daniel and Mary Neville. He was killed in action on 20 September 1944 while fighting around Arnhem Bridge, aged 29 years. He has no known grave and is commemorated on the Groesbeek Memorial, panel 2.

Name: Newell, Cecil
Rank: Private
No: 155998
Unit: 2nd Parachute Battalion
An ex-Royal Artilleryman from County Down, and a veteran of North Africa and Sicily, he was one of the few men of the 1st Airborne Division to actually reach Arnhem Bridge. Captured when the bridge fell back into German hands, no camp details are listed. After the war he served with the Ulster Defence Regiment.

Name: Nickle, W. J. (Bill)
Rank: Craftsman (Driver/Mechanic)
No: 915500
Unit: No 6 Light Aid Detachment REME
From Belfast, was attached to the 4th Parachute Brigade for 'Market Garden', and escaped across the Rhine at the end of the battle.

Name: O'Brien, Patrick
Rank: Private
No: 7047749
Unit: 3rd Parachute Battalion
He was the son of Captain D. O'Brien DCM MSM of Dublin, Eire, formally of the Connaught Rangers. Private O'Brien originally enlisted in the Royal Irish Fusiliers

before transferring to Airborne Forces. He saw service in Sicily and Italy before being captured at Arnhem, where he was a member of No 7 Platoon, 'C' Company. No POW camp details are listed.

Name: O'Brien, Thomas F.
Rank: Private
No: 5511421
Unit: 21st Independent Parachute Company
Reported as being from Ireland and listed as missing at Arnhem, he formerly served with the Hampshire Regiment. He was taken prisoner and sent to Camp VIII C, Kunau Kz Sprottau/Sagan, POW number 92157.

Name: O'Callaghan, Eric C. MBE MC
Rank: Captain
No: 243580
Unit: 9th Field Company Royal Engineers
Reported to be from Ireland, he served in No 2 Platoon at Arnhem and received a Mention-in-Despatches for that action. He was awarded the Military Cross for his actions on Sicily, and received a second MID for service in Palestine. He was also awarded the MBE.

Name: O'Connor, Herbert Francis
Rank: Private
No: 3776202
Unit: 1st Battalion Border Regiment
From Eire, he was killed in action on Sicily on 9 July 1943, aged 26, when his glider crashed into the sea. He has no known grave and is commemorated on the Cassino Memorial, panel 7.

Name: O'Leary, Peter
Rank: Lance-Sergeant
No: 4206855
Unit: 1st Parachute Battalion
The son of Irish parents, he had originally served with the Royal Welsh Fusiliers. He served with Jack Fryer in the 1st Battalion, and became a prisoner of war after Arnhem at Camp VIIA, Moosburg, POW number 140128.

Name: Oliver, George
Rank: Private
No: 7046170
Unit: 3rd Parachute Battalion
The son of Mr and Mrs David Oliver of Woodvale, Belfast, he was an ex-Royal Irish Fusilier and was killed in action on 14 July 1943 in Sicily, aged 23. He is commemorated on panel 12 of the Cassino Memorial.

Name: O'Neill, Joseph
Rank: Lance-Sergeant
No: 7043403
Unit: 11th Parachute Battalion
An ex-Royal Irish Fusilier from Eire, he was killed in action at Arnhem on 23 September 1944. He has no known grave and is commemorated on the Groesbeek Memorial.

Name: O'Reilly, Charles
Rank: Private
No: 6977913
Unit: Unknown
From Drumore, Stewartstown, County Tyrone, he enlisted in the Inniskilling Fusiliers in 1934. Listed as missing in action, then a prisoner of war at Arnhem, no camp details are listed.

Name: O'Reilly, John Joseph
Rank: Sergeant
No: 6979621
Unit: 156 Parachute Battalion
Born in Belfast on 8 July 1921, he originally joined the Royal Inniskilling Fusiliers at the age of 17. In 1942, while stationed in India, he transferred to the 151 Battalion, which later became the 156 Battalion, serving in 11 Platoon of 'C' Company at Arnhem. He was present at the Liberation of Copenhagen, being demobbed in the summer of 1945.

Name: O'Sullivan, Edward Delaney
Rank: Lance-Corporal
No: 1435732
Unit: 21st Independent Parachute Company
He first enlisted in the 108th Light Anti-Aircraft Battery in 1940, but in 1942 he transferred to the Glider Pilot Regiment. Failing to qualify as a glider pilot, he transferred to the 21st Independent Parachute Company. He later transferred again to the 22nd Independent in late 1943. He was killed in action on D-Day, 6 June 1944, and is buried in Touffreville Churchyard, Calvados. The Village Square was named in his honour – see main text.

Name: Parker, D. S.
Rank: Sergeant
No: 5586465
Unit: Glider Pilot Regiment
From County Cavan, he originally served in the Wiltshire Regiment. He was co-pilot to Captain J. A. Morrison in a Horsa glider of No 5 Flight, 'D' Squadron, flying from Broadwell Farm to LZ-X. The glider load contained elements of the 2nd Air-Landing Anti-Tank Battery. He was taken prisoner of war and sent to Camp XIIA, Limburg, SD Lahn.

Name: Percy, Robert
Rank: Flight Sergeant.
No: 1077628
Unit: 190 Squadron RAF (Volunteer Reserve)
The son of William and Elizabeth Percy, his aircraft, Stirling (LJ-982), flew from Fairford on 21 September 1944 on a re-supply flight to Arnhem. It was hit by flak at approximately 1545hrs and crashed 500 metres north of farm 'De Slop', 1.5km south of the Rhine at Zetten. There were no survivors and all are buried in the Airborne Cemetery at Oosterbeek, 4.D.10. Flight-Sergeant Percy died of his wounds, aged 25.

Name: Phillips, Edward
Rank: Lance-Corporal
No: 7013727
Unit: Unknown
An ex-Royal Ulster Rifleman from Lisburn, County Antrim, he had seven years service prior to being captured at Arnhem. He was sent to Camp XIIA, Limburg, SD Lahn. Recently married prior to the operation, his wife resided in England. Three of his brothers also served: Ivan was killed in action serving with the Royal Inniskilling Fusiliers in Burma, Joseph was taken prisoner serving with the Royal Irish Fusiliers in Italy, and Herbert served with the Royal Artillery in North West Europe.

Name: Place, J. W.
Rank: Lieutenant-Colonel
No: Unknown
Unit: Glider Pilot Regiment
From Dublin, as Commanding Officer of No 2 Wing he flew to Arnhem with Lieutenant Ralph Maltby (KIA). He also served in Sicily.

Name: Power, Sydney
Rank: Sergeant
No: 7013959
Unit: 2nd Parachute Battalion
An ex-Royal Ulster Rifleman from County Armagh, he was killed in action at Arnhem between 21 and 25 September 1944. He is buried in the Airborne Cemetery at Oosterbeek, 19.A.13.

Name: Pritchard, James
Rank: Corporal
No: Unknown
Unit: 1st Parachute Battalion
An ex-Royal Ulster Rifleman from Belfast, he was taken prisoner after Arnhem and sent to POW Camp XIIA, Limburg. His brother served in the Royal Navy during the war, while their father had been killed in the First World War.

Name: Probyn
Rank: Lieutenant
No: Unknown
Unit: Glider Pilot Regiment
It is believed that this officer served with the 1st Airborne Division in North Africa, before transferring to the Independent Squadron. He was the grandson of Irishman Captain Deighton Probyn VC of the 2nd Punjab Cavalry, the man responsible for the raising of 'Probyn's Horse'.

Name: Quick, Lew
Rank: Private
No: 19162164
Unit: 4th Parachute Battalion
From Dublin, he served in North Africa and Sicily with the 1st Airborne Division before transferring to the 2nd Independent Parachute Brigade. He received a Mention-in-Despatches for Palestine.

Name: Quinn, Peter
Rank: Sergeant
No: 14441146
Unit: 1st Airborne Reconnaissance Squadron
From Athlone, Eire, and an ex-Royal Ulster Rifleman, he escaped across the Rhine after the battle.

Name: Radcliff, Herbert C. N.
Rank: Lieutenant
No: 232560
Unit: 10th Parachute Battalion
Shown as being both born and resident in Eire, Herbert Radcliff served as officer commanding the Medium Machine-Gun Platoon in Support Company of the 10th Battalion at Arnhem. He was killed in action on 19 September 1944 close to the railway crossing at Wolfheze; he was 21 years old. He was buried in the Airborne Cemetery at Oosterbeek, 6.D.1.

Name: Redmond, 'Paddy'
Rank: Private
No: 5630388
Unit: 21st Independent Parachute Company
An ex-member of the Devonshire Regiment, he came from Eire and is believed to have served under an assumed name in No 1 Platoon.

Name: Reilly, Charles
Rank: Private
No: 6977913
Unit: 3rd Parachute Battalion
From Stewartstown, County Tyrone, he is listed as missing after Arnhem and later reported as a prisoner of war, although no prison camp details are listed. He had a total of ten years service.

Name: Roberts, William George
Rank: Private
No: 7013147
Unit: 2nd Parachute Battalion
An ex-Royal Ulster Rifleman from Belfast, he transferred to Airborne Forces and served in North Africa, Sicily, Italy and Arnhem, where he was taken prisoner when Arnhem Bridge fell back into German hands. No prison camp details are listed.

Name: Robinson, Jacob
Rank: Sergeant
No: Unknown
Unit: Unknown
From Belfast, he was reported in the local press as having been killed at Arnhem, but there is no record of a J. Robinson on the Roll of Honour or in the Commonwealth War Graves Commission records. He may have served under an assumed name.

Name: Robinson, Martin
Rank: Private
No: 6979407
Unit: 156 Parachute Battalion
An ex-Royal Inniskilling Fusilier from Belfast, he transferred to the 151 Battalion when it was raised in India. He served in Italy before going to Arnhem. The *Belfast Telegraph* of 14 October 1944 reported the following: 'The residents of Silvergrove Street, Belfast, this afternoon paid tribute to Private Martin Robinson, 40 Silvergrove Street, when they presented him with a wallet of notes. Private Robinson, who is a member of the airborne troops, has had service in India, Sicily, and Dunkirk. The collectors were Mrs Drummond and Mrs

McCaffery. Councillor S. K. Henry, JP, on behalf of the subscribers presented the gift to Private Robinson.'

Name: Robinson, William
Rank: Private
No: 7043192
Unit: 3rd Parachute Battalion
The son of Sarah Skelly of Linwood Street, Belfast, he had originally served with the Royal Inniskilling Fusiliers. He served in the 3rd Parachute Battalion at Arnhem, being captured at the end of the battle and sent to Camp XVIIB, Gneizendorf. A brother also served.

Private William Robinson

Name: Rodgers, Richard 'Dick' 'Doc'
Rank: Private
No: 6984167
Unit: 21st Independent Parachute Company
From County Londonderry, he enlisted in the Royal Inniskilling Fusilier on 10 September 1940, and joined the 21st Independent on 17 September 1943. He was a Pathfinder at Arnhem one year later, and escaped across the Rhine.

Name: Rogers, Terence P. W.
Rank: Captain
No: 124276
Unit: 156 Parachute Battalion
Born in India of Irish parents, he was commissioned into the Royal Ulster Rifles. He served at Arnhem as second-in-command of 'A' Company, and was killed in action on Wednesday 20 September close to Oosterbeek railway station, aged 30. He is buried in the Airborne Cemetery at Oosterbeek, 6.B.16.

Name: Ryan, Edward 'Eddie'
Rank: Private
No: 3961505
Unit: 156 Parachute Battalion
From Eire, he was a friend of J. J. Conway, also of the 156 Battalion, and they both served at Arnhem. Eddie Ryan was taken prisoner and sent to Stalag XIIA.

Name: Ryan, Joseph D.
Rank: Unknown
No: Unknown
Unit: 156 Parachute Battalion
A pre-war soldier from County Armagh, he first enlisted in the Royal Inniskilling Fusiliers in 1935. He was stationed in India when war was declared and shortly after transferred to Airborne Forces and was posted to the 151 Battalion. He subsequently served in the 156 Battalion in North Africa and Sicily, then transferred to the Special Air Service and served for the remainder of the war. he also fought in Korea with the Royal Artillery.

Name: Ryan, Joseph Patrick MM
Rank: Sergeant
No: 5333588
Unit: 1st Parachute Battalion
From Dublin, Eire, he was awarded the Military Medal for his actions at S'Nsir-Mateur on 18 November 1942 as a member of 'S' Company.

Name: Ryan, William 'Bill'
Rank: Sergeant
No: Unknown
Unit: Unknown
From Ireland, he went into hiding with the Dutch Resistance after the Arnhem battle and escaped across the Rhine during operation 'Pegasus I' on the night of 22 October 1944.

Name: Saunders, William
Rank: Private
No: 7018194
Unit: 2nd Parachute Battalion
An ex-Royal Ulster Rifleman from Belfast, as a member of 8 Platoon, 'C' Company, he served in North Africa and Sicily, where he was wounded. He was also wounded at Arnhem and taken prisoner, but no camp details are listed.

Name: Scullion, Tommy
Rank: Private
No: 6985123
Unit: 21st Independent Parachute Company
An ex-Royal Inniskilling Fusilier from County Antrim, he was one of the original members of the Company. He served in North African and Sicily prior to Arnhem, and escaped across the Rhine after the battle. He was one of those selected to return to Arnhem in 1945 to assist in the making of the film *Theirs Is The Glory*.

Name: Shannon, James
Rank: Private
No: 7021979
Unit: 2nd Parachute Battalion
An ex-Royal Ulster Rifleman from Cabra, County Dublin, he was the son of James and Mary Shannon, and was killed in action on Operation 'Fustian', the paratroop attack on Sicily on 14 July 1943, aged 18. He is buried in Catania War Cemetery, 1.D.6.

Name: Sheedy, John Joseph
Rank: Lance-Sergeant
No: 5730882
Unit: 1st Parachute Battalion
From County Waterford, the son of Francis and Mary Sheedy, he first enlisted in the Dorset Regiment, and was killed in action on Operation 'Fustian', the paratroop attack on Sicily on 14 July 1943, aged 26. He is buried in Catania War Cemetery, II.C.49.

Name: Siggins, Donald C. C.
Rank: Lieutenant
No: 143286
Unit: 1st Air-Landing Light Regiment Royal Artillery
From Portrush, County Antrim, he had five years service prior to 'Market Garden'. He was reported as missing and a prisoner of war after Arnhem, being sent to Oflag 79 at Braunschweig

Name: Simpson, Jack.
Rank: Corporal
No: 70134542
Unit: Unknown
An ex-Royal Ulster Rifleman from Belfast, he was reported in the local press as missing, then as a prisoner of war after Arnhem, being sent to Camp 357 Oerbke, near Fallingbostel, POW No 84764.

Name: Simpson, Thomas James Duncan
Rank: Sergeant
No: Unknown
Unit: Glider Pilot Regiment
He entered Queen's University, Belfast, in 1934 on a War Office Pre-Entry Course, and first served with the Royal Engineers before transferring to the Glider Pilot Regiment. He was reported as having been at Arnhem, but is not listed in the POW register, so may have escaped at the end of the battle.

Name: Singleton, A.
Rank: Private
No: 6984172
Unit: 3rd Parachute Battalion
An ex-Royal Inniskilling Fusilier from Hillsborough, County Down, he served in 'B' Company of the 3rd Battalion and was taken prisoner after Arnhem, although there are no prison camp details.

Name: Smellie, John Frederick
Rank: Captain
No: 158421
Unit: Glider Pilot Regiment
Born in Eire, the son of N. S. H. and Eileen M. Smellie, he lived in Holywood, County Down, at the outbreak of war, having entered Queen's University, Belfast, in 1932 to study Law. He transferred from the Royal Army Service Corps to the GPR, served in 'B' Squadron for Operation 'Market Garden', and was killed in action on 23 September 1944, while serving as OC No 4 Flight, aged 30. He is buried in the Airborne Cemetery at Oosterbeek, 6.A.4, and his name is listed on the War Memorial in the village of Holywood and on the Queen's University memorial at the OTC Building, Belfast.

Name: Smith, Albert E. DFC
Rank: Warrant Officer
No: Unknown
Unit: 575 Squadron RAF (Volunteer Reserve)
From County Armagh – see main text.

Name: Smith, John Taylor
Rank: Sergeant
No: Unknown
Unit: Glider Pilot Regiment
He entered Queen's University, Belfast, in 1943 on an RAF Pre-Entry Course, and first served with the Royal West Kent Regiment. He is not listed in POW records.

Right Captain John Frederick Smellie, Glider Pilot Regiment (on the right).

Below right The Airborne Cemetery at Oosterbeek in 1945. Patrick Sullivan's grave is on the right at the front. *Border & King's Own Royal Border Regiment Museum*

Name: Spiller, Harry Sydney
Rank: Sergeant
No: Unknown
Unit: Glider Pilot Regiment
He entered Queen's University, Belfast, on a War Office Pre-Entry Course, and first served with the Royal Engineers. He is reported as having served at Arnhem, and is not listed as a prisoner of war.

Name: Streeter
Rank: Sergeant
No: Unknown
Unit: Unknown
He escaped across the Rhine after Arnhem, according to an undated report in a local newspaper.

Name: Sullivan, Patrick
Rank: Private
No: 6978471
Unit: 11th Parachute Battalion
An ex-Royal Inniskilling Fusilier from County Wicklow, he was the son of Michael and Jane Sullivan, and was killed in action on 21 September 1944, aged 26. He is buried in the Airborne Cemetery at Oosterbeek, 5.C.15.

Name: Summerville, Gordon 'Slim'
Rank: Sergeant
No: 6980121
Unit: 21st Independent Parachute Company
From Northern Ireland, he led a party of ex-Young Soldiers from the Inniskillings to the 1st Airborne Division and in turn into the 21st Independent.

Name: Sunderland, J.
Rank: Sergeant Pilot
No: Unknown
Unit: 644 Squadron RAF
From Carrickfergus, County Antrim, he was reported as having towed gliders on D-Day, Arnhem and the Rhine crossing. For 'Market Garden', 644 Squadron flew 46 glider-towing missions without loss.

Name: Symons, Gerald
Rank: Private
No: 11412225
Unit: 133 Parachute Field Ambulance RAMC
From Grove Street, Belfast, he was taken prisoner after Arnhem, where he served with 'J' Section, and was sent to Camp XIB, Fallingbostel, POW number 117162. Private

Symons had a total of 17 years service, and two of his brothers also served during the war.

Name: Tallentire, Wilfred
Rank: Captain
No: Unknown
Unit: Glider Pilot Regiment
From County Down, he originally enlisted in the Royal Artillery. For Operation 'Market Garden' he served as OC No 1 Wing, and later served in the Far East.

Name: Tansley, George
Rank: Private
No: 6981799
Unit: 156 Parachute Battalion
An ex-Royal Inniskilling Fusilier from Northern Ireland, he was killed in action at Arnhem on 25 September 1944, aged 29, and is buried in the Airborne Cemetery at Oosterbeek, 32.B.2.

Name: Thompson, J.
Rank: Corporal
No: 5725314
Unit: 4th Battalion Dorset Regiment
From Downpatrick, County Down, he was taken prisoner within the Oosterbeek perimeter after crossing the Rhine, and sent to Camp XIB, Fallingbostel, POW number 117361.

Name: Towhey, John
Rank: Private
No: 7046990
Unit: 1st Parachute Battalion
From Eire, he enlisted in the Royal Irish Fusiliers, then transferred to Airborne Forces and was killed in action on 17 September 1944, while serving in 'R' Company, aged 24. He is buried in the Airborne Cemetery at Oosterbeek, 5.A.6.

Name: Trainor, 'Paddy'
Rank: Driver
No: Unknown
Unit: Royal Engineers
From Belfast, he left the 1st Airborne Division to serve with the 2nd Independent Parachute Brigade Workshop in Italy.

Name: Tucker, Edward W.
Rank: Private
No: 7013719
Unit: 2nd Parachute Battalion
From Belfast – see the main text.

Name: Usher, James
Rank: Private
No: Unknown
Unit: 1st Parachute Battalion
The son of Mrs Margaret Usher from Sydney Street West in Belfast, he had originally served in the Ox and Bucks Light Infantry. After the war he served in the Merchant Navy.

Name: Verral, C. A. D.
Rank: Private
No: 7023138
Unit: 1st Battalion Border Regiment
An ex-Royal Ulster Rifleman from Northern Ireland, he was taken prisoner of war after Arnhem and sent to Camp XIIA, Limburg, SD Lahn, POW number 075483.

Name: Vint, F. W.
Rank: Gunner
No: Unknown
Unit: 1st Air-Landing Light Regiment, Royal Artillery
Gunner Vint received a Mention-in-Despatches for his action at Arnhem.

Name: Walker, Joseph
Rank: Private
No: 3603968
Unit: 1st Battalion Border Regiment
From Moira, County Down, he was the son of Mr and Mrs Isaac Walker, and was killed in action on 18 September 1944 at Arnhem, aged 22, while serving in 'D' Company. He is buried in the Airborne Cemetery at Oosterbeek, 15.A.7. His brother was also killed in action.

Name: Walsh, Richard 'Dicky'
Rank: Unknown
No: Unknown
Unit: 1st Parachute Battalion
From Dublin, he later transferred to the 1st (Airborne) Battalion, Royal Ulster Rifles.

Name: Watson
Rank: Sergeant
No: Unknown
Unit: Glider Pilot Regiment
His name was mentioned in conversation with other veterans of the 1st Airborne Division.

Name: Watt, William E 'Billy'
Rank: Lance-Sergeant
No: 961356
Unit: 1st Air-Landing Light Regiment, Royal Artillery
From Coleraine, County Londonderry, he enlisted in the Army in 1940 and transferred to Airborne Forces in 1942. He served in North Africa, Sicily and Italy, and was wounded and taken prisoner after Arnhem, although no camp details are listed. Three brothers also served in the Second World War.

Name: Webber, Daniel
Rank: Unknown
No: Unknown
Unit: 156 Parachute Battalion
He came from County Donegal. According to POW records, a '5498825 Webber Pte D. G.' was interred at KRIE.

Name: Webber, Daniel R. W.
Rank: Major
No: 63580
Unit: 11th Parachute Battalion
Reportedly from Ireland, Major Webber, officer commanding HQ Company, was captured at Arnhem and sent to Oflag 79, POW number 00552.

Name: Wetherall, J. A. B.
Rank: Sergeant
No: 14414511
Unit: Glider Pilot Regiment
From Blackrock, County Dublin, he was mentioned in conversation with an Arnhem veteran as having been taken prisoner after 'Market Garden'. He is listed as having been at Camp 344, Lamsdorf, POW number 1087.

Name: White, Albert 'Bertie'
Rank: Sergeant
No: 6924849
Unit: 156 Parachute Battalion
From Northern Ireland, he served at Arnhem and was killed in action on 18 September 1944. He is buried in the Airborne Cemetery at Oosterbeek, 5.B.10; the position given for his field grave indicates that he died shortly after landing.

Name: Whitton, Robert Walter
Rank: Corporal
No: 3450725
Unit: 1st Battalion Border Regiment
From Eire, the son of Robert and Margaret Whitton, he was killed in action on 10 July 1943 during the attack on Sicily. He has no known grave, and is commemorated on the Cassino Memorial, panel 7.

Name: Williams, E.
Rank: Gunner
No: 1528726
Unit: 1st Air-Landing Light Regiment, Royal Artillery
From Omagh, County Tyrone, he was reported to have served at Arnhem. He is not listed as a POW or casualty, so may have escaped.

Name: Willis, Henry
Rank: Corporal
Number: Unknown
Unit: Unknown
It was reported in the *Belfast Telegraph* of 17 October 1944 that Corporal Willis was entertained to supper at the HQ of his local Home Guard unit. Henry Willis joined the Royal Ulster Rifles in 1928, then transferred to the Gordon Highlanders in 1937. He fought with the 8th Army in North Africa before transferring to Airborne Forces. While at home he stayed with his sister, Mrs Elizabeth Neill, who resided at Longstone Street, Lisburn. There is no Airborne unit listed for Corporal Willis, but considering when he transferred it is likely that he served with one of the parachute battalions in the 4th Parachute Brigade.

Name: Wilson, Robert
Rank: Corporal
No: Unknown
Unit: Unknown
An ex-Royal Ulster Rifleman from Belfast, County Antrim, he was listed in the local press as wounded in hospital in Wales after the airborne operation at Arnhem.

Name: Wilson, Thomas
Rank: Private
No: 7021594
Unit: 2nd Battalion South Staffordshire Regiment
An ex-Royal Ulster Rifleman from Belfast, County Antrim, he was taken prisoner after Arnhem and sent to Camp XIB, Fallingbostel, POW number 117370.

Name: Woods, Reginald Bryan
Rank: Lieutenant
No: 176460
Unit: 2nd Parachute Battalion
Born in Malahide, County Dublin, he was commissioned into the Royal Ulster Rifles, then transferred to Airborne Forces and served in North Africa, Sicily and at Arnhem, where he was officer commanding the Mortar Platoon. He was wounded and taken prisoner, but died of his wounds in prison camp. He is buried in Becklingen Cemetery, 8.C.3.

Remembrance Day, Belfast, in the early 1960s. The Northern Ireland Branch of the Parachute Regimental Association is on parade and several veterans of the 1st Airborne Division can be identified. The standard bearer is Joe Smith, who served with the 1st Parachute Brigade in North Africa. Wearing the light trench-coat is Bill Scott. Left to right in the first row are Campbell, Jackie Hegan and Tommy Lundy. Jim Bowden is behind Campbell, while the figure in the trilby hat is Bill Kerr. Directly behind Bill is Billy Saunders. Danny Gillespie is the last figure on the left-hand side. *D. Gillespie*

Appendix 2

The danger of the three-lift attack, and 'the phrase'

To tow the gliders of the 1st Airborne Division to Arnhem the RAF allocated ten squadrons from 38 Group and six squadrons from 46 Group. The USAAF was to make available Dakotas of the 9th Troop Carrier Command to drop the paratroopers. This was far from adequate.

Urquhart calculated he would need at least another 40 aircraft and was informed by Browning that this was impossible. Browning then used 38 aircraft to transport his Headquarters to Nijmegen, where he played no part in the battle whatsoever.

Urquhart gave the following reasons for avoiding the 'three-lift attack':

The first lift will not only have to seize the bridges, but also protect the landing and drop zones for the following drops.
The enemy will have time to build up strength around the zones.
German anti-aircraft will be ready for the following drops as they will have had ample warning from their positions on the coast.

To offset this danger it was suggested that the aircraft should make two trips on the first day. The RAF rejected this on the grounds that there would not be time for repairs, essential maintenance and rest periods for crews. 38 Group then suggested that the first lift should be taken in before dawn, which would give time for a second lift later in the day. The commanders within the 1st Airborne Division fully agreed with this, as a night landing had the advantage of surprising the enemy and hiding the true numbers of men in the drop. The further confusion caused by the dropping of dummy parachutists was also a vital factor.

This approach could not be adopted because American aircrews were not well enough trained on night operations. The landings in Sicily and on the Cotentin peninsula during D-Day showed this to be true.

'The phrase'

The oft-repeated story of how Browning is supposed to have voiced his doubts about 'Market Garden' to Montgomery with the phrase 'I think we might be going a bridge too far' proves to be false. The meeting was between Browning and Dempsey, and as Browning had been so keen on the operation known as 'Comet', from which 'Market Garden' derived, it is highly unlikely that he made any such remark, except later in the past tense.

APPENDIX 3

1ST AIRBORNE DIVISION ORDER OF BATTLE 1944

Division HQ
General Officer Commanding – Major-General R. E.
    'Roy' Urquhart
1st Airborne Divisional HQ and Defence Platoon

1st Parachute Brigade – Brigadier G. W. Lathbury
Brigade HQ and Defence Platoon
1st Parachute Battalion – Lieutenant-Colonel D. T.
    Dobie
2nd Parachute Battalion – Lieutenant-Colonel J. D.
    Frost
3rd Parachute Battalion – Lieutenant-Colonel J. A. C.
    Fitch
1st Air-Landing Anti-Tank Battery, Royal Artillery –
    Major W. F. Arnold
1st Parachute Squadron, Royal Engineers – Major D. C.
    Murray
16 Parachute Field Ambulance, Royal Army Medical
    Corps – Lieutenant-Colonel E. Townsend

4th Parachute Brigade – Brigadier J. W. 'Shan' Hackett
Brigade HQ and Defence Platoon
156 Parachute Battalion – Lieutenant-Colonel
    Sir R. de B. des Voeux
10th Parachute Battalion – Lieutenant-Colonel K. B. I.
    Smyth
11th Parachute Battalion – Lieutenant-Colonel G. H.
    Lea
2nd (Oban) Air-Landing Anti-Tank Battery, Royal
    Artillery – Major A. F. 'Bill' Haynes
4th Parachute Squadron, Royal Engineers – Major
    A. J. M. Perkins
133 Parachute Field Ambulance, Royal Army Medical
    Corps – Lieutenant-Colonel W. C. Alford

1st Air-Landing Brigade – Brigadier P. H. W. 'Pip'
    Hicks
Brigade HQ and Defence Platoon

1st Battalion, Border Regiment – Lieutenant-Colonel
    T. H. Haddon
2nd Battalion, South Staffordshire Regiment –
    Lieutenant-Colonel W. D. H. McCardie
7th (Galloway) Battalion, King's Own Scottish
    Borderers – Lieutenant-Colonel R. Payton-Reid
181 Air-Landing Field Ambulance, Royal Army
    Medical Corps – Lieutenant-Colonel A. T. Marrable

Divisional Troops
21st Independent Parachute Company – Major B. A.
    'Boy' Wilson
1st Air-Landing Light Regiment, Royal Artillery –
    Lieutenant-Colonel W. F. K. 'Sheriff' Thompson
1st Forward (Airborne) Observation Unit, Royal
    Artillery – Major D. R. Wight Boycott
1st Airborne Divisional Signals – Lieutenant Colonel T.
    G. V. Stephenson
9th (Airborne) Field Company, Royal Engineers –
    Major J. C. Winchester
261 (Airborne) Field Park Company, Royal Engineers –
    Lieutenant W. H. Skinner
1st Airborne Reconnaissance Squadron – Major C. F. H.
    Gough
250 (Airborne) Light Composite Company, Royal Army
    Service Corps – Colonel Michael St J. Packe
1st (Airborne) Divisional Field Park, Royal Army
    Ordnance Corps – Major C. C. 'Bill' Chidgey
1st (Airborne) Divisional Workshops, Royal Electrical &
    Mechanical Engineers – Captain A. F. Ewens
1st (Airborne) Divisional Provost Company, Corps of
    Military Police – Captain W. B. Gray
89th (Parachute) Field Security Section, Intelligence
    Corps – Captain J. E. Killick

Attached Units
Glider Pilot Regiment No 1 Wing – Lieutenant-
    Colonel I. A. Murray

Glider Pilot Regiment No 2 Wing – Lieutenant-Colonel J. W. Place

6080 and 6341 Light Warning Units, Royal Air Force – Squadron-Leaders H. W. Coxon and L. Wheeler

Dutch Liaison Team – Lieutenant Commander A. Wolters and Lieutenant M. J. Knottenbelt

Public Relations Unit – Major R. Oliver

US Air Support Signals team – Lieutenants J. Johnson and L. Geddes

GHQ Signal Liaison Regiment Detachment (Phantom) – Lieutenant-Colonel D. Heathcoat-Amory

'Jedburg' Team – Captain J. Groeneweg (Dutch) and H. A. Todd (USA)

Polish Independent Parachute Brigade Group – Major General S. F. Sosabowski

1st Battalion – Major M. Tonn

2nd Battalion – Major W. Ploszewski

3rd Battalion – Captain W. Sobocinski

Anti-Tank Battery – Captain J. K. Wardzala

Engineer Company – Captain P. Budziszewski

Signals Company – Captain J. Burzawa

Medical Company – Lieutenant J. Mozdzierz

Transport and Supply Company – Captain A. Siudzinski

Light Artillery Battery – Major J. Bielecki

ACKNOWLEDGEMENTS

A book such as this is never possible without the assistance of many people. I have been extremely lucky in having some of the best friends possible while writing *Brotherhood of the Cauldron*. To those who have given continued support throughout the course of the work, and some who have helped with only a word or phrase, my sincere thanks and probably many drinks in the years to come.

Many veterans have generously given their time in providing interviews and reminiscences during many years of research. It is my sincere regret that some of those veterans who gave me so much of their time have passed away before this work has been completed. My thanks must also go to my parents for their continued encouragement, my wife, Sharon, for putting up with my continued absence into 'the room', and to my son, Nathan, for teaching me how to use the computer in the first place!

Veterans interviewed (ranks and decorations are those held during 'Market Garden'): Corporal J. H. Bankhead 156 Battalion; Private T. J. Bannister, 181 Air-Landing Field Ambulance; Lance-Corporal Fred Budd, 181 Air-Landing Field Ambulance; Private George Curtis, 1st Battalion Border Regiment; Leading-Aircraftsman J. T. Dalkin RAFVR, Air Sea Rescue; Major Mervyn Dennison MC, OC 'A' Company, 3rd Parachute Battalion; Private Paddy Devlin, 1st Battalion, Royal Ulster Rifles; Private Norman Diffin, 156 Parachute Battalion; Private A. Dunbar, Royal Corps of Signals; Sergeant 'Jock' East, Glider Pilot Regiment; QMS H. W. Evans, 181 Air-Landing Field Ambulance; Lance-Sergeant Jack Fryer, HQ and 'T' Company, 1st Parachute Battalion; Private Danny Gillespie, 21st Independent Parachute Company; Sergeant D. A. Hall, Glider Pilot Regiment; John Hamblett, 1st Airborne Provost Company; Lance-Corporal Norman Harris, 1st Parachute Brigade HQ; Norman Howes, 2nd Battalion, South Staffords; Gunner George Jackson, 1st Air-Landing Light Regiment; Brigadier Osmond L. Jones DSO, South Staffords; Private Samuel John Kendrick, 1st Parachute Battalion; Private Bill Kerr, 11th Parachute Battalion; Captain James Magee, 21st Independent Parachute Company; Private William Magill, 'R' Company, 1st Parachute Battalion; Eric Milner, 'C' Troop, 1st Air-Landing Anti-Tank Battery; Private Harry Mitchell, 21st Independent Parachute Company; Staff-Sergeant Walter B. Naismith, Glider Pilot Regiment; Private N. J. Neads, 1st Parachute Brigade HQ; WO2 E. A. Neal, 181 Air-Landing Field Ambulance; Private Cecil Newell, 2nd Parachute Battalion; Private Pat O'Brien, 3rd Parachute Battalion; Captain Arthur O'Grady, No 1 Forward Observation Unit, RA; Private George Phillips; Private T. J. Phillips and Private S. G. Potter, 181 Air-Landing Field Ambulance; Private Lew Quick, 2nd Independent Parachute Brigade; Staff-Sergeant Harry Rathband, Glider Pilot Regiment; Corporal A. Reece, 1st Airborne Divisional Signals; Major Guy Rigby-Jones MC, 181 Air-Landing Field Ambulance; Lance-Corporal R. E. Roberts, 133 Parachute Field Ambulance; Private William George Roberts, 2nd Parachute Battalion; Sapper J. R. Ross, 9th Field Company (Airborne), RE; Private William Saunders, 'C' Company, 2nd Parachute Battalion; Staff-Sergeant J. Simpson, Glider Pilot Regiment; Private James Sims, 'S' Company, 2nd Parachute Battalion; WO1 Albert Smith, 575 Squadron RAF; Corporal James Swan MM, 1st Battalion, Border Regiment; Captain Douglas Swinscow, RAMC attached to 1st Airborne Reconnaissance Squadron; Captain Wilfred Tallentire, Glider Pilot Regiment; W. J. C. Turnbull RAF; Private V. N. Winter, 181 Parachute Field Ambulance.

Other sources:

Jan Aiken, for her translation of *Le Pont du Arnhem*

Airborne Battle Study Group archives

Marcel Anker, for his assistance in sorting out the chain of events regarding Billy Saunders on 17 September 1944

Derek Armitage, Museum of Army Flying, Middle Wallop

Arnhem Battle Research Group archives

Leslie Beattie, for all the coffee and encouragement

Stephen Blevins and the pupils of Millington PS, Portadown, for information on Private E Lynas

Mary Bradley, Holywood Public Library

Dominick Browne, for information on his brother Private Pat Browne, KOSB

Luuk Buist, for information on the Glider Pilot Regiment

Cameron family of Carrickfergus, for information on Private J. Cameron

Campbell College, Belfast, for information on Lieutenant John McFadden

Ian Campbell, for his attempts at straightening out my strangulated sentences

Tom Carter, for information on his uncle, Robert Carter

Martin Cassidy, for information on Richard Lonsdale

George Cholewczynski, for help with Cooney, the maps and the rest

Liz Consiglia and the Staff of Newtownards Public Library

Geoff Crump, Cheshire Regimental Museum

Matt Dillon, for information on the 4/7th Dragoon Guards (most of which will probably be used in the next book)

Richard Doherty, for assistance and friendship

T. Duncan, Headmaster, The Royal School, Armagh

Stuart Eastwood, for encouragement, friendship and guidance in the field of military research

Major John Ellis, Cheshire Regimental Museum

John Ellis, for the information on Private Jimmy Finn

Ted Flanagan, for information on Private Cecil Newell

Harry W. Foot, Museum of Army Flying, Middle Wallop

Philip R. French, Leicester City Museums Service, for information on Major Lonsdale

Bob Gerritsen, for the many e-mails and telephone calls on various subjects; if he had done much more I would have had to put his name on the cover

Sharon Gregg, Holywood Public Library

Adrian Groeneweg OBE, for friendship and assistance over the past ten years

Neill Hamilton, for information on his father Gunner Thomas L. Hamilton

The Very Reverend Brian Hannon MA, Bishop of Clogher, for information on Padre Buchanan

Mark Hickman, for information on Jack Smyth

George Harris, Larne and Inver Parish Church, for information on Padre Buchanan

Dorothy Hendren, for information on her brothers Sandy and Norman Dougan

Captain J. Knox, Royal Irish Regiment Museum, Ballymena, County Antrim

R. W. Kortekaas, for uncovering details of Irishmen involved in Operation 'Pegasus'

Jaap Kortsloot, for his kind assistance and advice.

Peter Loftus, for information on his cousin Jack Smyth

Geert Maassen, Oosterbeek, without whose help this book would have had a different cover

Vaughan McCracken, for the maps!

Gary McCrea, for information on those Royal Ulster Rifles who served in the 1st Airborne Division

Roy McCullough, for his magic with the computer in restoring many badly damaged photographs

Brian McMullan, for unending good humour and support

Martin Middlebrook, for the Dakota incident

The Right Reverend Thomas Moore, again for information on Padre Buchanan

Amanda Moreno, Royal Irish Fusiliers Museum, Armagh, not forgetting Billy and Iris

Steven Nicholls, for his assistance with the 21st Independent Parachute Company

Professor Eunan O'Halpin, Trinity College, Dublin, for information on spies in Ireland

David Orr and his then pregnant wife, Barbara, without whom this book would have a lot less photographs

Anthony Pas, for information on Private S. J. Kendrick

Bob Phair, for information on the Irish Guards in XXX Corps

P. Pouwels, of Elshout, Holland, for information on the Tallentire episode

Philip Reinders, for his assistance with research into the Polish Brigade and others (that flak jacket was very heavy)

David Rowntree, for you know what!

The Headmaster, Royal School, Armagh, County Armagh, for information on Lieutenant Siggins

David Scott, for information on his uncle, Charles McLaine Davidson

Scullion family, for information on Private Tommy Scullion

Robert Sigmond, for permission to use information from *Off At Last* and continued support

Charlie Smyth, for information on his brother Jack

Glen Thompson, for information on Sergeant Eric Matson

Robert Voskoil, for last-minute illustrations

Peter Vrolijk, for information on the 2nd Parachute Battalion

Eugene Wijnhoud, for information on the artillery at Arnhem

Hans and Els Van Wassenberg, for continued friendship and hospitality

Desmond Woods, for information on his brother Brian

Lori Woollacott, for permission to quote from her late husband's book *Winged Gunners*

Above Sir John Gorman MC, the author and Bert Smith DFC at the opening of 'Irishmen at Arnhem' exhibition held in the Somme Centre, Newtownards, County Down, in September 2002. During 'Market Garden' Sir John was Lieutenant Gorman MC, of the Irish Guards Group. He had been awarded the Military Cross for the destruction of a German King Tiger in Normandy, a feat achieved by ordering his driver to ram the enemy vehicle! Bert Smith was Warrant Officer Albert Edward Smith RAF from County Armagh, awarded the Distinguished Flying Cross for his actions on 17 September 1944. *Bernie Brown LRPS*

Left Bert Smith today. 'It was something that had to be done, then you got on with your life.' *Bernie Brown LRPS*

BIBLIOGRAPHY AND SOURCES

Published sources:

Adams, Jack *The Doomed Expedition: The Campaign in Norway 1940* (Leo Cooper, 1989)

Airborne Battle Study Group, *Just Ordinary Men* (Private publication, 1990)

Airborne Museum, Hartenstein *The Harvest of Ten Years* (1988)

Arnhem Battle Research Group, *'In Action to Repel': the 17lb A/T guns at Arnhem* (Private publication)

Arthur, Max, *Men of the Red Beret* (Hutchinson, 1990)

Badsey, Stephen *Arnhem 1944* (Osprey Publishing 1993)

Baynes, John *Urquhart of Arnhem: The Life of Maj Gen R. E. Urquhart CB DSO* (Brassey's, 1993)

Blanford, Edmund *Green Devils – Red Devils* (Leo Cooper, 1993)

Bredin, Brigadier A. E. C. DSO MC DL *A History of the Irish Soldier*

Breuer, William B. *Operation Dragoon* (Airlife Publishing, 1988)

Buxton, David *Honour To The Airborne*, 2 Vols (1993)

Cartwright, Lt-Col H. H. L. *Airborne to Arnhem* (Newsletter of Friends of the Airborne Museum, No 41, 1994)

Chatterton, Brig G. *The Wings of Pegasus: The Story of the Glider Pilot Regiment* (MacDonald, 1962)

Cherry, Niall *Red Berets and Red Crosses* (Robert Sigmond, Netherlands, 1999)

Cholewczynski, George F. *Poles Apart* (Greenhill Books, 1993)

Crookenden, Arthur *History of the Cheshire Regiment in the Second World War*

D'Arcy-Dawson, John *Tunisian Battle* (1943)

Dekkers, C. A. and Vroemen, L. P. J. (trans Bep O'Neill) *De Zwarte Herfst* (Gijsbers & Van Loon, 1989)

D'Este, Carlo *Bitter Victory: The Battle for Sicily 1943* (Collins, 1988)

Devlin, G. *Paratrooper* (Doubleday, 1985)

Divine, David *The Nine Days of Dunkirk* (Faber & Faber, 1959)

Doherty, Richard *Irish Men and Women in the Second World War* (Four Courts Press, Dublin, 1999)
Wall of Steel: History of 9th (Londonderry) HAA Regiment (North West Books, 1988)

Doherty, Richard and Truesdale, David *Irish Winners of the Victoria Cross* (Four Courts Press, Dublin, 2000)

Dover, V. *The Silken Canopy*
The Sky Generals (London, 1981)

Eastwood, S. A., Gray C. H. W. and Green, A. T. *When Dragons Flew: An Illustrated history of the 1st Battalion The Border Regiment 1939-45* (Silver Link Publishing, 1994)

Ellis, John *Brute Force: Allied strategy and tactics in the Second World War* (Andre Deutsch, 1990)

Ellis, C. and Chamberlain, P. *Handbook on the British Army 1943* (Arms & Armour Press, 1976)

Fairley, John *Remember Arnhem* (Patton Press, 1978)

Ferguson, Gregor *The Paras: British Airborne Forces 1940-84* (Osprey, 1984)

Fisk, Robert *In Time of War: Ireland, Ulster and the price of neutrality 1939-45* (Andre Deutsch, 1983)

Fitzgerald, D. J. L. *History of the Irish Guards in the Second World War* (Gale & Polden Ltd, 1952)

Frost, Maj-Gen John *A Drop Too Many* (Cassell, London, 1980)

Gerritsen, Robert M. *For No Apparent Reason* (R. N. Sigmond Publishing, 2000)

Golden, Lewis *Echoes From Arnhem* (William Kimber, 1984)

Graves, Charles *The Royal Ulster Rifles*, Vol III (RUR Regimental Committee, 1950)

Green, Alan *Arnhem, 1st Battalion, The Border Regiment* (The Museum of the Border Regiment, 1991)

Hackett, Gen Sir John *I Was A Stranger* (Chatto & Windus, 1977)

Hagen, Louis *Arnhem Lift* (Leo Cooper, 1993)

Hamilton, Nigel *Monty, Master of the Battlefield*, Vol II (Sceptre Books, 1983)

Harclerode, Peter *PARA! Fifty Years of The Parachute Regiment* (Brockhampton Press, 1992)

Hayward, J. B. and Son, *Prisoners of War, British Army, 1939-1945* (1990)

Heaps, Leo *The Grey Goose of Arnhem* (Futura, 1976)

Hey, J. A. *Roll of Honour: The Battle of Arnhem 17-26 September 1944* (Society of Friends of the Airborne Museum, Oosterbeek, 1986)

Heyward, John B. *Officers died in the Great War 1914-1919* (Suffolk 1998)

Hezlet, Sir Arthur *The 'B' Specials: A history of the Ulster Special Constabulary* (Mourne River Press, Belfast, 1977)

Hibbert, Christopher *The Battle of Arnhem* (Batsford Books, 1962)

HM Stationery Office *By Air To Battle* (1945)

Horrocks, Brian *A Full Life* (Collins, 1960)
Corps Commander (Sidgwick & Jackson, 1977)

Howarth, T. E. B. *Monty At Close Quarters* (Leo Cooper, 1985)

Jackson, Robert *Arnhem: The Battle Remembered* (Airlife Publishing, 1994)

Johnstone, Iain *The Arnhem Report* (Star Books, 1997)

Johnstone, Tom and Hagerty, James *The Cross on the Sword* (Geoffrey Chapman Ltd, London, 1996)

Keegan, John *Six Armies In Normandy* (Jonathan Cape, 1982)

Kent, Ron *First In: 21st Independent Parachute Company* (Batsford, 1979)

Kershaw, Robert *It Never Snows in September* (Crowood Press, Marlborough, Wilts, 1990)

Lagden, Alan and Sly, John *The 2/73rd at Waterloo* (Privately published, 1998)

Lewin, Ronald *Ultra Goes To War* (Grafton Books, 1998)

Longson, Jim and Taylor, Christine *An Arnhem Odyssey* (Leo Cooper, 1991)

Lucas, James *Storming Eagles* (Arms & Armour Press, 1988)

Mackenzie, C. B. *It Was Like This!* (Stiching Airborne Museum, Oosterbeek, 1991)

Marrinan, Patrick *Churchill and the Irish Marshals* (Pretani Press, 1986)

McKee, Alexander *The Race for the Rhine Bridges* (Pan Books, 1974)

Mead, Peter *Gunners At War, 1939/45* (Ian Allen Ltd, 1982)

Middlebrook, Martin *Arnhem 1944: The Airborne Battle* (Viking, 1994)

Montgomery, Field Marshal B. L. *Memoirs* (Collins, London, 1958)
Normandy to the Baltic (Hutchinson, 1947)

Montgomery, Brian *A Field-Marshal in the Family* (Constable, 1973)

Nicolson, Nigel *Alex: The life of Field Marshal Earl Alexander of Tunis* (Weidenfeld & Nicolson, 1973)

Norton, G. G. *The Red Devils* (Arrow Books, 1988)

Packe, Michael *Winged Stallion* (Blandford Press, 1988)

Powell, Geoffrey *The Devil's Birthday* (Buchan & Enright, London, 1984)

Roberts, Joe *With Spanners Descending* (Bluecoat Press, 1996)

Roekel, C. van *Who Was Who during the Battle of Arnhem* (Society of Friends of the Airborne Museum, Oosterbeek, 1992)

Ryan, Cornelius *A Bridge Too Far* (Hamish Hamilton, 1973)

Ryder, Peter *Guns Have Eyes* (Robert Hale, London, 1984)

Shannon, Kevin and Wright, Stephen *One Night In June* (Wrens Park Publishing, 2000)

Sigmond Robert, *Off At Last* (Netherlands, 1998)

Sims, James *Arnhem Spearhead* (Arrow Books, 1989)

Sosabowski, Maj Gen Stanislaw *Freely I Served* (William Kimber, 1960)

Stainforth, Peter *Wings of the Wind* (Guild Publishing, 1952)

Swiecicki, M. *With the Red Devils at Arnhem* (Max Love, 1945)

Terraine, John *The Right Of The Line* (Hodder & Stoughton, 1985)

Thompson, Julian *War Behind Enemy Lines* (Sidgwick & Jackson, 1998)
Ready For Anything (Fontana Books, 1990)

Truesdale, David *The First Eagle* (Redcoat Publishing, 2000)

Turnbull, Jack and Hamblett, John *The Pegasus Patrol* (Jack Turnbull, 1994)

Urquhart, Brian *A Life in Peace and War* (Weidenfeld & Nicolson, 1987)

Urquhart, Maj Gen. R. E. *Arnhem* (Cassell, London, 1958)

Warner, Philip *Auchinleck, The Lonely Soldier* (Buchan & Enright, 1981)

Weeks, John *Assault From The Sky* (David & Charles, 1978)

Whiting, Charles *Slaughter Over Sicily* (Leo Cooper, 1992)
'44 In Combat On The Western Front From Normandy To The Ardennes (Century Publishing, 1984)

Wood, Alan *The Glider Soldiers* (Spellmount Ltd, 1992)
History of the World's Glider Forces (Patrick Stephens Ltd, 1990)

Woollacott, Robert *Winged Gunners* (Quote Publishers, Zimbabwe, 1994)

Wright, Lawrence *The Wooden Sword* (Walter Beckers)

Zeno *The Cauldron* (Pan Books, 1966)

Unpublished sources:

Baillie, Lieutenant Pat, 7 Platoon, 'A' Company, 1 Border: Diary

CAB 100/12, PRO KEW

Charlton, Private D. J., 'R' Company, 1st Battalion: personal account

Curtis, Reginald, 1st Battalion: personal account

Devlin P., 1st (A) Battalion Royal Ulster Rifles: personal account

Fryer, Lance-Sergeant Jack, 'T' Company, 1st Parachute Battalion: personal account and audio recording

Gillespie, Denis Ivan, 21st Independent Parachute Company: personal account

Green, Corporal G. M., 1 Platoon, 'R' Company, 1st Battalion: personal account

Harper, Corporal Jack, 'C' Company, 3rd Battalion: personal account

Harris, Lance-Corporal Norman, Intelligence Section, 1st Parachute Brigade HQ

Magill, Private William, 'R' Company, 1st Battalion: personal account and audio recording

Neads, N. J., 1st Parachute Brigade HQ: personal account

Newell, Private Cyril, 'A' Company, 2nd Battalion: personal account and audio recording

Peatling, Private Robert, HQ Company, 2nd Battalion: personal account

Quayle, Sergeant T. R., 10 Platoon, 'T' Company, 1st Battalion: personal account

Reece, Lance-Corporal A. E., Signal Section, 1st Parachute Brigade: personal account

Sims, James, 2nd Parachute Battalion: personal account

Smith, Albert, 575 Squadron RAF: personal account and flying log, September 1944

War Diary, HQ 1st Airborne Division, Arnhem

War Diary, 21st Independent Parachute Company, Arnhem

War Diary, No 2 Platoon, 21st Independent Parachute Company, Arnhem

War Diary, 1st Battalion, Parachute Regiment, Arnhem

War Diary, 3rd Battalion, Parachute Regiment, Arnhem

War Diary, 1st Battalion, Border Regiment, Arnhem

War Diary, Krafft, Arnhem

Newspapers:

Armagh Gazette, Ballymena Guardian, Bangor Spectator, Belfast Telegraph, Daily Telegraph, Down Recorder, Newsletter, Newtownards Chronicle, Mourne Observer, Portadown Times, The Scotsman

Journals/periodicals:

An Cosantoir, journal of the Irish Defence Forces, various issues

Border Regiment Magazine, 'The Airborne Operations in Holland, September 1944' (September 1948 issue)

British Army Review, No 79, 'Battle for the Primasole Bridge', Part I

No 80, 'Battle for the Primasole Bridge', Part II

Legion Magazine, various issues

Pegasus, various issues

The Eagle, various issues

The Oak Tree, Regimental journal, 22nd Foot, The Cheshire Regiment

Armes Militaria, No 23, Paris, 1996 (trans Marie Bouchery)

Blackwood's Magazine, various issues

List of Personnel of the Irish Defence Forces dismissed for desertion in time of National Emergency pursuant to the terms of Emergency Powers (No 362) Order 1945 (SR&O 1945, No 198) or of Section 13 of the Defence Forces (Temporary Provisions) Act, 1946 (No 7/1946)

Libraries:

Newtownards Public Library; Holywood Public Library; Comber Public Library; Donaghadee Public Library; Bangor Public Library, County Down; Central Library, Belfast; Linenhall Library, Belfast; Prince Consort's Library, Aldershot

Museums:

Airborne Forces Museum, Aldershot; Airborne Museum, Oosterbeek, Netherlands; Border Regiment & King's Own Royal Border Regiment Museum, Carlisle; Cheshire Military Museum, Chester; Imperial War Museum, London; Museum of Army Flying, Middle Wallop; National Army Museum, London; National War and Resistance Museum, Overloon, Netherlands; Polish Institute and Sikorski Museum, London; Royal Ulster Rifles Museum, Belfast; Royal Irish Fusiliers Museum, Armagh; Royal Inniskilling Fusiliers Museum, Enniskillen; Royal Irish Regiment Museum, Ballymena, County Antrim

GLOSSARY

Ack-ack   Anti-aircraft fire – also called 'flak'. In the First World War it was known as 'Archie', a term familiar to 'Biggles' fans

AP   Armour-piercing, as in a round fired by an anti-tank gun designed to penetrate an enemy tank before exploding

APTC   Army Physical Training Corps

AWOL   Absent without authorised leave

BEF   British Expeditionary Force

Bocage   The name given to that area of Normandy infamous for its fields being surrounded by high earth banks topped with strong thick hedges, ideal for defence and murderous to attack

Bren   British light machine-gun, usually issued at a ratio of one per ten men. The name comes from the first two letters of the towns involved in its manufacture, BRno and ENfield

Compo   Pre-packed British rations, not liked by Americans – no coffee!

CMP   Corps of Military Police

DCM   Distinguished Conduct Medal

DOW   Died of wounds

DSO   Distinguished Service Order

DUKW   A six-wheeled American truck adapted for crossing rivers

DZ   Drop zone, an area designated as the landing place for paratroopers or supplies

Eighty-Eight   A name that seemed to be given to most German artillery pieces, but in actual fact a very powerful anti-aircraft gun that was adopted for use in the anti-tank role and was capable of knocking out all known Allied tanks of the Second World War. Most of the high-explosive shells that landed in and around Oosterbeek came from 75mm and 105mm guns.

'Faughs'   (pronounced 'Fogs') Nickname for the Royal Irish Fusiliers, from their battle-cry 'Faugh-a-Ballagh', meaning 'Clear the way!' (this is the clean translation)

GHQ   General Headquarters

GPO   General Post Office

GSO1   General Staff Officer grade 1

HE   High-explosive

HQ   Headquarters

IRA   Irish Republican Army

KIA   Killed in action

LG   *London Gazette*, followed by date of publication

MG   Machine-gun

MIA   Missing in action

MID   Mentioned-in-Dispatches. A 'mention' in a despatch from a commander-in-chief in the field is perhaps the oldest form of recognition of 'gallant and distinguished services', both in action and in administrative posts. During the Second World War a single oak-leaf emblem was authorised to be worn on the ribbon of the 1939-45 War Medal to indicate a 'dispatch'.

MM   Military Medal

Morning Hate   Enemy artillery fire delivered at the same time each day, usually in the early morning!

OC   Officer Commanding

Pegasus   A winged horse, the offspring of the Gorgon, Medusa, killed by Perseus. Pegasus carried the thunderbolt of Zeus and was the mount of Bellerophon when he slew the Chimera, and Perseus when he rescued Andromeda. Pegasus was regarded as a symbol of poetic genius; springs of pure water gushed forth at the strike of his hoof.

PIAT — Projectile Infantry Anti-Tank, a spring-loaded launcher that propelled a 2lb anti-tank bomb accurately for a distance of up to 110 yards. Although of shorter range than the American 'Bazooka', it had the advantage of not having a back blast, therefore making it hard to spot and capable of being fired from within an enclosed space, such as a room.

POW — Prisoner of war

QMS — Quarter Master Sergeant

RAF — Royal Air Force

RAMC — Royal Army Medical Corps

RASC — Royal Army Service Corps

Recce — Abbreviation of Reconnaissance, as in 'Recce Squadron'

REME — Royal Electrical Mechanical Engineers

RV — Rendezvous Point, as in 'let's RV at the pub'!

Schmeisser — German sub-machine-guns were often referred to as Schmeissers, but these were in fact the products of ERMA-designer Heinrich Vollmer and designated MP38 and MP40 by the German Army. They were superior to the British Sten gun in workmanship, but the Germans preferred the Sten, as with its side-loading magazine – the firer could lie flatter to the ground. Hugo Schmeisser designed the Bergmann MP18 in 1916, one of the first blow-back sub-machine-guns.

SHAEF — Supreme Headquarters Allied Expeditionary Force

Stick — Group of paratroopers in an aircraft; eg in a Dakota one group or stick sat on each side of the aircraft

Spandau — A collective name given by British troops to the German light and medium MG34 and MG42 machine-guns

Sten — British-made sub-machine-gun in 9mm having a crude metal construction and produced in large numbers – more than 2 million of the Mk II were produced. Airborne troops usually carried the Mk V, which looked better but performed much the same as the earlier models – poorly!

TD — Territorial Decoration

WIA — Wounded in action

WP — White phosphorus, smoke shells

INDEX

A Bridge Too Far 177
Adamson, Hugh 73, 169
Agincourt, battle of 14
Airborne Forces Security Fund 170
Alexander, Harold 13, 67
Allen, Thomas, W. 130
Allsop, David 154
Antopoulos, Anthony 50, 51
Armstrong, Thomas, G. 43
Arnhem Cup 172
Atkinson, J. R. 30
Auchinleck, Claude 13
Auchinleck, John 14
Auchinleck, William 14

Baltussen, Arnoldus 119, 131
Baltussen, Cora 131, 138
Barnwall, Desmond 58
Barry, Peter 100
Bateman, Jack 43
Baxter, Tony 102
'Beggar', Operation 50
Beja 58
Bell, R. F. 'Frank' 31
Bermingham, John 15, 31, 41, 62-3, 87, 123
Bermingham, Patrick 15
Bermingham, Richard P. 32
Bermingham, William Arthur 15
Beurling, 'Screwball' 44
'Biting', Operation 35
Black, Boyde A. 25, 73
Blatch, John 108
Bone, airfield 57
Boyd, James Frederick 53, 92, 143
Brackstown, Charles Thomas 90, 91

Breen, Tom 'Paddy' 30, 94, 118, 153
Briody, Michael 51, 52, 53
Brooke, Alan 13, 66
Browne, Patrick 49
Bruneval Raid *see* 'Biting', Operation
Buchanan, Alan Alexander 47, 120-121, 168
Budd, Fred 121
Burke, Joseph 43, 110
Butler, Thomas 14

Cadden, Gavin 59
Cain, Robert VC 134
Calloway, H. L. 'Cab' 30, 96, 111, 119-120
Cameron, James 23, 76, 138, 143, 157
Carter, Gerald S. 'Gerry' 78
Cassidy, James G. 61
Cassidy, Samuel P. 49, 93
Chatterton, George 49, 50, 53
Chobry, Polish troopship 51
Churchill, Winston 13, 14
Clarke, Anthony Leslie 34, 146-147
Cleasby-Thompson 58
Cockings, E. G. J. 'Paddy' 25, 126
Coffey, William VC 46
Coke, John S. A. 136
Collins, Kevin 57
'Colossus', Operation 19
Commando Order 59
Conboy, Martin Francis 65
Connell, Michael Burke 'Crow' 69, 71

Conway, Edward M. 45
Conway, J. J. 45
Conway, 'Paddy' 51
Cook, George 93
Cooney, 'Paddy' 119, 138, 151
Cooper, Astley John 50, 71
Corbett, David 138
Corry, Harry 40
Cos 43
Cotterill, Anthony 145
Couling, H. R. 'Chirpy' 139
Cousens, H. S. 47
Cowan, 'Curley' 25
Cox, 'Mick' 30, 86, 87, 94, 119, 120
Coxen, 'Vic' 63
Craske, Commander 51
Croute, Robert 'Bob' 28
Crumlin Road Prison 43
Cunningham, George 196

Dalkin, J. T. 90
Daly, John Joseph 28, 135
Davidson, Charles McLain 32, 155
Deelen, airfield 80
Deighton, Thomas Robinson 47
Dennison, Mervyn William 57, 59, 72, 98-99, 102, 116, 139, 158
Devlin, Brian 49, 136
Devlin, P. R. 'Paddy' 32
Devlin, William J. P. 32, 61, 130
Diffin, Norman 45, 109, 110
Dill, Sir John 13, 14
Dobie, David 31, 116
Dobrozyski, Frank 123
Dolaghan, Francis 43, 123

Dolaghan, Thomas 43, 123
Dorman-Smith, Eric 13
Dougan, Alexander 'Sandy' 32, 97
Dougan, Norman Arthur 32, 155, 167
Dover, Victor 100, 101
Down, Eric 'Dracula' 19
Dunkirk 39, 53, 55

Eastwood, H. D. 123
Eccles, Andrew 69
Eccles, D. L. 151
ELAS 22
Ellis, Sidney 33, 117

Feehily, Brian Patrick Sheridan 65, 155, 169
Fiely, James Vincent 25, 139, 140
Fitch, John 57, 103
Fitzpatrick, George Albert 40, 74, 99, 128, 134, 137, 142, 144, 156
Flynn, Hugh 48, 155
Fowler, 'Bill' 107, 108, 109
Frost, John Dutton 100, 104-105, 112, 123
Fryer, John 'Jack' 32-33, 61, 72, 91, 94, 98, 103, 117-118, 120, 127-128, 142, 146, 154, 158, 169
'Fustian', Operation 67, 71

Gamble, James 'Jimmy' 25, 123
Garibaldi, Guiseppe 66
Gillespie, Dennis Ivan 'Danny' 23, 75-78, 91, 137, 145, 156, 162, 175
Gordon, Hugh 61
Gough, C. F. H. 'Freddie' 15, 26-27, 99, 124, 145
Gough, Charles John Stanley 15
Gough, Sir Hubert 15
Gough, Hugh 14, 15
Gough, John Edmund 15
Gough, Matthew 14
Gough, Samuel 29
Grace, James 124
Graebner, Viktor 112, 114
Gray, W. B. 30
Grierson, R. H. 76, 77, 78
Grogan, Liam 175

Grundle, Robert 'Rab' 103

Hackett, John Winthrop 'Shan' 15, 42, 69, 75, 76, 107, 110, 111, 123, 129, 146, 159
Hackett, Robert Henry 16
Hackett, Thomas Bernard VC 16
Haddon, Tommy 107, 151
Hall, Denis 50, 51
Hamilton, John Mallon 45
Hamilton, Thomas L. 29
Harkin, James 'Jim' 44
Harland & Wolff 23, 192
Harrington, Patrick 130
Harris, 'Archie' 55
Hastings, battle of 17
'Hasty', Operation 22
Heath, Edwin 122
Hempel, Eduard 175
Henry, Edward 107
Herenthals 108
Hicks, 'Pip' 67, 110, 127
Hill, Herbert 71
Hillis, Samuel 33, 117
Hope-Jones, Ronald 107
Hopkinson, 'Hoppy' 21, 69, 76
Horrocks, Brian 13, 16, 17, 82, 170
Hughes, Charles 41
Hughes, Edward 46
Hughes, Victor T. 31, 40, 41, 63
Hunter, John 46, 130
'Husky', Operation 67

International Brigade 38

Jackson, Charles Ivor 19

Keddie, 'Jock' 87
Keneally, William VC 15
Kent, Ron 76, 77, 123, 148
Keogh, Ensign 14
Kerr, Harry A. 27, 147
Kerr, William 'Bill' 43, 110, 116, 136, 155
Kiely, Michael 157
Killingworth, Richard 109
King, Harry 124
Koch, Walter 60
Kremer, family home 138

'Ladbroke', Operation 67, 69
Lander, John 23
Lathbury, Gerald 67, 103, 105
Lea, George 44
Lewis, Peter 'Pongo' 105
Lindsay, Colonel 44
Lonsdale, Richard Thomas Henry 37-38, 44, 73, 110, 125, 127
Lord, David Samuel Anthony VC 124-125
Lynas, Ernest 45, 151
Lyons, F. 96

McClune, John 147
McCluskey see McCormick.
McCormick, Frank 142
McCracken, George 145
McCreedie, Leslie 27, 132, 134
McFadden, John Terence M. 32, 98
McKee, Andrew 'Adie' 35, 170
McKinley, Henry 107, 108, 109
McKnight, J. 'Paddy' 78
McMurray, James Isaac 34, 78, 79, 159
Magill, William 33, 96, 97, 128, 147, 169
Maison Blanche 58
Malta 44, 130
Maltby, Ralph 53, 90
Markey, Peter 33, 134, 157
Masterson, Patrick 14
Mateur 60
Matson, Eric George Wolf 51, 151
Middleweek, William 135
Millington Primary School 184
Mitchell, Harry 91, 138, 142
Mitchell, Henry 14
Mitchell, Robert 14
Model, Walther 100
Mole, 'Jackie' 94, 118
Monte Cassino 79
Montgomery, Bernard, Law 13, 17, 18, 65, 74, 82, 170
Montgomery, Robert V. 103, 120, 121
Montgomery, Samuel 48
Moore, William 'Barney' 23, 76
Morley, W. D. 96
Morton, Patrick 38, 40, 59, 60,

61, 74, 99, 128, 1034, 137, 142,
144, 156, 174, 181
Mullhall/Mulhern 63
Munford, Denis 114, 145
Murphy, James 65
Murray, Ian 146

Neill, 'Jock' 47
Neville, Daniel 30, 114, 131
Newell, Cecil 35, 36, 63, 72, 73,
94, 104, 114, 131, 168

O'Brien, Patrick 57
O'Connor, Richard 13
O'Leary, Peter 128, 155
O'Neill, John Joseph 143
O'Reilly, John Joseph 44, 153
O'Sullivan, Edward Delaney 26
Otway, Terence B. H. 26

Palestine 44
Patton, George 67
Payton-Reid, R. 135, 136
Pearson, Alistair 62
Peatling, Robert 96, 111, 120
Perdijk, police officer 96
Petrie, Hugh 'Big' 24
Pine-Coffin, G. 57
Place, John W. 53, 69, 90
Ponte Grande Bridge 67
Popski's Private Army 75, 78
Powell, Geoffrey 129
Primasole Bridge 38
Pritchard, James 61

'Quatre Bras', Oosterbeek 138

Quinn, Peter 27, 153, 154

Roberts, William George 114
Rodgers, Richard 'Dick' 'Doc' 25,
91
Ryan, Joseph D. 44
Ryan, Joseph Patrick 58, 59

Santa Agata patrol 76
Saunders, William 'Bill' 73, 100,
101, 115, 169
Scrivner, E. F. 130
Scullion, Tommy 73, 109, 137,
140, 147, 169
Sedjenane 60
Sicily 66
Sidi N'Sir 58, 59
Siggins, Donald 28
Sims, James 37, 104, 112, 122
Smellie, John Frederick 55, 143,
172
Smith, Edward Albert 'Bert' 107,
108, 109, 168
Smyth, Jack 87, 167
Sosabowski, Stanislaw 23, 132
Special Air Service 19
Sullivan, Patrick 43, 136
Summerville, Gordon 'Slim' 23,
148, 175

Tallentire, Wilfred 53, 54, 55, 89,
167
Tansley, George 151
Taranto 75
Tatam-Warter, Digby 161
Ter Horst, Kate 126, 127, 130

Theirs Is The Glory 176
Tiemens, Willie 155
Timothy, Tim 78
'Tonga', Operation 55
Touffreville 26
Towhey, John 34, 96
Tucker, Edward W. 131, 145, 169
Tucker, Reuben H. 132
Turno, 'Uncle', Polish pilot 89

Ulster Home Guard 24
Urquhart, Robert Elliot 23, 94,
105, 123, 146, 151
Usher, James 33, 87, 117

Vandeleur, Giles 16
Vandeleur, J. O. E. 16
Vienna Water Police 148
Vittoria, battle of 14, 16

Walcheren Island 89
Walker, Joseph 118
Waterloo, battle of 15
White, Albert 'Bertie' 110
White, David 93
Whittingham, 'Dick' 142
Willis, Henry 46, 153
Wilson, B. A. 23, 91, 135, 138
Wilson, Sir Henry 186
Winkworth, Charles 92, 93
Winser, John 93
Wolverine, HMS 51
Woods, Reginald Bryan 36, 73,
101, 104, 112, 122, 132
Wrigley's chewing gum 54